ONE SIGNAL
PUBLISHERS
ATRIA

THE FREE AND THE DEAD

The Untold Story of the Black Seminole Chief, the Indigenous Rebel, and America's Forgotten War

Jamie Holmes

ONE SIGNAL PUBLISHERS

ATRIA

New York Amsterdam/Antwerp London
Toronto Sydney/Melbourne New Delhi

An Imprint of Simon & Schuster, LLC
1230 Avenue of the Americas
New York, NY 10020

First One Signal Publishers/Atria Books hardcover edition February 2026

ONE SIGNAL PUBLISHERS/ATRIA BOOKS
and colophon are registered trademarks of Simon & Schuster, LLC

Interior design by Davina Mock-Maniscalco

Manufactured in the United States of America

1 3 5 7 9 10 8 6 4 2

The Library of Congress Cataloging-in-Publication Data has been applied for.

ISBN 978-1-6680-5061-3
ISBN 978-1-6680-5063-7 (ebook)

INTERVIEWER: You're writing for white people. Are you aware of that?

JAMES BALDWIN: I'm writing for people, baby. No. I don't believe in "white people." I don't believe in "Black people" either, for that matter. But I know the difference between being Black and white at this time.

—Paris, 1970

God made all of us, and we all came from one woman . . . we hope we shall not quarrel; that we will talk until we get through.

—Holata Micco, 1834

Contents

Personae Notabiles

MICANOPY, Chief of the Seminole Nation

ABRAHAM, Black Seminole chief, Micanopy's Sense Bearer and Interpreter

JUMPER, powerful chief allied with the Seminoles, known as "the Lawyer"

ANDREW JACKSON, seventh president of the United States

THOMAS JESUP, U.S. Quartermaster General, Commander of the Army of the South

ABIAKA, Miccosukee chief, influential war leader, also known as Sam Jones

OSCEOLA, vocal warrior and enforcer, loyal to the Miccosukee tribe

Inciting Events

March 10, 1818: U.S. troops led by Andrew Jackson invade Spanish Florida, attacking Native forces and pressuring Spain to relinquish the territory.

February 22, 1821: The Adams–Onís Treaty cedes Florida to the United States. Jackson will assume the role of the territory's first governor.

September 18, 1823: The United States and the Florida Indians agree on terms confining them to a reservation in the interior in return for livestock, rations, and $5,000 annually for twenty years.

May 28, 1830: President Jackson signs the Indian Removal Act into law, setting the stage to displace tribes to the west of the Mississippi River.

December 1, 1833: Jackson's pick to facilitate the Seminoles' removal, Wiley Thompson, arrives as the new Indian Agent at Fort King, Florida.

November 24, 1834: Duncan Clinch assumes leadership of U.S. military operations in Florida.

February 16, 1835: Jackson mandates the removal of all Native people in the peninsula.

Prelude

The writer Zora Neale Hurston was working in Florida as a folklorist, in the 1930s, when she recorded the tale about the man with the unusual name. "Uncle Monday," locals said, was "a great African medicine man" of the crocodile clan that practiced kinship with the fierce reptiles. Soon after he was stolen from his home and forced to America, he escaped from "Georgia or South Carolina and made his way down into the Indian country which is now Florida." He and others settled among the Seminoles—this was the 1830s, "the days of that haughty Osceola"—and when the white men attacked, he led the "Indian-negro forces" in battle. They "fought as fiercely as the best," but were overcome, in the end, by greater numbers and weaponry.

Uncle Monday and the survivors met in the woods near Blue Sink Lake, to debate and decide what to do. He explained to the people what the deities had revealed: that continued warfare would be of no use. Still, the medicine man vowed that he would never yield to enslavement or death at the hands of the invaders. He promised that he would change himself into an alligator, and that he would reunite with his reptilian kin in the Blue Sink until the trouble was over. When the fighting was done, he would emerge and once again walk the earth in peace. And so there was a ceremony on the banks of the Blue Sink, where the people drummed African and Indian beats on their instruments.

As Uncle Monday danced, he began to shift in form. His face turned "longer and very terrible," his limbs shortened, his skin grew dense and rough, and his voice "came like thunder." His roar echoed over the Blue Sink, and in reply a bass chorus rumbled like distant shock waves, and a thousand alligators surged forth from the lake in two columns. Uncle Monday was now the largest of the reptiles, and he strode regally through their lines and "glided majestically into the water." Bellowing all together, the legion of alligators plunged after him. It was said that he lived on in the Blue Sink Lake for many years, and that every so often, he would transform back into a man and roam the land, and cast his spells on the people.

The true story behind the legend is what follows.

I

1

The Functionary

Not everything in Wiley Thompson's life was unpleasant. The site of his impending death, at least, was beautiful. He spent most of 1835 in the outback below a picturesque hillock, surrounded by pristine forest in what is today north-central Florida. To the northwest, a tangled and primordial thicket flourished. An open pine grove stretched south. Beyond gentle slopes, lush woods extended as far as the eye could view.

Thompson lived and worked in a spacious log building known as the Seminole Agency house. It was likely built on limestone piers, with a tall roof and grand porches. Its rooms would have been well lit by dormer windows of rare sash glass and floored by plank wood, which was difficult to obtain in the interior so far from the sawmills.

He had reason to feel secure and protected. Above the Agency house, a hundred yards away, Fort King's sentinels scanned the area. Under a flagpole where thirteen stripes and twenty-four stars rippled in the breeze, over two hundred armed troops busied themselves in the barracks, mess hall, and ammunition and weapons depots.

The soldiers had access to basic amenities and comforts. A blacksmith forged nails. Surgeons tended to the sick. The sutler, who sold goods, was well stocked in beer and even champagne. Officers bathed in a fresh spring where the waters were as "soft as a lady's hand," and bedrocks glittered clearly far below, and even the fish glided idly.

The fort was as agreeable as Thompson could have possibly hoped. His problems were not rooted in where he was stationed. The headaches came with the job itself.

The U.S. government did not send the fifty-three-year-old to the hinterlands simply to evict Native Americans from their homes. The government had sent Thompson to the Florida Territory to force Native Americans from their homes as cheaply as possible.

Removal without war. That was the goal.

Treaties were trifles compared to armies and bullets. Treaties could be printed in newspapers so that citizens knew it was all super fair and aboveboard. Thompson was the guy hired to grin and shake hands. He spent late March 1835 in meetings with Seminole chiefs and other leaders, encouraging their imminent departure, and futzing over logistics. Transporting an estimated three to five thousand Indigenous people west of the Mississippi involved tons of paperwork. He was a man of forms and procedures.

For six months, his lithe, graying figure—he not only supported Andrew Jackson's commitment to the Indian Removal Act of 1830 but, by total coincidence, physically resembled the president—could be seen pacing up and down the promontory, performing drudgeries. He completed many of his unsavory chores alone. His new assistant, Yancey, was a drunk. Thompson sat dutifully inside the Agency house and toiled away with his quills and letter paper. The Indians had been promised frocks if they relocated westward. But what kinds of frocks? His boss assured him that the frocks should be homespun and sewn in a "workmanlike manner." Mock-ups had to be stitched. Bids procured.

The envoy, a former U.S. congressman from Georgia, was not

ignorant of the risks. He had only traded in his seat on Capitol Hill, after all, after falling into debt and filling out a will. His job title, Office of Indian Affairs *Superintendent of Seminole Removal,* was just as dicey as it sounded, and Fort King—for all its rustic pleasures—*was* recklessly isolated. Supply runs to Palatka, some forty-five miles away, took all of two weeks.

The camp was situated within the boundaries of the Indian reservation, a central enclave cordoned off in the years after Spain ceded the peninsula to the United States, in 1821. The systematic process of forcing Indigenous peoples from their homes, spearheaded by the War Department's troubled Office of Indian Affairs, was now in full swing, and Florida, with citizenry from the Deep South, was eager to join the Union as a slave state. But the project was lagging. Apart from Michigan, nearly all lands east of the Mississippi River had been carved into states, while Florida remained sparsely inhabited and in large part unconquered. No colonial power had ever controlled the swamps and savannas of the interior—an alien land of lagoons, glade marshes, prairies, and hardwood thickets. If America chose a war of eviction, it would face terrain closer to the mangrove-choked waterways and swampy forests of Vietnam than the landscapes of Alabama or Thompson's native Georgia. If he failed, the entire territory could plunge into chaos.

President Jackson's Indian agent, who would soon be a pile of bones under his wife's bed back home in Elberton, knew all this and accepted it. He knew his job would be tedious and lonely, and that his duties might kill him. What he did not expect—what he could not have foreseen—was that in April of 1835, with negotiations at their most delicate, his boss, the president of the United States, would paint an even larger target on his back.

April 21, 1835. More campfires meant more people. The nights were growing brighter. Under starlight, the flames encircled Fort King. For three days, leaders of the Seminole, Miccosukee, Tallahassee, and

Creek Indians gathered in the surrounding woods, until a hundred blazes glowed like votive candles under the canopies.

For the colonists, it was another surreal sight in a landscape full of them. Fresh army recruits found themselves among whizzing insects, screeching owls, and bellowing gators. Newborn reptiles scampered on the riverbanks. Neon parrakeets flocked over live oaks draped in Spanish moss. Dead fruit rotted on withered evergreens, remnants of a record-cold February. Wild oranges hung, black from frost. Glowworms lit up uncanny forests. Stars, one officer wrote, "were the only familiar objects."

Below the outpost on the hill, around the multiplying fires, families of cultures just as alien to the outsiders relaxed in shelters of poles and bark ripped from huge pines. Curious artillerymen drifted down, and the families welcomed them and shared their corn, which they baked in kettles, sifted, pounded soft, and sweetened with molasses. The troops snacked on coontie root and gawked at the women's beads and at their silver ornaments—brooches of flattened quarters, shillings, and picayunes.

The Seminoles hosted a welcoming ceremony two miles away. The officers who attended were fearful they would be killed on the long night walk. The dancing didn't end until after two o'clock in the morning, until the earth by the fire was left trampled "like a circus ring." Moonbeams brightened packed dirt.

After sunrise, the leader of the Seminole Nation walked into a clearing near the Agency house. Chief Micanopy was the head of a fragmented coalition of tribes and their constituent bands of loosely allied guerrilla fighters. The Americans knew that there were many factions but often called them all Seminoles anyway, which made it easier to convince the public that the treaties were valid. The designation derived from the Spanish *cimarrón,* or "untamed," a reference to Indians who left the troubled Creek Confederacy to build new lives.

Chief Micanopy was, in fact, a Seminole. Hefty, gentle, and in his fifties, he was known to be faithful to friends and to enjoy a glass and a fine meal. He and other chiefs shook the officers' hands with firm grips that left the Americans with sore digits. Thompson opened the meeting with an "altogether too grandiloquent" speech about an old treaty signed by leaders who did not speak for all bands or families.

The details of the talks were nothing. The pattern was everything.

Thompson was only following a script. The government had a playbook, it turns out, for kicking Native people off their lands without any unseemly, costly bloodshed. The scheme involved several moving parts. First, settlers pushed in on Indians and drove away their game. Once families were starving, Washington sent envoys to meet with them in a clearing. After sharing a meal and laying out gifts, the emissaries would insist that the Indians move to where the animals were plentiful. They were starving, after all, and the government was only trying to be a friend and to help, and to protect them from the corrupt settlers and unfair local courts that would cheat them. If they didn't leave, the army would attack, but since the government was a friend, it hoped to avoid war.

"The white people are settling around you," Wiley Thompson announced, reading directly from a letter written by President Jackson to the chiefs. "The game has disappeared from your country. Your people are poor and hungry."

White people were not settling all around like in Georgia and Alabama. Much of the interior was no good for farming. Some bands were hurting, but Micanopy's people were flush with livestock. They weren't hungry. They weren't poor.

"Every true friend would advise you to remove," Thompson continued, numbly reciting the president's address verbatim. "But you have no right to stay, and you must go. I am very desirous that you should go peaceably and voluntarily."

Talks continued for two days. Thompson ran the scheme, regardless of whether it really fit. An American general placed "his sword upon the table" and brashly informed the chiefs that "he had been sent here to enforce the treaty; he had warriors enough to do it; and he *would do it*. It was the question now whether they would go of their own accord, or go by force." The ultimatum was plain: Leave or it's war.

Hints of the tragicomedy to come surfaced on the second day, when heavy clouds threatened rain and the meeting was held in the barracks. Micanopy had "a pain in the stomach" and did not show, which offended Thompson.

"Tell him," the agent sputtered, "he is stricken from the list of chiefs!"

The proclamation had little effect on the room. So the envoy composed himself, "rose slowly and imposingly from his seat," and with "every eye fixed upon him," extended his arm in a grand gesture. That was when the floor collapsed, and men, benches, tables, ink, and paper tumbled four feet to the earth in a tangled mess. An alarmed warrior yelled. Indians rushed from the barracks. It took a moment for the chiefs to be sure that it wasn't a "stratagem," and both sides laughed, and Wiley Thompson resumed the absurd theater that required him to hide his true face behind a thin mask of friendship.

Eight chiefs voted to emigrate. Five, including Micanopy, refused to.

News of trouble in the Florida hinterlands could take nearly a month to reach the Oval Office. Replies took another three-plus weeks. From the Agency house, outgoing mail traveled by horse or mule to a hamlet about twenty-five miles north. Contractors then humped it east around Orange Lake to Jacksonville, an eighty-mile slog. From there, letters were ferried by boat and trotted by stagecoach up to North Carolina, where important correspondence was loaded onto a steam locomotive to Virginia. In Washington City, completing the sprawling 902-mile trek, vital messages would have been delivered by courier to Pennsylvania Avenue, and placed among the piles of incoming mail addressed to the office of the president.

"His Excellency" Andrew Jackson was sixty-eight when he caught wind of Thompson's irksome message, and in the final days of his second term. Wild, cotton-white hair decorated a slender, wrinkled, beady-eyed face. He looked increasingly anxious in his old age, and especially unhappy when he removed his dentures, as he did for portraits, and his lips frowned over toothless gums.

Years of rough living had ruined the president's health. His digestive system was wrecked by recurring dysentery and colic, and the calomel prescribed by his doctors only made things worse. A duel in 1806—Jackson killed the man—and an 1813 gunfight had planted two lead bullets in him, including one still lodged near his heart. He exhibited many of the symptoms of lead and mercury poisoning, including paranoia, irritability, violent mood swings, excessive salivation, hand tremors, diarrhea, and pallor. He often bled his arm with his penknife.

He may not have been in the best mood when he received Thompson's letter.

The agent's message, dated April 27, 1835, arrived in mid-May. Forwarded from the War Department, the gist was that the envoy refused to serve the president's wishes. Despite clear authorization, Thompson would not help enslave any "Indian negroes."

"Application was made to me," the dispatch read, "for permission to purchase negroes of the Seminole Indians." With Jackson's blessing, white slavers had shown up at the Agency house. Thompson explained why he had turned them down:

> The negroes in the nation dread the idea of being transferred from their present state of ease and comparative liberty to bondage and hard labor under overseers, on sugar and cotton plantations. They have always had a great influence over the Indians. They live in villages separate, and, in many cases, remote from their owners, and [enjoy] equal liberty with their

> owners, with the single exception that the slave supplies his owner annually . . . with corn, in proportion to the amount of the crop . . . in no instance . . . exceeding ten bushels. . . . Many of these slaves have stocks of horses, cows, and hogs, with which the Indian owner never assumes the right to intermeddle.

Tribal law prohibited the sale of any so-called Indian "slaves," Thompson reported, and the Seminoles would resist all attempts to violate that precedent. Most seemed to be "slaves but in name" only. Tribute was little more than an in-kind tax, and there was legitimate doubt over how seriously even that obligation was taken. (Florida's former governor complained, in 1826, that the Indians exercised "no controle over their slaves" and derived "no advantage from their labour.") It was too dangerous, Thompson advised, to test the bonds between the Black and Native peoples. If the government allowed enslavers to divide the families, the agent warned, "God only knows what the consequences will be."

Jackson must have been disappointed by his appointee. Like the president, Thompson was a Southern slaveholder. The emissary understood perfectly well how vital slavery was to the economy of the adolescent Florida Territory. As of 1830, nearly 45 percent of the population was enslaved. Total inhabitants numbered 35,000 or so; only 844 were marked as "free colored." Florida did not welcome free Black people. That was the Louisiana model—a legacy of French and Spanish occupation. That model helped produce a violent revolt, in 1811.

Thompson knew that there was a "rulebook" for holding people in bondage just as there was one for eviction. Enslavement without rebellion. That was the goal.

Not all toxic recipes were identical, to be sure. At Jackson's private forced-labor-camp retreat in Tennessee known as the Hermitage, the president denied some one hundred souls access to education, real assets, and freedom of movement. Southerners openly discussed plantation "laws" and their psychological effects. One Louisiana slaver even wrote up a five-page document laying out his restrictions and detailing their intended results. The idea was to prevent trafficked people from realizing that they were equally capable and could live freely. "Never allow any man to talk to your negroes," the slaveholder cautioned, "nothing more injurious."

Evidence and information posed a mortal threat to the "peculiar institution" of slavery. Communities of apparently free, "Indianized" Africans and African Americans were intolerable no matter what they were called. The Florida Territory's governor whined that they were a "serious nuisance," that they seemed to have "unbounded influence," that they were "all hostile to the white people" and "constantly counteracting the advice and talks given to the Indians." Slavers in the territory saw them as a haven for "runaways" and wanted them all reduced to chattel. No more bad examples of free, dignified Black people. No more bad advice to Indians. That's what Jackson had authorized his emissary to make happen.

Florida was personal to Jackson. He took possession of the land from Spain himself, after invading in 1818, and served as the first governor. The most powerful Americans in the territory were his men. Clinch. Gaines. Gadsden. Eaton. Call. Butler. And Thompson. The board controlling land claims was made up of "a remarkable combination of former Jacksonian associates" dubbed the "Nucleus." President "Jackson's Cronies in Florida Territorial Politics" was destined to be a topic of scholarly interest. The two enslavers backed by the president, turned away by Thompson at Fort King, offered a case study in local power: Two men, hearing about a bargain in the woods, asked the territory's next governor—Jackson's former aide-de-camp—if they could purchase "Indian negroes" from the Seminoles; the future governor wrote to his pal the president on behalf of his dear "friends at Tallahassee"; and voilà, the Office of Indian Affairs replied that *of course* the close friends could separate the families.

Except Thompson refused to play ball.

Jackson overruled his envoy, ignored the agent's explanation and warning of grave risks, and instructed him to follow the original mandate. Jackson did not reply personally. Instead, the acting secretary of war conveyed the president's position that "the condition of these" families would be the same if they were sold. The letter flatly denied that the targets held rights that chattel slavers strongly opposed: That the Black men were all armed, that many were worldly, bilingual or trilingual, that they traveled freely, and that they owned vast livestock.

"Indian negroes" had no place in the Territory of Florida.

2

Abraham's Town

The Native shout echoed over Hope Hill, on the St. Johns River, announcing his arrival. The gentleman would likely have been traveling on horseback, armed with a musket and knives and crowned with a stately turban, in the Seminole style, with handkerchiefs around his neck for pockets. His title was Sawanok' Tustenuggee, or Shawnee Warrior. He was a chief and man of God, hailed as a prophet for his prescience, and was likely also known to the Seminoles as Yahola: Crier, orator, the one who speaks. He was over six feet tall and dark-skinned, a "full blooded negro," in the parlance of the invading categorizers. Keen observers said that he had "a great deal of fun about him," that he was brilliant and "artful," and that he had more wit in his left eye—his right eye angled inward—than most held in both. He played different roles on different occasions, and did not mind turning prejudices to his advantage. To his people, he was shepherd and commander. To Americans, he was Chief Micanopy's Interpreter. In ways, he was Thompson's opposite number: an emissary and a negotiator.

The army called him Abraham.

The chief was accompanied to the settler's home by two enslaved people. Several years prior, a forced labor camp had been attacked by Indians. Hogs shot dead. Horses stolen. A bondservant and her child carried off. The slaver escaped with only the clothes on his back. His wife was found under the bed—stabbed, shot, and scalped in an unknown order. Abraham was asked to recover the settler's human property.

He could not have enjoyed the task, but such gestures were the price of peace. The bands of the interior and their new American neighbors maintained a fragile truce, and the issue of human trafficking was especially sensitive. Out of over five hundred men, women, and children of African heritage living among the Indians, locals believed that four-fifths of the population were "runaways, or descendants of runaways." The situation had always been tense and ripe with the potential for violent confrontations. Rules, however uncomfortable, had to be negotiated by both sides. Indians promised not to harbor or take bondservants in raids; locals learned not to dispatch bounty hunters into the interior.

Concessions had to be made. Lessons had to be taught. An Alabama woman known as Gray once sent her son and a party of stalkers into the reservation searching for her human chattel; Abraham's people killed some of them, wounded Gray's son badly, and sent them all scuttling back north. In 1830, a man called Waters dared to venture into Indian lands to "obtain negroes"; he was caught, flogged "pretty badly," and promptly expelled. Waters did not much like getting whipped like a bondservant and promised to use his gun next time. There is no record he did. A disturbed denizen recommended that locals form a militia to punish Abraham for the white man's whipping—a proposal sent to the secretary of war. There is no record that happened. The central region of the territory was ruled by Indian law, not American. Abraham, along with a chief named Jumper, was one of the lawmen. They were Chief Micanopy's top advisors.

Of five known African Seminole or Black Seminole towns, Abraham's was the most prosperous. As many as 160 men, women, and children lived under his protection, forty miles or so west of present-day Orlando. Thirty or forty well-built homes of timber, thatch, and daub, some of "considerable size," dotted the rises in the lowlands known as hammocks—"islands" of hardwoods of twenty to three hundred acres. In the rainy seasons when the ponds filled, the tree islands acted as sheltered sanctuaries of jade. In the dry seasons, from November to April, the land became a "most beautiful open savannah country." Hundreds of ponies, cattle, and gentle calves grazed. Green "fields of the finest land" sprouted "large crops of corn, beans, melons, pumpkin," rice, and peanuts. Fresh beef dried to jerky. The orange trees flowered bright in late winter. Men who dressed and hunted more or less in the Seminole way smoked from clay pipes and enjoyed tunes of the Native flute and the percussive rattle of a box-turtle shell filled with palmetto seeds. A game of stickball, maybe, during the day. A sip of rum from an emerald bottle as the sun sank.

This was Pilaklikaha. In the Muscogee language of the Seminole and Creek, it meant "scattered hammock." It was also known, simply, as Abraham's Town.

Residents here and in the other independent Black Seminole settlements held biblical, classical, or African names. Peter, John, and Rebecca. Caesar, Venus, and Diana. Juba, Cudjo, and Dembo. Some used aliases, and many, like the Indians, held one title for themselves and offered another to outsiders. Abraham's wife Tainy was also Betsy; Tenebo was Charles; Kelina was Carolina. In the African tradition, some were named for the occasion of their birth: In the Twi language of present-day Ghana, *Cudjo* meant "born on Monday"; Monday, July, and August were Black Seminole names.

For nearly 150 years, Africans and their children and grandchildren had traveled a lesser-known Underground Railroad leading south. The weakness of the powers vying for control of the peninsula—Spanish, Indian, British, and American—opened doors to new lives. Many men seized offers as old as antiquity: Soldiery for civil rights. Africans fought for the Spanish against the English, for the British against the Americans, and for the Seminoles against Georgia militia. Hundreds of warriors perished when the U.S. army sacked the African Fort, a British outpost abandoned after the War of 1812. In 1818, a sizable African army fought off Jackson's forces on the Suwannee River. In the "land of flowers," guns were needed, a gun was a gun, and a gun meant freedom.

Few who found safety among the Indians of Spanish Florida left records of how they earned their liberty. One young woman's story survives. Tena walked to La Florida. She was born with her mother's red hair on a cotton plantation among the Gullah people on the northern Georgia coast, where she came up speaking a variant of Creole. She never imagined leaving her plantation home until the owner, "a part-Cherokee Indian who had adopted the white man's ways," seized and sold her firstborn infant daughter. She and others set out one morning before the sunrise, following the Suwannee south, "through swamps with thick clumps of mangroves and dense palmettos and brush that scratched her arms and face." They survived on berries and roots, evading slave hunters following on horses. She was only seventeen.

Tena's party reached the open Alachua prairies of the interior, where they found protection under a Seminole chief, King Payne. There she met Kelina, and the pair jumped over a broom to signify their marriage. Kelina had darker skin and strange markings on his face, and spoke a language unknown to her. He could still remember "the smell of rain hitting the dry mud-walled houses of his village in Africa and the smell of dusty rice on his mother's winnowing basket." Kelina had escaped to Abraham's Town from the South Carolina rice fields, by hiding a "cypress canoe in the gnarled mangroves by the sea." He stashed food and rowed down the coast with his brothers Plenty, Hardy, and Cuffee.

Kelina, Plenty, and Cuffee added three guns to Abraham's army.

The towns allied with the associated tribes and bands included several groups of Africans and African Americans. Black Seminole royalty, like Abraham (formally liberated by Micanopy in 1830), were legally free. Most families, at least four hundred self-liberated people and their descendants, whose men offered to fight in exchange for protection, "all pretend[ed] to have been purchased" to guard their freedoms. The others, an estimated one hundred enslaved people, lived under lenient terms of service and tribute, likely a mixture of Spanish and Native practices. The Seminoles, as with the Muscogee or Creek peoples they broke off from, had enslaved other Native Americans before they encountered Africans, but they "associated servitude with capture in warfare rather than an organized system of labor." Seminole bondservants had never been cogs in agricultural machines, and the chiefs had no interest in overseeing the hard labor of vast numbers of enslaved people on plantations. Warriors, they could use.

Over the years, the practical exchange of rights for soldiery evolved into something deeper. Time had turned trust into fondness and, in cases, feelings close to love. Abraham had known Seminole children since birth. Micanopy had known Black Seminole families for nearly his own entire life, and had lived beside them at Pilaklikaha for decades. To outsiders, Abraham's people appeared to "have been reared among" the Indians or, at least, in "language, mode of living, [and] habits" seemed to have been "a long while living among" them. According to a free Black Seminole woman, at least two hundred of her people had "been living with the Indians since they were born." By 1835, Indigenous and African Seminole warriors were resolved to fight and to die for each other, and for each other's families.

Black Seminole politics, at least at the top, mirrored the Seminoles'. Abraham was the principal chief, but at least eight others were listed as chiefs or subchiefs, including Toney Barnett, Hokepis Hadjo or John Horse, August, July, Murray, Robert, and Juan Philip, who may have been married to Abraham's eldest daughter, Rachel.

Sometimes called maroons, their people built communities

that were profound creative acts. In the peninsula, they laid fresh paths from cobblestones of past customs. Uniting African and Indigenous heritages, they wove mixed cultural fabrics from fast-unraveling threads. Traditions of the Igbo, Egba, Ashanti, and Mandinka—of some of the noblest "fighting tribes of Africa"—blended with Seminole practices. Afro-Indigenous alliances forged in the 1790s strengthened. Families raised roof beams and babies. By the 1830s, two generations of Black Seminoles had come of age among Indians, in independent and allied villages. Boys and girls who had never endured the nightmares of American slavery had grown to adults.

Abraham's task was to protect their freedoms for as long as he could.

Chattel slavery was a monster that Micanopy's advisor had likely never known. Asked directly, he could not say when or where he was born. White officers who spent little or no time with him described him as a crafty "runaway" from Spanish Pensacola. Alternatively, four men who lived with or near Abraham for up to a year reported that the Interpreter was raised among the Seminoles and that their language was his mother tongue. His freedom papers apparently traced his origin to Alabama, while other sources point instead to Georgia—both of which were then, in part, Creek territory. The best we know, he was born within the Creek Nation or among the Seminoles who left it.

Later records list his birthplace as Florida and suggest that he was raised amid the empire of King Payne. That would make him a child of the rich Alachua prairies of north Florida and the ward of a kind leader. King Payne was known to prioritize "the happiness of his people" over any "vicious passions." In an "era that was prone to border raids and other conflicts," he "often faced the thankless task of being a peacemaker." Above all, Payne aimed to avoid any senseless fighting.

Raised among Seminole royalty, Abraham would have known the wealth of the Cowkeeper Dynasty. Verdant lands and abundant fauna, the taste of honey water, and meals of venison, corn cakes, and hominy. Gardens outside every home. Wild potatoes in the woods. Fresh bread baked of coontie-root powder. Payne's family, heirs to Cowkeeper, owned fifteen hundred cattle and four hundred horses—not to mention countless goats, sheep, and pigs. As a boy in Spanish Florida, among warriors, hunters, cowboys, and rogues of all sorts, Abraham would have had strong Black Seminole role models. As early as 1802, the Black Seminole Harry was not only King Payne's translator, but a trusted negotiator in colonial diplomacy. Abraham would have been in his twenties when they fought off Andrew Jackson's forces at Suwannee Old Town, in 1818. By the early 1820s, he was working alongside the African Seminole Juan, the tribe's new principal translator—apparently as Juan's apprentice. Payne's world of alliances and conflict mediation would have prepared Abraham well to visit Washington City in 1826, when he and Micanopy stood toe-to-toe with President John Quincy Adams, to successfully petition for access to richer lands.

Payne was succeeded by his brother Bolek, who was succeeded by Micanopy.

By 1835, Abraham was around forty-five years old, with as much to lose as he had to protect. Like other leaders, he had two wives. Hagar was mother to his small children Renty and Lucy. With Tainy, he shared Washington, nine, and Rachel, twenty-three. He had two infant grandchildren, both by Rachel, who that year was expecting or was about to be.

For all of them, the stakes of the looming war were stark. Losing their homes and starting over would be arduous and painful. But being forced into chattel slavery was a fate even worse than death. All of the bands knew that fighting to defend their lands meant risking their lives. But Abraham's people also risked their most basic freedoms—everything that they and their parents had fought for and built for over forty years.

Abraham remained calm in the face of American imperatives and threats. As President Jackson insisted that the Seminoles "must prepare" to go. *Takuecetv*. As Thompson predicted that the Indians would face "hopeless poverty" if they did not leave soon. *Estemerketv rakkē*. As the envoy promised that Micanopy would be as poor as an "Indian dog." *Este-cate em efv*.

The Interpreter met with the latest Indian Agent, as he had with the ones before him, and translated the demands and insults, and did not let on how he felt. Not to the army. He was prudent in his dealings with the Americans. "Abram," as the soldiers sometimes called him, carried himself with dignity, smiled politely, and betrayed no reaction to bravado. A white officer complained that he had "a countenance which none can read," and compared him to Napoléon's chief diplomat, the shrewd French statesman Talleyrand. Others cast him as a political animal, a real "Martin Van Buren." Many Indians knew English: his was clear and accurate. He spoke in a low tone, softly, with a "genteel emphasis."

American intentions and pain thresholds remained difficult to gauge. Clearly these men were a far cry from the Spanish of Abraham's youth, who held more lenient views of servitude and welcomed free people of color. The outsiders nurtured dreams of a great nation, but their true commitment to fighting Natives and their allies in the Florida wilderness remained untested.

The soldiers were slow to appreciate that Micanopy's solemn Interpreter doubled as his honored confidant. In the beginning, officers puzzled over Abraham's dual roles as they tried to measure his influence. To them, a Black translator was little more than a servant. Abram was not that. It took time for them to accept that he was also a "sense bearer" to Micanopy, a formal position akin to "prime minister" or "privy coun[selor]." At one point, the Americans put two other interpreters in the same room to double-check his translations. In every case, however, Abraham's renderings were faithful and authentic. The advisor had no reason to warp their words. Their talks were tangled enough.

Wiley Thompson claimed he was acting as the Seminoles' "friend," but that was not the right term for what he was. Slaveholders called themselves "planters," and that sounded a lot nicer than what they were. The forced labor farms sprouting up along the rivers were "frontier plantations"—idyllic bastions of Eden braving the very heart of darkness. Africans were "negroes" whether they were Mandé or Igbo. Europeans were "whitemen" whether they were Dutch or Prussian. All Indigenous people were "Indians," and all Indians in the Florida Territory were "Seminoles." "Settlers" insisted on these words and wrote them down. Everything was written down and almost all the records were theirs.

Thompson claimed that there were several different kinds of white men. He claimed that he and the president were among a group of friendly white men. He said corrupt locals who had once cheated the Seminoles were still alive and plotting against them. He warned them that "all bad men are not yet dead." He said he represented better white men who could protect them from worse white men but it was difficult to tell the difference between the two.

Both envoys who preceded him were crooks.

In 1822, Gad Humphreys had been appointed to the position of Indian Agent. An undated sketch portrays him as a plump man with sagging jowls and heavy eyes, in apparent need of sleep. To avoid a conflict of interest, the U.S. government forbade him from buying enslaved people from Indians. Humphreys did it anyway, enriching himself by "speculat[ing] in Negro claims"—purchasing dubious titles for rock-bottom rates, leveraging his position to enforce them, and reaping high rewards.

Humphreys was not above using "a bill of sale from a desperate and notorious scoundrel" as evidence. He targeted one woman known as Lydia and obtained "several of her children by fraud." He seized Abraham's ally, Toney Barnett, who had liberated himself from a Creek slaveholder around 1816. (Toney also had children with Abraham's wife Hagar.) Humphreys acquired Barnett from a man "without any authority whatever" to sell him. Illegally purchased, illegally sold, and enslaved for five years. Humphreys retained Barnett on his own labor camp, on lands he was likely squatting on. In the end, Barnett and his wife Polly, widow to Chief Bolek, bought his freedom. Abraham's disputes with Humphreys were far from over. Twenty-nine Black Seminoles remained illegally enslaved by the former agent.

Humphreys was charged with corruption and fired.

John Phagan was the next agent to arrive. He proved even more bent than Humphreys. Instead of tyrannizing one of Abraham's peers, he stole the prophet's money. Abraham's trouble with Phagan began in 1832, when the translator accompanied an Indian delegation to present-day Oklahoma, to see the lands the government had set aside for them. His salary was $1.25 a day, standard for an interpreter. The Americans also promised him an additional $200 to curry his favor, a pledge later described as a bribe. When the "bribe" didn't help to evict anyone from their homes, the army painted Abraham as doubly corrupt. After all, he accepted a so-called bribe and then that "bribe" had absolutely no effect.

The kicker was, Phagan never paid the Interpreter his $285 salary. Abraham applied for his money, but Phagan "put him off by some excuse or other . . . and on every occasion offered him a gun, at a very high price, as part payment." The Sense Bearer already owned a firearm. He had no need to buy another gun at over double its fair value. Rebuked, Phagan forged a receipt with Abraham's "mark" and invented a witness named William Davis. The commander of the Territorial Militia in East Florida had never heard of any William Davis. Neither had the Marshal of the Territory.

John Phagan was charged with corruption and fired.

Thompson was a better man than Humphreys and Phagan, but not by much. He was not particularly intelligent. He promised that the Indians and Black Seminoles would not be separated. He promised, but it was difficult to trust him, especially after the enslavers showed up at the Agency house in April. Thompson tried to keep it quiet, but news of their visit reached the tribes and profoundly unnerved them. Was Thompson another Humphreys? A swindler who would seize the vulnerable for profit? Was he a Phagan type? A liar and a cheat? Did the emissary mean what he said, and if he did, did he have the power to follow through on his word? Official policy was in flux, with Thompson assuring the African Seminoles that they would be safe and secure on the journey west, and the president of the United States, spurred on by citizens of Florida, urging him to reverse course and enslave Abraham's people.

Chief Micanopy, for his part, revealed little, even as the functionary kept asking him, over and over, as if he could not understand the answer.

"The old man says today the same he said yesterday," Abraham told Thompson, in one meeting. "The Nation . . . decided in Council to decline the offer."

"I say what I said yesterday," Micanopy told the agent.

"We do not feel disposed to go west," Jumper told him.

Micanopy and his advisors saw no cause for bluster. They hoped to remain in Florida and to avoid bloodshed. Threatening Thompson would accomplish nothing. Barbs and taunts, in fact, would hurt their chances. Best if the Americans had no clue that many chiefs and warriors were preparing to defend their homes. The more poise they maintained—the less said in anger—the better.

3

Things Lost

In May of 1835, a warrior strutted into Thompson's office and "insulted [him] by some insolent remarks."

Foreign troops claimed that the man had no right to the land, so now he told Thompson that it was the agent's people who had no right to it, and "ordered him to leave the place." The outsiders had swaggered and predicted his total ruin, so he brandished his blade and delivered his own dire forecasts. He seized on his enemy's logic, twisted it, and hurled it against them. "Am I a negro? A slave?" he prodded. The foreigners seemed to hate dark skin, so he promised to kill them and leave their corpses in the sun and rain until their hides were ebony, and wolves caught the scent of their rotting persons, and vultures tore the flesh off their bones.

Osceola was well-known at Fort King. Thompson had singled him out as a determined upstart who was "more virulently opposed to removal than any other." In negotiations, his resistance to emigration was clear and consistent. His loud voice and temper were duly noted in reports to the War Department. During one discussion, with Abraham absent, Osceola had appeared tormented, as if afraid that Micanopy would prove vulnerable to persuasion without his Sense Bearer. Osceola stalked about outside the cabin and wielded "his knife, and flourished it around his head," as if desperate to ply the blade.

His righteous anger, and Abraham's distrust of Southern white Americans, formed the basis of their alliance.

Born to the Muscogee, or Creek people, Osceola was the enforcer for the Miccosukee Indians of Florida. More or less, he was the muscle. Yet he would become, by his overt deeds and by U.S. propaganda, the face of the conflict to come. His profile remains the logo of the Florida Seminoles football team.

Reporters of his era, as if cataloging a new race, detailed his physique: his ease, the athleticism in his "oiled" joints, his slight stoop, quiet eyes, the hollow and arch of his feet, his "long, dark lashes," Grecian nose, and the space between his mouth and square chin. Writers ogled him with perverted gazes, like those of entomologists admiring the butterflies they prized so much they killed them, stuck them under glass, and inventoried them. Later on it was deemed important to index his beaded belts, chintz tunics, ostrich plumes, silver bracelets and earrings, his pendants, his wampum beads, his otter-skin bullet pouch, his tomahawk, and even his skull.

He would be presented as the ideal Indian warrior, a "bold and dashing" rebel, a brazen savage to justify U.S. schemes. Miccosukee leaders would find a complementary use for the warrior, one that frames his ascent into legend within shadowy tribal politics, psychological warfare, and counterintelligence. A man of moderate status, neither a Seminole nor the leader, would be propped up as the "leader of the Seminoles" as much by white folklore as by a mysterious Indian chief, an elder who concealed his own power. A quiet patron who ushered Osceola into the spotlight also helped forge the myth, as we'll see, as he masked himself behind it.

In 1835, for all that, Osceola was still only human. The foot soldier who stormed into the Agency house that day was a sleek man with strong features, dressed plainly in a hunting shirt, leggings, turban, and moccasins. Abolitionists would claim that he was upset because he had a wife of African heritage who was seized as chattel. Others said he was drunk or that Thompson cut off his access to the sutler's liquor. All accounts agree that he was deeply upset.

After he finished his tirade, Osceola left the room without hurting Thompson. But the thin-skinned U.S. emissary simply could not bear the threats and indignity. An example would have to be made—something public. Osceola was two hundred yards from the barracks when the four soldiers snatched and subdued him, "after a hard scuffle." They locked him in irons and secured him in the guardhouse where, for some hours, he "remained in a state of frenzy." Thompson was glad to keep the dissident in chains. He believed that he understood the Native American psyche, that the "idea of a jail" caused "terror to the Indian mind," that such penalties imbued a "good effect."

Imprisoned, the warrior stewed and plotted, full of thoughts of revenge for things lost and the obstacles ahead. For all of Thompson's self-regard and inane pomp, the functionary was winning. The tribes were divided. Eight head chiefs, of thirteen, were pledged to travel west with their warriors, gutting the armed resistance. Osceola longed to fight back, but the tribes could not go toe-to-toe with the army if their ranks were sharply reduced. He viewed those chiefs who had voted under duress against war as turncoats to the cause. The "friendly Indians" clearly had to be punished, severely, for their disloyalty. An example would have to be made—something public.

As a boy, Osceola had witnessed the schism. He watched it all fall apart.

For centuries, residents referred to by colonists as Creeks controlled much of present-day Georgia, Alabama, and north Florida. Their traditions followed those well-known to the ancient world. Muscogee leaders treated their prisoners of war much like the Romans. Captives faced execution, enslavement, or if they were lucky, integration into the group. Creeks raided rival towns and forced labor camps in Georgia and South Carolina, took captives of all colors, and killed them, kept them as servants, or embraced them. The children of prisoners were welcomed as full members of society.

Over time, the logic of the Anglos distorted the old ways. After the American Revolution, as the population of the Deep South ballooned, some Muscogee men were seduced by the new culture of acquisitiveness and the riches promised by plantations and unfree labor. The "most radical innovation" in Creek captivity practices began to take root: the transgenerational enslavement of Africans. Converts accepted skin-based servitude and the notion that bondage extended to children. Like other Southerners, some Creeks now laid claim to servants and to their kids, and kids' kids, forever.

The large numbers of Africans among the Creeks in the early years of the American republic provoked "a terible uprore" [*sic*] and a rupture. Many Muscogee people did not accept the ideologies of white Southerners, found their practices corrupting, and "voted with their feet," joining Native allies in Spanish Florida. The Alachua band of Seminoles of Abraham's youth had already broken off from the Creek Confederacy in the mid-eighteenth century. They practiced the old customs: The status of prisoners was not based on looks and did not extend to children. In the peninsula, Native Americans did not turn servants into hard laborers on plantations for cash crops.

Men and women who liberated themselves, who became known as the Black Seminoles, found a place among old traditions. Lucy, aka Lydia, likely freed herself as a young woman in the 1790s from a white man in Georgia or was captured in a Creek raid as a prisoner. She lived among the Creeks until one of them killed her son Sampson, and then she escaped to the safety of the Seminole Nation. She had five other children, including a daughter, Flora, who married the interpreter Cudjo. Flora and Cudjo had Ned and

John. These were Abraham's wards. Many of them spoke English, Spanish, Muscogee or Hitchiti, and a Gullah dialect known as Afro-Seminole Creole.

Abraham's people embraced new traditions as Osceola's witnessed the destruction of old ones. Americans settled the land, and novel competitions supplanted conventional communities. Common lands became private. Consensus yielded to coercion. Traders came with mass-produced products that devalued the crafts practiced by women. Calico, osnaburg, and stroud fabrics replaced customary garments of mulberry bark and deer hide. Woolens replaced buckskin blankets. Rum diminished the hunters.

Osceola was around ten years old when his world was shattered by civil war, in 1813. Upper Creek "Redsticks," named for crimson war clubs, resisted encroachment. Lower Creeks joined forces with Andrew Jackson, then major general in the Tennessee militia. Osceola was a Redstick, reportedly born to an English father. He and his mother arrived in Spanish Florida around 1814, after the brutal Redstick defeat at the hands of fellow Creeks and General Jackson, and the cession of 23 million acres of land.

At the Battle of Horseshoe Bend, in March of 1814, Jackson's forces slaughtered some eight hundred Redsticks, effectively ending the war, and mutilated the bodies. Only fifteen or twenty Redsticks reportedly survived. Widows and orphans, Osceola among them, escaped to La Florida and its various allied bands. He grew to manhood, to see the general who'd butchered his people elected U.S. president. He sat in the negotiations with the pompous functionary, livid, forced to listen to Jackson's bullshit.

He never made any secret of what he thought about the chiefs who resolved to head west. In 1834, he had argued in Council that "any person who should consent to remove should be looked upon as an enemy, and should be held responsible to the Nation." Before the Creek Confederacy fractured, "there [was] no coercive power . . . their kings [could] do no more than to persuade." Chiefs used "storytelling, not chains and jail cells" to maintain "order in their towns." Now, under U.S. pressure, Osceola and others advocated harsh punishment for any leaders who yielded to American threats of war.

In particular, the enforcer blamed Chief Emathla, a muscular Apalachee cattleman known for his "amiable, sociable countenance and manners." Emathla had hoped to stay. He *had* protested, pointing to the 1823 treaty that prohibited immediate expulsion. He "consented," almost literally, with a rifle to his head. No matter. His life and his people were threatened. Thompson took the danger seriously enough that he allowed some of the "pro-removal" party to relocate outside the reservation, to the Tallahassee region, to avoid reprisals.

After a day in Fort King's guardhouse, in irons, Osceola cooled off. He sent word to Thompson that he would leave Florida. If the agent would summon Chief Emathla, Osceola would persuade him, of all people, that he was serious. Emathla, the warrior proposed, would convince Thompson. The cattleman was summoned. His talk with the prisoner was not put to paper, but after they spoke, Emathla vouched for Osceola: the rebel seemed to grasp the costs of war with the army; despite his passions, he was not governed by anger.

After six days, on Emathla's word, Thompson released him. Soon afterward, as a show of good faith and "true to his professions," Osceola returned to Fort King with seventy-nine others to pledge their loyalties. From that moment, he seemed to be "an altered man . . . on the most familiar terms with the" soldiers. He visited them "in the most social and friendly manner; invited [them] to his town, and performed many little acts of kindness, which could not be forgotten." He organized a cordial competition—a game of stickball—to engender good feelings. In the following weeks, Thompson hired him "on several delicate and important trusts," to discipline Indians who had committed "any depredation" on settlers, and the Creek "never failed" to inflict punishment on the culprits. The agent was so pleased with Osceola's "good conduct and valuable service" that he gifted him a "handsome rifle" as a reward.

"I now have no doubt of his sincerity," Thompson bragged, brimming with certitudes, in a letter to Washington, "and as little that the greatest difficulty is surmounted."

Summer came, and dense rains drenched the lowlands. In the Everglades, in the south, the dance between the wet and dry seasons was so peculiar that the land could not be described as one thing or another, as if the territory would not submit to words. Not quite lake or river. Not prairie or savanna, either. Salt water mingled with fresh. Sawgrass welcomed alligators and sharks. Great ponds washed on teardrop islands of tangled hardwood roots and aquatic flowers. Camping grounds vanished. Wagons yielded to canoes. Trails surrendered to the sun and North Star.

Even at higher latitudes, the changeful clime ravaged the land. Low waters halted ships and floods carried off bridges. Storms felled timber and clogged rivers with old rafts and snagging debris. As of early 1835, the Chipola in the Panhandle remained obstructed. So did the waterway from Fort King to Palatka. Earth muddied until entire regions became impassable by horse.

U.S. surveyors were grossly ignorant of vast swaths of the interior, and the infrastructure being built was a matter of fragile trial and error. Stretches of road—mere dirt paths with tree stumps sawed off low enough for wagon axles—were often shabbily strewn and in need of frequent repair. One lane stretching west from Jacksonville snaked through terrain so interspersed with "numerous boggy swamps & ponds" that even in the wintertime it was unsafe for heavy cargo.

Ten years earlier, in 1825, there was no major military path through the Indian reservation. Before the Fort King Road was constructed, the outpost in Tampa Bay later known as Fort Brooke, located on Florida's central Gulf Coast, was isolated from the northeastern cities. The camp's lifeline for monthly supplies had been a water route to Pensacola, in the Panhandle.

It took a full year to snake the crucial, sixteen-foot-wide, hundred-mile-long artery from Tampa Bay to Fort King through the unforgiving southern hinterlands. This sort of work required hard labor, scythes and reaping hooks for the long grass, mules or oxen to drag landfill, axes to fell trees, spades to shift dirt. Streams of considerable width were bridged in five places, and swampy, wet grounds were patched with log causeways.

Laborers stalled until autumn 1825 to avoid the malarial diseases and parasites that came with the mosquitoes and sand flies that came with the rains. The surveyor avoided beachy hills and ridges in favor of the eroding limestone plains in the valleys, steering east of the Wahoo Swamp, skirting west of Abraham's Town. Even that prudent pathway was vulnerable in the summers to the flashing thunderstorms, winds, and waterspouts.

The Fort King Road still traveled rugged and painful in the wet seasons.

In August of 1835, when the soldier's cadaver was found in a pond alongside the road, the route was still the most essential umbilical supporting the garrison.

Private Kinsley Dalton left Tampa Bay for Fort King on a mule, on August 11, carrying military letters. The express rider and his lumbering mount started out on the eastern bank of the Hillsborough River, where today stands the pirate-themed bar and grill known as Harpoon Harry's Crab House, and navigated northeast through thickets and marshland. Dalton passed the spring the troops used for water, which was barely drinkable, crossed through pine woods, over a sugar-sand elevation and beyond a red-clay hill, into a rolling wilderness. He was attacked within twenty miles—discovered shot, scalped, disemboweled, and floating, the letters gone. From what the Americans could glean, he was killed by Miccosukees allied with "old red sticks."

The brass in Washington expected to see the criminals punished: That task fell to a general called Clinch. Grizzled, over 250 pounds, dark eyebrowed and gray haired, the military commander was a slaveowner and self-professed Christian who had been killing Africans in the peninsula since 1816. He knew the Florida Indians as well as any other white man, which is to say that he didn't. At news of the murder, for all his wisdom and experience, he could only speculate about Miccosukee intentions. Was the Dalton killing an act of war, or something less sinister? The Indians said it was something less sinister—only a cultural thing—a necessary tit for tat for a prior dustup where an Indian died. The culprits would be turned over promptly. Dalton's death was no harbinger of hostilities. The missing mail was of no concern.

"Measures have been taken," Clinch assured the War Department, "by the officers of government and the Indian chiefs, conjointly, to apprehend the murderers."

"I have no doubt that by this time they have been secured."

But the killers were not secured. No Miccosukees or Redsticks were ever delivered. Weeks passed and all Clinch heard was crickets. By October of 1835, the general had begun to question himself—troubled by the hit-and-run tactics employed against Dalton. He had been operating with the idea that ten companies of fifty men could handle the Seminoles and their allies. Now, he grasped that if the Indians used the jungle, five hundred soldiers would not be nearly enough. If his adversaries spread out "over a large extent of country," into "marshes & swamps that are almost impenetrable to the white man," he did not have the troops to keep Florida safe. Suddenly, the forces at his command felt "entirely inadequate."

4

Labyrinths of Doubt

Before the war began, Abraham recruited soldiers along the rivers of sugar.

He visited forced labor camps and whispered of daring plans. The Seminoles had their eyes on the cane plantations in the east, along the intracoastal waters south of St. Augustine, and below Jacksonville on the St. Johns River. It was said that, in the Indian way, enslaved men and women at the labor farms were handed bundles of sticks dipped in red paint, and told to burn one stick each day. A countdown to zero hour.

Some Black Seminoles had husbands or wives trapped on the plantations; Abraham and his companion, "a chief of distinction," would have reached out to those they knew. One contact they would have visited or gotten word to was Romeo, a fifty-one-year-old bondservant at the Cruger and de Peyster property, south of what is today Daytona Beach. Romeo's African Seminole wife was "a near relation of Abraham" and sister to the prophet's close confidant August, who was "raised amongst" the Tallahassees.

Cruger and de Peyster were New Yorkers who had acquired the six-hundred-acre plot in 1830 and developed it, using other men's money. Wiser investors would have stayed away. By 1835, the pair had already been sued by creditors desperate to recoup losses. Their bungling operation was both inept and cruel. The first "apprentices" the duo brought to the site—reformed juvenile delinquents from New York's House of Refuge—were abused so severely that the authorities in St. Augustine intervened and "liberated them."

The sugar mill at the heart of the Cruger and de Peyster project was a squat stone factory dominated by a imposing, industrial chimney reminiscent of a death-camp crematorium's. Countless insects buzzed electrically around the locally quarried coquina of mollusk shells and quartz sands. Romeo was trapped on a "fully evolved" plantation equipped with a thirty-horsepower steam engine, scorching firebox, and barbarous boiling room with its train of massive cast-iron kettles capable of distilling hundreds of gallons of precious "white gold." The graceful archways of the doors and windows contrasted eerily with the primal flora and sucking bugs, the titanic cane crusher, giant steampunk sprocket wheel, and the dual, towering cast-iron boilers. Underneath coats of white lime plaster, shoddy masonry bound by improvised metal lintels betrayed the haphazard project for what it was: someone's violent pipe dream, a ruthless roll of the dice.

During the "boiling season" in the fall, bondservants on sugar farms were forced by overseers with whips to work day and night to process the cane before it spoiled. Behind shuttered windows, inside scorching fire-and-smoke-filled rooms, they suffered third-degree burns from blistering glucose, which could reach 240 degrees Fahrenheit. Bone-tired men and women lost limbs and died feeding cane into the inexorable crushers. In the Deep South, for this reason, a minder "was often stationed nearby with a sword to sever the mill feeder's arm before she could be pulled to her death in the rollers."

For Abraham and Romeo, their conspiracy was a matter of life and death. Fomenting a "servile revolt" was a capital crime. If the Interpreter was caught, he could expect to be tortured before he was killed. The leader of the rebellion in Louisiana in 1811, Charles Deslondes, had his hands severed and was shot in both thighs before he was placed inside a bundle of straw and burned alive. Amputated heads of his insurgents were placed on raised pikes on the road to New Orleans. A feral, ghoulish display stretching forty miles. The leader of the more recent revolt in Virginia, in 1831, had been comparatively lucky. Nat Turner's body had been mutilated, cut into pieces, and distributed for keepsakes after he was executed. Of course, the entire region then was terrorized. White supremacists dealt out punishments to anyone with dark skin. In "little more" than a day, 120 people were murdered. Folks who had nothing to do with the revolt "were tortured to death, burned, maimed and subjected to nameless atrocities."

Still, Abraham recruited. Still, it was said, enslaved men and women at the camps took the bundles of sticks dipped in red paint, and burned one stick each day.

Plantation owners and overseers were already on edge. Throughout the summer of 1835, while Osceola was performing friendly deeds, the Deep South had been shaken by an ambitious pro-abolition campaign carried out by William Lloyd Garrison's American Anti-Slavery Society. Targeting the notable and affluent, the organization mailed southward 175,000 copies of the *Emancipator*, the *Anti-Slavery Record*, the *Slave's Friend*, and *Human Rights*. In late July, in Charleston, South Carolina, a "vigilance society" called the Lynch Men broke into the local post office and stole the pamphlets before they could be delivered.

Threatening ideas carbonized at a public bonfire.

Increasingly, the Deep South stood alone. The United States had banned the transatlantic slave trade twenty-seven years prior. Great Britain formally abolished slavery across much of its empire in 1834.

A European observed, after visiting New Orleans, that slavery had been "confined to a single tract of the civilized earth." To Western "men of letters," the rite was increasingly distasteful. Southerners feared that it was the beginning of the end.

Nervous farm owners and investors in Georgia, Alabama, Virginia, and the Carolinas fumed at Northern "lunatics" who dared to print that slavery was a sin: "always, every where, and only sin." In Washington, soon enough, abolitionist petitions in Congress would push "southern members almost to madness" and rattle, in their view, "the very pillars of the constitution." Between August and September of 1835, over 150 anti-abolition meetings were held across the South, including in the Florida Territory. Local legislators strengthened laws banning antislavery materials. Diligent citizens scoured for troublemakers, who, if caught interfering, were tried and hung "without a word."

In Florida, violence and doubt were kindred. In St. Augustine, a "hotbed of slavery," a visitor was warned that if he showed sympathy to enslaved people he "might be found tomorrow lying stabbed in the gutter." In Jacksonville, residents urged laws "necessary to avert the evils intended by the Fanatics and Incendiaries," formed a "vigilance committee," and arranged regular patrols. The *Courier* assured readers of how "infatuated" and "perfectly insane" abolitionists were. Their insecurities did not arise from moral concerns. On the contrary, townspeople watching a slaveholder separate a family "did not take any more notice of it than of selling so many cattle," even as the mother, father, and four children "when they parted . . . all shook hands . . . and seemed to take it very hard, for it was not probable they would meet again." Local anxieties were more primal. Paying for labor scared them. Payback scared them.

The Florida Territory was only fourteen years old. Dreams of easy fortunes, spurred by incentives, attracted investors and settlers to the newfound backcountry. In 1833, the Legislative Council chartered the Union Bank of Tallahassee to serve as the local "planters' bank." Backed by bonds sold by the Territory of Florida, it opened with a staggering $1 million in authorized capital. After one year, the board raised that limit to $3 million. With a simple offer of collateral, "by pledging property on a loan . . . which property could be bought with money thus obtained," speculators could find themselves "suddenly rich . . . offhand the proprietor of land, negroes, houses and equipages." Bargains were everywhere where money was free.

But the colonists remained vulnerable. Jacksonville was home to some 250 people. The first school on record opened in 1835. The city paper started up that January. The town was several dozen scattered buildings, mostly log cabins, six stores, a courthouse, and a jail. One woman described it as "not much of a place. Perhaps 50 buildings . . . & plenty of pigs & children," the people generally "as rough as their houses." The riverfront was undeveloped. There was no bank or railroad. In a country of shoddy paths, rivers made the best roads. The town's prospects were tied to its location on the St. Johns: The city named after the president was an important port and point of commerce. While cotton production was centered in the north, around the territorial capital of Tallahassee, speculators in the east gambled with cane. Steamboats pushed down the waterways, delivering sugar boilers and enslaved people. "Huge plantations stretched into Florida's interior as far as the St. Johns River steamers could reach." Armoires, human chattel, and machines south; sugar, molasses, and rum north.

The riverine labor farms, exposed to attack, were first to sound the alarm.

In October 1835, a holdover from Spanish Florida named Hernández alerted the territorial governor that the Black Seminoles might be preparing for war. Hernández was a local militia commander who owned three plantations on the coastal Matanzas River and lived on one of them, Mala Compra ("Bad Purchase," in Spanish), as a country residence. Son of a carpenter from

Minorca, he had married the wealthy widow of a North Carolina slaver. In 1822, he was the first territorial delegate to represent Florida and the first Hispanic member of Congress. Now, he was growing uneasy. The "community at large," Hernández warned his governor—Jackson's former secretary of war—was filled with "much apprehension" about the "large number of Negroes amongst the Indians, who may be under the influence of the Abolitionists of the North, whose machinations are now endangering our safety." He proposed a "cordon of" militia along the St. Johns River of at least 150 men, requested two hundred to three hundred muskets, and forwarded the letter to the War Department, petitioning for the attention of the president.

In St. Augustine 1835, General Clinch was equally disturbed by the swirling, foreboding rumors. He warned Washington that "some of the most respectable planters fear that there is already a secret & improper communication carried on between the refractory Indians, Indian negroes, & some of the plantation negroes." The stocky officer owned two endangered estates. One was a sugar plantation called Auld Lang Syne, the other an orange grove on Lake George, a riverine expansion of the St. Johns.

In late October, Indians attacked the latter property and torched the cabins.

"This outrage, as a matter of course," the commander complained to the U.S. Adjutant General, on November 3, "has produced a great deal of alarm & excitement in the country." He begged the War Department brass to send guns "with as little delay as possible" and reminded them of his plea to recruit volunteers.

Jacksonville militia captains received orders to muster troops on November 10.

President Jackson, unconcerned, did next to nothing. To him, the "alarm of the southern men" over the abolitionists, "the burst of feeling" at their growing power, felt excessive. Their fears seemed unwarranted; the planters were crying wolf. Jackson's Secretary of War, Lewis Cass, denied Clinch's request for mounted troops. By

Cass' reasoning, if there was any trouble, the commander would have some seven hundred soldiers at his disposal, more than enough to handle a few Indians. Cass also rebuffed Hernández. The Seminoles would be removed west. The Florida project was on track.

By the end of 1835, Thompson had rebuffed Jackson's attempts to subjugate the Black Seminoles not once but twice. The agent would have hoped that the matter was closed. After the turmoil in April, he had focused on preventing speculators who were possessed by the "impression that the Indian negroes can be bought for little or nothing" from sneaking onto the reservation. Thompson even tried to obtain military "orders to turn back every white" civilian who dared "to cross the Indian boundary." When the president, unexpectedly, insisted on a policy of enslavement, the startled envoy drew a line in the sand.

"I venture to suspend further operations on the subject," he wrote, directly to Jackson. He did not bother explaining his warnings again in a diplomatically worded letter. Two officers visiting Washington from the Florida Territory would instead provide "a more comprehensive and correct view of the state of things" than he could "possibly give in writing." Scant record exists of Jackson's meeting with the officers, but when it was finished, the president backpedaled. He heard the message and reversed course. Maybe Thompson threatened to quit. Maybe Jackson finally grasped the damage he'd already done.

The president replied, in effect, that he had been informed and now understood that Indians in the peninsula appeared to be unusually fond of their bondservants:

> It is made known to me by Colonel Gadsden and Captain Thruston, now here, that the Indians in Florida have no disposition to sell their negroes, and the very idea that any

> individuals are permitted to come into their country to buy has disturbed them very much, and all say they will neither sell nor leave their negroes. You will therefore instruct the agent . . . to permit no individual to go into the nation to buy any of their negroes without his written passport, and to inform the chiefs of this order.

Jackson refused to recognize that there was anything unique about the Indian and African Seminole bonds. He seemed unable, or at least unwilling, to accept or acknowledge in writing that the term "slave" could be used protectively.

After all, Abraham owned his son Renty as a "slave." To Black Seminoles, titles and claims of ownership were instruments of self-defense. When possible, it was important to have these things written down in U.S. record books. After Renty was born, Abraham made sure to have Thompson make a notation of his parentage. In cases, Indians "sold" children to their parents, who ensured that the transactions were duly transcribed. One mother and father, Rose and Plenty, had their three children's freedom documented not only at St. Augustine but again at Fort King and for a third time at Garey's Ferry.

Paperwork could only accomplish so much. Southern "negro stealers," with their trained dogs, didn't care about titles of ownership, and corrupt speculators used forged documents. One of the greatest risks of emigrating, for Abraham's people, was simply having to gather in one place for the trip. For Indians, too, congregating outside the reservation made them marks for scoundrels. Roving "designing, unprincipled white men," as Thompson called them, circled "like so many hungry Vultures," ever eager to cheat Indians out of livestock, pelts, and corn. Prospectors would swindle people as readily as horses.

The date for emigration, for the party of "friendly Indians," had been set for January 8, and the departing families had to be fairly paid for their livestock. But if an auction was held near the reservation, speculators might pour in. And if locals claimed any of the Black Seminoles, Abraham's warriors—known to the army as "bold, active, and armed"—would likely kill them. If that happened, the odds of all-out war would skyrocket.

In the end, Thompson had little choice. He announced the "Sale of Indian Cattle" in local newspapers and set a date for December 1. The bidding would take place twelve miles from the Agency house, beyond the border of the reservation.

Tragedy struck on November 26, but not in the manner that the agent had most feared. That day, Abraham and Osceola visited the "friendly" Chief Emathla at his home, to convince him to remain and to resist. The cattleman refused to reverse his decision. Osceola "raised his rifle and was about to fire," before Abraham, "thrusting it aside," saved the chief's life. Hours later, Osceola returned with "a small party" and killed Emathla.

In another recorded version of events, the Creek enforcer came upon his victim after Emathla had sold his cattle. Acting on behalf "of the hostile chiefs," Osceola struck him down, scattered Emathla's payment of gold around his dead body, and warned Abraham: "It is the price of your blood!" According to a more mundane report circulating in Jacksonville, the ill-fated chief had not yet sold his livestock when he was executed. Instead, Osceola killed him as he was leaving Fort King, where he had presented a list of the horses and cows he planned to sell. When Emathla died, in fact, the auction was still five days away.

For months, the Miccosukees had applied "threats and persuasion" to dissenters, culminating in the murder. Most accounts agree that Abraham had hoped to sway Emathla, while Osceola was eager to kill him. The victim either "charged his attackers" before nine or eleven bullets dropped him, or "upon the first fire of the Indians" he "fell prostrate upon his face, and covering his face in his hands, received the death blows of his enemies without uttering a word."

One of Emathla's daughters was with him. Ick-ko-ho-lay (or Betsy) was twenty-three; Li-yo (or Nannie) was seventeen. He was also survived by a seven-year-old son.

The message was as clear to the tribes as it was to the Americans. The choice was war. If Emathla's murder strained relations among the bands, the alliances held for now. Chief Micanopy and the Seminoles would stand with the Miccosukees, and Abraham would fight beside Osceola as the rebel's fame grew. By the enforcer's hand, "friendly Indians" joined the resistance as white journalists spread word of his deeds. He was the leader who had led the Miccosukees in the attack on the "most intelligent" Emathla; Osceola had "fired the first gun."

Hearing the news at Fort King, a one-armed colonel named Fanning immediately messaged commander Clinch, who was holed up in St. Augustine. "A deep laid plan of villiany [*sic*] is just now developed," Fanning wrote, with Osceola apparently "at the bottom of it" all. "War is determined," he informed the general, from the isolated outpost inside the reservation. "You are marked as a Victim; therefore, be wary, come quickly, but come with force," he warned. "It is their determination with the mass of their force to attack this place." He begged Clinch to bring backup as quickly as possible:

> Raise fifty or one hundred mounted men with Rifles; pick up every man who is willing to join you on your march.—Bring Drane's Company. Order in Captain Grahams' as you come along. . . . Again I must say—lose no time—make every exertion to reach this post, where your presence is absolutely necessary.

Thompson appeared to react more calmly. "The consequences resulting from this murder," the envoy noted, dryly, "leave no doubt that actual force must be resorted to for the purpose of effecting the removal, as it has produced a general defection among those Indians, now in the nation, who were pledged to remove." He pulled the newspaper ads for the auction and published a new announcement in their place: "An indefinite postponement of the sales is unavoidable. . . . Citizens are warned to consult their safety."

5

The End

St. Augustine's harbor ran narrow and crooked. Navigating the tricky waterway was difficult enough that vessels often sat in port indefinitely. Captains risked wrecking their ships on the "St. Augustine bar," a shifting sand mass lurking six feet beneath the surface. Passengers scheduled to leave by sailboat, instead of steamship, could be detained ten days by the "tyrant wind"—northeastern gusts roaring down the Atlantic shore like nature's jail keeper, taunting its captives. Old-timers knew unlucky air currents as "orange winds," in honor of the trademark fruits decaying pungently aboard trapped schooners.

In the old rectangular city, ocean breezes lifted loose soil off slender streets, peppering horses' and pedestrians' eyes. February's brutal frost had reached eight degrees here, withering hundreds of citrus trees. Bright orange ornaments were absent.

Compared to Jacksonville, St. Augustine was a behemoth, easily the biggest city in what locals still called East Florida. Founded in 1565 by the Spanish, the city was crowned by the Castillo de San

Marcos, a moated coquina fort with fat, thirty-five-foot walls. At the change of flags, the town was already three-quarters of a mile long and a quarter mile wide, encompassing nearly a thousand domiciles "of all descriptions," including many two-story limestone homes. By the mid-1830s, some two thousand people called the city home.

Travelers described the port as stagnant and slothful. One visitor rebuked it, simply, as "small and dull." Another complained that he had never "been more disagreeably disappointed" by any place he had ever seen. The town felt grossly polarized, mired in purgatory, as if the partying white elites, who loved drinking and dancing above all else, had learned from enslaving others to be "idle, licentious, and useless." The naturalist John Audubon dismissed the locals as "all too lazy to work," and the site itself as "the poorest hole in the Creation—The living very poor and very high."

The Deep South had a grip on the city, but not a monopoly. Northerners passing the "sickening sight" of the "negro quarters," it was true, could find "human beings chained and ironed like wild beasts." Scottish merchants who had arrived in Florida "with a conscience that would scorn to keep a negro" learned that buying and renting people was a fast path to cash and were soon "overcome by the prevailing fashion." But Spanish, French, and Minorcan residents—descendants of indentured servants from the Mediterranean—also lent the town a distinctly multiethnic flavor. Spanish beaus serenaded lovers from the streets. Women danced to the harmonies of the Black fiddler Marcellini. Cross-dressing festivals still had their place in the "Ancient City." In the summer, for St. John's Eve, Minorcan ladies representing the "chivalry" paraded as men on decorated steeds. Masked gentlemen donned the "costumes of the ancient dames." "Damsels" visited candlelit altars decorated with draperies and accepted flowers from lady proprietresses. Over one hundred free Black people resided in or near St. Augustine.

Abraham visited in November of 1835. The prophet had likely frequented the walled settlement, to procure goods, for over a decade at least. His people, like all Indians in the interior, bartered for or bought many of their most vital necessities. Nearly 55 percent of items later unearthed at Abraham's Town were made in "European or Euro-American shops and factories." "Indian goods" included blankets, felt, woolen cloths, fine and heavy linens, and decoratively striped and checkered cottons. Osnaburg fabric was for workwear. Platillas were for blouses. Rumals made for head coverings and neckerchiefs. Britannias made good shirts. Armbands, finger rings, beads, mirrors, and fiery vermilion war paint were all acquired at traders' stores.

Abraham and the Seminoles also had to buy flints, gunpowder, and lead.

The apparent purpose of the Interpreter's visit, in the closing weeks of 1835, was to organize the covert delivery of armaments of war. He was not alone in St. Augustine. When the American artilleryman known as Drane spotted the Sense Bearer in town, he was in the company of Micanopy's brother-in-law Cooper. Drane harbored no suspicions that they were readying for war, or that, through the freeman Stephen Wright, Abraham was arranging for Spanish fishermen to smuggle gunpowder disguised as barrels of flour into Florida from Cuba.

White residents of St. Augustine, as tensions rose that November, kept their eyes on the local free Black population. Afro-descendant men and women could, they feared, help supply the tribes or leak critical information that exposed their defenses. As of December a single company, fifty-three armed men in all, protected the former Spanish capital of East Florida. Following the report of Chief Emathla's murder, the mayor of St. Augustine struggled to marshal a minimal security force. He confiscated all the guns that he could from the city's free people of color, and mobilized elderly veterans of past wars to guard the homes at night.

Terrifying hearsay spread wildly through Jacksonville's streets and shops. "The Indians," rumor was, "have commenced war uppon the whites, and are a killing on them in every direction." The land on the Gulf Coast north of Tampa was apparently "in flames." The "war whoop," they said, had sounded at Fort King. In Newnansville, the largest white settlement of "inland Florida," Chief Emathla's execution, and Thompson's public announcement of potential bloodshed, had unleashed deep "agitation and alarm." Residents were evacuating in horror. "Houses and property have been abandoned," a witness reported, "and women and children are flying from the *threatened* danger."

Commander Clinch arrived at Jacksonville on December 2, 1835, and camped on the St. Johns opposite the city. Crossing the river the next morning, finding "every one in a state of much allarm and excitement," he immediately appealed for 250 mounted volunteers. On paper, he had seven hundred soldiers, but most were unavailable or scattered. He called on the "gallant sons of Duval and Nassau Counties" for more men, "completely armed and equipped for active field service." The plea was a long shot at best. Two hundred and fifty militiamen could be found. Two hundred and fifty efficient, well-armed troops could not be. Not quickly. Horses and firearms were scarce, and not just any gun would do. Locals couldn't fight off Indians with twenty-year-old birding rifles. "Among many guns in the hands of the men in Alachua," a judge lamented, "I have seen but two that seemed to me really fit for service." In a letter to the Secretary of State, the justice pleaded that "*the country wants arms.*"

When Clinch reached Newnansville, he learned that the houses near the Indian reservation were on fire. By the time he reached the inland town of Micanopy, he realized how difficult it would be to recruit men as they ran to safety with their families. He found it "truly distressing to witness the panic and sufferings of the white frontier inhabitants," running about like headless chickens with nothing "save a few articles of clothing." Settlers who had lived comfortably were "now reduced to want." Overnight, colonists lost properties built by people they'd enslaved. Outsiders hoping to evict were evicted and made homeless, war refugees. Destruction came, in early December of 1835, "with the suddenness of the whirlwind and the storm," with roaring fires, crackling cabins, smoke clouds. "It is difficult to imagine or describe," Clinch bemoaned, "the alarm & confusion that pervades the whole of the citizens of Alachua & Columbia counties."

In the east, the militia commander Hernández ordered his troops to protect the forced labor camps on the coast, including his own. Militiamen moved into position to guard three of Hernández's investments on the Matanzas River, along with the Rosetta, Bulowville, Dunlawton, and Carrickfergus plantations. His personal finances were at risk. Earlier that year, he'd borrowed $38,000 from the Union Bank using his properties as collateral. When St. Augustine's mayor asked him to help guard the city, he declined.

Clinch pledged to counterattack. "My first object," he informed the War Department, on December 9, "is to throw a sufficient force on the Indian line to drive these incendiary and murderous wretches within their limits." Andrew Jackson, apparently also feeding off rumors, agreed. The president advised his commander to "with his whole concentrated force move into the Indian Towns, seize the women & children, and inflict merited chastisement for these atrocious murders so unprovoked."

But Clinch did not invade any towns, or drive anyone back inside their "limits." The general couldn't even manage a slight skirmish with any of the warriors who were traveling in small bands. Instead, the officer abandoned his pledge to march to Fort King and, like Hernández, prioritized his private interests. At Clinch's Auld Lang Syne labor camp, every year, over fifty enslaved people produced some 180 sugar casks, 80 cotton bales, and 2,000 corn bushels. (These laborers included Primus, a man with a Black Seminole wife.) In today's currency, the sugar alone was worth over a half million dollars annually.

Several hundred troops gathered at Auld Lang Syne, twenty-six miles northwest of Fort King, and Clinch's plantation became the official beating heart of the conflict. The soldiers built pickets 12 feet high, 80 yards wide, and 150 yards long, with loopholes for guns and defensive perches facing north and east, and the commander christened his dystopian farm with a more dignified title: Fort Drane. The site remained, to be sure, as everyone knew, "neither more nor less than General Clinch's sugar plantation." Clinch then ordered all but one company stationed at Fort King to his new headquarters, reducing the soldiers who were protecting Thompson to around fifty men in total.

The Agency house, along with the storekeeper's shop, remained outside Fort King's defensive walls, unprotected. Above Thompson's office, on top of the promontory, soldiers were still shoring up the defensive barricade of towering split pine logs that surrounded the barracks in an irregular pentagonal shape. On the southeast end, facing the Indian reservation, the troops had erected a "blockhouse": a large wooden "square room raised high above the ground on a pedestal-like base" that was typically entered from below using a ladder, through a door cut into the floor. Gunports allowed soldiers both to shoot out at attackers and down at enemies with torches attempting to burn the logs.

Indian forces intercepted U.S. couriers and confiscated mail. Communications between Tampa Bay and the forts and cities of the interior ceased. Fort King—isolated, exposed, and cut down in strength—took extra precautions. The sutler moved his wares inside the palisades for safekeeping. Both he and Thompson now slept inside the barricade. The agent was warned "not to expose himself out of the lines of Fort King."

Only a few years earlier, the envoy's future was auspicious. He had strolled the marbled halls of the U.S. Capitol. His contributions to the national interest had filled newspapers for all to read: There was Thompson, pushing to evict the Muscogee peoples from Georgia, defending his militia, and plotting out policy with Jackson, who was fresh off of winning his first term in office. Following one session with the president, Thompson was so enamored with Jackson's ideas for removing Indians "peacefully" that he published their talk in the *Georgia Journal*. But their shared scheme had floundered, along with any hopes to fast-track Florida to statehood. The envoy had failed; his failure was nearly complete.

In Washington, too, Jackson had lost stature. Bedridden, a lame duck, he complained that "nobody of no party had confidence in him." He puffed on his long pipe incessantly, "eternally whiffing," and pondered his "'little Jackson Family in East Florida." The president himself had only been governor of the Florida Territory briefly. He resigned soon after he watched the Stars and Stripes hoisted high in Pensacola, in 1821. When Jackson's wife saw the city, she was horrified to find a melting pot in the South. "Fewer white people by far than any other," she complained, and in their place a "mixed multitude." They left in boredom; his protégés remained with a mandate to extend the Deep South into the fledgling annex. Roads and railroads. Loans and land grants and labor camps. Books and newspapers peddling a Southern Eden to investors. The region would be less Spanish, less multicultural, and without Indians. Free Black people would have fewer rights. Removal on the cheap. Slavery without revolts.

A costly war and a rebellion loomed. Jackson had applied both "scripts" at the same time, against allied Indians and Africans, and mixed them up. Masks of friendship were less convincing flanked by faces of terror. Abraham and his people knew Jackson's intentions. Osceola had not forgotten his boyhood. La Florida retained its memories. The land of the "Atlantic Creoles"—men and women of color known for "linguistic dexterity, cultural plasticity, and social agility"—would not submit to the Jacksonian way. Old Florida was international, an enclave where African families gleaned the knowledge enslavers tried to deny them, where "all speak Spanish and French. Some speak four or five languages."

Florida itself—the very flora and fauna—defied the colonists. Torrential rains rebuffed their roads. Liana vines guarded the swamps from their cavalrymen. The Gulf of Mexico and the Atlantic allowed the Seminoles access to Spanish traders and the spoils of wrecked ships. Canoes connected them to the unmapped tree islands of the Everglades. Primeval forests protected the wild game. Unsullied rivers, lakes, and estuaries offered abundant fish and softshell turtles. Malaria guarded the marshlands. Alligators lurked in every mudhole. Scorpions, rattlers, and moccasin snakes waited in the summer heat with other biters: "gally-nippers, red-bugs, fire ticks, seed-ticks, fleas." Even the plants—sword ferns, Spanish bayonets, and Spanish daggers—warned off the Americans.

Far from the crisis, Jackson conveyed his instructions to Clinch to "subdue [the Indians] as quickly as possible" with the men available. He was "anxious," his secretary of war wrote, "that no greater number of troops be called into service than is requisite, on account of the expense." Jackson was not aware that Clinch was camped at Auld Lang Syne and had deserted Thompson, or that on December 26, 1835, Clinch withdrew troops from Fort King.

On December 28, around three thirty in the afternoon, Thompson and a lieutenant named Smyth dined at the Agency house below the fort walls. Afterward, they enjoyed a leisurely post-supper stroll away from the pickets toward the sutler's store, seven hundred yards below the hill, over a quarter mile from the stockade, soldiers, and guns, toward the warriors waiting in the woods.

6

Prophecy

> Before the death of [Wiley] Thompson, Abram had prophesied that he would be killed by Indians while walking about his place. . . . Such had subsequently been the fact.
>
> —*New York Evening Post*, 1836

In the early years of the nineteenth century, Native seers spoke of a return to past ways, to before modernity made men lazy, and liquor numbed wits. Prophets sermonized of a pan-Indigenous alliance, a rejuvenation won through battle, and martial triumphs over the colonists. Holy women protested the "plows and looms that had upset older gender roles" and the European goods replacing the Indian wares they had once crafted.

A Shawnee clairvoyant saw the vision in a dream, and spread the lesson, and the lesson inspired thousands. In 1811, his brother Tecumseh made a pilgrimage to the Deep South, to meet with Muscogee leaders. The "age of prophets" reached La Florida. Oracles preached a new gospel, and a meteor tore across the sky, and the earth shook.

The Redstick prophet Francis rose to power, inspired by the Shawnee and the diviner Seekaboo. In time, he became the most important Muscogee holy man and took on many subordinate sages. The mystic assured his followers that he could live underwater and fly in the sky, and proved his devotion to spiritual and practical war.

Francis galvanized followers to fight the Americans, including Jackson, leading to what textbooks called the First Seminole War but for Seminoles was the onset of a colonial assault that lasted over fifty years. Francis negotiated with Spanish authorities and helped secure gunpowder and lead. His speeches lent strength. His prophecies were tools of warfare, inspiring belief in all rebels that the spirit world was on their side.

God, Master of Breath, Giver and Taker of Life, was beside them all.

Help was on its way to Thompson, if the reserves could reach him. The troops were dispatched to Fort Brooke, the eleven-year-old outpost in Tampa Bay that looked more like "an ornamented College Green" than an army station. The southwestern fort sat off a grand shoreline, in "one of the most beautiful and regular groves" ever seen. Majestic live oaks, "the most superb trees" of "enormous limbs, as large as the trunks of common" hardwoods, extended nearly horizontally some dozen feet before branching and rising to a height of fifty, forming "a perfect *parasol*" and shading the "wonderful quarters of logs" under a lush canopy, a natural awning decorated with "long pendants of the Spanish moss, and with festoons of the yellow jessamine" and lemon-gold flowers.

In mid-December 1835, panic loomed over the camp. Ammunition was dangerously scarce. Soldiers slept with their rifles, lightly. All available hands, including the officers, worked to fortify stockade walls and to erect defensive blockhouses. The hundred-some local civilians were so fearful of Indians that every night they crowded inside the newly erected fences and slept among the troops. The pickets touched the shore twice and pointed north like an A-frame, toward the Indian reservation. Most buildings, including the cantonment headquarters, the stable, and the hospital, were beyond the palisades. So were the "friendly" Indians camped to the west across the Hillsborough River, north of the anchorage point and the oyster bed. The emigrants—families allied with the late Chief Emathla—included only one hundred men. Three hundred were women and children.

Four companies of soldiers—two hundred additional troops—had been ordered to Florida to join Clinch, who planned to attack the Seminoles and their allies on December 31. The trouble was, Fort Brooke made little sense as a staging point. The reserves should have been sent down the Atlantic coast, not the Gulf of Mexico. If the requisitioned soldiers had taken steamships from South Carolina or Georgia down the St. Johns River, Clinch would already have the extra troops he badly needed. Instead, the additional companies were ordered to report to Tampa Bay at a time when the outpost could not make contact with either Fort King or "Fort Drane," with "the centre of the disaffected & hostile part of the Seminole Nation" positioned between them. Clinch's army was "equally divided"—its effective force reduced by half—with neither part, in the commander's opinion, "strong enough to effect much in a Country like this." Newly dispatched artillerymen and infantry who arrived at Fort Brooke were left with few options. To meet up with Clinch, they had to march up the Fort King Road, through the heart of the Indian reservation.

A hundred-mile travail. A trial by fire though the enemy stronghold.

The other problem was that some troops were late. By December 21, 1835, ten days from Clinch's planned assault, only two of the four companies had arrived in Tampa Bay. When the schooner *Motto* made anchor that day, at long last, the ranking officer disembarked with a mere thirty-eight infantrymen and "a small supply of musket ball cartridges" scavenged from scattered Gulf Coast depots. Fort Brooke's ranking officers—a captain called Belton and a major named Dade, in particular—faced an unenviable choice.

They could either trek up the Fort King Road with half the troops, or fail to reach Clinch in time.

Belton was Maryland-born, a former Virginia lawyer who might have preferred a life as a London barrister. He would have been one, too, if his ship to England had not sprung a leak and been forced to limp back to port. Belton hated the idea of a march into the reservation and was troubled by the communications blackout. "Gen Clinch last is dated Fort King, 15 Nov," he noted. "He is not aware of the state of this garrison." To him, leading a hundred men up the Fort King Road was lunacy. He preferred to resign.

Most officers agreed. A shorthanded march would be "virtually doomed."

Dade was a more rugged, braggadocious sort then Belton. His black beard reached below his waist, so far that it was difficult to tell where the nest of bristles "stopped and his boots began." His tall officer's hat, a stovepipe shako, towered absurdly on his gigantic cranium, stretching some twenty-four inches in circumference—an XXL, by today's standards. He was the type of officer who insisted on wearing his long crooked sword at all times, even indoors, where it clanked "as he walked about and . . . dragged on the floor and struck against the furniture." One woman who met him described him as "covered in dirt from head to foot."

On December 22, the urgency of their decision was impressed on both officers by an unexpected event. That evening, a patrolman found the adjacent Indian camp abandoned. On hearing the news, Belton took a "small guard," crossed the Hillsborough, and quietly followed the trail northward. After a quarter of a mile, he came upon a "large Indian council in session." Three envoys, "deputies from the hostile party," stood in the center of a circle and addressed the families. Belton spied on the mysterious proceedings until he was discovered by children playing in the trees. Then he barged in on the talks and arrested the three emissaries.

Back at Fort Brooke, he and Dade interrogated the prisoners.

The envoys didn't hide their purpose for long. They had been sent to "stop the whole emigration."

Even the "friendly" chiefs seemed to be losing faith in the Americans.

That night, "in a council with" one of the chiefs, Dade reassured the would-be emigrants that the army remained completely in control. He preached of his "confidence in Indian character," and spoke of his faith in the positive "influence of *Abraham*" on Chief Micanopy. The major boasted that he could "march all over Florida with his single company."

Dade pledged to lead the march himself. The army could not wait for the hundred-some soldiers still on their way. Belton would stay behind and try to get word to General Clinch that Dade was coming. Given the geography, Belton had no choice but to hope that Micanopy would allow an army courier through the reservation. The captain tasked one of his Indian captives—"holding the other two as hostages for his fidelity and return"—with delivering letters to both Thompson and Clinch. He promised the prisoner twenty silver dollars as a reward. The messenger, he knew, had to pass right "through *Abraham's Lands*."

Naturally, Belton's message to Clinch "was upon the subject of the premeditated attack of the 31st December and involved many details," including "numbers and other facts" of strategic value. Abraham could "read but little," Belton recognized, "yet was likely to have with him a well educated" comrade who could. "To guard against treachery," to protect the most sensitive information, acutely aware that the letter "might pass through Abraham's hands," he wrote "numbers and other material facts in *French*."

Belton sent his Indian courier north, ahead of Dade.

On December 23, Dade said his goodbyes to the gathered crowd, "thanking them for their concern." The "friendly" chiefs bid farewell to his officers, certain that "they would never see them again alive."

Belton saluted Dade, and 108 U.S. soldiers embarked up the Fort King Road, stepping to the patter of a drum. Pomp and circumstance disappeared over a low ridge, bonded by flag and fabric. Cool gray double-breasted greatcoats, trousers the color of a cloudless day, gilt and silver buttons. Ivory leather belts. Epaulettes. Alabaster gloves. They were armed with swords or bayonets and 1816-model flintlock long guns that weighed eight pounds and measured an ungainly five feet. They hauled gunpowder and shot, canteens, and heavy rations. At the rear, a horse dragged a supply wagon over bumpy, jolting dirt. Four oxen lugged a heavy-wheeled cannon capable of firing six-pound iron orbs and making a loud boom that officers hoped would terrify the Indians.

Dade was no stranger to the Territory of Florida. Nine years prior, he destroyed a host of Native settlements and drove "about eighty men women & children" from their homes on the Suwannee River, leaving them in "the most perfect picture of distress." A year prior to that, in 1825, his men strutted down the Fort King Road, stopping at Micanopy's primary residence, twelve miles north of Abraham's Town, as a show of force. They found the village deserted, before meeting a messenger who emerged from the woods to explain that the people "had taken to the swamp, and would fight if followed." Dade did not follow. In 1821, Dade had answered to Jackson in Pensacola. Before that, he served under Jackson during the invasion of La Florida.

His soldiers were four miles away from Fort Brooke when their oxen gave out. The draft animals were trained to pull plows to till fields, not lug iron-shod carriage wheels and cannons over rugged, rutted grounds. Nostrils flaring, wheezing and rasping, they planted themselves stubbornly in the road, leaving the army with no choice but to unhook the beasts and abandon the cannon amid the yellow palmetto blossoms, muzzle stuck in the dirt like an ostrich, as if terrified by the surrounding forest.

Dade sent a message back to Belton in Tampa for horses to haul the weapon forward, and his army marched onward. "All in fine spirits," he assured the captain. U.S. troops had not traveled the Fort King Road for months. The sandy dirt was "nearly covered with a green and healing growth." Hound dogs bounced back and forth, circled the soldiers, howled and yelped. Swamps and marshland, settlers' log shelters, pine barrens, hammocks, ponds, and palmettos led them to the first of the bridges, a "strong, substantial" overpass at a narrow stream bordered by silvery cypresses. Pine needles carpeted the earth.

At Fort Brooke, Belton purchased the three best civilian horses he could find, and dispatched men to retrieve the six-pounder, and haul it to Dade's camp. He also sent forward an interpreter. The linguist Louis Pacheco, "good-looking, intelligent," "able-bodied . . . in the prime of life," was assigned by chance. He was only in Tampa Bay because his Spanish enslaver had died, and he was traveling to meet the executor of the estate to be delivered to the widow. He spoke English, Spanish, French, and at least one Native language, either Muscogee or Hitchiti, and had learned to read and to write. Belton "rented" him and ordered him north.

The six-pounder cannon reached Dade after nightfall, after Pacheco caught up with the detachment, after the quarter moon had risen in darkness. The enslaved interpreter, "ambitious to learn, and quick of perception," had acquired "a good deal . . . of book learning"—more than many Americans were comfortable with. He found himself among campfires of mostly illiterate troops, a mix of Northern rabble and foreign-born transplants from Ireland, Scotland, England, and Germany, children of some "farm or small town [who] joined up in a confusion of boredom and patriotism."

The next afternoon, after another tiring march, Dade messaged Belton again from the twisting Hillsborough River. He asked the captain to send along the troop reinforcements due at Fort Brooke "as soon as possible," and requested a supply of ammunition and more provisions "without delay." He wrote, in his last message to reach Tampa, "There has been no hostile attempt made on us as yet . . . but they have burnt the bridge here, and I expect all others."

Belton's Indian courier returned to Fort Brooke two days later than expected, carrying a blunt message and a strange assortment of sticks. The captain's letter—and its secret details—*had* fallen into Abraham's hands. According to the courier, the Interpreter appreciated its contents. Baldly, the Black Seminole chief had asked the messenger to tell Belton that his "talk was good" and to gift him a clutch of kindling, with instructions to throw away one stick every day. When the bundle was gone, Abraham promised to meet the army on the battlefield.

Belton counted the sticks: Their number "indicated the 31st" of December.

The captain could scarcely believe that the information had been "freely rendered," that the Sense Bearer had admitted "that he would be *at the attack* fixed for Christmas week." The message was an open taunt. The officer had no way, after all, to tell Thompson or Clinch that the army's plan was compromised. Abraham's gall flustered the captain. Days after the incident, he still did not seem to understand why it was a bad idea to code military intelligence in a Romance language and send it through lands controlled by linguists raised in Spanish Florida.

Abraham prophesied Thompson's death, and Halley's Comet tore across Florida's nightscape. Spies sent word that "two companies were preparing to march" the Fort King Road, and the Seminoles and Miccosukees assembled in Council. Both Dade and Thompson were on the agenda. The Indian agent had "put irons on our men," as one chief recalled, "and said we must go." Osceola argued that the emissary was "was *his friend*" and insisted that "*he would see to him,*" and the chiefs agreed that Osceola "should attack Fort King, in order to reach" Thompson. That done, he should "return [south] and participate in the assault mediated upon the soldiers coming from Fort Brooke."

Thompson first. Dade next.

Osceola and some fifty Miccosukee warriors advanced to Fort King as Dade's men strutted north toward Abraham's Town. By December 27, Osceola and his men had reached the forest flanking the sutler's shop, below the hill. The warriors stayed clear of Fort King and kept their distance from the Agency house, opting instead to wait to ambush Thompson. They held fast in the woods in "dense foliage and palmettos," as the hours ticked away. A day of doldrums. On December 28, pleasant weather drew the envoy from his Agency house, in the company of an officer, to enjoy a cigar. It was said that when Osceola saw Halley's Comet he prayed to the heavens, and had lured Thompson's spirit.

The agent neared, until he reached a slope "in full view of the fort," three hundred yards from the Agency house. Osceola shouted—a shrill battle cry—and the warriors emerged from the thicket, from thirty feet away. The attackers included two chiefs "whose attire denoted them to be leaders" but whose names remain unknown. The sequence of the injuries that Thompson endured was not recorded. He was scalped, impaled by "a deep knife wound in the right breast," and riddled with fourteen bullets. The lieutenant at his side was shot twice. The raiders "proceeded at once to the sutler's" shop and killed the storekeeper.

A clerk's head was discovered "so broken that the brains had come out." An enslaved woman, the murdered sutler's cook, "concealed herself behind some barrels under the counter" and watched as Osceola "came into the room, battering down the furniture and whatever else chanced to be in his way."

He shouted again, acutely, and he and his men were gone.

Forty-six able-bodied American troops were reportedly shoring up defenses when they heard Osceola's war cries and retreated inside the stockade. Several diners escaped from the sutler's and confirmed the attack. Smoke from the burning store followed the fumes from the guns. The garrison did not recover all the bodies at once. Thompson, the lieutenant, and the clerk were retrieved quickly. The sutler's body was left outside where it was discovered the next day, "shockingly mangled," the head "very much broken." Messengers rode to apprise Clinch. Two days later, they had not returned. The soldiers worried that they were cut off to the north, as well as to the south.

Thompson's body was buried, for the time being, at Fort King. For the fourth quarter of 1835, for duties performed in service of "Florida Removal," he earned $500.

7

Trespass

But I will punish you according to the fruit of your doings,
saith Yahweh: and I will kindle a fire in the forest thereof,
and it shall devour all things round about it.
—Yiremiyah 21:14

At one time, the Seminoles routinely burned the forest undergrowth, and the fresh grass brought wildlife to them. Near the capital of Tallahassee, the land was covered in virgin timber with no brushwood, only lawn and flowering weed. Trees blanketed "undulating hills and valleys" into the distance: "magnificent extensive parks" of geese, bucks, bear, and turkey. A banker's son remembered it as a "veritable hunter's paradise," and recalled how the deer loped fearlessly in front of the path, in herds of ten to fifteen, and how a half dozen flocks of wild turkeys had once lingered beyond the doorframe.

At first, when Americans arrived in numbers, their cattlemen continued the Indigenous practice of burning the bushes and scrub. But after the forced labor camps "and their extensive fencing became numerous," the cleansing fires could no longer be used to rejuvenate, and repellent underbrush clogged the woods.

Poor stragglers who lived off the land were the first to wander into the territory. They were "cast-off Americans," so-called clay eaters, piney woods people, sand hillers, mountain whites, river rats, rednecks, and crackers. Pickpockets, alcoholics, gunfighters, and swindlers drifted down to the "rogue's paradise" in search of an edge. According to Napoléon Bonaparte's nephew Achille Murat, who lived in exile in St. Augustine, early settlers were known for their "idle and drunken habits." Among "poor citizens," he wrote, "there exists no form of government; every dispute is amicably terminated by the fist." A society woman called them "the most miserable squalid creatures in the world."

White elites preferred the high-society "planter" who followed by coach—seduced by "extravagant promises of land speculation." This man arrived from Virginia, the Carolinas, and Georgia, with "goods and provisions in carts, his Negroes on foot, himself and his family in a wheeled carriage, or on horseback." Roads were shoddy and partial; enslaved people cleared woods and built bridges along the way. Arriving in the territory, the "planter's entourage continued to camp" until the bondservants constructed houses from the tree trunks. Down came magnolias, oaks, and laurels.

Lower-class slaveholders represented a third stratum of colonial society. One cattleman of this sort lived in a "badly-built, wind-cracked, fenceless, vineless, paintless mansion in the Pine Lands." His "face was sallow, his lips thin and stained with tobacco, his dress loose." The cowboy was "wealthy in land and slaves, and he had sired many of his younger Negroes. He lived a crude sort of life, enjoying few luxuries except his artful loafing and hunting." He was badly in debt but "bountiful with wine . . . and with whisky at all times." In general, migrants were either the "rich vulgar" who "belonged" and owned "negroes and lands," or among the poor who traveled southward "in hopes of getting them."

Progress toward American statehood and the full rights of the Union advanced slowly. As of 1830, there were only 0.6 inhabitants per square mile in the Florida Territory. The U.S. Census Bureau would not even consider a frontier minimally occupied until there were at least two people on average per square mile. By the standard of the Northwest Ordinance, the 1835 territorial population—counting more than twenty thousand enslaved people among the total—remained over ten thousand settlers shy of the sixty thousand required to demand recognition as a state. Aiming to lure Southerners, colorful advertisers championed the soil. Come to grow cotton, coffee, or indigo. Come cut down trees to produce tar, pitch, rosin, and turpentine for shipbuilders. Take out a loan and try your hand at sugarcane and at hemp. Feast on olives and tropical fruits. Join life on the frontier, where rugged housewives fight wolves using "only a club," and women display a considerable amount of the "alligator and the snapping turtle in their dispositions."

Even as 1835 neared its violent end, Florida newspapers pledged rosy futures and tempted hopeful speculators. A five-hundred-acre labor camp on the St. Johns. Over two hundred acres of oak forest "for cash, or prime Negroes." Eighty acres "under good fence." A whopping 1,520 fertile acres with "20 Negroes, 18 of which are good effective hands."

Yuletide was as exuberant, shoddy, and wild as the population. The colonial elite indulged in roast turkey, plum pudding, absinthe, "Havana segars," galas, and never-ending hours of "frolicks," while the "plain folk" raised pathetic sand pines too spindly for heavy ornaments. Boisterous men howled out for their Savior and shot pistols after dark.

Christmastime in Florida always brought joy, yelling, and gunfire in the night.

Micanopy, Jumper, and Abraham mustered one hundred eighty men to meet Dade's. The Interpreter commanded eighty warriors; that day his ranks numbered around fifty. Black Seminole forces were also subdivided into companies. Old Primus captained fighters who stood with the Miccosukees. Juan, a trusted counselor and skilled soldier old enough to have seen action in 1818, had charge among others over Ishmael, the son of Sarah and brother to Phoebe and

Caesar. Juan's son Toby, not yet twenty, also marched under his direction. Toney Barnett's son Boston fought under Abraham, likely next to his father. So did Ben, husband to Jane and father of eight. African-born brothers Kelina, Plenty, Cuffee, and Jesse—siblings to Nancy and uncles to Sue, fourteen—took up arms beside them. "Abram's company" also included Old Charles, who had just become a grandfather, and Sandy, in his sixties, who already was one. The Sense Bearer led fighters as young as thirteen.

The Seminoles and their allies had been preparing for war for over a year. Chiefs had purchased gunpowder and lead in bulk from Fort King and from the traders in St. Augustine. By October, the tribes had stowed away forty to fifty kegs of black powder, and by December, they had purchased most of the stocked supply in the Ancient City. Weeks prior, women and children evacuated the villages and moved to the safety of the Cove of the Withlacoochee and the Wahoo Swamp. By the end of the year, Abraham's Town, Big Swamp, and Long Swamp were all empty. The families settled into new homes, likely at least eight miles west of Pilaklikaha and four west of the Fort King Road. The Wahoo Swamp took its name from the wahoo tree, native to thickets and stream banks, whose bark made good head-collars for horses. The adjacent Cove was a foreboding sixty-three-thousand-acre wetland made up of "a chain of lakes or ponds, communicating with each other by boggy sluices" dotted by "pine islands, cypress swamps, [and] hammocks." Within its limits stood elevated hardwood stands large enough for cabins, crops, and even grazing land for livestock.

The wetlands' natural fortifications embodied the "same principles" as those "used in [the] systems of defense" of the time. At one massive hammock, a stream formed an organic moat, splitting and bleeding into two marshes of tall saw-toothed grass, each seventy-five yards wide. Protruding above and hidden below the surface, knifelike remnants of cypress tree outgrowths—spiderlike roots known as knees—projected like spears, their spikes "almost as pointed and dreadful as the stakes of war pits." Sinkholes offered other deadly obstacles. Vines webbed paths like giant spiderwebs, spinning a disorienting tangle. The "prevailing dankness" seemed designed to have "an unfavorable moral effect" on any enemy who dared enter.

On December 28, before daybreak, Abraham's company stood ready in the Wahoo Swamp. Within hours, Dade would bypass Abraham's Town at a juncture hugging the edge of their swamp refuge. Osceola and his warriors were still at Fort King, but if Abraham and the others waited, Dade would advance beyond the ambush site and they would lose "the favorable moment." Jumper argued for immediate action.

Six-foot-four, in his fifties, and "exceedingly intelligent," he was one of the most influential chiefs in the Nation. Known as "the Lawyer" for his sharp advocacy, he often led negotiations with the Americans, with Abraham interpreting. As a young man in Alabama, Jumper—now also a sense keeper, as Micanopy's close advisor—reportedly battled against Andrew Jackson's forces. He was happily married to Micanopy's sister and had six children, "to whom he seemed much attached." Some claimed that he was Creek, others that he was of the Yamasees—a people pushed into Spanish Florida in the early eighteenth century and in part absorbed by other tribes. He insisted that he came "from a distinguished race, of which he [was] the sole survivor," the last of an "ancient tribe." He described himself as a "rogue."

He was one of Abraham's closest allies. All three Seminole leaders—Micanopy, Jumper, and Abraham—were deeply loyal to one another. Special relationships between men of the Nation were later described as bound by "Fellowhood," wherein "young men agree to be life friends 'more than brothers,' confiding without reserve in each other and protecting each the other from all harm." If Jumper chose to fight, Abraham and Micanopy would fight.

Jumper did not command any warriors to obey him. On the contrary, he "requested that those who had faint hearts" stay behind. The Lawyer had made his decision, and was "going, when Micanopy said he was ready" and joined him. The sunrise warmed the wetlands and 180 fighters, included Abraham's, left the swamp and ventured east. After a few short miles they entered a pine barren and reached the Fort King Road.

On the far side of the road, a pond was guarded by "tall grass, brush, and small trees." If they could pin down Dade's army here, the bladed grass and growth would complicate, if not outright halt, any eastern retreat. Each fighter carefully "chose his position on the west side," protected by pine trees and high palmettos. Abraham's warriors, with Jumper's, settled into a long line that stretched and bent around the pond in a semicircle, a perfect shooting gallery, and waited for Dade's troops.

The literate, enslaved man led the illiterate army. Louis Pacheco walked ahead of Dade's march, alone, to the "Big Hillsborough" River, to scout for hostile forces. Dade deployed him as a human shield, a minefield sweeper sent first into danger so that the 108 American troops could safely follow.

Pacheco reached the Native town of Thlonoto-sassa only to find it silent. Palmetto-wood homes stood abandoned. Playing children were absent from the shores of the lake down the hill. No anglers fished or dug for clams. Pacheco followed the high road west of the water and turned at the north shore, where the route descended to a small creek. Where the forest opened into the clearing, he found the burned ruins of some cabin or trading post and an evil omen in the road.

A bloodied cow, split open, lay dead in the middle of the pathway. A message, blinking red, for Dade's command. Beyond the bovine, up the slope at the Big Hillsborough, the wooden beams of an army bridge were charred and smoking, the overpass wrecked. Low flames licked the planks. Pacheco knew that the torched bridge and mutilated carcass were signs "of warning and danger," and when the army caught up, he confronted Dade.

"Hostile? No," Dade lied, blaming it on a recently jailed Seminole known to the Indians as Capikch Achulee. "Old Bowlegs did that, Louis," he claimed. "He's been in the guardhouse at Tampa. He got away a few days ago, and he did that out of spite."

"More than Old Bowlegs did that," Pacheco said.

Deserted houses lined the Fort King Road, cattle missing from the pens. At night, the soldiers felled trees and slept behind the trunks while Indian scouts jeered and shot, tormenting their sleep. Dade expected an attack, if one was planned, near the forks of the Withlacoochee River, directly below the Cove of that name, south of Abraham's Town. Pacheco harped on the risks, but "every time Major Dade would laugh at him."

"If you are afraid, Louis, I will not send you," the officer said.

"Did not you tell me that the Indians were not hostile?" Louis said.

Dade promised it was perfectly safe but he kept sending Pacheco on ahead. The linguist advanced by himself "to explore every bad place" on their route. On December 26, on Pacheco's thirty-sixth birthday, the major gave his "guide" more specific orders. "If you see a black man in the road named Sam," Dade said, "tell him I'll see him—to wait." But when the interpreter arrived Sam was gone, and grass was "trampled down in the woods."

"I guess Sam's gone to Wahoo Swamp to keep Christmas," Dade offered.

"It's worse than 'keep Christmas,'" Pacheco said. "Wasn't a soul on the place."

"I'll go through if I have to fly sky-high," Dade said, and they went on.

The major had a vision that night. "I had a strange dream," he told one of his captains, on December 27. "It was one of the strangest dreams of my life. I dreamed that I was among all the old officers that died in the [War of 1812]." The soldiers who had perished beside him in battle appeared again and spoke, and he called out their names.

The detachment neared Abraham's Town on December 28, after marching five days and covering some sixty miles. Dade dispatched dogs to search the surrounding forest, but the hounds behaved strangely that morning, and lingered in the roadway. The canines "did not hunt through the woods nor bark with any spirit."

The advanced guard marched two hundred yards ahead. The Withlacoochee River—the rumored attack point—flowed behind them, and Dade was calm and confident. "We have now got through all the danger," he told the men. "Keep up good heart, and when we get to Fort King, I'll give you three days for Christmas." At around 9:00 a.m., the soldiers spotted another lone animal by the road, this one living: a silvery mare.

Dade called for Pacheco, pausing in the pine barren, pines and palmettos to the left, pond and high grass on the right. Micanopy yelled Dade's name, and at "the sound of his voice Dade threw up his head and Micanopy fired, the ball striking him in the throat and going through." He was hit while snacking on a cracker, according to a Black Seminole witness. Another account stated that Jumper gave the war cry before Micanopy discharged. Others reported that Micanopy, to the end—up to the moment he shot Dade and the major shrieked "My God!" and fell off his horse—did not want to kill him and hoped to avoid the war that followed.

8

Kinship

> The Florida War was occasioned, not so much by the indisposition of the Indians to emigrate, as by the attempts made by our own citizens, under the sanction of officers of the Government, to obtain [the Black Seminoles].
>
> —General Jesup

In Seminole marriages, women ennobled men. Children joined the mother's clan, and uncles, not fathers, taught boys "manly pursuits." The royal line did not descend from father to son but from uncle to nephew. Sisters of chiefs were literal kingmakers, and a chief with many sisters could find many allies through their unions.

Micanopy had three sisters. Their husbands were all chiefs: Jumper, Cooper, and King Philip. Among his allied brothers-in-law, Philip was most formidable. Known for his high character and now "very aged," Philip reportedly commanded 350 Seminole warriors—nearly double Micanopy's total forces, and 55 more than the Miccosukees.

By law, Micanopy's successor would be the first son of his oldest sister. In practice, succession rules were flexible. Micanopy himself had been a compromise candidate. The true heir to the Alachua line was Holata Micco Chee—Little Chief Governor—nephew to the late rulers Payne and Bolek and son to their sister, Buckra Woman.

Micanopy had been elected during the rightful leader's "minority"—until he was of age—as a placeholder king. He married two women, one a Black Seminole, whose brother was made a chief, a warrior of "herculean size" known for his red turban. Micanopy's wife, as the sister to a chief, could then become the mother to a chieftain herself.

Florida's multiethnic bands and tribes were bound by four decades of shared triumphs, failures, and struggles. Figurative and actual kinship fortified loyalties. Unions made armies. Among the elite, marriages between Indians and Africans were not uncommon. White taxonomists pretended that "the two races" remained distinct. But those who were candid saw "the negro and the Indian . . . rapidly approximating," united "in interests and feelings."

At the onset of hostilities, while Abraham's command targeted Dade and Osceola killed Thompson, Philip's forces took on a special role. With a Black Seminole warrior named John Caesar, Philip attacked the forced labor camps on the intracoastal rivers south of St. Augustine. Near the Cruger and de Peyster property, where Romeo labored, servants at a yuletide dance were interrupted by nine Indians painted for war.

Dade fell. The horse bolted. He lay motionless. Animals in the woods froze. Warriors rose up in a long line and fired rifles and muskets. Lightning flashed across the surface of the earth. Half of the soldiers fell under the first volley, including the entire advanced guard. Within seconds, fifty troops hit the dirt. After the opening shot, Pacheco collapsed in terror and crawled to a pine tree, praying and banging his head on the bark. He saw the Americans "waver and tremble." Seminole sharpshooters snapped arms and punctured lungs. Bullets scorched soldiers' skin and hummed around their ears, deadly metal mosquitoes. An American, "a little man, a great brave . . . shook his sword" and screamed and it seemed that "no rifle ball could hit him." A dazed lieutenant stumbled, mute, mortally wounded. He died against a tree, where he remained for fifty-four days. Troops drew from cartridge boxes and poured black powder in gun pans and filled rifle barrels with one-ounce lead balls and packed them down with flared rods. Native forces kept powder in pouches or horns and bullets in their mouths.

Seminoles charged, swinging muskets like clubs. The Indigenous line extended, executing a flanking maneuver that brought the warriors to within a hundred yards of the dwindling survivors of the assault. Men met in a clinch, sliced at each other with sabers, bayonets, and tomahawks, and then men retreated. Dade's troops manned the six-pounder and Seminoles shooters picked them off from afar, one by one, after the cannon smoke cleared. Cannonballs crashed against pine trees and showered warriors with needles. When the gunners switched to grapeshot, fragments sprayed the fighters taking cover in the grass. Seminole forces pulled back, and the pace slowed. Soldiers axed down trees light enough to carry for a makeshift fortification, stacking trunks horizontally in a triangle. Survivors hid inside. A doctor tended to the wounded from a scarlet velvet case.

Abraham, Micanopy, Jumper, and Chief Alligator minimized the risk to their men. Hours passed, snipers shot from a distance, and morning turned to afternoon before the warriors made their final, intimate assault. Around 1:00 p.m., a private named Clark was shot in the thigh before he staggered inside the crowded triangular stacks of logs. He was raising his musket from inside the "breastwork" that was already filling with blood when a musket ball shattered his right arm above the elbow. Another bullet entered near his temple and exited the top of his head. A third struck him in the back, and then a fourth, around 4:00 p.m., courtesy of one of Abraham's men, ripping open his shoulder blade. Peeking between the logs, he witnessed a man who resembled Micanopy addressing the warriors and "pointing to the breastwork."

The Native army emerged from the pines and palmettos and descended upon the remnants. Abraham's fighters taunted them in English before killing them "with axes and knives," face-to-face. "What have you got to sell?" they asked the soldiers. Clark played dead as they removed his shoes and hat. Only one officer of eight was breathing. Captains Fraser and Gardiner, and Lieutenants Mudge, Keais, and Henderson had all fallen. So had Assistant Surgeon Gatlin. His medical case lay in the road. The final officer, a lieutenant named Basinger, pleaded in vain for his life. An African Seminole tomahawked him—the same fate dispensed earlier to Keais. Abraham's command took their blades and carved up the dying foreigners. "Loud cries and groans" echoed through the pine barren. Their knifework included a castration.

"Don't," Jumper said. "It is bad enough as it is. It'll bring us bad luck."

Seminole forces completed the ambush. Losing three warriors, with five wounded, they sent 105 of the 108 U.S. troops in the detachment to their graves.

Louis Pacheco was spared. "He is not his own master," Jumper's son had yelled, as the fight raged. "Don't kill him." One of Abraham's men guarded him during the battle. Afterward, the families marveled at how Pacheco had escaped without a scratch. Some claimed that he had mastered the uncanny arts and had made himself invisible.

The victors returned to their stronghold in the Wahoo Swamp. That night, Osceola rejoined them from Fort King, and the Seminoles and the Miccosukees danced around a pole of scalps. Warriors teased Thompson's severed crown as if speaking to the agent himself, mocking his mannerisms. The bands drank and celebrated and danced until sunrise.

News of the "massacre" reached the colonial army in the form of a dog, wounded in the neck, that had hobbled sixty miles back down the Fort King Road to Fort Brooke and staggered into camp. Two bleeding men followed. Neither soldier had dared try for the closer outpost of Fort King. Like the canine, they dragged themselves back to Tampa. Private Clark, somehow still mobile, was stalked by beasts. Wolves picked up his scent and tracked him on the second night and "came very close." His right arm was worthless; one leg dragged. He used his left hand and knees and "crawled and limped through the nights and forenoons," sleeping off the path during the day in tangled scrub. He arrived barefoot, ragged, and starving.

He was treated in the hospital, in a ward with four double bunks, four singles, and six windows. Two surgeons cleaned five wounds and removed splintered bone as he cursed, coughed up a piece of his coat, and joked that his bone shards might make for good broth. His right arm was ruined and his back would never heal. Six months later, his shoulder blade still regularly broke the skin.

Belton gathered the "horrid story" of the defeat. He swallowed his fury—and fears for Fort Brooke—long enough to pen a "cold official letter to Washington" covering all known facts. He was more honest in a letter to his wife, raging over how the soldiers had been sent, "by an order of *two lines*," into an ambush: an "Indian ambuscade of 100 miles." It reeked of gross negligence—nothing less than "indifference to the army." Beyond that, he still had no clue where exactly Clinch was. "I have been three weeks in command here," he ranted on, "and in all the time have not a line from any superior whatever."

"All our friends are dead!" he scribbled. "Oh God oh God."

Belton set fire to his headquarters, the log building directly outside the pickets, and ordered that the officers' quarters be incinerated, so that attackers could not torch them. He burned his own outpost and hid inside the palisades.

The warriors at the Christmas dance were invited.

Enslaved laborers at the Cruger and de Peyster plantation—including, almost certainly, Abraham's associate Romeo—"secreted an advance party of Indians" into position before the attack began. Risking execution, the bondservants even "supplied the raiders with a boat" to ferry across the intracoastal river. When they arrived in full, Philip's Indian and African force numbered as many as 120, enough to terrify the overseer and his wife, who caught wind of the plot and fled. Romeo and an estimated seventy-five others helped free themselves.

"During the night, a large body of Indians," a witness recalled, attacked the settlement of New Smyrna "and burned all the residences." Hunter's cotton house was torched, with "four or five negroes taken." Judge Dunham's roof collapsed to loud cheers. Everything at the Dunham plantation was burned to the ground, as were "all the buildings on Cruger and Depeyster's plantation," except for a corn shed.

The mill went up in fire and smoke. So did the entire sugar works: the state-of-the-art engine house, boiling room, and purgery. Flames embraced and then consumed roof beams and melted chunks of white plaster, exposing the coquina stones and blackening them by the eaves. When the fuel was exhausted, the flailing investment was left so completely destroyed that it was never used to produce sugar again.

Still today, the old ruins bear the scars of Philip's torches. Romeo's former overseer, when the warriors caught up with him at a nearby plantation, was shot in the right arm and again "in the head between the eyes." Removing the latter bullet, which he survived, proved to be "a very painful operation."

In wide-ranging bands, the Seminoles moved on, gaining warriors in freed bondservants while slaveholders and their overseers ran fast and far and lost fortunes and so-called livings. At the Spring Garden forced labor farm by the St. Johns, 160 souls were liberated. At Heriot's plantation, another 75 enslaved people joined up with the insurgents while they "burnt everything to the ground," including the sugar works.

Corn and provisions were spared for the fight to come. Forage was saved for the horses. Cane growing in the fields was cut down. Barges floated away under new captains. Cloth sails of boats were "cut up and carried off." Sugar boilers were stripped of removable lead parts. All sorts of settler properties found new uses: horses, mules, hogs, fowl, sheep, gunpowder, a shipment of cigars, and twenty-one gallons of Madeira wine.

On December 30, "a considerable light in the sky" was reported in the direction of the labor camps south of the Carrickfergus plantation. Within days, a witness confirmed that the properties between New Smyrna and Rosetta had been destroyed. Cruger and de Peyster's former laborers were spotted "with painted faces."

Lenders lost investments as borrowers were "left in fiscal shambles." Many enslavers, including Cruger and de Peyster, Hernández, and Williams, were already in debt. The Anderson family would later claim $38,000 in damages; the Bulow family, another $40,000. Orlando Rees—the city may have been named after him—lost an estimated $140,000, the equivalent of nearly five million dollars. The Union Bank of Tallahassee, the "slavers' bank" known for shady lending, could do nothing.

Colonists retreated to fortified plantations or to the relative security of St. Augustine, where "strong apprehensions were felt" that bondservants would sack the town. Citizens called a meeting and discovered "that there were only about seventy men left in the city," and "these were generally old men or invalids." Locals "cast about for arms and ammunition," only to find "about thirty or forty old rusty muskets, rifles, and shot-guns . . . not ten of which would fire." Residents learned too late that the Indians had bought up most of the gunpowder.

Eastern Florida, outside of a few sheltered cities and fenced-in camps, lay abandoned. Tomahawks decorated ceilings and walls. Bureaus, sofas, tables, mirrors, and beds were "cut and broke in all shapes." In some areas, not "a window or door" was unbroken. Goose plumes floated through the air from ripped mattresses. Cracked chests lay open, valuables removed, the unwanted contents scattered. Brick and stonework stood shattered, smoking. Settlers caught off guard or too dumb to run were killed. Woodruff was shot and scalped near his family's forced labor camp. Raiders at the Baya plantation, twelve miles outside St. Augustine, killed Llenovar and threw his body into the flames. Reports of new attacks circulated hourly. Evacuees poured into the old Spanish city "destitute of food and almost naked." Some were forced to trek up the coast for seventy miles. Refugees watched fires burning in the distance. The scarlet glow was visible for forty miles.

9

Fidelity

The Indians seem to have been, at times, partial in the destruction of property, and to have had favorites among the white settlers.

—"Extracts from the Journal of a Private," 1837

Like the bundle of sticks said, Abraham met the enemy on December 31, 1835, by the Withlacoochee River, by the Cove of that name. Black Seminole and Miccosukee forces were waiting for Clinch's 200 men with 120 warriors, and attacked from a well-protected thicket. The Miccosukee chief, a fisherman the army called Sam Jones, was absent that day and left Osceola in command. The rebel fought beside Abraham and his men, bravely, moving in and out from cover in a pilfered navy double-breasted military jacket. He was spotted by multiple U.S. witnesses, the most visible man in the fight. Clinch and his command lost only four soldiers, but fifty-nine were injured. His troops withdrew to his labor camp in a morbid line of stretchers and wagons of wounded that spanned for nearly a mile.

The Indians lost three, according to an American, including one of Abraham's men. Cudjo's brother, a Black Seminole reported, did not survive.

Instead of basking in victory, the Americans accused each other of cowardice. The controversy centered on Richard Call, the former aide-de-camp of President Jackson's known for his knack for storytelling and self-promotion, "a man of great ambition whose abilities were just a step behind." During the skirmish, Call had been on standby on the other side of the river, with five hundred militiamen. He stayed waiting, and ordered troops not to join the fight across the water, where Clinch's men were under heavy assault.

Blame games followed. The army of the era was still small—consisting of seventy-two hundred regulars—and too often led by commanders with skewed priorities. Feuds were common among officers who "owed their commissions to political patronage," who even occasionally disobeyed orders over petty quarrels. Many commanders seemed most interested in their careers and "regarded their peers" as "rivals in an unending competition for better positions and more awards. They guarded their prerogatives jealously and viewed their competitors with suspicion." There "was so much quarreling," one historian remarked, "that it could be considered a major characteristic of the nineteenth-century army." Generals "worked the newspapers" like the best politicians as carefully worded letters from the field were published for all to read. Reputations were made and destroyed by reports about far-flung skirmishes.

Generals composed perfect self-portraits in prose they knew would shape their legacies. When Clinch publicly outed Call for inaction during the army's "death struggle for victory," Call took it as a threat to his name. The militiaman had to reply in print to the general's "ungenerous and illiberal remarks," his "fictitious reputation and vainglorious boasting," and his "garbled and faithless representation" of the fight. Clinch, in his view, understood less about what had gone down "than any general who ever made report of a battle."

Clinch was the coward. When Richard Call's services were required by the Territory of Florida, according to Richard Call, he "hastened immediately across the river," straight into the "yells and heavy firing." He mounted the first horse he found saddled "and galloped to the field." Clinch, when Call came to his rescue, was not even on his horse, but was instead cowering "on *foot,* standing very close to the rear rank of regulars." The notion that Call had ordered his troops not to cross the river was "utterly false."

In turn, Clinch, published a reply to Call's "*malicious* and *vindictive* tirade." Couldn't readers tell that the militiaman's self-depiction as a "*protective angel*" who "shielded and saved" them was phony? Clinch sent evidence to the *Army and Navy Chronicle,* including testimony from a colonel who served under Call. "Every officer and soldier in my regiment," the colonel corrected, "will make oath that they were not permitted to cross after the action began."

Five officers and enlisted men testified that Call was lying. The few volunteers who did cross the river to fight alongside Clinch were not of much help. "The fact is," a witness declared, "the Militia were so badly frightened that they did not know whether they saw any Indians . . . many discharged their guns at, they could not tell what!"

In the months after the battle, Jackson's secretary of war blamed Clinch, Clinch fired back, and Clinch and Call went at it as Floridians demanded to know who had caused the "present disastrous state of our Territory." "To whose shameful neglect is it owing," one resident challenged, "that our Citizens have been slaughtered, their houses burnt, their fields laid waste, their wives and children compelled to flee from their homes, abandoning . . . all, to escape from the tomahawk and scalping knife"?

Why weren't there more American troops in the peninsula? Who had been asleep at the wheel when the express rider was killed on the Fort King Road, in August? Why did it take Emathla's murder to wake Clinch from his "dreams of peace"?

The Indians were "in complete possession of the country," with the military "disgraced and humbled." The army was unable to protect the people, its troops hiding, holed up in fortified positions. Black warriors had routed white soldiers in a slave territory. Bondservants were in revolt. The failures and the panic were "infinitely humiliating." The abolitionist William Lloyd Garrison was gloating in private letters:

> The numerous Indian tribes on our southern . . . borders, having been robbed of their lands, and goaded to desperation by the cruel oppression of the whites, are up in arms . . . and [are] not only defying but absolutely out-generally the U.S. troops. They have ravaged many plantations, killed many inhabitants, and emancipated a considerable number of slaves. . . . In Georgia, Alabama, and Florida, all is consternation. . . . This war will cost much blood and treasure, petty as it may seem. It is thus slaveholders are bringing down vengeance upon their heads.

Who messed up? How could whites even tell the story? When would it end?

President Jackson's January 2, 1836, bill for "Furnishing the Hermitage" included seven mahogany bedsteads, four silk curtains, a wardrobe, two marble washstands, twenty yards of crimson carpeting for the stairs, and twenty-four "Fancy Chairs" of blue and gold. He ordered three sets of Parisian wallpaper depicting scenes from a French epic about a boy with an absent father who was burdened with power and misunderstood by his critics.

Florida smoldered as Jackson redecorated; in 1834, a blaze sparked from his Tennessee dining-room chimney had destroyed most of his second-floor furniture and ripped down the roof. He was pleased that the repairs to his countryside home were nearly complete, even while he was convinced that he would not "be long on earth to enjoy its comforts in retirement." In fourteen months he would be out of office, and then he could retreat to his estate, and be pampered by captive workers, and enjoy the renovations. Most dramatically, a faux Grecian colonnade—fluted wood painted to resemble stone—would grace the home's false façade, mirroring the White House.

For the greater part of a month, he was entirely ignorant of the events in the territory. Fourteen days after Dade's death, Secretary of War Lewis Cass was issuing placid directives to Clinch as if the commander was in firm control. "I am instructed by the President to say to you that you will continue your operation against the Indians until they are reduced to submission," he informed Clinch, in a note dated January 11, 1836. Jackson, Cass emphasized, would not accept a peace deal or any negotiations.

Washington expected a total victory and the "unconditional surrender" of Indian forces. Jackson's secretary of war also wrote that day to Thompson, ordering the late emissary to prepare transportation to remove the enemy after Clinch defeated them, which would certainly be accomplished soon. "You will . . . exert yourself to remove them as promptly as possible," Cass informed the dead Indian agent.

Reports of Thompson's murder, the torched labor camps, and the Seminole victory over Dade spread slowly, south to north. Once the facts emerged, citizens in Charleston, South Carolina, and Savannah, Georgia, held public meetings, raised volunteers, and sent provisions to help the territorial settlers, a population that would come to be known as the "suffering inhabitants of Florida." In Congress, a Jackson ally insisted on bipartisan unity, arguing that the nation faced bigger problems, with trouble on the Mexican border and a brewing crisis with France over war reparations owed to U.S. merchants for seized ships. In Massachusetts, an editor blamed troops in the peninsula for exaggerating Native forces, and for not protecting the property of locals. In Burlington, Vermont, the *Weekly Free Press* published a column expressing alternative sentiments about Florida's disputed lands:

> We, by a forced and corrupt treaty, call it ours. We send armed men—men armed with the whisky bottle, a weapon more

> terrible than the rifle—to persuade them to abide by a treaty which they never made. . . . The preventative power of this government is nothing; but its vengeance is terrible. . . . Every Indian and every negro suspected of having been allied to the Indians will be slaughtered in less than two months.

News of Thompson's death reached the War Department on January 16.

When Jackson heard of the envoy's murder, and the catastrophes plaguing large swaths of the Southern territory, he barely flinched. Not even when he received the stark doom-and-gloom warnings on January 26. Frantic complaints only annoyed and wore on the president, as if panic itself were the problem, and not all the dead soldiers and locals, abandoned lands, burning houses, and severe economic damage. The jittery letter, from an old ally, arrived to as much welcome as the flu:

> The People of Florida are in a most distracted and distressed state—We are literally without a Government . . . a universal distrust seems to pervade the whole Community . . . all seem distracted in the general cry of "something must be done," while all oppose every measure which can be suggested—We are literally like a Ship tossed on the waves of an angry Ocean, without a helm, the Mariner asleep . . . the crew divided among themselves. This is no exaggerated picture. . . . Thompson the Agent I presume you have heard has been killed & the whole country of Tomoka, Lower Allachua, &c Destroyed & laid waste—The Peopel [*sic*] of the East are in a truly deplorable state & something must be done & that speedily to relieve them.

Jackson scribbled a reply on the back, urging calm. He regretted the "Spirit with which" the complaints were written, as he communicated to the sender. The trouble was much ado about nothing, a little "Punic war, waged by a few desperate Indians, not more than 500 gunmen." Hardly cause for alarm. "Ample & prompt means" were already mobilizing to put down the rebellion. Floridians could fight as militia. Alabama, Georgia, and South Carolina would supply soldiers as well. Ships were incoming, and a new general was already on his way to assume command. All would be put in their place.

The president's estimate of Native forces was short by roughly one thousand warriors. He was sleepwalking into one of the longest American wars prior to Vietnam.

On January 21, 1836, at 11:00 a.m., the Legislative Council of the Florida Territory met in a modest two-story brick building in Tallahassee. Like the fledgling town, the Capitol was not much to look at. Four slim pillars adorned the masonry edifice, anemic echoes of a grand plantation house. The headquarters was statelier than the rustic cabin that first housed the seat of government. But the building was incomplete, a fraction of its intended size. Ambition wasn't the issue. Locals had planned a "large and commodious" statehouse. They just couldn't find the money to cover the costs of the building materials, or even pay the contractor his due salary. The man sued; they countersued and lost. The government did find the cash, in 1832, to plaster the walls and paint the building, prune the trees, and tidy the grounds.

The Legislative Council—two dozen officials who worked with the territorial governor—was determined to respond to Dade's defeat. The men knew that "a large force of Indians & negroes," fighting together, had decimated Dade's soldiers. In the initial write-up of the incident, Belton had made no attempt to censor the full participation of Abraham's warriors. His report was excerpted across the nation, and by February, word of the shocking "Slaughter"—and the active engagement of Black warriors in the carnage—had spread to the North.

In the Deep South, the account was censored—to reduce the risk of servile revolts and, likely in part, out of plain old-fashioned denialism. In one version of the "Massacre!" published in an Alabama newspaper, in January, Dade's soldiers were attacked by "an overwhelming number of Indians." Indians descended to the field at the end and finished "the slaughter of the whole corps." There were no Black Seminoles at all.

Black Indians and enslaved people who razed the plantations received the same treatment. In February, a *New Orleans Commercial Bulletin* entry made no mention of a rebellion. News *was* bad: Everything south of St. Augustine had been "laid waste," with "not a building of any value left standing" for some three hundred miles, all the way down to Cape Florida. In the second week of February, the paper said, losses exceeded the equivalent of over $6 million. But these were only "INDIAN DEVASTATIONS."

In January 1836, the legislators in Tallahassee who knew better drafted an "Act respecting the hostile Negroes and Mulattoes in the Seminole Nation." The statesmen explicitly blamed Abraham's warriors for the "massacre of Major F. L. Dade." "The present insurrection of the Seminole Nation of Indians," they proclaimed, "has been chiefly excited by diverse mischievous Negroes and Mulattoes." By their decree, anyone of African descent captured among the Indians would be treated as "a slave for life." Black prisoners would be property to be sold, with proceeds going to the Territorial Treasury. The governor could also lawfully "put to death any white person, Negro, Mulatto, or Indian" who engaged in warfare or helped "the hostile Indians or Negroes."

The resolution was approved on February 13. The legislators also renamed the district near present-day Miami, to Dade County.

Before the ambushes, raids, and fires, Black Seminole messengers visited the "white families they did not wish to injure, advising them to remove." U.S. troops commonly discovered "the dwellings of Northern men or Englishmen remaining untouched in a vicinity where cracker houses had been destroyed." Settlers known for decency were spared as Native "acts of generosity . . . manifested much good feeling and gratitude." A soldier who fashioned an ax handle was spared by the Indian he made it for. Osceola, during the battle of December 31, had asked his warriors not to hurt an officer who had been kind to his daughter.

Men also used the war to redress grievances. Philip's Seminoles singled out a man named Cooley, a squatter and the first lawman and judge in what is today Broward County, in the southeast. They knew him as a liar who shielded white murderers from justice. Cooley was barely literate but qualified enough to satisfy settlers. He spelled "today" as "to Day," "doctor" as "Docktor," "esteem" as "a Steame," and "immediately" as "a mediatety." "For the good of my country" was "for they good of my Countery." That was Mr. Cooley, "Justice of they Peace for . . . they Teritory."

Cooley had proven his loyalty to people who looked like him. That's what so many colonists did—in military reports, newspapers, court rulings. Sometimes they died for it. After "swaggering white" ruffians killed an Indian chief, Cooley took the assassins into custody. But he soon dropped the charges due to "insufficient evidence." The Seminoles accused the judge of withholding information "essential to conviction," and in early 1836, in the opening weeks of the war, Philip's men raided Cooley's estate. The lawman was not home on that day. In his absence, his wife and three children paid the debt.

Philip's son Wild Cat rode a stunning ivory horse. He was famous for decorating his headdress with glistening fragments from a lighthouse mirror. In daytime, when he attacked, enemies fled from the sunbeams' sharp reflections.

10

Grace

They said they could supply us with provisions . . .
that we could fish on the river bank if we chose.
—Captain Thistle, 1836

Regulars and volunteers from Louisiana, Alabama, Georgia, South Carolina, and Tennessee—as tender as fourteen and as senior as seventy—assembled in the hundreds in the port cities, for schooners and steamboats. "Old and young, lame and blind were enlisted," an astonished private observed. Recruiters promised to target citizens of "good character," ages thirty-five and under. In reality, all generations of miscreants found their way into the corps. In a single company of fifty-five men, one survey found, nine-tenths enlisted "on account of some female difficulty," thirteen signed up using fake names, and forty-three of them were "either drunk, or partially so" when they took the oath to faithfully serve.

Greenhorns yearned for "victories and national renown," the "honor of killing Oseola [*sic*]," and legacies of heroism. Reporters seized on Thompson's killer and made up the rest. Osceola, the Creek rebel who fought for the Miccosukees, suddenly became a Seminole, and not only a Seminole but a chief, and not only a chief, but the prime mover of the entire fight. Newspapers promised soldiers and settlers alike that Osceola was a "savage of great tact, energy of character, and bold daring," destined to achieve the stature of Tecumseh. He'd cost the United States a million dollars and proven "superior to *Black Hawk*." He was honored so that Southerners could earn honor in the hunt.

Glory could be won in the Florida Territory. If it couldn't, at least they would have an adventure. If that turned out to be a lie, at least it was a fresh start. Patriots seemed eager to put down the Native "war of extermination." In New Orleans, word spread that "Clinch and 400 men had been butchered," Tallahassee had fallen, Fort Brooke was under siege, and that among the hostiles were "1,000 able-bodied negroes." The American flag was unfurled by the customs house, the governor spoke, and by January 29, 1836, some four hundred volunteers had enlisted. In the Gulf of Mexico, a few days later, choppy waters churned their stomachs and stole color from their faces.

On the steamer *Merchant*, on February 7, a recruit testified, the voyage was rough and vulgar. "Most all hands in the cabin sick. Sick myself. Men on deck also sick. Every body looks pale, and they are throwing up all over the boat. An interesting sight!!!"

The contingent reached Fort Brooke on February 9. Some thirteen hundred troops assembled on the waterfront. Soldiers were "anxious to have a 'fight,'" but were disturbed to find "almost every house in this beautiful spot . . . torn down or burnt," with the inhabitants "compelled to fly for protection to the vessels in the bay." Dade's name had been painted on a cannon. Surrounding the fencing, inside eight-foot pits, wolf traps of sharpened stakes waited, hidden by straw. After sunset, a jumpy Dutch sentinel shot at a stray dog.

U.S. forces in Tampa Bay finally seemed sufficient. These included not only the Louisiana Volunteers but U.S. Marines, 1st Dragoons, 3rd Artillery, 4th Regulars, and 4th Infantry. At last, they could stop hiding and waiting at Fort Brooke and attack. "We all hope for glory," Belton explained to his wife, on February 12, after hiding and waiting at Fort Brooke for two months. The army set out the next day with eleven hundred soldiers, toward the decomposing bodies of Dade's men.

Loaded down with ten days' provisions, the troops moved slowly. Military staples of the era, for men stationed at forts, included pork, bacon, flour, beans, rice, salt, vinegar, sugar, tobacco, and coffee. Candles and soap came in boxes, onions and corn in bushels, molasses in gallons, and pickled onions and sauerkraut in barrels. On the march, grunts generally carried coffee, sugar, crackers, and twelve ounces of preserved meat per day—pickled pork or beef. Even that was a burden for a large army. Stuffed into the marchers' haversacks and loaded onto horses were over eighteen thousand pounds of "salt meat" and either flour or "hard bread"—biscuits baked to last and often infested with weevils.

Humping food was the least of it. The Americans needed axes and hatchets to fell trees to prepare firewood. A camp of twenty tents could burn through a half dozen ninety-foot-tall pines a night. Ordnance and weapons were essential burdens. Buckshot and howitzer cartridges, rifle and cannon powder, bayonets and blunderbusses. Companies required canteens, medical supplies, and horse litters—drawn stretchers—for the sick and wounded. Horses needed blankets and nose bags and twelve pounds of corn, hay, or oats a day. Camp kettles, greatcoats, wool overalls, snare drums, fifes, mouthpieces for bugles. Each little impedimenta of warfare came with a cost in calories.

The men made only seven miles the first day. Sweltering, heavy air wore down the soldiers and tempered their enthusiasms. "Many of them threw away their provisions" within hours of leaving Fort Brooke. Twenty-five troops gave out and had to be ferried back by boat. The columns marched for seven days in the sun and dust, through high waters, without a battle. A lieutenant's pistol exploded in his pocket, injuring him badly. They burned an empty village. "Volunteers became dissatisfied & threatened to go home," upset that the "fighting was not what it was cracked up to be": There wasn't any.

Troops were wilting marchers, not fighters. When they reached Dade's battlefield, on February 20, they became gravediggers. For nearly two months, sun and rain had weathered the corpses. Nothing had prepared them for the smell that hung over the gruesome site, or the vulture cloud that rose from the breastwork logs coated white with their excrement. Under hovering scavengers, bleached bones and blackened fragments of a hundred corpses lay "denuded of muscles," picked apart by beaks and wolves' teeth. "The lower jaws of all the bodies" had dropped, "leaving the mouths wide open . . . the fingers were all drawn up and contracted by the drying of the muscles."

As if on public display, thirty or so bodies—the soldiers who had survived the longest—remained as "mostly mere skeletons," many in sky-blue uniforms, inside the triangular breastwork by the road. Decomposition made it difficult to know if they had been scalped. Sallow skulls rested on the topmost horizontal beams of their last desperate defense, or directly below it, their bodies apparently arranged in a ghoulish dollhouse pattern, at right angles and regular intervals. A witness noted that they resembled "toy-soldiers arranged by a child in his sport." Pine sap leaked from bullet holes in the logs.

"The best in the army," Belton wrote, lay "bleaching in the air."

The "bodies were collected together" and "the army then marched round the whole while the shrill fife and muffled drum" played a patriotic tune of Scotland. Eight officers were recognized "with great difficulty" by their height, dental work, and jewelry and buried as a group. Rank-and-file were interred in a larger mass grave.

Sounds of the funereal song drifted west, three or four miles, until they spread over the fields where Abraham was planting and met his ears. The Wahoo Swamp and the Cove may not have been suitable for all of the crops they had harvested at Pilaklikaha, but he and his people could plant rice in the wetlands, and they could fish. Oranges, plums, and grapes grew wild on many hammocks.

Beef could be preserved into jerky, there was plenty of dried corn to make sofkee, and they could harvest coontie root and set it in the sun, and mince it to a fine powder, and bake fresh bread in their kettles.

"God was in our favor," as Abraham said, as the battles so far were one-sided, and so few warriors lost. His men had kept the families safe, after dispatching Dade's troops, for over seven weeks. By now, their wartime hideaway—also referred to as "Abram's town," by one of the few outsiders who heard about it—may have been complete. One of several strewn in the wetlands, the village was situated near "a large pond or lake from which a considerable stream, forty or fifty yards wide, puts out and runs into the river," in "the forks between this stream and the river."

Hewn-log homes were "small and built of pine" and "laid out like the towns in a civilized country," with beef and food stored in "places in the shades." Most importantly, the site was hard to find. Reaching it required the army to cross the perilous Withlacoochee River and trek several miles "through one continuous swamp and hammock." It had to be well-hidden: The enemy targeted civilians. The burial party's drums, and news of the gathering soldiers, signaled a renewed threat to children, wives, grandfathers, and grandmothers. Eleven hundred troops from Tampa Bay. Five hundred more at Fort Drane.

In the past, the Americans had been content to burn villages. They marched, and made their shows of force, and went away for a while. After King Payne's army had routed the Georgia militia in 1812, Southern white men invaded Alachua, seized livestock, destroyed crops, and torched Payne's Town. But the settlement was empty. U.S. troops did not follow the Indians and Black Seminoles southward. It was the same when Jackson had attacked Suwannee Old Town, in 1818. Fighters clashed as families escaped across the Suwannee. Jackson's forces claimed few warriors and did not follow beyond the waterway.

Terrible losses had been endured, and the risks were real. But the Americans had never made a sustained attempt to dislodge them from the hammocks and swamplands. Let the proud army march and peacock their uniforms and guns. Let them burn Micanopy's empty abode by the orange tree and destroy the ghost town of Pilaklikaha, so long as the Seminoles and their allies survived to rebuild and plant anew, so long as the families could live in peaceful quiet, at least for a while, as they had before.

Sixteen hundred soldiers meant this time could be different.

Abraham lowered the plow, took up the gun, and readied his men.

Seven days later in the rainy cold, around 4:00 p.m. on February 27, the U.S. army reached the border line, the Rubicon of the rapid, 120-foot-wide Withlacoochee. Over one thousand troops, preparing to cross, assembled on the shores. Seminole forces on the opposite bank fired on their position within minutes.

Louisiana volunteers took the brunt of it, with at least one killed and six wounded in what felt like ninety minutes. In the morning, the troops found that they could still not cross the Withlacoochee, the "river being very deep, and hammocks very dense on either side." Warriors followed them to a fording point and opened fire again.

A bullet struck a soldier named Izard in the corner of his eye, disfiguring him. He was found "on his knees with his face in the long grass, his arms partly supporting his head," with both his eyes "thrust from the sockets and hanging apparently half cut out." He was "placed into a blanket" and taken away, to die slowly over six days.

Gunfire again made it "impossible . . . to cross the river without great loss."

The Americans made camp on a deep U-shaped meander of land, a bend outlined by the river. Firing at a brisk pace, Indian and Black Seminole fighters kept the army engaged. Unwilling to retreat and unable to cross the water safely, U.S. troops instead built another defensive log breastwork while projectiles flew over their heads.

Night fell. Abraham's men forded the river silently, in the shadows. Hundreds of warriors waded the Withlacoochee in the damp and gloom, at a crossing unknown to the army, in an eerie silence. "No one could tell why" the Indians were so "very quiet." The mystery was not solved until after daybreak, when northwest gusts blew fire toward the breastwork.

Searing "flames, driven by the wind," ravaged dry grass and "came down upon [them] like an infuriated enemy" as gunfire erupted. Palmettos had concealed the warriors' approach. Lead balls rained down, and only then did the soldiers realize that "every tree seemed to have" an Indian or Black Seminole behind it.

Smoke and fire "came rolling towards the breastwork like a heavy sea," warriors in the wake, until the flames were "coolly extinguished." The U.S. commander, a prideful Virginian called Gaines, was shot through the lower lip. "It is mean," he muttered, catching two dislodged teeth, "to knock out my teeth when I have so few!"

Crossfire continued for two hours. Native forces, which reportedly numbered over eleven hundred, used small-caliber bullets and gunpowder of inconsistent dosage or quality. In cases, balls hit with the same force as "what might be produced by throwing [them] forcibly with the hand." A soldier died. A dozen more were injured.

The Americans found themselves surrounded. Impassable river guarded three sides. Guns guarded the fourth. Throughout the next day, warriors fired shots "from time to time," and let off rounds at night and shouted to "give alarm." On March 3, a U.S. scouting party was attacked and forced to retreat. The battle settled into a siege.

Seminoles and Miccosukees blockaded the colonists, lighting large fires around their camp at night and keeping a "strict look out." By March 4, the troops were suffering from a severe "want of provisions" and were forced to kill a horse "to keep the men from starving." Frozen in place, waiting for backup, their ammunition grew scarce.

Recruits fresh from New Orleans were reduced to "living skeletons." Soldiers foraged for roots, butchered mules and horses—the malnourished equines themselves "in a dying state from starvation"—and devoured them, including their guts. The going rate for a dry biscuit reached $8. A "quarter of dog meat"—a dog's leg—went for $5.

While the Americans suffered, the Seminoles and Miccosukees held a Council meeting. According to a Native scout, five hundred U.S. troops were on the march to rescue the stranded soldiers. Should the warriors slaughter the army before backup arrived?

A Miccosukee chief proposed sending 250 fighters to meet the 500, to turn them back. "Many of the Indians" were eager for "a general butchery of the whites." Seminole leaders were less interested in bloodshed. Defending the families was a given, but standing against the U.S. military long term was not practical. If a deal could be made, maybe the army would let them rebuild beyond a new boundary line. Given no other option, Micanopy, Jumper, and Abraham, at least, had "resolved to make peace and move to the West." The Miccosukees wanted blood; the Seminoles pushed for negotiations.

Jumper "& others" overruled the war party.

"There have been enough killed," they said.

On Saturday, March 5, around ten o'clock at night, Abraham approached the besieged U.S. camp to restart peace talks. A soldier on guard duty heard the Interpreter's loud, "very articulate" voice in the woods and asked that he "come nearer."

"What do you want?" the guard asked.

"How far are your sentinels posted out?"

"You can come up nearer, they shall not fire on you," he said.

Abraham approached to within a hundred yards. "Is Colonel Twiggs there?"

"Yes!"

"Tell him we don't want to fight him anymore, and as tomorrow is a good day, we'll come in and shake hands."

"Very well. If you come in with a white flag you shall not be harmed."

"We'll come in for breakfast tomorrow morning, around nine o'clock. Good night."

Word of the promised visit spread the next morning among the troops. "Everybody is talking about the probability of the negro's being sincere. And everybody sneers at the idea of his coming in," a white man wrote. "All laugh at the idea." Around 8:00 a.m., one hundred Indians and Black Seminoles warmed by blankets approached with a white flag. To the "utter astonishment of the whole camp," Abraham stepped forward "without his gun!"

The Interpreter, Jumper, and Osceola—the Creek rebel looking "much dejected, and apparently subdued in spirit"—settled on a log north of the breastwork, south of the Indian trail. Jumper led the talks, through Abraham. *Enough blood has been spilled. The Seminoles "had revenge enough" for past wrongs. Both sides should put down their arms.* "We were sorry that white people forced us to fight them," Abraham translated.

Jumper proposed a new demarcation line to separate the colonists and the tribes, at the Withlacoochee River. If the army did not cross the boundary, the Seminoles and their allies would leave the settlers in peace. "There have been enough killed," they kept repeating, and offered to let the famished men fish without firing on them as a gesture of goodwill, and even proposed to share their brandy and tobacco. "There was nothing like treachery on their part," a witness testified. "I believe every officer and private considered them sincere, and looked for a speedy termination of the war."

Recruits warned of savages discovered discerning, clear-eyed diplomats. In the afternoon, the same envoys met with the Americans again. The emissaries could not finalize terms of peace without consulting Micanopy, but both sides had agreed on a ceasefire and to a future "grand Council" when "at that moment a noise was heard" in the distance and men were "seen running towards the river." The five hundred U.S. reinforcements had arrived. "Not knowing the purpose" or meaning of the gathering, they had opened fire. Abraham, Osceola, and Jumper escaped safely with the others, back across the Withlacoochee.

When the emaciated soldiers were rescued, many of them "could scarcely stand . . . the whole party leaned over the breastwork crying pitifully for food." Some "were even seen picking up the horse feed, or single grains of maize that had been spilt" around the mounts. The newcomers shared their hardtack and pork, and cattle to slaughter. Either that night or the next morning, the Seminoles sent men to the riverbank, to find out if the Americans "were still of the same mind" to end the fighting. But the messengers were rebuffed by the sentinel, who replied that "the whites would come over and kill them all, the next day."

"Go to hell, Goddamn you!" the whites said.

The Seminole and Miccosukee alliance had fractured, if not broken, with Abraham on one side and Osceola on the other. The Sense Bearer believed that the costs of war had grown too high; Osceola was eager to continue, to press their advantages. By firing upon the talks, the army had weakened Jumper's hand, with many families left to "so strongly believe that they were cheated" and tricked, that there was no use for further discussions, that the enemy could not be reasoned with. But not a single U.S. soldier crossed the river, and no Indian or Black Seminole fired on them. The starving troops were allowed to fish, and to eat.

11

Contagion

> Last night 2 Privates, Humphrys & Madden died, & this morning Morrow, after coming out of his tent as well to appearance as he had been in five or six weeks past, fell down and died in a few moments . . . found the spleen, liver, lungs, heart, and intestines greatly diseased.
>
> —Assistant Surgeon Cushman, 1836

Clouds gathered in the west, collecting and "accumulating darkness until they wore a most frightful aspect." Raindrops pattered and the ashen sky unleashed in torrents, and wild gusts, "lulled into a severe gale," torqued and ripped. Aeolus, the Greek God of Wind, uncracked his jar, and from all around "huge pines were torn from their roots." The lid of the earth flashed like a fired musket, the flint on the frizzen, the black powder in the barrel, a "liquid sheet of flame over the whole expanse." Thunder like mortar fire followed. "Peal after peal and shock after shock," salvo after salvo. The dazzling light and explosions, "as loud and long as though ten thousand thousand pieces of artillery had simultaneously burst," detonated over the flats and the glades and shook the ground.

At Black Creek, the army depot twenty-two miles southwest of Jacksonville, summer deluges came "violently, every afternoon." Tempests and thundershowers tormented the soldiers and beat down on the refugees who had abandoned their homes and fled to the outpost for safety. Seven or eight hundred poor settlers—colonists with nowhere else to go, who could not evacuate on the crowded steamships, and leave it all safely behind—huddled in the heat by the waterway, a tributary of the St. Johns. Sleeping on wood boards in makeshift huts that let in the elements, they endured colds, "raging fevers," measles, diarrhea. Orphaned children cared for young siblings.

Dry seasons brought rare gusts to fell oaks and lightning to kill cows, knock down horses, and shatter mainmasts in the harbors. But in the never-ending summers, when temperatures soared and waters steamed, the skies escorted a "continued succession of the most violent storms of wind and rain." The air itself saturated, waterlogged. Malarial biters laid eggs in pools in the wetlands, and in the brackish waters of the swamps and marshes. Wriggling larvae hatched faster in the humid warmth. When the humans came, they marched past the stagnant infected ponds and drank from them to quench their thirst. Men's traces lingered in the breeze, alluring beacons.

Troops burned empty villages, including Pilaklikaha, and shot the "tame and gentle" calves roaming Abraham's former home. Soldiers marched toward the Cove, got lost, ran out of rations, marched back. A general named Scott, who dreamed of war in open fields, in "serried lines and columns," arrived with ornate furniture and left in disgrace. Napoleonic gambits were no match for "Indian bush fighting." The military pamphlet, "Artillery Tactics; *or*, Rules for the Exercise and Manœuvres *of* Field Artillery. *Translated from the French Regulations of* 1836," was of limited use. Strangely enough, the Indians and Black Seminoles refused to line up neatly on a prairie to be shot.

The territory killed the soldiers. After April, the "heats of Florida" settled in and marches became "exhausting and desolating." Troops returned "half-naked and barefoot, dirty and sick." Diseases multiplied in limestone sinks, the liquid "nearly a mass of animal life." Measles debilitated a South Carolina brigade. On the Suwannee River, maladies were so "violent and fatal" that "often a guard would stand his turn at night and next morning would be found dead with the yellow fever." Surgeons recorded the terminal causes as "Disease unknown."

Gastritis, hepatitis, consumption, chronic dysentery, bilious fever, typhus fever, and "brain fever" plagued the Florida Territory's "sickly season." At the headquarters of the U.S. Army, the toll was shattering. At least Fort King was elevated; Clinch's forced labor farm occupied the lowlands, a few feet from a mosquito-infested marsh. The site "long had the unenviable notoriety of being one of the most unhealthy places in Florida," and northern Europeans were vulnerable to subtropical diseases. The farm's own overseer claimed that "no white man could pass a summer" there safely.

Clinch established Fort Drane's headquarters in his overseer's home, a "half dismantled log house" with four open holes for windows. Soldiers slept in the slave quarters, in mud-floored windowless huts where gaps in the logs let in "snakes and other reptiles." Other troops retired to the temporary shed badly roofed with bark and open to the elements. When the clouds poured, weary troops crawled through the picking holes of Clinch's maize sheds and passed out on the corncobs. Grunts dozed in their clothes, buckling their forage caps to prevent "ear-wigs, centipedes, cockroaches, etc." from crawling into their ears.

As of April 1836, most soldiers at the forced labor camp were healthy. By July, dysentery and fever had spread to "almost every individual at the post." Desperate cases filled the hospital tent and overflowed into seven makeshift sheds, where scorpions and "immense spiders" were "daily tenants," fleas and chiggers packed the sandy floors, and wolves and frogs serenaded patients by moonlight.

Army doctors did not generally wait for bodies to heal themselves. Surgeons practiced "heroic medicine" to treat afflictions. Aggressive interventions included amputations, bloodletting, blistering, cupping, enemas, and purges. Bodily "secretions," they believed, had to be regulated and brought back into natural balance. Physicians were governed less by hard evidence than by cryptic guesswork.

Thumb and spring lancets weakened patients and led to infections. Tartar emetic used to treat fevers made men vomit. Plumbic acetate gave them lead poisoning. The sulfuric acid in elixir of vitriol damaged organs. Opium addicted. Many antidotes did nothing or had only moderate benefits. "Hospital stores" requested at Fort Drane in 1836 included chocolate, ginger, coffee, cinnamon, cloves, rum, wine, and lavender.

Eleven regulars died of illnesses at Clinch's camp that summer. Militia fatalities were not comprehensively recorded and were far higher. A "great sickness in the fort" claimed many names, "sometimes five daily, at the minimum two or three." Patients in the "out-of-the-world place," roasting in the heat and drowning in the air, were all "delirious at the full heat of the day." A doctor fell ill and hallucinated all-consuming flames outside the window. He woke up, at one point, to find seven soldiers dead in the surrounding beds.

After one grueling march, in a "fit of insanity produced by brain fever," a young colonel known for his "finely wrought and extremely sensitive mind" placed the hilt of his saber on the ground and fatally pushed the blade into his eyeball.

"Indians! Indians!" a man shrieked, before perishing of "dread." One went singing Psalms; another gently, like an "infant, falling asleep." Many went numbly. Bodies were buried quickly, as it was "dangerous to keep a corpse over six hours."

Clinch's "grave yard" outpost was finally evacuated. Fort King, sickly and isolated, was also abandoned. Native forces burned it down. American soldiers fled and their enemies came "out of the woods and resumed the undisputed possession of the settlements; occupying the houses of Alachua, and reveling in the deserted plantations of the settlers." Osceola and several hundred Miccosukee warriors took over Fort Drane and camped there for over a month, sleeping in U.S. tents, their livestock feasting "on General Clinch's corn and sugarcane."

The rebel and his men took torches to "every house on [the] large farm, including the dwelling house, outhouse, shugar house, and almost a town of negro houses." Clinch resigned from the military that fall, on September 21. Before leaving Florida, he croaked out a hoarse speech in St. Augustine about his own dedicated service that skipped over the soldiers who had died, for no good reason, on his failed labor camp.

Philip's army, reinforced by fighters from the plantations, remained active in the east. In all, raiders freed or forced off an estimated five hundred bondservants and destroyed at least twenty-two cash-crop estates, including the three owned by the militia commander Hernández. The Miccosukees also kept on the offensive, firing on convoys and forted camps. Osceola "sent frequent runners to Micanopy and Jumper . . . asking them to come help him destroy [U.S.] garrisons."

"They inevitably reply," a soldier reported, "that they will not come."

Micanopy and his advisors apparently refrained from raids that summer, with one exception. In May 1836, Jumper led a feigned assault on Fort Defiance, the outpost at the settler town of Micanopy. Near Defiance—roughly three hundred yards east of the fort proper—stood a cluster of houses and huts of particular interest: the plantation of Gad Humphreys.

Twenty-nine African Seminoles, "purchased" by Humphreys illegally, remained captives at his labor camp. Abraham may have joined the offensive staged to free them; Toney Barnett, himself enslaved by Humphreys for five years, certainly did. On May 18, Barnett spread word to local bondservants that in two nights time, on May 20, 250 warriors would distract the armed soldiers by firing on Fort Defiance. During the scrum, the hope was, their friends could escape.

Jumper instigated the jailbreak after 11:00 p.m., assaulting the picketed city named after his chief simultaneously from the east and north, from the cover of hammock woods, from at least one hundred yards off. His party fired 250 rounds over a half hour, during which time all twenty-nine Black Seminoles "walked off very quietly" from Humphreys' farm "without being observed." A soldier was baffled by how easily they had been "captured."

"One cry for help would have saved them," he insisted.

Humphreys endured his "heaviest loss" of the war. When Fort Defiance was evacuated, for health reasons, the army burned Humphreys' property so Natives could not make use of it. Up in smoke went his five houses, fancy armchair, mahogany table, carpenter's tools, corn house, kitchen, library, blankets, and pillows, along with his two feather beds.

The president had already elevated Richard Call to territorial governor. Jackson now also handed him command of all forces in the peninsula. On October 12, Call's Tennessee Volunteers attacked a Native camp north of the Withlacoochee, killing a woman and a child and taking four women and eight children prisoner. His captives revealed the location of the village where "there were a considerable number of the enemy, chiefly negroes, it being the town of Abram." Militiamen tried to cross the river to attack the settlement the next day, but were fired on at the water's edge. A Black Seminole sniper was spotted in a tree, fifteen or twenty feet in the air. Two U.S. soldiers were killed along with their Muscogee guide. Eight were wounded—including the Tennessee governor's son—in an hour-long fight, before the army retreated.

One month later, at the same crossing, the Tennessee Volunteers forded the river and entered the Cove unopposed. They found Abraham's sanctuary abandoned. The prophet and his people had left "several days before," reportedly for the Panasoffkee Swamp. Militiamen burned the empty homes, which were "quickly consumed." Two of the volunteers dug up a grave they hoped was the Sense Bearer's. A Native commander had been killed, reportedly, during the battle of October 13, "and many believed it to be the celebrated Abram." A "little bird was perched" on the grave, which was built of "small pine poles," moss, and pine bark. The skeleton inside still had remnants of straight hair, and could not have been Abraham's.

Governor Call led his men to the Withlacoochee, twice, devouring rations and returning hungry. "He was like the French King," a soldier remarked. "'Marched his army up the hill and then—marched down again.'" On his second try, with a reported fifteen hundred troops, he had "3 days' provisions besides enough to carry him back." Instead of attacking, he waited two days for additional men. On reaching a "deep and boggy stream"—actually only three feet deep—the soldiers retreated because, "as they say, their provisions gave out." Call rejoined the settlers as a failure, "having nearly starved his Army twice and accomplished nothing."

At a dinner party held in his honor, a guest openly mocked the military. "The Army of the United States—Paralyzed and Powerless!" the heckler goaded, in a toast. "Too feeble to chastise one tribe of wandering savages. How hath the mighty fallen!"

Jackson seethed. "Put an end to this Punic war," he instructed Call, "or your *military fame is gone forever.*" The president ranted that with "fifty *women*" he could still "whip every Indian that had ever crossed the Suwannee." When a Florida representative visited Washington, Jackson commented that it would be better for militiamen "to run off or let the Indians shoot them." At least that way, he scolded the delegate, widowed "women might get husbands of courage, and breed up men who would defend the country."

Senator Henry Clay, one of Jackson's fiercest opponents, attacked him for his "disgraceful Seminole war" and its failures. Boston's *Columbian Centinel* bemoaned the "everlasting Florida war—a war which has already proved a grave for the glory of four American Generals." In England, the *Morning Post* assailed the president for lawlessness, arguing that his ascendency to power had "in itself been an encouragement to a contempt for the law," and questioning why Americans championed him as "the greatest and the best of men" and the "rock of ages." Much of the rest of the so-called civilized world was too busy, and too far away, to care much about a trifling Indian war in the alien American South. In Paris, Frédéric Chopin composed his études. In Japan, the aging printmaker of the wood-block masterpiece *The Great Wave off Kanagawa*, Katsushika Hokusai, forged ahead with his visions. On the HMS *Beagle*, a young naturalist named Charles Darwin pieced together a theory of evolution.

That year, as commander after commander failed and receded, nature reclaimed Florida's interior. Clinch's "Lang Syne Plantation was left in desolation," until verdant growth "covered its once productive acres." Of the twenty-two destroyed plantations in eastern Florida, only two were ever even rebuilt. Rains spread moss and mold. Fences leaned and fell. Leaves shed and mulched, replenishing soil, insects chewed on charred roof beams, vine tendrils gripped exposed bricks. Seeds turned to saplings and cleaved apart coquina. Goosegrass, goldenrod, and wild savin erased pathways and concealed shards of "old iron and pieces of earthen ware" debris. Flora enveloped sugarcane fields and orange orchards, and the seasons changed, in good time, until everything "grew . . . in the rankest luxuriance," and all that was left were old ruins.

II

12

The Quartermaster

He didn't look like much of anything. Physically average, he had brown eyes and brown, graying, thinning hair. He was not plump, puny, handsome, unattractive, tall, or runty. He struck a dour pose for portraits, like other army men.

At forty-seven, General Thomas Jesup was the youngest of the top-ranking officers. He had always been an eager achiever. As a bookish young man, he had planned to excel in all aspects of military service. But he was severely wounded early in his career—in the shoulder, chest, neck, and hand—and soon abandoned the battlefield for a desk. Instead of perfecting warfare, he had mastered prices, transportation routes, depots, and the costs of army outposts. He became one of the best bureaucrats in the U.S. military, the "Father of the Modern Quartermaster Corps," a bespectacled expert on inputs and outputs.

Since 1818, the quartermaster had led a life of arithmetic, not steel and lead. He was the man who could tell you, if you were really asking, that a one-horse cart hauled 850 pounds, a two-horse wagon could handle 1,332, and a four-horse unit pulled 2,000. A march, after all, was essentially a math problem. Two thousand men at full rations, for ten days, needed thirty-five thousand pounds of biscuits and pickled meat. Assuming a distance of ninety miles from a central depot to a field encampment, and an average wagon speed of fifteen to twenty miles per day, as Jesup's office informed the secretary of war, keeping troops fed would require either fifty carts or twenty-five wagons "kept in constant motion." Even Indian Removal, to him, was a numbers game. By his estimate, "Transporting One Thousand Indians to West of the Mississippi" necessitated 13 wagons for 120 days, 80,000 rations, 200 ponies, and 3 hired hands. He calculated the cost to American taxpayers at "26 dollars per head."

He was raised fatherless, poor, and proud. Jesup's first job, as a store clerk in Kentucky, suited his "happy facility for administration." He was only fired because, a biographer wrote, "his sensitive conscience exacted too high a standard of commercial morality for the purposes of his employer." The quartermaster had retained a "sensitive conscience." He was shrewd, vain, thin-skinned, and hot-tempered. He was no "*boy to be lectured*," as he once scolded another general. But if Jesup still nurtured any high moral values, they did not extend beyond bookkeeping. As a strategist, he was amoral, calculating, and ruthless.

Jackson tapped him to take over command in Florida in November, as Call was floundering. The president was desperate for the entire embarrassing mess to be done with. "I have been brooding over the unfortunate mismanagement of *all the military* operations in Florida," he grumbled, "all which are so humiliating to our military character . . . it fills me with pain, & mortification." The "sooner that a remedy can be afforded the better."

The president was reportedly "raving because the war" was not over.

Even before he heard of Call's failures, Jackson had been frustrated and impatient. In July 1836, with eight months remaining in office, he had left Washington for Tennessee with a lot on his mind and more on his schedule. He did not reach his labor camp for nearly a month. Rains melted the roads into mud. Ten horses struggled to tow one wagon. The muck degraded the steeds' feet until the animals were "left almost without hoofs." The grueling crawl gnawed on Jackson's nerves. Downpours slowed him to less than two miles an hour. In the days after arriving at his retreat, on August 4, he suffered "violent spasms of coughing."

He barnstormed for his vice president, Martin Van Buren, to succeed him in the upcoming election and mulled over ways to improve his candidate's odds. The prospect of a protracted conflict in the peninsula did not help matters. Jackson sought to limit federal spending, yet the war budget was ballooning. An initial $120,000 proved useless. So did the next $500,000. In April of 1836 alone, the tab amounted to $1.5 million. The costly humiliations of one inept general after another seemed endless. Dade strolled into an ambush, Clinch prioritized his property, Scott got lost, and Call was all talk. Good help was hard to find.

Leadership was a problem at all levels. Military officers saw service in Florida as a dirty, thankless job. Dreams of glory had wilted as high-ups realized that the Indians would "not fight in a mass." Duty in the territory felt like a pointless test of survival. "I am now of the opinion that this campaign will not end the war," a sergeant concluded, that summer. "I intend to get out of Florida as soon as I honorably can." Salaries were skimpy, and promotions came slowly. It could take eight years to reach first lieutenant. The president's little war in Florida, as another officer phrased it, offered "neither thanks, profit, nor honor."

U.S. policy, a soldier in Florida wrote, was "inhuman, unjust, and therefore unwise." Disheartened grunts even "sympathized with the Seminoles." As troops grew more "sick & disgusted," Americans found it easier to cite moral concerns. The unjust war shouldn't be fought; the army couldn't win, so the war must be unjust. Both answers were the same.

"All means possible are used by officers to avoid coming," a surgeon wrote, "and if not successful they prefer resigning to running the gauntlet between being kill'd by Indians or the climate." Orders to fight in the Everglades in the summer felt tantamount to "a sentence of death." Officers didn't like the local "crackers" or care much for the volunteers.

Desertions were common. One militiaman in the Middle Florida Regiment simply "pushed off for 'Old Leon County'" in the north without a guide. He became lost in the "pathless woods" and returned to camp in shame. The "spirit of dissatisfaction" bred insubordination. Entire companies of recruits began to discuss "quitting the Campaign and returning" home. Men quarreled and uttered "threats, oaths, and murmurs."

West Pointers quit in droves. Between 1835 and 1837, 202 officers resigned; 155 had attended the academy. A shocking 117 officers—over 18 percent of the authorized officer corps—resigned in 1836. One hundred and ten were captains and lieutenants. Men who'd planned long careers of service abandoned them at the word "Florida." Terse notations in army notebooks scarcely conveyed the simmering resentment in the ranks: "Resigned, under orders to join his company in Florida, on being promoted"; "Resigned under orders to join his post in Florida"; "Never joined his regiment. Graduate of 1836."

In May, in eleven artillery companies, there were six officers. Eight "infantry companies had no officers at all." In July, August, and September, three field officers served with the troops. "We are entitled to fifty-five officers," a colonel noted. "We have here only *six* for company duty." During Scott's 1836 campaign, he didn't have "a single officer for duty in his personal staff," no adjutant general to manage personnel, communications, and records, and no inspector general to enforce discipline. He didn't even have an aide-de-camp. Troops "did not know their officers and consequently knew not who to obey." Discharged soldiers waiting to cash out couldn't find anyone to pay them. Basic reports went unfiled.

Topographers were scarce. Supply lines for equipment and rations were "in a miserable condition." The depots in Tampa Bay and Picolata were too far away. "The wagons are few in number and old, weak, and rickety," an officer complained. "The army is in constant danger of starvation." Famished horses stuck their heads forlornly through tent flaps, reduced to eating the "tents, shoes, saddles, harness, wagon covers," and even the wagon frames. "Were one so unfortunate to leave his coat out in the night," a Northerner explained, "nothing could be found of it in the morning but the buttons."

Jackson could barely stand to hear the reports from the field. "This condition of the Army," he insisted in October, to his War Department, "must no longer be permitted to exist." The Florida War needed organization; Jackson needed an organizer.

In August 1836, when Jesup pitched a plan for defeating Seminole forces, the president was eager to hear it. Jesup had devised the scheme from his recent experiences in Alabama and Georgia fighting Creek Indians—his first field assignment in nearly twenty years. He suggested to Jackson that they raise a "friendly" Indian force for tracking and bush fighting. He also proposed that they extort Abraham and Osceola. "I have been informed that Osceola's brother," he explained to Jackson, "and other members of his family, are with a chief in the Creek Nation. I shall cause them to be seized and held as hostages." Using Abraham's ally Jumper as leverage, likewise, they could "detach Abraham from the Seminoles" and force him to reveal "the plan of concealment of the Seminole families." The president, replying from Tennessee, could hardly contain his zeal:

> I highly approve of your plan of raising an Indian force . . . as well as that of seizing Powell's alias Osceola's brothers and family, and holding them as hostages—this done, and Abraham, the friend and warrior of Jumper, influenced to come over to the whites, the whole of the Seminole Nation will at once surrender.

By Jesup's reckoning, Osceola and "Abraham, the negro who rules Jumper & Micanopy," were the linchpins. "Abraham will come over to save Jumper," Jackson agreed, "and thru him and his clan all necessary information can be splendidly obtained." They would kidnap people close to both men and hurt them if the warriors refused to surrender.

Months of fighting had taken their toll on the Native families. Unlike the Americans, Abraham and his men could not retire after their service contracts expired, or rotate in and out, or resign and switch careers. The longer the war lasted, the more painful it would become. The Seminoles and their allies had also suffered sickness, "something like the cholera." Jumper lost many men, it was said, in the clashes in November. Dearly departed had been buried in log coffins covered with bark or thatched palmetto. Mothers and fathers were put to rest aside the items they would need for their journey. Warriors were laid next to decorative brooches, cooking utensils, liquor, knives, coins, and tobacco. Women were buried beside beads of amber and coral, cups of sofkee, and bags containing needles, thread, flint, and steel.

Some souls left families; others joined. Toney and Polly Barnett welcomed a boy named Martinus. Chloe birthed Dennis. Nelly had Sandy. Mary brought Scipio into the world. Morris, George, and Mundi were all newborns. Abraham's granddaughter was born sometime in 1836. Rachel and Juan received her and named her Nancy.

The Interpreter learned of the law passed by the Legislative Council, by the statesmen keen on targeting his warriors, their wives, and their children. Every encounter the Black Seminoles had with U.S. forces, by decree, now risked their enslavement or execution. Abraham's burden—to protect the families—remained fixed. His strategy had shifted: He hoped to negotiate. The trouble was that the army would not let him.

In the final months of 1836, the tribes left the Cove and fanned out in small groups across the territory. The chiefs decided it was safer to keep moving than to defend permanent settlements. With any luck, the soldiers would get tired of wasting their "time and labor in exploring their country and trailing them from swamp to hammock and hammock to swamp." If and when the Americans did find "one of their strongholds," they could simply "vanish to another," trapping the army on a hamster wheel, locked in an endless cycle. Only they knew Florida's inlands, the terra incognita that was as alien to their enemy as "the interior of China": the creeks and river crossings, the depth and strength of the streams during the wet and dry seasons, and where to find coontie root, wild deer, and turkey. The places where, as Jumper said, "the lakes and ponds so abound with fish that our little boys can shoot them with bow and arrow." The climate could fight for them, its diseases their guns. The unmapped land could be their army, its hidden trails camouflage, the hammocks forts, the marshes moats.

Abraham's people traveled east around high sand hills, to Lake Apopka west of modern-day Orlando, to where pines, red and black oaks, and cypresses dotted rolling vistas of "beautiful little lakes of transparent water." The region was "one of the most romantic and delightful" landscapes in all of Florida, a country so magical that it might have been occupied by "fairies, Naids or Nymphs." Abraham, Micanopy, and Jumper resettled or at least paused here, likely joining Micanopy's brother-in-law Cooper.

Jesup arrived in Tampa Bay from "Creek Country," after following the Chattahoochee River past Snake Shoals, through the swamps. Carrying a brown-leather journal, he recorded diary entries in which he referred to himself in the third person, as "Genl. J."

He gathered all the intelligence he could. He recruited and hired over 750 Creek warriors, as proposed, at a cost of $10,000. It amounted to $1.07 a month per warrior—less than Abraham earned in a day as an Interpreter. As extra incentive, Jesup promised them all the Indian property that they could take, including so-called slaves.

The new commander's allies were acculturated Creeks, the sort who claimed that the Seminoles were illegitimate and should be reabsorbed into the Creek Nation. The hired guns were also children of the old Muscogee people. But these brothers and uncles had been twisted, warped by outsiders as if by a fun-house mirror, until they had accepted white ideas about skin color, superiority, and wealth. Jesup hired bent versions of the Seminoles to kill them and force their allies into bondage, to pull money from dirt.

13

Prisoners

The mercenary was good-looking and did what he was told. Tustenuggee Emathla, Creek commander, stood six feet one. He was "well proportioned, of manly and martial appearance and great physical strength." He flaunted a scarlet headwrap. Whites said that he was a "firm and undeviating friend of the whites," the most handsome Native American they ever saw, and also "the most intelligent Indian, known." He fought beside them to remove his own people from their Alabama homes. He bragged that he had once marched with Andrew Jackson. He had a record of assault and fraud. Some said he "had negro blood" and that he exhibited "all the vices of white, Indian, and negro, without the virtues of any." They once called him Gun Boy. Now he was Jim Boy.

Jim Boy and other Creek chiefs came down the Chattahoochee with 776 strong, to join Jesup's army of 1,050 artillerymen, Marines, and Alabama Volunteers, all preparing for winter hostilities. After arriving, after a delirious U.S. officer in his camp committed suicide, Jim Boy soothed his warriors by explaining that their white brother had only fulfilled his destiny. He may even have believed that he and his men were destined to fight for the Americans for an eighth of the monthly pay earned by Mounted Dragoons, or one-sixteenth that of a sergeant major. He trusted in fate.

Creek proxy fighters had made useful colonial grunts for decades. When Clinch laid siege to the African Fort in 1816, under Jackson's orders, U.S. forces stayed in boats. Muscogee warriors did the dangerous, hand-to-hand clashing. When Jackson's army destroyed Suwannee Old Town in 1818, Creeks did most of the fighting, against Black Seminoles. Creeks handled the unpleasantries; Americans took the credit.

Even with Jim Boy's men, Jesup's ever-expanding "Army of the South" faced a discouraging task. The quartermaster's adversaries were dispersed in small groups, according to him, from Cape Sable on the southern coast to the Okefenokee Swamp in Georgia, an expanse of roughly four hundred miles covering five degrees of latitude. The job was to "go into an unexplored wilderness and catch them," into a country "so extensive, and at the same time so difficult, that five hundred warriors could hold it for five years against an Army of ten thousand." The army was drowning in ignorance. One general had to rely on "booksellers' maps," which "only afforded outlines filled up with unlucky guesses." At Clinch's battle on the Withlacoochee, "there was not, perhaps, in the Army, a single individual who had ever explored the fastnesses on that river, or was competent to act as a guide." Awareness of who was who among the bands was just as spotty. Americans assumed Osceola was a chief. They had almost no insight into the Miccosukee leadership that he answered to.

Jesup seized Jumper's nephew along with one of Osceola's relatives—a philanderer known as Young Powell—and while neither man was important enough to use as leverage, they could be deployed as envoys and spies. The quartermaster also formed "Spy Companies," units of Creek warriors and frontiersmen tasked with reconnaissance. Hostage taking and interrogation became the centerpiece of Jesup's plans.

Fighting battles, "not a single" Black Seminole or Indian warrior had been captured. Fighting battles, U.S. troops had failed to defeat Seminole forces for nearly a year. Slow marches made sense for a conventional land war, but not for seizing families who were spread out in small groups. Native warriors will "neither be captured nor destroyed unless they can be surprised," Jesup concluded, "which can be accomplished only by the sudden and rapid movements of mounted force." Creeks would hunt the families.

Jesup began taking prisoners in earnest on December 3, 1836, on a march to Volusia on the St. Johns, in the company of 350 Alabama Volunteers and fifty Mounted Marines. He passed the ruins of Abraham's Town, where the road was strewn with dead horses, traversed two hammocks, and camped by a pond. A Spy Company found fresh footprints, spotted a lone Indian warrior, and arrested him. The captive, a scout of Osceola's, betrayed the location of a "Negro town" on a lake fed by the Ocklawaha.

Jesup dispatched an Alabamian named Cawlfield, with two companies, the prisoner, and an interpreter. While the quartermaster waited by "a beautiful lake," the hostage led the troops to the site, where they "surprised the village, captured the greater part of its inhabitants, and burnt the houses and property." Cawlfield returned around 9:00 p.m. with forty-one detainees, "including the women and children."

A man named Chambers spearheaded the interrogations.

"The prisoners whom I have taken inform me," Jesup wrote on December 18, "that it is the purpose of Micanopy, Jumper, and Abraham to fly before the Army & avoid a battle—they will hide themselves in the dense hammocks & swamps of the Everglades." The captives revealed that the bands were "scattered off and were scarce of provisions and ammunition," and that Osceola was in the Wahoo Swamp with eighty warriors, "determined to live and die there." Jesup dispatched Jim Boy and two hundred Creek "scouts and spies" to search the mazelike morasses in and near the Cove, to find the rebel, but the henchmen reported, after a careful survey, that the wetlands were empty.

On January 9 and 10, 1837, Jesup's Creek forces captured fifty-two Black Seminoles who had taken refuge in the Panasoffkee Swamp, north of the Wahoo. Many were close with Abraham. They were now spoils of war. Forty-eight of the fifty-two detainees were women and children. Of the four men, one was seventy, one fifty-five, another nineteen, and the last, a twenty-five-year-old, was suffering from a "wound in [the] right knee."

A captive taken on January 9, described as "a boy," gave up Abraham's location. "Jumper, Micanopy, & Abram are at Ahapopka," aka Lake Apopka, the interrogator wrote, in his report. "The prisoner is quite communicative." On January 19, Jim Boy and forty-seven warriors took another twenty-one prisoners, described as "9 negroes and 12 squaws and children." By January 21, the hostages had divulged Abraham's smuggling connection in St. Augustine as Stephen Wright, and named Cudjo's son as the go-between. "The prisoners say," Jesup recounted, "that Wright has sent Barrels of Flour to Abraham by Ned. These barrels, in place of flour, no doubt contained powder. This matter should be looked into."

"I shall march tomorrow to attack Micanopy and Jumper," he pledged.

The quartermaster and his huntsmen traveled east toward Lake Apopka, toward Abraham, Jumper, and Micanopy. Advancing slowly, opening the road as they marched, the colonists continued to seize and interrogate noncombatants and to terrorize children. During one raid of a campsite, an American officer discovered a petrified five-year-old, "her ears filled with little silver drops," in addition to orange-peel scraps and peltry. Sometimes the ransackers found deerskins and cattle hides. Sometimes clothing, axes, lead bars, gunpowder, coontie root, alligator meat, kettles, tins, pots, Dutch ovens. Sometimes people.

Jesup's forces reached Lake Apopka on January 23. The reported camp of "a body of negroes & Indians" stood abandoned, but the soldiers surprised and seized another prisoner at a nearby "negro settlement." Guided by the hostage, the army marched for the camp of Chief Cooper. Reaching a hammock swamp, the Alabama Volunteers had trouble entering the thicket. The hired Creeks explained that there was no entry trail at that point, so the Americans sent them ahead with instructions to report back "if they found a trail or made any discovery." Next came the gunshots. Following the sounds, the troops discovered that the Creeks had "*killed* Cooper, his son . . . and one other Indian." The U.S commander apologized for the snafu in his report, "as it was very desirable to make prisoners of them."

Sixteen more detainees, Indian and African, mostly women and children, were seized in the raid. Among them were Cooper's surviving family and widowed wife—Micanopy's sister. When Cooper's son was pulled dead out of the water, his fifteen-year-old brother "was observed to shed tears." Jesup wrote up the accident as if it were planned, claiming he had "succeeded in surprising Cooper . . . killed him and three of the warriors, and took nine Indian & eight negro prisoners." The hostage takers continued southward toward Lake Tohopekaliga, to scour for Abraham, Jumper, Micanopy, and their families.

Osceola was dead.

He died on January 2, 1836, a week after the war began. "Twelve friendly Indians," reported that he had been shot twice on December 31—once in the hand—and passed two days later. February reports of his demise could not be rejected.

The rebel died again in June. An Indian on a pony rode into the Little River settlement, where Miami is today, and told of how Osceola was in a fight with a chief who struck him with a hatchet "in the left side near the heart," killing him instantly. But only weeks later, in July, Osceola's death had still not been confirmed, and by September 10, oddly enough, news came that Osceola was once "again in the field."

If he didn't die, he "barely escaped." Soldiers almost had him after he abandoned Fort Drane. Word was that he was sick, and that "they had to put him in a two wheeled wagon to get him away." Troops could see the wagon tracks. A prisoner said that Osceola had departed the Panasoffkee Swamp with the Miccosukees on January 5, only four days before the Black Seminole women and children were taken. Another close call.

Even Osceola, after a year, with supplies dwindling, would not risk a serious engagement. Captives claimed that the enforcer was "flying from one place to another with only three warriors." By another report, he had "six or eight men."

Abraham walked south, meanwhile, with all he owned, with the Americans on his trail. He led the families from the high, rolling country, below brackish lakes of rotting limestone, toward Lake Tohopekaliga, toward Philip's settlements, below modern-day Orlando. He led them west of the lake, east of the Big Cypress Swamp, north of the Hatchee-Lustee Creek, into a maze of prairies, creeks, lakes, rivers, footpaths, sand hills, pine barrens, and low, dense, boggy swamps, where prickly briars were sharp enough to shred shoes.

The Interpreter's people forged on, their possessions loaded onto fifty ponies along with the beef jerky and coontie root. Abraham's belongings included blankets, pots, kettles, powder, and $100 in silver, along with papers that proved his free status.

Alabama Volunteers, Mounted Marines, Creeks, and Jesup himself were combing the region on January 27, when an officer discovered "fresh signs of women's and children's tracks." A rapid pursuit resulted in the capture of "two Indian women and three children" and twenty-three Black Seminoles, "young and old." Abraham and an estimated fifty others escaped into the Big Cypress Swamp, toward where the ponies carrying the guns, lead, powder, and food were stashed. The U.S. soldiers and mercenaries followed them into the wetlands, wading through the muck, sinking to their knees, and at times to their waists.

After a quarter mile, the huntsmen reached a river in a ravine that could only be crossed by walking over a tree, which had been felled over the water as a bridge. "Here," according to an American, "the Indians had left their packs and ponies; and here, they . . . commenced a fire." Abraham and Alligator "commanded the Indians," engaged the attackers, and fought them off, killing two Marines. A Black Seminole woman lost her life, and Abraham's warrior Ben was taken prisoner, along with his wife Jane and one of their children. The warriors held the position for as long as they could, defending the scarce provisions. Then all who were able fled deeper into the wetlands, under heavy pursuit. The army took the ponies, food, all the armaments, Abraham's money, and his freedom papers.

The chief eluded them. Alone in the swamp that night, in the darkness, he crept up on the American camp, close enough to see the metal of their rifles glinting in the firelight. He could not see his family among them.

14

The Warden's Rations

The Sense Bearer stepped into high waters, into the swamp. After four miles he stopped and whistled, and made noises: First like an owl, then like a deer, to see if his people were near. The night was cold. He built a fire and sat by the warmth. After some time, two Indians found him and showed him where the others were camped. He sat and he thought about the raid, about his loved ones and friends, about what the war was coming to.

Rains beat down on the American tents the next day, dripping through the canvas. Abraham did not expect the army to send a familiar face to him. His soldier Ben, taken the day prior by the Creek Volunteers, arrived alone. By the time he found Abraham, on January 28, at least sixty Black Seminoles were being held hostage.

Jesup wanted to see Abraham, Ben claimed.

"Did he call me Abraham?"

"He appears to know your name very well."

Ben handed him a plug of tobacco, courtesy of the quartermaster, and Abraham sat and smoked and thought, and did not sleep that night.

"Maybe it is a trick," he thought.

"Go back," he told the messenger, after the sun rose. "If the general send[s for me] again, I will go." Ben left for Tohopekaliga and returned with confirmation.

The Indians advised against the trip.

"They will kill you."

Abraham left for the camp filled with white men who wanted him dead. He came upon a wolf in the woods, howling, standing still, and wondered if it was a bad omen. He had never seen a wolf wail that way in daytime. Fortune had turned against him. Micanopy's brother-in-law was dead and his sister was a prisoner. Their ally and friend, Jumper, had recently fallen ill, and was in "decline from [a] pulmonary infection." Days earlier, John Caesar, Philip's advisor, had been killed near St. Augustine. Every week, more friends were taken.

Between December 1836 and January of 1837, Jesup claimed over 130 captives. Records suggest but do not confirm that these included Abraham's wife, their children Washington and Rachel, and their four grandchildren. Many of those dear to him, in any case, were in grave danger, including Ben and Jane and their young children Charles, Polly, Joe, Betty, Elsey, and Robert. The hostages' ages spoke for themselves. Nelly's boys Scipio and Sandy were three and one. Elsey's daughter Katy was three, Nancy was nine, Linda was eight. There was Ishmael, six, Cyrus, five, Tamar, three, Lucy, seven, Pompey, four, and Matilda, three. Sylvia was nine months.

The Interpreter reached Lake Tohopekaliga, stopping at the outskirts of the sprawling outpost known as Camp Childs. The lake seemed a hundred miles long and seven wide and abounded with fish. Eagles soared aside white cranes and geese. A description of the site at the time provides some idea of the "great confusion" the Sense Bearer saw: "a camp of thirteen hundred men, six hundred horses, [hundreds of seized] cattle; men cutting wood to keep themselves warm; cows lowing; asses braying; horses stamping." Many of the soldiers were Southerners who knew all about "the celebrated" Abraham, about what had been done to Dade and his troops.

The chief walked into the camp, into the heart of Jesup's Army of the South.

"Is that the negro they are going to hang?" the first white he saw said to another.

Ben's wife was in "much distress." Jane could only guess whether her husband would find Abraham, let alone if the chief would follow Ben back or allow Ben to return at all. She and the other hostages could have been held inside the guardhouse. They might not have witnessed Abraham's walk through over one thousand white troops and Creek fighters. Micanopy's imprisoned sister could have missed it when the Interpreter strolled by the soldier who wondered aloud if he was the one they would hang. The child hostages may never have seen the Sense Bearer's deliberate steps past ogling militiamen. But white men saw him approach, on January 31, at around three o'clock in the afternoon:

> Abraham made his appearance, bearing a white flag on a small stick which he had cut in the woods, and walked up to the tent of Gen. Jesup with perfect dignity and composure. He stuck the staff of his flag in the ground, made a salute or bow with his hand, without bending his body, and then waited for the advance of the General, with the most complete self-possession.

The Interpreter was afraid because he "expected to be hung" but did not show his fears. He had "concluded to die, if he must, like a man" to "make one effort to save his people." He planted his flag by the American one, "by the flag-staff," and entered Jesup's marquee. The spacious traveling nerve center of U.S. forces, a stately combination of pole, frame, and canvas, provided an office and areas for dining and sleeping.

You are as safe as if you were at home, Jesup said, welcoming him. The headquarters would have been filled with a commander's paraphernalia: a collapsible desk or writing box, chairs, iron chests, inkstand and quills and powdered ink, envelopes and blotting paper, logbooks and ledgers. The tent cloth glowed with daylight. It was not yet time for candles. Face-to-face, yards from the hostages, the quartermaster and the chief discussed terms.

Jumper is nearly two days' journey away, Abraham told the general. *He is in poor health, and though desirous of peace, he might not be able to meet you in person.* The Indians hoped to broker a truce, the prophet said, and if possible, to remain in the territory. Abraham told Jesup that the lands west of the Mississippi were "too far North and that the Seminoles, accustomed to a warm climate, could not live in one so cold." *We prefer to stay in Florida, but we will leave, reluctantly, on Micanopy's orders.*

Jesup served dinner. Abraham had no appetite and could not eat. He had not yet determined the army's intentions. The commander's behavior made little sense: Jesup was the one who had unleashed Creek stalkers on the wives and children. Now, just like that, the quartermaster wanted them to share a meal and talk like reasonable men?

The chief was ready to leave. Jesup would not let him. "No, not now," the commander insisted. "Towards dark." And the Interpreter grew nervous once again. Maybe they would hang him, and he would fail the prisoners and families. But Jesup only talked, and offered him tobacco, and seemed serious about "peace." Abraham departed in the evening, escorted by a mounted guard to protect him from the hired Creeks.

When he returned that night to the Seminole camp in the woods, the people gathered all around him, to debate and decide what to do. Jumper, gaunt and sickly, stayed up all night with him and Alligator, deliberating. "What can this mean?" they wondered. "Fighting us, one day, and then [asking] us, the next day, to come to their camp." Jumper went with Abraham to meet again with

Jesup, this time near a deep morass outside the army camp at Tohopekaliga. The Lawyer warned the quartermaster that they "could not be accountable" for the Miccosukees. But he and Micanopy and Abraham and Seminole leadership, at least, would agree to a ceasefire, to further talks, and to send out runners to relay news of the armistice and stop the fighting.

The messenger sent north did not reach King Philip until after he had attacked Camp Monroe. On February 8, 1837, an estimated 350 Indian and Black Seminole warriors surprised the Americans before dawn. Troops "flew out of their tents like lightning, some naked, some in their shirts only." Bullets pierced sleeves, and tents, and lodged in logs. Like bomber pilots eager to dump munitions and exit the danger zone, some 650 cautious soldiers and warriors shot at each other for three hours and missed. Two men reportedly died and the Americans dubbed it the Battle of Lake Monroe. They stopped their aimless shooting after word of the truce arrived. A private wrote an ode to "the constant firing of 1000 rifles and muskets, the reverberation across the bosom of the calm and placid beautiful Lake Monroe, the stillness, darkness of the hour, the smoke remaining solemnly around our camp." He noted names of heroes. He claimed in his diary that "the celebrated Osceola" led the attack, but Osceola was not truly there. Three hours, 650 guns, two dead. "No pen can describe the scene."

Abraham, with Chief Cloud's nephew, arrived at Fort Dade for the next round of negotiations around 2:00 p.m. on Saturday, February 18.

The Americans worried that the talks were a tactic to stall until the sickly season, when Indians knew the army could not fight. Abraham assured them that his people "had all started from different camps, and would probably be in, the next day," and eight or ten did come that Sunday, twelve or fifteen on Monday, and five or six more on Tuesday. But the other chiefs had still not arrived, and the army grew skittish.

The Sense Bearer could not allow talks to fail. If the colonists sensed foul play, the prisoners would have no chance. And so on the fourth night, he mounted a steed and "started out of camp—the object not known—but a thousand rumors afloat." In the following days, his reputation as a "shrewd diplomatist" grew. He "talks a great deal and fluently," a traveler reported, and yet proved to be "astonishingly successful in avoiding every expression which might be turned against him," or against Micanopy.

Jesup did not release the hostages. Not all of them. As an act of "good faith," after a misunderstanding, he did release Micanopy's sister and her immediate family. The others remained confined. The general also allowed Cloud's nephew to visit his sister, "an interesting young Indian woman" jailed at Fort Brooke, along with her "only and small boy." She was happy at the visit because "she had only one brother, and she did not know that she should ever meet him again." From her prison, she sewed him a hunting shirt. She requested a candle to finish her gift after sunset.

Abraham came and went from the army camps. He spent many hours in conversation with Jesup, and the quartermaster noted each meeting, often referring to himself in the third person:

> **MARCH 4:** Abraham came in and reports that Jumper had arrived with his family, and that Davy or Holach Toochee would be in today. . . . Jumper sent Genl. J a message that he desired to come in and shake hands with him, & that he would talk to him tomorrow.
>
> **MARCH 7:** Gl. J. had long conferences with Holat Toochee, Cloud, Jumper, & Abraham.
>
> **MARCH 8:** Abraham complained that Major Fagan had cheated him out of $280. Genl J. gave him fifty dollars.

> **MARCH 16:** Gl. J. had a long talk with Abraham. Not satisfactory. He evidently has information which he is unwilling to communicate.
>
> **MARCH 18:** Micanopy and Alligator with Abram spent the whole evening with General Jesup.

The "negotiations"—the snatching of families, the brutal extortions—led to terms of so-called peace that satisfied few. In exchange for leaving the territory, Jesup offered the warriors clemency and pledged to free the hostages. They could start over again in the west, as they had before. At least, they could start over together.

Abraham gathered his livestock. He caught a turkey weighing seventeen pounds and brought it into an American camp to sell. He rode alongside a U.S. officer past the Dade battleground, and could not resist a bit of gaslighting:

> "Ah!"—said he "Here is where those poor fellows were killed!" (Here he heaved a deep sigh) "Poor fellows! I was not there but I heard a great noise!"

Jumper and Micanopy came and went as well, the latter bearing "the appearance of a man with authority." Micanopy wore a bright handkerchief around his head, tied "with peculiar gracefulness," a blue-and-white hunting shirt, and "handsomely beaded" red leggings. After news spread that the chief had agreed to leave the territory, the white men no longer described him as a plump decrepit zero. "Micanopy is not the fat old fool we thought him," a surprised American explained, in an *Army and Navy Chronicle* letter, "but [is in fact] certainly possessing good sense, and actually exercising *regal* powers." The chiefs dined on Jesup's fried ham, stewed turkey, and salmon, and drank his wine.

Jim Boy sauntered in, after one meal, "evidently disappointed that he had not been invited." The mercenary did not yet grasp that his claims on Abraham's people were mere points of leverage: threats for the negotiations, to be bargained off.

The demands of local white residents, many of whom had lost friends and fortunes, were a trickier matter for Jesup. The commander likely did not expect the absolute vitriol directed his way by angry settlers.

Floridians were beyond upset at the terms of the peace deal. "The opinion is very generally expressed here that Gen. Jesup has begged the Indians off," the *Florida Herald* reported, "and that the honor and dignity of his country have been entirely overlooked." Every advantage to the Native peoples granted by an older treaty, it seemed to locals, had been upheld, with every disadvantage ignored. No provision had been made "to our despoiled citizens for property destroyed and captured."

"Is this justice?" the editorial asked. Florida planters were just as blunt in a public letter to the Secretary of War. "Such a termination of the war would be . . . an absolute and clear triumph to the Indians," they warned. Any peace deal on "such extraordinary terms" was a "virtual *sueing* for peace, on the part of the United States." The army's misnomer "capitulation" was no win: It was "a sacrifice of the national dignity."

Jesup had to spell out the political sway and martial power of the Black Seminoles to Hernández, the enslaver who lost three forced labor camps. "The Indian negroes have heard of an act passed by your legislative council directing that they be . . . sold to satisfy the claims of citizens who have lost their property," Jesup wrote the militiaman. "If such an act has passed, it would be the extreme of madness to attempt to carry it into effect." The commander petitioned the governor on the same point. "The negroes control their masters," he warned Call, "and they have heard of the act of your legislative council." Any "attempt to interfere with Indian negroes," he cautioned, "would cause an immediate resort to hostilities."

To Abraham, in early April 1837, the Miccosukees remained the greatest unknown of many. Jumper believed that they would fall in line, that without the Seminole majority, the Miccosukees were too weak to "hold the country." But there remained the threat of warriors who, regardless of the loved ones held hostage, viewed any deal with Jesup as a betrayal, and saw Abraham as another Chief Emathla, and wanted him dead.

15

Waiting for Osceola

Washington was close to eleven, but small enough that the officer guessed he was six. Abraham's son seemed to have "hardly ever seen a white person before" visiting Fort Armstrong, on April 2. In camp, Washington recognized his "Indian pony"—fast and slim, and "about as large as a two-year-old colt"—which had been taken by the army in a raid, and wept. Abraham explained the child's tears, and "the officer gave him up the pony," and the "beautiful boy" brightened up, "took the bridle; ran and caught it; and rode it off."

The Sense Bearer's family were free and safe. If they had been prisoners, Jesup released them. The family was delayed in reaching the emigration site in Tampa Bay, and arrived late to Fort Armstrong, a stop along the route. The army heard Abraham coming around sunset, "a great hallooing in the woods—a noise peculiar to people of this country, driving cattle." The major on duty was so pleased to see him and his wife and child that he nearly helped them herd their livestock into camp.

"Well! Abraham," the officer exclaimed, with the cattle in the pen. "What shall I tell General Jesup? I must send an express, to Tampa, tonight, as the general is anxious about you."

"Tell the general I should have come before, but I waited for Juan and Juan's father. . . . My father-in-law was sick and had to be carried, two days, on the black people's shoulders. I'm afraid he won't live to get to Tampa."

"Have you heard anything from the Miccosukees?"

"No."

"Orderly!"

"Sir," the orderly said.

"Show Abraham the mess tent."

"Yes, sir."

The aide escorted the chief to the dining area, and the major penned an urgent letter reporting Abraham's arrival into camp, dispatching an express rider with instructions to travel through the night. Cattle tussled in the pen. Dogs barked. A ceremonial snare drum beat. In the dimness, "under whip and spur," the rider tore into the woods. Sentinels cried out, "Who comes there?" All around the pickets, soldiers shouted back their names. Abraham's wife was "frightened to death."

Tainy, Washington, and her husband slept in a tent aside the camp commander's. "We have to treat them with great consideration," the officer wrote, to his own son, "for fear they will not come in." The major explained to his little boy that the renowned Sense Bearer had been "the terror of the white people, for the last year," and that "no action was complete unless Abraham was reported to be in it, with his *big gun*."

The Black Seminole chief left twenty-one bovines in the pen, a fraction of his "large number of cattle," and left Fort Armstrong the next morning with his family and the rest of his herd, heading south on the Fort King Road toward the ships that would take them west, hoping his father-in-law would survive the journey. They passed the battlefield where he defeated Dade, and a sinkhole of "sweet, cold water." Crossing the Little Withlacoochee through a "low-lying swamp," they reached Fort Dade on the Big Withlacoochee on April 3. Oak and blackjack led to sandy savanna, to Hagerman's Hole, "where travelers were wont to camp." Twenty-one miles to Fort Foster, fourteen to the Little Hillsborough, and seven to Fort Brooke.

The sick man in their care may have been King Philip, possible father to Abraham's son-in-law. The chief was reportedly "badly burned by his clothes taking fire" in March. When Abraham's party finally reached the emigration camp, nine miles outside of Tampa, a U.S. surgeon recorded the case as "Abram's father—burn." In May 1837, Philip was apparently "too sick to go about."

Micanopy's coalition was increasingly fragile. With Philip's injuries, Micanopy himself and his three brothers-in-law and allies were all either compromised, sick, or dead. Hostage taking had forced him and Abraham into talks. The Creeks had killed Cooper. Jumper was in decline. When Abraham reunited with Micanopy near Fort Brooke, the Chief of the Seminole Nation was as weak politically as he had ever been.

Osceola and the Miccosukees sent word they were coming to Tampa, as Micanopy had ordered. In the early summer, as the Americans waited for them, sickness began to spread at the emigration camp. Abraham's and Jumper's grandchildren came down with rubeola, or red measles, as did eight others. The prophet's family—Tainy, Washington, and Rachel—suffered intestinal pains. Micanopy's wife was stricken with dysentery.

The Interpreter and his family camped and drew rations. Black Seminole fathers and husbands of hostages endured. "Many of the Indians" inspected a steamboat waiting in the harbor to take them to New Orleans, to start their journey. The African Seminole John Horse stole some horses. Jumper informed the army that "his life and that of his son had been threatened by the Indians." Micanopy and Abraham deposited money with the army, for safekeeping. Micanopy left "a considerable sum of money . . . about

1,000 dollars"; Abraham also put down "a considerable sum." The Miccosukees needed more time: to sell cattle; to gather their people; to reach Tampa. Jesup twiddled his thumbs, and stewed, and hoped the war was over. April turned to May, and the Miccosukees did not arrive. The army waited for Osceola, the killer—the "leader of the war"—but he did not show.

Judge Reid, the next territorial governor, knew that the laws were made for him. He was surprised when an acquaintance argued that "a black man, a free man, had as much right to be President of the United States" as Andrew Jackson. "This is a government of white men," Reid noted in his diary, disturbed by the comment, "made by whites for the benefit of whites."

Locals expected their pound of flesh. Reid deposed suspected enemy collaborators personally in St. Augustine. So did Mayor Gould. When Gould learned that the Seminoles had smuggled gunpowder through his city, he petitioned Jesup to send him all those with knowledge of the plot. But the quartermaster did not. Abraham was not summoned. The prophet's go-between, Ned, faced no punishment. The statesmen in Tallahassee repealed their law aimed at the Black Seminoles. Jesup shielded Abraham's people. White supremacists bristled.

Reid and Gould were the least of threats to the truce. Indignant officials, majors, and judges could be reasoned with; profiteers were harder to control, and they could just as easily torpedo Jesup's deal. The quartermaster feared that crooks would claim Abraham's wards using false titles, or charge their allies as debtors and seize Black Seminoles as payment. The widower Cooley, "Justice of they Peace," had teamed up with lurking speculators whose pockets were "full of powers of attorney." As Jesup heard it, Cooley was "a cunning knave, and . . . head man in Florida" who had been locked up "in the Georgia Penitentiary for stealing negroes."

U.S. troops remained vigilant. In March, a major reported that a local man was at Camp Armstrong "to look up his negroes." "Abraham is here," the officer warned, "and has no doubt discerned the object of his visit." Jesup was compelled to issue Order No. 79 in April:

> The Com'g General has reason to believe that the interference of unprincipled white men with the negro property of the Seminole Indians, if not immediately checked, will prevent their emigration and lead to a renewal of the war . . . he will not permit such interference under any pretense whatsoever, and he therefore orders that no whiteman, not in the service of the United States, be allowed to enter any part of the Territory between the St. Johns river and the Gulf of Mexico, south of Fort Drane.

The general also banned civilians from approaching by water. All vessels, merchant or transport, had to be "immediately examined" and all names registered. No one without government business could step off their boats.

Mayor Gould chaired a public meeting in St. Augustine, where residents vented over Jesup's order. The outraged gathered off the Plaza de la Constitución, in the courthouse on King Street, where Spain had once ceded the land to General Jackson. The former Indian agent Humphreys, among other locals, filed into the Moorish coquina building near the market where they sold humans, and slave patrols met.

Humphreys and others drafted a resentful letter to Jesup "*most solemnly*" objecting. Securing their "negro property" was as vital to them as peace. They simply had to recover the last "remnant of their wrecked fortunes," which would otherwise "pass from their power" forever. If citizens couldn't visit Micanopy's camp, how could they know who was who? Would Jesup rely on "negro or Indian testimony"?

Tempers boiled over. For fourteen months, settlers had cowered in villages and outposts, dependent on the military for necessities. In Newnansville, 330 "women, children & old & infirm" were living off U.S. rations. Fort Mills, ten miles north, fed another 190. At Fort Lancaster, 319 were on the dole. After her husband was "killed by Indians," Martha Hull drew aid in Jacksonville. The orphan Quinn, whose family had been "murdered by Indians in 1836," collected food at Garey's Ferry. Carter's widow was forced on welfare after he "died from excessive fatigue while in service." Graves' partner "died of disease contracted in service, after losing *all* of his property by Indians." Another husband "died soon after being driven from home by Indians" in 1835. Not to mention the "Orphans of Capt. Hollerman," the widow and mother of Seely, and the widows of Granger and Ellis—all on government rations.

No stratum of society was untouched. In St. Augustine, as funerals plagued the city, an enslaver who had lost property and kin told a visitor about Abraham and his "powerful control over the Seminoles," and of the destruction of a forced labor camp. Gad Humphreys was "smarting" under his "injuries" like the rest, and he had no intention of sitting idly as his fortunes crumbled. Two days after he helped draft the protest letter to Jesup, he flaunted the general's decree and set out for Tampa. He made it to Black Creek, thirty-five miles away, before he was informed that the army had instructions "to use coercion if necessary" to force him off.

Under Jesup's peace deal, the Seminoles were "not bound to surrender runaway negroes" from prior years. Bondservants liberated or taken during the war—*if* they were found—would return to their enslavers. But all Black Seminoles were protected, and no white claims "of dubious origin," like Humphreys', would be honored.

Cooley made it to Tampa, briefly, before Jesup removed him. A man called Warren, carrying military dispatches, also appeared to be on business, "in a measure at least, to urge claims for negroes said to be with the Indians." In fact, "most all citizens" who snuck into Fort Brooke were there representing claimants. Circling citizens threatened the African Seminoles, jeopardizing Jesup's plans to end the war.

Black Seminole hostages began to die in May. Lydia, eighty, and Mundy, one year six months, passed on May 11, as did one-year-old Maurice. Philip, four, died on May 17. George, one, on May 23. Clauda, two months, left on May 27, as Abraham waited.

Osceola looked "like a man worn down by hard usage." He arrived late at Fort Mellon, 115 miles or so to the northeast of Micanopy's emigration camp, in what today is Sanford, Florida. He seemed "crestfallen" and "agitated." At the fort by the lake, as the days were warming, Indians sold cows and calves, beef cattle and stock cattle and yearlings, and traded buckskins and bearskins for fabric, and ate army corn. The families pledged to begin their march soon to Fort Brooke, where the ships would take them to where it was colder and they doubted they could plant twice yearly.

For Mellon was a sprawling "city of canvas" occupying over one square mile of shoreline. A wharf would soon extend into the shallows of Lake Monroe, for the steamboats and fortified flat-bottom barges. At night, long rows of campfires extended down the "avenue of tents" and wolves' howls echoed around the encampment.

When Osceola arrived, the troops were eager to see him. But most could not pick the warrior out. He "sat with his head down," gaze fixed on the earth. Once in a while, he picked up a chip of wood or stone. He walked alone with folded arms, lightly and with a mild slouch, and avoided eye contact. He spoke softly and never in English.

The Creek enforcer only seemed to transform into an "entirely different man" after starting up a ball game, after the warriors stripped down to their breechcloths, after the athletics began and he lost himself in competition. His voice sounded out the loudest. He yelled in a high pitch that had likely scared Wiley Thompson before he died.

Ball games were played every evening behind the camp "on a wide level plain," on a "perfectly" cleared "parade ground, an area about 200 acres." Different types of ball games had distinct rules and often pitted men against women. The variation that Osceola played at Fort Mellon, in May of 1837, seems to have been the "brother of war," two-goal style, where the objective was to launch a ball the size of a fist, of deer hide sewn with sinew, through two perpendicular poles at each end of the field using sticks resembling lacrosse rackets. In that version, bands vied against each other in an "exceedingly rough" game where "deliberate efforts were made to put good players out," and "limbs were frequently broken."

The "brother of war" version was "used to settle disputes rather than resorting to open conflict." Osceola may have matched up against the "friendly Creeks" assembled at Fort Mellon. If he did, the contentious contests truly did pit brother against brother, with Creeks who fought for the army facing a Creek fighter who wouldn't. In his youth, Osceola was known as a powerful athlete and "a ball-player of some skill." Townspeople would wager trade goods on his performances. But this time, he injured himself or an opposing player hurt him. His foot became inflamed and swollen, and he had to raise the limb to quell the pain.

Newspapers marked his surrender. Troops scribbled in journals about him and wrote about him to relatives. A soldier described him in a letter to his parents as the "most active and smartest Indian in the nation." Fort Mellon's commander wrote up jittery reports to Jesup regarding Osceola's intentions.

The rebel said all the right things. The Miccosukees wanted peace, the enforcer promised, and would move west as soon as they had gathered their people. The ranking officer gave him tobacco and let him sleep in his tent. Osceola dined and drank with the colonel and promised that he was a trustworthy man and would abide by Micanopy's order.

The news from Fort Mellon was encouraging. "I will pledge my life," a report read, that "all will go well." The mercenaries had done their jobs. Kidnapping the families had worked. Americans could finally enjoy the "successful and glorious termination of this horrible war." Soon enough, the country would have no choice but to sing General Jesup's praises, and even the most "slanderous & bitter tongues" would concede his triumphs. The quartermaster had "covered himself with glory," and would soon subjugate the "malignant, but truly brave Oseola."

"They are anxious for peace, there is *no doubt at all*," a letter promised.

In late May, a report shook Jesup from his stupor. According to a recently seized prisoner, Micanopy had been dethroned as the head of the tribes. The Miccosukees now ruled the Nation. Micanopy was blindsided and first heard the news from Jesup, who also had no idea how the Miccosukees pulled it off. Not even Abraham saw it coming. The army knew close to nothing about the new leader, a man locals came to call, simply, "The Devil."

16

The Old Man

He was "feeble," "senile," "wrinkled," "old," "small and bent." A lowly beggar, a parody of a pauper. Before the war, Abiaka appeared at the American camp as a meager, withered fisherman, hawking his catch to support his poor family. In Tampa, troops bought his trout and dismissed him as a gossip, the "town-pump." None of them knew his name so they borrowed one: "Sam Jones," taken from a burlesque tune about a dunce, an angler out to "catch a load of clams."

To the soldiers the aged fisherman was nameless, guileless, chatty, while in reality he was spying on the colonial army that was growing in strength and readiness. The Americans did not think much of him because he did not want them to. Later, he seemed to be nowhere, everywhere, right behind the curtain. "No white man has seen him since the war began," a surgeon wrote, three years into the fight.

When the army learned his status, they sent for him. But his messengers said he was so sick "they thought it doubtful whether he would ever get up again." He couldn't come, another time, because of "*severe illness*." Abiaka was "very sick and perhaps by this time dead." Really, he was not even so old: in his fifties, "entirely destitute of the infirmities of old age," "hale and hearty," he was "in a perfect state of heath."

He had a long nose and mustache and gray hair, white by the temples. His "slight elastic frame" was spry enough to command men, kill seamen on ships wrecked on the rocks, and pole a "laden canoe across the length and breadth of the Everglades." He was reportedly married to Micanopy's niece, who was "very fair to look upon," and also to her daughter, who was said to be "about sixteen, and very beautiful."

Abiaka dressed plainly, disguised his intentions, and did not speak in anger in meetings with the colonists. By 1837, three instant books written by soldiers had already appeared about the "Florida War." ("How comes on your book?" troops taunted one Northerner, who complained that he would "rather have a nickname.") None of them had anything of substance to say about the fisherman. He was one chief of many, a name on a list of strange names. Osceola was the one who'd killed Emathla and Thompson. Osceola was the commander spotted by more than one man that first December, in 1835.

The Americans confused the gunman for the boss who ordered the hit, focusing on Osceola in their ignorance, and for his usefulness. Indian wars needed untamed warriors, and Southerners were uncomfortable with the centrality of slavery to the conflict. Osceola *had* to be the face of it. But a soldier with a bull's-eye on his back can be useful to both sides. To Abiaka, functionally, Osceola was the shiny object. He was the "noble savage" dangled in front of colonists unable to credit Natives with political savvy, placed in the spotlight as the chief stayed out of it. The old man was the face of nothing.

Abiaka was not a man to change his mind once it was set. He promised that he would die in Florida, and he did not need to profess a romantic attachment to the land to justify his decision. "I never consented to do it," he once told a soldier.

"There is no use to talk any more at all about it."

In late May of 1837, before Micanopy lost power, the bands held "a great many dances and talks" in the woods near Lake Jesup, thirty-five miles south of Fort Mellon. Many tribal leaders were weary, and "before the Miccosukees" came, "all talked a great deal about peace" and about "going to Arkansas." But when Chief Abiaka joined the Council meetings and laid out his case to continue fighting, the "fisherman" began to turn the tide in his favor. Attempting a coup d'état was remarkably bold: Of 1,454 warriors remaining, Abiaka only commanded 280. A smaller Miccosukee band provided just 15 more men. For his power play to succeed, he needed to forge alliances.

Seminoles comprised most of the fighting force. Including Abraham's warriors, they had 1,010 men, and the Tallahassees added another 119. Abiaka applied various tactics to attract converts. The Miccosukees threatened Chief Coa Hadjo, captain of 100 fighters, that he "would have his throat cut." The usurper also applied subtler means, persuading Philip's son Wild Cat with promises of power. He may even have promoted him and Osceola to the rank of *tustenuggee*, elevating them to young "lieutenants." Wild Cat and Philip broke with Micanopy; Abiaka gained 350 men as Micanopy lost them.

Abiaka demanded that Micanopy "leave Tampa Bay and join" the Council, then used his refusal as a pretext to depose him, solidifying the takeover with a savvy political bargain. As one chief reported, "the Miccosukees . . . elected a new king of royal blood; but . . . he was yet a boy, and [for now] Sam Jones ruled the nation as Chief." Abiaka would hold the throne until the Seminole heir came of age—the identical compromise that had brought Micanopy to power. The young king of royal blood, Holata Micco

Chee, nephew to King Payne, would indeed later succeed Abiaka as the leader of the Nation.

The calculating Miccosukee chief and his advisors plotted a strategy to obtain badly needed supplies. Agreeing "in council on a story" to fool the Americans, the Indians would pretend to follow Micanopy's orders while they acquired "all the provisions from the whites that they" could for the coming campaign. (The people were "always laughing at the lies they tell the whites.") Jim Boy's men would soon leave the territory, and the sickly season would weaken U.S. troops. Abiaka planned to hide the women and children in a swamp and to "*commence fighting*" again "*when this moon is small*." Before, the tribes spoke with two voices but now they would speak with one. Whites had "but one & they will have but one."

The Council passed a law that would "treat as enemies any who attempt to emigrate," and Abiaka dispatched warriors to the embarkation site, which likely only harbored two hundred or three hundred people. Alligator's brother Capikch Achulee, or Old Bowlegs, reported that Philip's son Wild Cat led the march to Tampa, with eighty fighters.

The revolution went off with a whimper. Bowlegs did not list Osceola as among those who executed it. Abiaka had as much need to be there as Jackson did at Fort Brooke. The "old chiefs in council" gave the orders and subordinates carried them out. Wild Cat prevented another band from reaching Tampa, then confronted the former head chief.

Bellicose warriors may have wanted to punish Micanopy and Jumper, but Miccosukee leadership had prescribed restraint. Diplomatically, Abiaka gave explicit instructions that Micanopy was "not to be hurt or insulted." If the Seminole chief flashed his temper, Wild Cat and his warriors were told "to hold down their heads & say nothing."

If he resisted, they could "carry him off bodily."

Abraham was absent when the raiders arrived, at around 7:00 p.m. on June 2, 1837. Jumper insulted the captors as they forced the camped families off. The Lawyer called them cowards. He goaded that "formerly when he wanted them to fight he could not persuade them to come," but that "they had got very bold now." He said "that by carrying them away, they made them appear like liars and disgraced their chiefs," that "he and Micanopy loved them, and had come to make peace and save them." The families were escorted east toward Lake Tohopekaliga, across the Kissimmee River.

"My tongue and heart remain the same," Abraham dictated, in a letter to an allied chief, as officer Linnard transcribed. "I have one tongue and one heart only. If you can believe me listen to me. I have been known to you so long that I think I have a right to expect credit for my talk. Come in with as many of your people as you can and if you can bring none come alone. Do not sacrifice yourself to the advice of crazy men. My heart is heavy for you and Micanopy and Jumper. If my advice was ever friendly to you believe it to be so now. The Miccosukees threaten me and you and others—why fear them? Are the Seminoles conquered by the Miccosukees? *I* am not, for one, and I expect yet to see some of them by a want of bread at my door, as they have done heretofore. . . . Think in a minute as much as in a day and act."

When the coup unfolded the Interpreter was nine miles away, near the pickets of Fort Brooke, guarding his family and the interests of the ninety African Seminole hostages and an estimated fifty-five Native American captives—mostly women and children—who were now imprisoned at Tampa. Land could be replaced, painfully. Loved ones could not: By June, eight Black Seminoles and thirteen Indigenous prisoners had died in custody.

The army recorded their names phonetically, with tin ears: "Wookar," "Queoka," and "Wilikipa." A "Daughter to Sahopaya." On May 31 alone, three captives died, including a one-year-old boy, a "Son of Sally," and a "Niece to Rosa or Lucy." That was the day

Abraham had heard the news that "100 Indians" were on the march to Micanopy's camp, and the Sense Bearer moved his family to Fort Brooke. He learned what Abiaka had done on June 1.

Jesup urged Micanopy to move closer to the fort, so the soldiers could protect him. Micanopy replied that "his people [were] not his enemies." The chief did not believe he was in danger. He would simply wait "at his present ground . . . till they come." He explained to the commander, "When the 100 men come [I] will find out what they want to do."

"What good will that do?" Jesup protested. "They will carry off your women and children and talking will do you no good."

"Yes," the chief muttered.

Micanopy and Jumper returned and waited, without Abraham.

After he was deposed, Micanopy sent an envoy to Jesup with assurances that he would still "abide by the treaty," that "whatever others might do, he would never raise his band" against the army again. But the general was so infuriated that he seized the messenger and shipped him to New Orleans with the other prisoners. By Order No. 116, twenty-three Indians, the envoy, and ninety Black Seminole hostages were dispatched to Louisiana. Jesup promised to enslave the latter group, "the greater part of them having been captured by the friendly Creek Indians [as] their property." Abraham would have watched the prisoners depart.

That summer, he and his family lived among the extorters. Toney Barnett was with him, likely with his own family. (Forty eight Black Seminoles came into Tampa the day after the coup, but were turned away.) The Interpreter could not know if his deal remained valid. He had to wait, day in and day out, by the outpost. Drums and bugles at sunrise, breakfast, dinner, and end of the day, and other rhythms to call the sick to the hospital, and grunts to their labor. Hostlers tended to the horses, sawyers sawed, carpenters built, blacksmiths hammered, wagoners drove in and out of camp, and the collier burned wood to make charcoal.

Troops indulged in debauchery. Soldiers *had* to drink. The water at Fort Brooke was so "horribly bad," so filled with iron sulfate, it cramped stomachs. Even coffee hurt to drink. Claret wine, at least, kept them hydrated. At one point, 11:00 a.m. rations included a half cup of vinegary whiskey mix dubbed "Catalonia wine." Troops didn't only sign up for service "on a drunken dare"; men stayed drunk, played cards, gambled, picked fights, challenged each other to duels, and generally proved to be troublemaking "rowdies." In St. Augustine, soldiers enjoyed "all sorts of rioting and drunkenness." The "rampant problem" was so severe that most troops were ordered to a fort seven miles outside the city, "in consequence of their being constantly in a state of drunkenness." At Fort King, an officer nicknamed The Baron kept getting arrested for his hedonistic tastes. "Nearly the whole garrison is, at this moment, drunk," an officer reported. At St. Marks, "many of the soldiers" were found intoxicated. Men were so undisciplined and reckless they went on "drunken raids" to loot settlers' homes. A doctor was "awoken once by the howling of wolves & once by the howling of a drunken soldier." Pages of the army Order Book at Tampa filled up with charges of "Unsoldierlike Conduct."

Militiamen had the worst reputations of all: "*full one half* were extremely ignorant men, capricious, acknowledging no rule of action but prejudice." Indian families feared the militia, and nicknamed them "round hats" for their circular headwear.

Abraham had no good options. The army could not be trusted. Even Jim Boy's loyal mercenaries, who left Florida "entirely broken down," had been betrayed, their wives and children forced West in their absence. The ship carrying Jim Boy's family sank and four of his children drowned. Abraham's hopes could end just as horribly.

If he had abandoned the prisoners, the Miccosukees might have forgiven him, as they had Micanopy and Jumper. But after the Sense Bearer rebuked Abiaka's orders, he became a marked man. Not long after the coup d'état, the Miccosukees ordered a hit on the Interpreter and assigned twenty warriors to kill him. The chiefs were now opposed: Abiaka, the "old man," who would not abandon the land; and Abraham, the prophet, who would not abandon the people, who faced death on all sides, with only the slimmest path out.

17

Live

We do not live for ourselves only,
but for our wives and children.
—Abraham, 1837

Hesaketv /hisa:k-itá/: live

Jesup sat inside his headquarters, dejected, composing disappointed, demoralizing reports. "I have now to acquaint you with the entire failure of the scheme of emigration," he began, in his letter to the Commissioner of Indian Affairs. "I have the honor to report that this campaign," he dutifully informed the Adjutant General, "has entirely failed." Despite his "military" successes, he explained to the U.S. Secretary of War, "the measure of immigration has entirely failed." The American general blamed everyone and everything he could think of for the implosion.

He blamed the measles and insulted Micanopy. He indicted locals, in particular the white "negro hunters." He rebuked the African Seminoles who wouldn't wait around while enslavers circled their camp. He didn't know the land. There weren't sufficient topographers. What's more, the climate was too punitive, restricting his offensive efforts to roughly six months a year. Did the public understand that forts had to be abandoned each summer, so that every fall the army had to start over? The Florida Territory had to be "the worst country for military operations on the globe."

Bitterness consumed him for weeks. They had botched their own scheme: There were no colonists crowding out the Indians like usual. Too many soldiers were dead, with too many horses. Jesup had never known of "such a consumption of horses" in a campaign. The effort was exorbitantly expensive. By January of 1838, the war's price tag had surpassed $8 million. (In 1835, the entire U.S. government had expended $17.5 million.) "The country is certainly not worth a [tenth] of the lives and treasure it has already cost," Jesup brooded. "My opinion is that emigration is impracticable."

The general wanted to hang up his hat. In fact, he had definitely never pursued the job in the first place. He longed to be relieved of command and leave the peninsula behind, "the sooner the better." He wrote an acquaintance, "The moment my failure becomes known at Washington I shall no doubt be suspended. At least I hope so." He dreamed of retiring and of living out the rest of the life on his Kentucky farm. "We are perfectly helpless," he confided bleakly. U.S. Removal policy truly was "lawyer legislation" passed by "pettifoggers," corrupt legalists who controlled the country.

"It is most unfortunate that emigration was ever thought of," he concluded.

Jesup stopped writing in his "Seminole Campaign" diary. His journal ends May 30, three days before the coup. Most of the twenty-six ships that were idling in the bay, intended for the emigration, slinked off unused, while Jesup waited to be fired. His foot slipped through a floorboard and he cracked his ankle. Hobbled, he left Tampa Bay in late June 1837, and rode up the Fort King Road to survey his forces. Fort Dade was so unhealthy, so overrun with scurvy, that he evacuated the camp. Stopping at the outposts of Micanopy and Garey's Ferry, he arrived in St. Augustine on July 7.

He hunkered down at the Florida House on Treasury Street, in the heart of town, confined to his hotel room for ten days by his ankle. The mood among residents was grim. "*Our prospects.*— They are as bad as bad can be," the *Florida Herald* announced. The "affliction" hanging over the territory showed no signs of lifting. Economic damage had compounded the human costs. Stores had shuttered. Merchants had gone broke and pulled up stakes. "Property can't be sold at no price," a Jacksonville resident complained. The war in the peninsula was bad for business, vile to investors, repugnant to would-be settlers, and poisonous to the goal of statehood.

"Let us be a state!" an inhabitant declared, that Fourth of July. "Florida in the present war has suffered *most*, done *most*, and has been abused *most*. . . . Instead of begging for, we will then *demand* our rights." Locals felt the territory was ready *now* to join the Union, "to take her stand among the matrons of the Confederacy, and become the mother of statesmen and Patriots." They had to blame someone for the fiasco that had dampened their dreams. "It is now ascertained, and is honestly admitted, that General Jesup's policy has been a complete failure," the St. Augustine newspapers reported. The same "men who were prepared to glorify [the quartermaster] as the 'hero of the Seminole war'" now railed "against him as a dupe and an imbecile." One of Jesup's top officers agreed, reckoning that the enemy had "completely outwitted" the commander.

For as little as the army understood about the tribes, finger-pointing was natural. A year and a half into hostilities, military leaders still had scant idea of how bands were organized or how power was wielded. Reporters who described all the Indians as "Seminoles" could hardly grasp the Seminole and Miccosukee fissure, let alone explain it to a baffled public. Colonists concluded that the "lying Seminoles" had tricked them. Everything Jesup learned pointed to Abiaka, but he could not accept that the chief had outfoxed him.

The general grew "much depressed in spirits." Punitive fits punctuated his sorrows. He spent his hours ordering courts-martial and approving penances. He had deserters tattooed with the letter *D*, locked drunks in solitary on bread and water, and sentenced miscreants to hard labor for up to twelve months "with a ball and chain." He ordered men's heads shaved, forty lashes on bare backs, busted men in rank, and had them "drummed out of service."

His letters to officers were blunt and bloodthirsty: "Secure all the chiefs you can get hold of, and all the warriors too"; "Seize all the Indians you can"; "seize Wild Cat and his brothers"; take King Philip and "all the family and as many of the people as possible"; and "if the chiefs come in and you can make them drunk seize them in that state and secure them all in irons." If the Creek warriors caught Osceola before leaving, they could "dispose of him in their manner." Any who couldn't be grabbed had to be "hunted and fought," meaning killed. "As for the negroes," Jesup ordered, "they should be hung up as they are taken." He saw "but one way to remove these people" and that was to "exterminate them." Despondence yielded to rage. If the public could stomach it, he could use bloodhounds. Maybe, instead of quitting, he would recruit a thousand Shawnee, Miami, Delaware, and Sioux Indians to his cause. "They kill all men," the commander boasted, "drink their blood, and make the women & children slaves." Maybe then he would succeed in sweeping his adversaries "from the face of the earth."

Cooped up in the Florida House, ankle swollen, he aimed his wrath at the Sense Bearer. "Abraham," he insisted, to the ranking officer in Tampa, "must be closely watched." The quartermaster was certain that when hostilities renewed, the Interpreter would "take the first opportunity" to abandon the army. He ordered Fort Brooke's commander to move the chief inside the pickets and arrest him and Barnett at the first signs of Indians.

July 23, 1837. The interrogation of Chief Sawanok' Tustenuggee, known as Abraham, was notable for the information that the subject refused to provide. The interview probably took place inside Fort Brooke's Seminole Agency, in a log cabin west of the saltwater swamp and the ancient Indian Mound, a bygone relic.

The Interpreter named the heads of sixteen bands, with robust estimates of their strength—a rough sketch of the players. He would not divulge anything about Black Seminole bands, the location of the enslaved peoples freed from the camps, or where the warriors might be. "The number of runaways cannot be obtained," the interrogator reported. "Nor can Abram give any accurate information about the Seminole negroes."

A Creek captive contributed three additional bands to the grand tally. Osceola and Wild Cat, "fierce warriors" ranked highly by Jesup, did not make the list. Of nineteen chiefs and subchiefs in the final report, Abraham commanded more fighters than twelve of them. A third prisoner interviewed gave up a list of "negro warriors" captained by Abraham, and names of the African Seminole company commanders and their soldiers.

An interrogation of Chief Alligator's brother Old Bowlegs, on July 24, yielded current locations. Philip, Abiaka, and five smaller bands were camped on the west side of the St. Johns, two days south of Fort Mellon, with 870 warriors. Micanopy, Jumper, John Horse, Alligator, Cloud, and a number of minor bands were across the Kissimmee with 440. The Tallahassees were a "short-day's" walk northeast, with 119.

Chiefs Micanopy and Jumper, defying Abiaka, were not swayed to his cause. A sizable contingent remained faithful to them. Forcing the two Seminole leaders from the emigration camp was far easier than forcing them to fight. Abiaka yielded great influence when they were not in Council, but with their return to the field, both Micanopy's and Jumper's voices countered his, refuted the coup, and resisted the call to war.

In his way, Micanopy protected Abraham, sending word to Tampa that he missed and "wished to see" his old friend. Abraham likewise reminded a lieutenant of his close "friendship" with the Seminole chief, which was "no doubt reciprocated." He reaffirmed his worth to the anxious Americans—and their need for him.

"I have watched Abram closely since he has been here," the officer wrote, to Jesup. "I beg leave to state to you some of the circumstances [of] his conduct . . . in the hope that you may be induced at least to suspend the order for his confinement. . . . He knows that . . . by deserting us he would forfeit the liberty of his family and his property—if not his life, and he has too much sense to risk all these interests." The Interpreter made "no professions of gratitude to the whites." He acted from cold logic. Locking him up would be a tactical blunder.

"Abraham is obviously a great man," the lieutenant wrote.

Indian signs were found near Fort Brooke. In August, "parties of considerable strength" circled, and horses were stolen. But Abraham was not placed in irons.

Seven storms hit Florida. Five soldiers drowned. A packet schooner disappeared, killing another fifteen. Gale-force winds flattened nineteen houses in Fernandina, tossing trees over the roads. A market house was "carried away." In St. Augustine, gusts cracked the hull of the steamboat *Florida* and grounded another ship at the mouth of the St. Johns. In Jacksonville, the public wharf was shredded. The storms were not matched by gunfire. The frontier was mostly quiet. Indians visited the reconstructed Fort King "in a most friendly manner." Express riders passed through the interior unmolested. Forts abandoned earlier went untouched. The "influence of Micanopy and Jumper" had "prevailed . . . to prevent a renewal of hostilities."

On August 20, 1837, Jesup met near Fort King with a Seminole chief, a Seminole subchief, and a Miccosukee subchief. The Native emissaries explained that it was the "desire of the whole people to be at peace," but that the tribes "had an old man among them, Appiacca [*sic*] [Sam Jones], who gave them bad advice, and . . . caused most of the recent difficulty." They said all, "except Jones, expressed their anxiety for peace."

"I have one hundred eighty of your prisoners, including negroes," Jesup told them. "If you spill a drop of blood, I will execute them man for man."

The quartermaster refused to "acknowledge Sam Jones as a

Chief" and dismissed him as "a fool, a knave, and a liar." But even Jesup saw that Abiaka could not be both a lone irritant and Chief of the Nation. He believed that the envoys' true goal was to convince him to open a trading house. The families were running low on necessities.

Following the meeting with Jesup, the tribes held a private Council in which Coa Hadjo argued that the fight was not practical because of their limited supplies:

> He addressed old Yakky, (Abiaka) from morn to midnight. . . . Yakky became so mad that he several times left the council. [Osceola] coincided in the views of Coa-hadjo, stating that they could not maintain the war another year, and that he for one would make peace with the whites. Sam Jones replied that he would not give up as long as he had a single ball and a charge of powder—that when he could no longer shoot game, he would live on fish—when his lines are worn out, he will make others of horse hair—and when his hooks are broken, he will cut up his old tin pans and make others. He concluded by saying that he had 700 warriors, and that he would fight as long as they would stand by him; and that if every other Indian should leave Florida, he would find a retreat among the islands of the Everglades, remote from the face of white or red man.

A Miccosukee subchief with family among Jesup's captives agreed with Osceola and pushed for a truce. Abiaka, to be sure, was less burdened than many Seminoles: Of the 180 U.S. prisoners, 18 were Miccosukees. But the chief also exercised what a witness described as "a hundred times the power and influence" of Osceola. Above all, Abiaka inspired the will to endure.

Jesup decided to retain command, resume his terror campaign, and try to salvage his damaged reputation. He planned to muster an additional forty-one hundred regulars, two spy battalions, mounted brigades from Georgia, Kentucky, and Florida, and a regiment from

Louisiana. He was also intent on hiring the one thousand northern Indians who, he repeatedly bragged, "kill all the men—take their hearts out and drink their blood, and make slaves of the women and children." On August 13, he pledged to enslave *all* captives:

> All who shall not have surrendered by the 1st of October, both black and red, will either be killed, or made slaves to the northern Indians. After these Indians arrive no peace can be made, for they will claim, and must have, the Seminoles and Miccosukees as slaves. All the prisoners already taken will be given up to them, unless their relations come in immediately and go to the west. . . . If they determine on war they must be destroyed or be slaves.

On his return to Tampa Bay in late August, Jesup met with Abraham. They spoke of slavery, and of freedom, and of terms of peace they could both live with.

18

Walk

The Indian runner was also furnish'd with a horse for the use of Jumper whom he stated [is] incapable of walking.
—Captain Jarvis, 1837

Yvkvpetv /yakap-itá/: walk

Jackson usually avoided liquor on account of his health, but this was a historic occasion. "Gentlemen," he told gathered friends, "let us drink a little Madeira." Jackson drank the wine and set it down and lit his cob pipe and puffed on it. Smoke whirled around his thin ice-white locks. He turned his thin frame toward the old clock in the corner. Enduring a long, painful silence, he watched the seconds tick off to midnight. "I am no longer president of the United States," he announced. "I am very glad to get away from all this excitement and bother."

Before bed, he read from the Bible until his head hurt. He slept in the gloom of the White House after the oil lamps went out. In his 8,247-word Farewell Address—still the longest presidential goodbye in American history—Jackson did not bother mentioning any of the tribes in the Florida Territory. He only expounded, generally, on how he sought to "protect" Native peoples, on how Removal of "that ill-fated race" was humane and paternal. Then the so-called

Great White Father left Washington City for good, for his private forced labor farm.

By the end of Jackson's second term, approximately 45,690 Native Americans had been forcibly relocated west of the Mississippi. The Cherokee, Chickasaw, Choctaw, Creek, and Seminole Indians—the Five Civilized Tribes—were a fraction of the story. The Sac and Fox tribes surrendered lands in modern-day Iowa. Members of the Quapaw Nation were removed from Arkansas and Louisiana. The Pawnee people were forced to relinquish tracts in what became Nebraska, the Otoes and Missourias forsook acreage in Missouri, and the Shawnee and Seneca tribes were pushed from Ohio. The Chippewa, or Ojibwe, Menominee, Miami, Ottawa, Potawatomi, and Winnebago peoples. The Kickapoo, the Wyandot, the Kaskaskia, the Peoria, the Piankashaw, the Wea, the Iowa, the Delaware, and the Osage. Michigan, Wisconsin, Indiana, Illinois, Kentucky, and Kansas.

The Florida War would prove to be the longest, costliest, and deadliest of all of these efforts. By the time Martin Van Buren took office, Jackson had been singled out as responsible for the losses in lives and treasure in the peninsula. Removal was ugly enough when it was cheap. When failing was this expensive, it looked like madness. The Florida mess held up an unflattering mirror to the nation. To Jackson, the quagmire was a stain on his legacy.

Back in Tennessee, the ex-president—a father of American Florida—could not get the territory out of his thoughts. He had deeply offended the settlers. "Let the damned cowards defend their country" was not a nice thing to say, and locals punched back when his words appeared in print. "Gen. Jackson vs. Florida," a headline read, above all the sordid details. Was Jackson senile? Maybe he *should* take fifty women, like he bragged he could, and "whip every Indian that had ever crossed the Suwannee." The old man should "mount his war horse," instead of making Floridians "subjects of ridicule."

In late 1837, as a retiree, Jackson exchanged at least six private letters with Secretary of War Joel Poinsett regarding how to "put down the Punic war in Florida." For the life of him, Old Hickory couldn't understand the problem. "1000 well organized Tennesseans," he promised Poinsett, could defeat "all the hostiles" in three months. If the recruits were good woodsmen and marksmen, he was sure that "one thousand [additional] volunteers, bayonets or riffles, will be all sufficient . . . to put an end to the Florida War."

Abiaka, the war leader—"said to be the most aged Indian in the Territory at the time, being upwards of seventy-eight"—did not appear in the correspondence. An idea of Osceola, instead, occupied Jackson's thoughts. The warrior, according to him, had been loyal to Emathla and had killed his own chief. Jackson also falsely believed that the rebel had been in the fight against Dade. Osceola, "when he came in," the old general argued to Poinsett, on August 27, "ought to have been hung or kept in irons. Except in this, I have no doubt Genl Jesup [has] performed his duty *well*, under all the circumstances."

Jesup may never have read those lines verbatim. He did at some point read an "Excerpt of a private letter from General Andrew Jackson to the Secretary of War dated Hermitage, October 1st, 1837." In the extract, Jackson doubled down on seizing "the Indian women and children" as hostages and insisted for a second time that the quartermaster should have arrested Osceola. "Jesup, I hope, will profit by experience," the ex-president wrote, "and the moment he gets [Osceola] and the chiefs in his power, will hold them fast."

Twenty days later, Jesup seized Osceola under a white flag.

Newspapers wrote up how the tawdry scene should have gone. "LATEST FROM FLORIDA—SURRENDER OF OSEOLA . . . the Florida war is ended, by the surrender of Oseola and his warriors, in number three hundred," the announcement read. "The great Chief formed his men into line—leaned himself against a tree—and when the United States officer, who was deputed to receive him, came up, he approached him, and gave up his rifle, with all the grace of a fallen hero." "Our correspondents," another paper reported, "need be under no apprehension respecting the truth . . . *the war has terminated*."

The scene was invented from whole cloth. The rebel had never commanded three hundred warriors loyal to him over Abiaka. He didn't harmoniously surrender his gun like "a fallen hero" after leaning against a hardwood. The real thing went down eight miles south of St. Augustine, on the northern bank of a "large cypress pond." He was waiting for the colonists, within "a short distance by a white flag flying." When fabric was scarce, the bands used heron wings or feathers tied to sticks, or "the skin of a heron" on a rifle. In this case, Jesup had "provided them with a quantity of white cotton cloth to be used as flags," under his authority. The symbol of truce, emblem of sacred rules of war, was authentic.

Seventy-five warriors allied with Abiaka were present. Osceola seemed content, and a "continued smile played over his face, particularly when shaking hands with the officers present." Chief Coa Hadjo and the U.S. militiaman Hernández led the discussion. As they negotiated, 150 Mounted Dragoons circled.

"What people have come with you?" Hernández asked.

"All that were well and that could gather."

"Have you come to give up to me as your friend?"

"No."

Osceola watched as the enemy formed "to enclose them." He "evinced a good deal of uneasiness [and] kept his eyes constantly and quickly wandering about" as the Dragoons made their move. But he did not raise his rifle when they rushed in to arrest him. The "moment he found himself a prisoner, he became perfectly quiet and calm," with "not the slightest symptom of emotion." The "Indians bore it like philosophers." No gun was fired. The detainees left behind Jesup's cotton flag and began an eight-mile walk to St. Augustine. Three days later, Jesup apprised Jackson of the operation. The quartermaster reckoned, he informed the ex-president, that his Army of the South had killed only thirty men in nearly two years. But he now held over five hundred prisoners, including King Philip and his son Wild Cat.

The 1st Infantry stared at the strange markings carved into the Fort King Road, between Abraham's Town and Fort Brooke. The "hieroglyphical representations" had been drawn in "a smooth place made in the sand": two "acute angles thus crossing each other," somehow resembling two arrowheads, which were etched beside an emblem of a heart. The Americans gave "various interpretations . . . some quite playful." But when they reached Tampa they asked Abraham, who they knew had been "born and raised among the Seminoles," and he told them "the *cross marks* was the private *sign* of Micanopy."

The journal of a U.S. Indian agent may have recorded the image they saw:

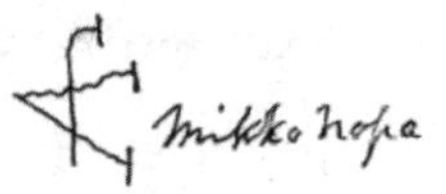

mikko nopa

Abraham—like other Seminole chiefs, he apparently had his own private sign*—"gave it as his interpretation that it indicated the desire for peace but that fear prevented their showing themselves." Micanopy and Jumper were, in short, only waiting for a "favorable opportunity to join" Abraham, to emigrate west together.

On November 13, the Sense Bearer dictated his Last Will and Testament to the Acting Paymaster at Fort Brooke. "Abram desires that in case of his death the following arrangements may be made in relation to his property," the officer scribbled, in a small bound notebook. To "Washington, his son, 1/3 of all." To "Tenny, or

*At the end of a letter dictated letter by Abraham, in place of his signature, an icon appears:

Betsy, his wife, one third." The final third would go to his daughter "Rachel & her children Fanny, Katy, [and] Nancy." The title for Tenebo, who seemed to be "owned" protectively, as Abraham's relative, would pass to Rachel.

Abraham's two other children remained in the interior, likely with their mother, Hagar, in serious peril. He allotted a few dollars for them as well, in case he did not find them before they were captured or surrendered. "Renty & Lucy if coming in," the officer recorded, "$10.00 a piece." On November 14, Abraham and Toney Barnett departed the scenic waterfront outpost together, in the company of U.S. troops, on a dangerous mission. The Interpreter's wife, son, daughter, and three grandchildren would stay behind, within the safety of Fort Brooke.

At seven in the morning, a rainstorm hit "quite suddenly." From the west, mist and showers rolled in on ashen clouds. In the east, the sun shone brightly. A double rainbow formed in front of Abraham and the troops. Bright colors arched in the heavens, forming "the most brilliant & splendidly perfect of any thing [one soldier had ever] seen or heard of."

Abraham and Toney led the army toward the sun, toward the Kissimmee.

Six hundred and fifty soldiers advanced east: two regiments of infantry, a squadron of mounted men, artillerymen bearing a "6 Pounder" cannon, ten Citizen Companies, a company of Citizen Pioneers, 120 wagons, and 120 armed wagon drivers who could fight in a pinch. The forces marched fourteen miles, stopping at Lake Thonotosassa.

The Sense Bearer camped amid the mass of motley characters: the bootless, the idle, the plump, the lean, the laughing, and the glum. Next to "the man of prayer," an officer reported on November 15, you would find "the infamously profane." The scholar settled in beside the "consummate ass." Veterans dined aside newbies, the "abstemious & the drunkard, the eaters of pills and of oysters," the "busiest of the busy & the lounger of perfection." A ruffian with a "nasty obscene moustache" supped with a "boy of new-sprung beard," the "musician, they of the flute; & he of the violin," and with the "clans, clubs, gangs," the "hunting, riding, singing & sighing," the "sick[ly] & dying." A portrait of the new America.

The colonel in command was skittish. "I go to a part of Florida never before visited by white men," he wrote, to his wife. "Pray for me Betty. . . . Abraham the Prophet & Prime Minister of Mickanopy accompanies me with Antony his waiter. He is a perfect noncommittal man . . . a shrewd cunning man, but he has in me a Yankee of the first water to deal with. *I shall use him*." In truth, both men were using each other. For all of Jesup's menacing, promises of enslavement and blood-guzzling, the colonists remained in a weak position. The army might win a fight, but they could not fight tribes who did not wish to be found, who spread out over millions of acres and knew how to live off the land. Jesup needed to deal, and Abraham also had leverage. The Interpreter could bring families in.

Before joining the march, he secured concessions. The chief had only agreed to act as a guide, at $2.50 a day, "on condition that in the event of Miconope or Jumper, or either of their families being taken, the lives of all shall be saved . . . quite a magnanimous trait in Sohanac's [*sic*] character." Every prisoner captured by the Creeks would be released, and all twenty-nine African Seminoles who had been enslaved by Humphreys, who were liberated in Jumper and Barnett's raid, would have their freedom.

Abraham walked the finest of lines. Miccosukee hitmen wanted his head. Florida statesmen wanted revenge for Dade and the ruined plantations. He was surrounded by Southern white men. Jesup had threatened in writing to hang him if things went sour. Step by step, in concert with Micanopy, he balanced on a tightrope over a minefield, acting more as a mediator than guide. At least nine other Indians and Black Seminoles would also work with the army. Two would be killed in the course of their efforts. It was no time to be "full of sofkee"—soft as corn porridge—as Abraham would say.

On the second day, they hiked ten miles east to a tributary of the Alafia River. A soldier was shot by accident. A mule plagued by glanders was shot on purpose. Troops cleared roads, leveled a thicket, built a bridge over Pease Creek, and constructed a fort. Rain poured, and the prophet came and went from camp. Jesup met with Micanopy, Abraham found Jumper, and the chiefs set out together to gather their friends. By December 1837, Jumper was too sick to travel by foot. A horse was summoned to carry his weight.

19

Run

For some weeks we watched the moon, in order that the night of our attempt it should be as dark as possible.
—Wild Cat, 1848

Pefatketv /pifa:tk-itá/: run

Jesup's army paraded the prisoners through town at sundown. The "whole population" of St. Augustine turned out to watch, to gawk at Osceola, at his blue calico shirt and bright red leggings with their glinting buttons. He seemed "in no manner cast down by his present situation." He flashed the same gentle smile, even while he seemed sickly and weak. Osceola and two others rode horses but the rest walked the narrow streets toward the fort, past settlers who did not know what they were looking at.

The Castillo de San Marcos was built to defend St. Augustine from pirates, to ensure safe passage to the Spanish galleons carrying silver from Puerto Bello, gold from Vera Cruz, and pearls from Cartagena. Convicts, Indians, and Africans axed out 150 million pounds of coquina from the earth, from the barrier islands, over twenty-three years, and barged the blocks over for the builders. Time, fire, oysters and clams, water and sand became brick, plaster, whitewash, and tabby. By 1837, the stone behemoth was already over 140 years old, and more useful as a jail than as protection from roving seamen.

Viewed from a bird's eye, the squat Spanish fortress formed a Japanese throwing star. Four protective bastions extended like blades from a square body. The outer walls were weatherworn and pockmarked from bygone battles. Above an inner courtyard, rows of cannons on the gun deck pointed muzzles at the Atlantic.

The prisoners crossed the moat and the eighteen-hundred-pound drawbridge, passed beyond the sliding grated gate, and entered the thickset stonework. Jesup bragged about capturing seventy-one warriors, but his men only seized forty-seven rifles, "old and much worn," and the forty-three pouches and horns of powder were "generally not more than a fourth full." Troops confiscated the warriors' "large knives" and "a barricade was erected to prevent a rush upon the passage" to the exit. "The Indians are perfectly secure," a surgeon wrote, "and do not dream of escape." Guards were warned to remain alert.

Among the detainees were high-level subchiefs, children, mothers, sisters, and wives. They slept on forage bags stuffed with straw, above dungeons where they once held outlaws, where the Americans had found "human bones—or stones, resembling those of man." Communal cells in the walls were furnished with "police tubs"—barrels for human waste. Light beamed from slits near the arched ceilings. In daytime, captives were allowed into the courtyard, and maybe up the stairs to view the ocean. At night, they were locked until sunrise in their cells, with bodies and barrels, in dank stone rooms roughly eighteen by thirty-three feet.

Rumor had it that Osceola had poisoned himself, and that he was dying. His fever came and went. He may already have had malaria. He now likely contracted head lice. He sent for his loved ones and settled into the routine, as Jesup seized more families, until over two hundred captives moldered inside the jail. Despondent hostages became increasingly sick from the diseases that had killed so many of the colonists: measles, diarrhea, dysentery, and infections of the nose, lungs, and throat. Abiaka's subchief John Hicks died on November 25.

In a cell in the southwest of the Castillo, at night, inmates gazed up from hay mattresses at a sliver of darkened sky fifteen feet off the floor, where the faintest promise of freedom peeked in through a slender opening. Philip's son Wild Cat stood on a friend's shoulders and worked a knife into the masonry, into a "crevice of the stonework," pulling himself up on the perch of the blade to examine the loophole. The opening was five feet tall, eight inches wide at its narrowest, and caged by two iron bars. If the prisoners managed to pry loose the metal, to squeeze through to the outside, they would find themselves dangerously suspended above the waterless moat, staring down the outer wall at a fall of perhaps forty feet.

The plan was desperate and absurd. They feigned illness, pleaded with the guards for sliming roots to treat their maladies, and fashioned a rope from torn forage-bag bedcovers. Roots and fasting turned them thin as they waited for the waning moon to dim, to try their luck with the cramped, cragged loophole that opened high above the dizzying drop.

The sun rose and fell until the moon was positioned between the sun and the earth, and its shadowed side faced the prisoners, and only the stars shown. The night of November 29, 1837, came under a nearly moonless sky. The guard seemed drunk, barging into the cell, "talking and singing." The captives pretended to sleep until he left, until his muffled snores rumbled beyond the locked door. Somehow, the prisoners removed an iron bar. Wild Cat fixed the makeshift rope to the remaining one and lowered the cord, and one by one in turn they gambled their lives, hidden from view from the town by the southwest bastion. Pumice-like coquina ripped skin from their chests and backs. Dull silhouettes slipped down the wall and escaped St. Augustine, past the sentries and city dwellers. A warrior fell and thumped on the ground, unconscious. After some time, he was helped to his feet. Guards passed in darkness. By morning, by carefully lowering themselves down to earth, twenty men and women had escaped.

Wild Cat made it out, with two of his brothers. So did the Black Seminole subchief John Horse. Eight Miccosukees escaped, including two women and one of Abiaka's lieutenants. Troops from Fort Peyton chased the jailbreakers but lost the trail in a cypress swamp. The 530 Tennessee Volunteers dispatched east of the St. Johns came up empty. Wild Cat ditched a mule to throw them off track and escaped through the thickets, surviving on roots and berries for five days before finding his people.

Jesup lost "two or three of the most important characters." He retained Osceola, who had remained behind, ill and weary. Still, Americans did not like the part of the story where the rebel was seized under a white flag. Jesup expected to be lauded. Instead, he drew scorn. Newspapers slammed him for the breach of martial decorum. Calls for an investigation and his resignation followed. He tried to wriggle out of it by framing Osceola for Abiaka's takeover. It wouldn't matter: For the rest of his life, the commander's reputation was sullied for capturing Osceola "*by treachery and fraud.*" Countrywide, the condemnation was nearly universal. "The conduct of Gen. Jesup in detaining Oseola and his band as prisoners," a Vermont press noted, "is censured by many of the papers." If the story was true, a Washington paper professed, it would represent a "treachery disgraceful of the character of the country, and a foul stigma on the American soldier." North Carolina's *Newbernian* warned that Jesup's betrayal had damaging practical repercussions. "Will they respect treaties or keep faith with us in the future?" the editorial asked. "Never—never! . . . Oh shame, where is thy blush!" The general's actions, the *South-Western Farmer* insisted, stood "solitary and alone in the annals of the Republic." At least parts of the Deep South were on the quartermaster's side. In Mississippi, the *Natchez Daily Courier* declared that the beleaguered general should have snatched Osceola sooner, to save lives.

The rest was mockery. In Pennsylvania, a paper ribbed him in verse:

> Truly it seems our Gen'ral Jesup
> Found't hard to mix his *Indian mess* up;
> For though some of the chiefs he caught
> And them to prison safely brought,
> The [Indians] broke through the jail,
> Giving for their return *leg*-bail.
> By violating flags of truce,
> He caught Oseola in a noose—
> A breach of faith by every nation
> Esteem'd a stain on reputation;
> But though the Gen'ral thus by tricks
> Thought he the [enemy] could fix—
> And though in bragging very tall,
> He could'nt clime a *semi-knoll*

The Memphis Inquirer wisecracked that as of its "last intelligence," Jesup was busy scheming to capture a couple of Indigenous women "under a flag of truce!"

In Congress, a South Carolina representative admitted his "unmeasured condemnation of . . . the first instance in the history of this country, where an American officer had refused to respect a flag of truce." The congressman also lashed out at "the sympathies [of Northerners] for the Indians," which he believed derived from "a hatred of their own race." A delegate from Florida likewise wondered why the "public sentiments at the North called for sympathy—for sympathy with any thing that had color, whether red or black." Others worried about the financial toll, particularly after the bank runs that May—a crisis known as the Panic of 1837—which led to a national recession. Contractors were stuffing federal cash into their pockets and "growing fat on the spoils of Government." Wagons that should have been hired for $5 were leased for $10. The original treaty was a sham. The war was based on fraud and lies. Turtles all the way down. The North forced into a Southern war in a slave territory. Abolitionists forced to fight for values they detested.

Blame for arresting Osceola extended beyond Jesup to the War Department and White House. "Indeed, there is good reason to believe," *The Recorder* informed readers, "that this treacherous capture was planned in Washington; and that Jesup, in the part he acted, was merely a subservient tool." Jackson did not defend Jesup. Neither did President Van Buren.

Osceola remained in the national spotlight. Many Americans seemed to feel that the enforcer—their villainized, romanticized, invented chief—deserved a better ending, one that helped them wash their bloody hands. Instead, indignity hung over the conflict as Osceola languished in sickness, while the real torchbearer, Abiaka, planned his next move.

Abraham was unfamiliar with the lands in the southeast beyond the Kissimmee River, north of Lake Okeechobee. But his children Renty and Lucy were reportedly at a Seminole camp in that region. He had no choice but to convince the American colonel, the future U.S. president Zachary Taylor, to let him look for his boy and girl "or make arrangements for their coming in." Taylor believed the excursion could cost the Interpreter his life, but he allowed it after the prophet's "earnest solicitation," and Abraham set out with Jumper for the labyrinthine network of lakes and swamps across the waterway.

Micanopy, true to his word and sincere "in all he promised," met with Jesup in December, under the "the white scarf of peace," to make good on his difficult decision to emigrate. But when Jesup learned that Abiaka refused to attend the talks, the general grew "increasingly imperious and ill-tempered," and ordered guards to seize Micanopy and his men and force them onto a steamboat to St. Augustine. The chief accepted his fate calmly. Another "unprecedented violation" of a flag of truce, and a pointless betrayal. Days later, Jumper and thirty-seven of his own people came in, to travel west.

Abiaka may have had five hundred fighters. The army had eighty-nine hundred. Colonel Taylor alone had over a thousand soldiers on the Kissimmee. The "old man" kept him and Jesup guessing, projecting weakness. The army was told that he was no longer head chief. Jesup received word that he was losing power, that he had been "disabled by a fall from his horse," that he would surrender soon, and would have already if he wasn't so afraid. "The Miccosukees are leaving Sam Jones," the messengers insisted.

To the contrary, Abiaka positioned his warriors to the east of the Kissimmee, off the northern shore of Lake Okeechobee, in a thicket that the soldiers could not enter with their horses. The battlefield was expertly chosen: a large cypress hammock, bordered by a deep creek on one side and a "very muddy swamp" on the other. A newly captured Indian prisoner told Taylor's army that Abiaka's fighters were "in a very bad place where we could find it hard to get at them," but the soldiers dismounted and marched straight at them anyway, trudging some thirteen hundred yards through the sawgrass and knee-deep mud.

The Americans were "completely tired out" before they reached the clearing that Abiaka had laid out like a place mat. Bullets came from behind trees and from the tops of them, from "snipers skillfully camouflaged with Spanish moss" in the cypresses. Shooters targeted officers, troops panicked, some soldiers ran for their lives and some didn't, and men argued about it afterward. Taylor's troops were so exhausted after the battle was over, and so "jaded, that it was with the utmost difficulty" that they retrieved their dead, hauling them off on stretchers through the swamp after sunset.

Taylor described the scene as "one of the most trying" of his life. Twenty-six of his men were dead or dying, with another 112 injured. Out of the 6th Infantry, Abiaka's command had killed or wounded "every officer of four companies, with one exception, and every orderly sergeant . . . killing its gallant commander and adjutant . . . and mortally wounding the sergeant major." In casualties, the Battle of Lake Okeechobee marked the "highest losses on any American force" during the war. In fatalities, only Dade had suffered worse. For the first time, two years into the fight, the army took Abiaka seriously.

The Miccosukee chief lost eleven warriors, Taylor claimed "victory," and the resistance slipped away in canoes in parties of ten to fifteen, melting into the eastern Everglades. In January of 1838, they whipped the army again near Jupiter Inlet, at the edge of the glades. A meager "old squaw leading a pony" tricked sixty U.S. sailors with offers of surrender, then led them into a swamp where fifty or sixty warriors "kill'd 5 or 6 [of them] and wounded ev'ry officer," seizing their boat, gunpowder, rum, whiskey, and nautical books. The sailors held the woman prisoner but she escaped, was caught, and escaped again.

Jesup marched south along the coast, in pursuit of Abiaka. Little had prepared him or the dragoons for the alien landscape. At first, they crossed pine barrens with shallow ponds of high grass. But then came white sands, saw palmettos turned from green to blue, and waters rose, nearly drowning Jesup's horse. Even in January the heat here killed mules, and "a number of the men gave out." Rattlesnakes slithered around flowering pennyroyal and myrtle, tangled mangroves, and regions that "might have been pass'd in boats."

Troops met Abiaka near the Loxahatchee River, where the land was "a little more dry." Tennessee Volunteers panicked at the first gunshots, "running out of the hammock in utter confusion." The quartermaster "himself lost his temper and his judgement," and "ordered the regulars to charge" but sent no forces to cut off an enemy retreat. He rallied his men, and one of Abiaka's shot him in the face, knocking off his glasses, the "ball laying open the left cheek just below the eye." A surgeon described Jesup's injury as a "severe flesh-wound in the face."

The army lost nine men, with thirty-one wounded.

20

Trust

We wish to get in writing from the General
the agreement made with us.
—Abraham to Jesup, 1838

Fvccetv /facc-itá/: trust

Osceola was transferred with the other captives from the Castillo in St. Augustine, where detainees were dying, on the final day of 1837, to Charleston, South Carolina, on the steamboat *Poinsett*. The prisoners arrived on January 1 at Fort Moultrie, on Sullivan's Island—later known as the Ellis Island of American slavery—where the ships docked after the Middle Passage, and Africans were quarantined.

Sullivan's Island was long and sandy, the prison built of pine. Charleston sat six miles west in full view, beyond "a scarcely perceptible creek, oozing its way through a wilderness of reeds and slime." Beyond the Charleston wharf, the city gardens were "decked with green foliage and roses." The flashy port boasted promenades of fine shopping, a new theater, four bookstores, and at least three newspapers.

Osceola landed in South Carolina a celebrity. As soon as citizens heard news of his arrival, they flocked to the isle. Noteworthy ladies and gentlemen *had* to see the man, to show "their good feelings by many acts of attention and kindness," which was easier now that he was imprisoned. Osceola was deathly ill, but the demand was so great that U.S. troops "were forced to bring him to the window, where he nodded his plumes to the admiring multitude" like a crown prince. "You have no idea of the curiosity raging here to see the Indians, more particularly [Osceola]," a colonial soldier wrote, in a letter home. "Old & Young and more especially female throng the place. . . . Van Buren would be a small personage here at present."

A "crowd thickened from morning till afternoon," and in the evening, Osceola attended a play in town—a romantic comedy of disguised identity. He did not seem to enjoy the performance. "He was usually pensive," a witness wrote, "and not overly fond of conversing." The Americans were less interested in the chiefs at Fort Moultrie who outranked him and who seemed at peace and were "not disposed to grieve." The draw was Osceola, the "fallen Prince and Hero of Florida," the "*restless spirit*" who sat and mulled "over his nation's calamities with a broken heart": the only prisoner who appeared "sad and tired of the world."

Poets, painters, and writers gathered around the Creek captive and composed romantic and false tributes to his sufferings. Portraitists worked two at a time, in the same room, "while Osceola occupied a seat in the center, or moved about" when he needed a break, as spectators came and went. For "6 or 7 Days" he was whisked from space to space for artists "who wished to take his likeness." The warrior spent "day after day . . . pent up in small warm rooms" that were so hot and crowded "he could scarcely breathe," where even the Americans seemed "in danger of being suffocated."

He was confused and "thought it very strange" that even President Van Buren wanted a painting of him for the collection in Washington. On January 26, he "was attacked in the night with a violent" throat infection. Tonsillitis, complicated by an abscess. The U.S. surgeon at the fort called for a doctor in Charleston, who arrived to find Osceola "lying on his blanket before the fire" in the candlelight, his two wives bathing his neck in herb water. His throat was so swollen he could barely breathe. The doctor tried to put leeches on his ears, but a medicine man in the room forbade the odd procedure.

The "press & confusion yet continues," the physician wrote, on January 28, "the hospital constantly besieged, to see Oceola, notwithstanding he is unable to speak, and can only make signs for people to keep out of his room." Osceola professed that he had "no wish to live," "regretted his country had been taken," and protested that he had played a minor role in the conflict and "had done nothing except killing [Wiley] Thompson." On January 30, the doctor informed the family that he was dying, and the warrior's belts, feathers, turban, and knives were brought. He took his whalebone cane in his right grip and knife in his left, placed both hands at his sides, "adjusted himself and died 20 minutes past 6" p.m. Before he passed, he asked the physician a favor. He wished to be buried in the Florida Territory, at a site where his bones would not be disturbed. The surgeon, finding himself alone with the body, cut off Osceola's head as a personal keepsake, took it home, and embalmed it. Later, the doctor would hang the head on his children's bedstead, as punishment for misbehaving. The rebel's remains are still interred on Sullivan's Island, skull-less, not far from a plaque commemorating the "tens of thousands of captives" from Africa who were disembarked there from 1700 to 1775.

The region between Lake Okeechobee and Jupiter Inlet was no place for feet or hooves, a "most hideous region, in which nothing but serpents and frogs" lived year-round. At the northeastern edge of the Everglades, the sawgrass and saw palmetto sliced the soldiers, "destroying not only their shoes and clothes, but severely lacerating their flesh." Roughly four hundred troops no longer had footwear. Many men were "almost naked." Jesup predicted that his command would be "entirely disabled by marching" within forty-eight hours, with "nearly all the foot soldiers being barefooted, and many of them disabled by wounds inflicted by the saw palmetto." Of between 1,300 and 1,400 horses, 150 remained "effective." Two hundred and eight "fine mules" had left Fort Mellon; 80 were still serviceable.

Jesup learned that his adversaries were five miles away and "ready to give battle." A scout said that Abiaka had occupied a thicket skirted by a "nearly impassible swamp, the mud & water up to a man's waist & cover'd with tall thick saw grass." The warriors were "effectually screen'd & . . . could have pour'd in a deadly fire . . . killing some 10 or 20 & as usual with impunity." The general faced "another Col. Taylor's affair." A death trap.

The commander caved. Smarting from his wound, he requested peace talks with the Miccosukees, asked the Secretary of War to suspend the policy of Indian Removal, and dispatched a messenger to Washington to appeal to Van Buren directly. No harm could be done, he rationalized, in letting the tribes remain in the southern peninsula on lands uninhabitable by settlers. Jesup must have understood that the War Department would rebuke him. He also knew it would take over a month to hear back, and the sickly season was fast approaching. He waited for the president's decision, and for the summer hiatus.

He marched the Army of the South to Fort Jupiter by the coast, as the last days for fighting ticked away, and his soldiers knew what it was. "When I saw upwards of a thousand effective troops filing off on a retrograde march, the enemy close in their front," an officer recorded, "I felt disgusted, and have felt so all day till I am sick." Downpours followed them on their trek east. Troops struggled through "but one slough of mud." Winds blew from the south, thunder cracked, "scattering drops" turned to a roaring deluge, and then the northern gusts came, a "perfect gale" of "torrents of rain mingled with hail."

Military leaders described Jesup's timely retreat as "the most disgraceful move ever made," and the general himself as "a disgrace to the army—the most fickle, inconsistent man that ever lived." The "mountain has labored," a West Point graduate remarked, "and brought forth a mouse." At first, the warriors who accepted the quartermaster's truce and came in for talks were optimistic. "Nine Seminoles" entered the American field camp "as cheerfully, and moved as freely, as belles in Broad Way." It wasn't until negotiations continued at Fort Jupiter, in full view of everyone, that Jesup revealed his face-saving scheme.

Talks began in earnest on February 24, two days after Abraham arrived. One hundred and seventy-five Black Seminoles also came in, appearing "well cloth'd," a surgeon noted, and "well supply'd with venison & turkey and considerable quantities of Coonti [*sic*]." A man named Motte fumed that Abraham's wards displayed "none of the servility of our northern blacks" and whined about how they offered out handshakes with disdainful pride. The Seminole chief Tuskegee (brother to the late Cooper) led the meetings, with Abraham and Cudjo interpreting. A woman, "the eldest in the tribe," spoke first, of her hopes for peace. No troops recorded how she had earned her status or even her name.

Before his audience, Jesup adopted a punitive tone, as if from a position of authority. "Who desired this talk?" an astonished chief asked. "We did not."

Jesup outlined a strange agreement. He claimed that the Indians had promised to accept Van Buren's decision regarding their future. If the president said so, they could stay in Florida. If not, they had already agreed to emigrate. In effect, Van Buren would have their total surrender by demanding it. The commander pretended, after two years of bloodshed, that a flimsy rhetorical trap could achieve what millions of dollars and the military could not.

Would the chiefs abide by Van Buren's reply, regardless of what it was?

Tuskegee and the others, once they understood Jesup's question—and his insistence that they had already answered it, and only wanted confirmation—"very coolly and determinedly evaded a direct answer," avoiding Jesup's ploy so calmly and consistently "as to amount to a negation," replying finally "that they wished to hear the talk of the president before they decided." Negotiations adjourned. The fighting stopped. They waited.

Washington's response arrived on March 17. The government would not suspend its policy of Removal. The plot dissolved; the tribes camped nearby did not surrender as Jesup had hoped. Four days later, on his orders, an army detachment ambushed the families at sunrise, capturing 513 prisoners. Three hundred sixty-two were noncombatants.

That winter and spring, Abraham finalized the terms of Black Seminole emigration. He petitioned to purchase Romeo, husband to his "near relation," who had liberated himself from the Cruger and de Peyster plantation. Mr. de Peyster didn't appreciate the idea and named an exorbitant price. But Jesup knew not to risk "any dissatisfaction" among the Black Seminoles, so he paid for Romeo and billed Congress. Dade's "guide" Louis Pacheco, and Primus, from Clinch's forced labor camp, were also freed.

Humphreys' illegal "purchases" of twenty-nine African Seminoles remained void, and all hostages would still rejoin their families. Jesup further promised Black Seminole leadership that the U.S. government would guarantee that all of their people who emigrated would live in independent villages, as "slaves" in name only, never to be sold or separated. Historians have described the general's vow as an early "Emancipation Proclamation," but in reality Jesup pledged freedoms they had already won: the status quo.

Between January and April 1838, as Abraham's wards traveled between American outposts, a number of lively episodes played out. U.S. troops admired the several Native "noble ladies" who came into Fort Jupiter "well and tastefully dressed," including "Micanopy's sister and one of his wives (half Indian and negro)." An officer tried to catch a quick glance from Tuskegee's daughter, "young and handsome and coy," but the "chiefs and ladies" spotted him and laughed, so he stopped trying.

At New River in the south, troops watched a Black Seminole prepare coontie flour, and Cudjo's son won a debate with a doctor over whether the "African race is inferior to the Caucasians," as proven by "Craniology" and anecdotes. "Ned showed so much originality of thought and knowledge of the world," such "genius and knowledge," an abolitionist witness recorded, "as to give the Dr.'s principles a manifest refutation." The physician, "not wishing to be shaken in his belief . . . withdrew . . . to save his conscience."

Ned also praised "the beauty of the negresses and squaws that he had seen while on his way from Fort Jupiter," holding forth on their ankles and describing "in a very unconcerned manner . . . how a fair one had cheated him in his purchase of a deer skin."

Indigenous people watched a demonstration of a rifle, invented by a man named Colt, that fired eight shots a minute. A ship full of rice ran aground, and Abiaka's men rescued the cargo. Soldiers marched past burnt ruins of plantations, wrecked houses and lighthouses, and abandoned fields where the soil was too thin for the fallen coconut trees, where bondservants had once harvested plantains, oranges, limes, figs, and sea grapes. Seagulls dived for fish. Troops shot a puma. The New River camp was dubbed Fort Lauderdale.

Abraham visited Fort Jupiter in the east, Fort Basinger on the Kissimmee River in the interior, and Fort Denaud in the southeast, on the Sanibel River. Alligator came in with his people, along with John Horse. Plans were finalized for nearly all African Seminoles in the peninsula to travel west, and as the prophet gathered his friends and their families and told them of Jesup's promises and asked for their trust, he grew worried.

Reaching their future home, off the western edge of Arkansas—designated as the Indian Territory—could prove dangerous. In villages and camps, with weapons and hammocks to retreat to, his people were relatively safe. To relocate they had to assemble, turn over their guns and—with few freedom papers or protective titles of ownership—unarmed and legally vulnerable, survive a voyage through the worst of the Deep South.

The emigrants' journey meant boarding ships in Tampa Bay, gathering in New Orleans, and then traveling together up the Mississippi and Arkansas Rivers. Seminole chiefs had insisted on going by water because they knew what rogues, schemers, lawyers, and corrupt local courts would do to them on land. Abraham didn't have to imagine the worst: It had already happened. In 1834, when one of the first displaced chiefs stepped foot in New Orleans, he was ambushed by the sheriff and jailed "on spurious charges of absconding with stolen funds." Two Afro-descendant people were confiscated to pay off the so-called debt. Without federal help or money, the chief and his band had to traverse Louisiana on foot. He died soon afterward.

Abraham's wards would travel by river. But there was still the waiting area of New Orleans, where they would have to stop and gather. New Orleans was a problem. So, in late April 1838, while at Fort Denaud—a fenceless little camp on a hill—Abraham dictated a letter to General Jesup, asking for formal guarantees and details on the bargain they'd made:

> I have the honor to present my best respects to you. Myself and Toney Barnett have done everything promised by us, and expect the General will do by us as he said at the beginning of this campaign. I send Toney to see you, and he can afterwards come and join me wherever I may be. We wish to get in writing from the General the agreement made with us. We will go with the Indians to our new home, and wish to know how we are to be protected, and who is to have the care of us on the road. . . . When we reach our home we hope we shall be permitted to remain while the woods remain green, and the water runs. I have charge of all the red people coming on to Pease's Creek, and all are satisfied to go to Arkansas. . . .

> Whoever is to be chief Interpreter we would wish to know. . . . I hope Tuskegee is satisfied. All his Seminole brethren are coming in. Holatoochee has done well. All the black people are contented I hope.
>
> P.S. John [Horse] is in and contented. Glad to hear of the peace. Abram

Before Jesup could reply, he received new orders from the War Department. He was fired.

21

Stand

I have been informed that persons are ready to arrest some of the [Black Seminoles].
—Lieutenant Reynolds, New Orleans, March 22, 1838

Vsvpakletv /a-sapakl-itá/: stand

Mary, Isaac, Dinda, and Sulla arrived in Tampa Bay from Pease Creek, above the river of that name, where cowpeas and black-eyed peas grew on the shores. August brought in Friday, Daphney, Cyrus, and others to Fort Gardiner on the Kissimmee, where the lakes were. July, Cudjo, Thursday, Monday, and Dembo met the army roughly 160 miles from Fort Brooke. Over one hundred of their party journeyed from Fort Jupiter in the southeast to Fort Van Swearingen near Lake Okeechobee, north to Fort Basinger and then westward, with twenty-five packhorses, through lands that were "nearly impassible on account of the high water."

They arrived in New Orleans on steamships: eighty-seven on April 9; forty-seven on May 11; seventy-four on May 14. Most transports traveled at a snail's pace. Ships could take nearly two weeks simply to navigate up the coast from Tampa and across the Panhandle. The vessels had shallow wooden hulls and usually stretched around 130 feet, often with single decks, and had names like *Liverpool, Caroline, Chamois,* and *Itasca.* Often they had only a single wood-fed boiler to spin the huge paddle wheel on the side or stern. The emigrants were well stocked with water and rations, and used little galley stoves called cabooses to cook meals.

Abraham was eager to follow them. "I cannot do any more than I have," he stressed, in his letter to Jesup. "I have done all I can." He would have regretted that he could not join them on the journey up the Mississippi, to help with any problems. Health risks were one issue: About 5 percent of passengers would not survive the trip. Recalled trauma was another: Some African Seminoles, like Kelina, who survived the Middle Passage, reportedly "trembled because they remembered crossing the ocean in chains from Africa." But the greatest threat to the families was the dishonest local profiteers. Jesup's sudden dismissal heightened that danger.

The quartermaster left Florida, and the next commander, Zachary Taylor, forced Abraham to stay. A number of Seminole bands allied with Abiaka remained in the territory, and Taylor believed that he could still be useful as an envoy. The Interpreter's family waited in Tampa while their neighbors boarded ships. On May 15, the day that command was transferred, Jesup left a note for Abraham guaranteeing his family's freedom. But the general kept his other promises unwritten. The quartermaster was gone by May 21, when the New Orleans sheriff disembarked Abraham's friends and lined them up to be claimed as property.

By March of 1838, the hostages at Fort Pike, Louisiana, twenty-four miles northeast of New Orleans, had suffered nine months of captivity. Twenty Indigenous people and sixty-seven Black Seminoles had persevered as captives at the station, inside a double moat. Resting on a raft-like foundation of cypress logs, the red-brick outpost was shaped like a wedge of mincemeat pie. A triangular end pointed landward; a semicircular arc faced the Gulf of Mexico. A drawbridge and sally port were the only ways in and out. The French originally called the marshy strait the fort was built on the Rigolets: the "Furrows."

Twenty-four Black Seminole children at the military jail were ten years old or younger. Abraham's warrior Ben and several of Ben's family members were among them. The army paid very little attention to the hostages until Abraham and Jesup's initial agreement, in September of 1837. Only after Jesup raised Abraham's salary, on September 1, did Jesup order the army to purchase the prisoners' freedom from the Creek soldiers, for $8,000. Only after they negotiated did Jesup instruct an officer to take down their names, check on their health, and arrange for new clothes. Only then were they well cared for.

Florida hostages were also being held below New Orleans, at the U.S. Barracks, a compound located three hundred feet northeast of a wharf on the Mississippi River in what is today the Lower Ninth Ward. By March, Micanopy and an ailing Jumper had joined them in Louisiana and were waiting to travel as a group to Arkansas. The military base's walls enclosed at least four enlisted men's barracks and ten other buildings of red brick and white-painted pillars, in the "colonnaded plantation" style. As an embarkation point, the site made sense, but it was too close to downtown and too accessible to speculators.

Reynolds, the officer in charge of logistics, knew crooks were lurking. The U.S. Marine Corps lieutenant was confident that schemers were eyeing the emigrants. "I am convinced many individuals with fraudulent claims are in a state of readiness," he wrote, on March 22, "and only wait the arrival of the [Black Seminoles] in the city to carry into effect their design. The measure that I shall adopt will bar their intention." He planned to pick up the captives from Fort Pike at the last possible moment, stop only briefly at the U.S. Barracks, load the necessary supplies, and cast off up the Mississippi immediately. "Everything will be in a state of readiness to embark as soon as the boat arrives," he noted.

On March 28, the Fort Pike prisoners reached the U.S. Barracks and were about to depart, when an order to delay them arrived from Washington.

The directive came from Commissioner of Indian Affairs Harris, a Tennessean holdover from Jackson's administration and one of the former president's inner circle. On the face of it, his order made no sense. When Reynolds received it, there were "about 500 [Native and Black Seminole emigrants], all well," and had he "taken them up immediately, there would have been no sickness no discontent among them as they were all anxious to go." Instead, as summer diseases set in one month later, there were at the "Barracks 1,150 Indians and Indian negroes, half of them sick." Harris' directive was not even practical. They needed two steamboats for that many people anyway. The acting quartermaster in New Orleans couldn't understand it.

The mandate imperiled Jumper's failing health and stranded Abraham's people at the Barracks—exactly what Reynolds hoped to avoid. As a result, in early May, on "the eve of their departure," a character named Buisson, Sheriff of the Parish of Orleans of the State of Louisiana, served a writ of sequestration, forbidding any Black Seminoles from leaving the city.

On May 21, at 3:30 p.m., Buisson and a lawyer arrived at the compound and demanded, by order of Judge Buchanan of the First District Court, to "examine and select . . . claimed" individuals. Roughly 290 Black Seminoles were apparently gathered on a ship below the Barracks, waiting for clearance to depart. Reynolds now ordered them all to disembark.

Families walked up the wharf, toward the base, past the privies, and entered through the gate between the watchtowers on the Barracks' south end, assembling on the field between the chaplain's, surgeon's and officers' quarters. Emigrants waited under the American flag, as the lawyer went through his list. Men, women, and children were "pointed out and set aside." Thirty-one people were removed from the group, their names and heights "marked upon canvas and sewed" on the backs of their clothing.

Prince, 5 feet 10 inches.
Daily, 5 feet 5 and a half inches.
Fanny, 5 feet 7 inches.
Dolly, 5 feet 4 inches.
Ishmael, 3 feet 11 inches.
Cyrus, 3 feet 7 and a half inches.
Scipio, 2 feet 4 inches.

Chief Micanopy and the Seminoles protested, and when that didn't work, they "rose in a body, determined" to stop the proceedings by force, "and to such a pitch of excitement was their anger raised, that the troops were called out to suppress the tumult." Threats of brute force ultimately "compelled the captive" Seminole warriors to back down.

A man with a misfitting name was behind it. Hugh Love, a "vulgar and disrespectful" trader in the "Creek Nation West," where the Muscogee people were being forcibly resettled, was known for his "corrupt and evil practices." According to the local Indian agent, Love had operated for years without a trading license, illegally selling liquor to Native people. On January 10, 1835, Love's story went, he had met an impoverished old Creek woman named Gray, who informed him that years ago in Alabama she had enslaved a man and woman named Pompey and Dolly. Around 1795, the husband and wife had liberated themselves and their children and found protection among Abraham's people. Pitying the poor Creek woman, Love purchased her claim for $5,000 in "money, goods, & provisions" and set out for Florida to seize the couple and their descendants. But Wiley Thompson had turned him away. Love died soon afterward.

His two brothers revived his claim in New Orleans, naming Dolly and sixty-six others who they declared were her progeny. Even if the story was true, the family would be hard to identify after over forty years. But if the Love brothers succeeded, given a valuation of $1,000 for each person, they would reap a windfall equivalent to over $2 million.

John Love later insisted that he had hired someone to identify Pompey and Dolly and their family, someone "acquainted with them from his infancy." But the list of people identified by the lawyer at the U.S. Barracks tells a different story. The prisoner roll from nearby Fort Pike, from September 1837, listed sixty-seven Black Seminole captives total: the exact number claimed by the Loves. Many of those listed by their legal filing appear on the Fort Pike list in an identical order. The brothers bribed someone, or accessed the Fort Pike roll, and fit their claim to it. No one present could identify the claimed. They were called by name.

The lawyer would have read off the sixty-seven listed names, and thirty-one confused and anxious people would have stepped forward. Many of those announced were brave enough not to react when they heard their names. Tena and Taina were both taken, even though they were not named in the court filing. The wrong Flora stepped forward, and was separated along with her granddaughter Abby, who wasn't on the Love brothers' list either. Louis Pacheco, the late Dade's "guide," also somehow ended up among the victims, making for a total of thirty-three. After spending one last night at the military compound, the group was hauled downtown in the custody of the sheriff.

News of the incident reached Tampa Bay, and within days Abraham was dispatched to Louisiana. He apparently left Fort Brooke on or shortly after June 5, on the U.S. Transport *Columbia*. At eighty-seven-feet, smaller and faster than other transports, the ship was a twin-mast schooner that was also outfitted as a steamship. The vessel made the Alabama coast after five or six days. On June 11 off Mobile Point, the furnace burst, "badly" scalding five enginemen. A deckhand leaped overboard, paddling around for a half hour before he was fished out. The *Columbia* likely sailed onward, reaching New Orleans on June 13.

When Abraham stepped onto Louisiana soil, the 257 Black Seminoles who were not in jail had already departed for Arkansas. After the seizures of May 21, they had embarked in the middle of the night, at 2:00 a.m., on the *South Alabama*: Abraham's people, Micanopy, and 401 Indians. Later that day, another lawyer showed up in New Orleans, with another claim. He learned that his targets were gone, found a ship, and chased them upriver.

22

Tell

The following account may be relied on; and though, from the circumstances, *of course* incapable of being sustained by white witnesses . . . [it] must carry with it a certain weight inseparable from a true story.
—Lieutenant Casey, 1838

Nak-onvyetv /nâ:k-onay-itá/: tell

The *South Alabama* was not built for speed. A lumbering workhorse, it was designed to lug heavy loads into harbors and up shallow rivers. The steamship navigated at three knots, about the speed of the average person strolling along the banks. The crawl came with a clamor: the metronomic churn of the massive paddle wheel, the clatter, huff, and clunking of the pistons, pipes, and boiler, the hissing steam blasting from the safety valve, the creak of the shallow wooden hull, and the roar and vibrations of the firebox. Roughly an hour passed after leaving the U.S. Barracks before New Orleans came into view. From the deck, the emigrants would have seen the glow of gas streetlights from the French Quarter riverfront, and maybe even the dim aura of the candles and oil lamps farther inland, where Judge Buchanan had his court, and Sheriff Buisson had his jail.

The riverboat carried Micanopy and Abraham's people west beyond the city, away from the rising sun, as the moon faded. In daylight, they skirted the German Coast, a land of forced labor farms, of cotton and sugarcane and grand estates, where the severed heads of enslaved people had been displayed on the shores not thirty years prior. Up the narrow river corridor, the Deep South lurking on both sides, the transport puttered and clanked. Louisiana endangered their left flank; Mississippi menaced on the right. Humid, mucky air blanketed assorted river scenery. Flatboats, rafts, keelboats, cargo ships, and their weatherworn rivermen. Sandbars, river islands, and cypress swamps. Alligators, herons, live oaks, and Spanish moss. The travelers passed the towering bluffs of Natchez, named after the Natchez people, stopped for fresh beef and a short break, and hit Vicksburg, Mississippi, on May 26.

Reynolds, the officer in charge, dispatched a boat to shore for provisions—likely a skiff or a yawl—took a muster roll of passengers, and then took a trip into Vicksburg himself. When he returned he was in the company of a civilian. Reynolds introduced the newcomer to the emigrants after they cast off for Little Rock, Arkansas. He requested an audience with Micanopy and informed the chief that he had just received a letter from Commissioner Harris, of Indian Affairs. The Creek mercenaries, Harris explained, never accepted Jesup's offer of $8,000 to free the African Seminoles they had seized as prisoners. A Creek delegation had visited Washington, were promised their spoils of war, then sold the claim for $14,600. The buyer was a speculator from Georgia who, with an associate, reportedly loaned Harris $3,000, the value of a half share in their company. (Harris would resign amid scandal before Christmas.) The civilian was the buyer's lawyer and brother-in-law, Collins. Harris had ordered all Black Seminoles captured by the Creeks turned over to Collins, who had trailed them from New Orleans.

The mandate had been approved by the U.S. Acting Secretary of War.

Micanopy considered Harris' directive and refused to abide by it. The War Department's order, he told Reynolds, was "contrary to the express words of Genl. Jesup." The guards on the *South Alabama* were armed but few, and as the Seminole chief later explained, he had known the families in question for fifty years. He had over one hundred warriors on board with him. Did Reynolds really want to enforce the decree, with only ten guards?

The answer was no, for now.

In Arkansas, on June 3, the lieutenant forwarded a letter to Little Rock requesting additional armed men to make the Seminoles comply as he continued to pressure the chiefs. "I told them it was needless to object," he reported to Washington. "My orders were positive and must be obeyed." Micanopy held his ground, daring the army to impose the claim with more than mere words. He and other Seminole leaders "became, if anything, more vexed than before," leaving the lieutenant "excessively perplexed with these Indians and negroes." The acting governor of Arkansas, meanwhile, refused to supply troops. The executive knew what had happened in Florida—what was *still* happening there—and wanted no part of the "hostile band of Indians and savage negroes" docked off his port. He ordered Reynolds, the *South Alabama,* and its cargo to depart Little Rock immediately, to avoid the "massacre" of civilians.

Reynolds tried to enforce the directive again at Fort Gibson, off the Arkansas River, after the passengers had arrived at their destination. He petitioned the outpost commander for the armed troops he needed, but the officer, after "much reflection," also declined "compliance" with the baffled lieutenant, Commissioner Harris, and the War Department. Orders meant one thing in Washington. In the Western wilderness, when push came to shove, they were slips of paper patterned with ink scratchings. The lawyer left the Indian Territory empty-handed and returned to Louisiana, to target the jailed Black Seminoles who were stuck in New Orleans.

New Orleans Parish Prison was tucked behind the city, away from the tourist shops. Built on the inner edge of a swamp in what is today Tremé, the complex could handle six hundred inmates, more than most state prisons. The monstrosity towered three stories and stretched an entire block of "stately and gloomy" mortared façades, decorative moldings, macabre stairways, sooty chimneys, cells, and dungeons. Blueberries grew nearby in wet woodlands, where rattlesnakes, water moccasins, and alligators roamed. At dusk, in later years, cauldrons of bats spun in sunset colors over the edifice, squeaking "like ghosts about its naked sentry towers," reeking flying mammals circling on high like Transylvanian phantasms. Inside its walls, Afro-descendant men and women were separated and forced into hard labor in chain gangs. Outside, hangmen executed the disobedient in public, for watchful crowds.

Abraham's first task, after arriving, was to find out who had been claimed and taken. The chief and his companion Holatoochee (Micanopy's nephew) must have visited the captives in person. From the mooring area on the Mississippi River, the path to the Parish Prison began with the merchants and sailors at the levee and led northwest through the heart of town, through the vibrant French Quarter where wrought-iron balconies, Spanish courtyards, colorful Creole town houses, ornate hotels, and infamous brothels lined the cobblestone streets.

Holatoochee didn't care much for the Crescent City. Too many white people crowding around for his taste, thick "like ants ... rolling over and over each other." Street smells wafted: horses, dogs, humans. Within another two years, total residents would surpass one hundred thousand, ranking the burgeoning city as the third-largest in the United States. As the enslaved population soared, prison committals climbed. Slavery and jail went hand in hand.

Jackson was the town hero here. Ten years prior, he had been "paraded through the streets in a carriage of State, drawn by six milk-white steeds." But New Orleans, like the Florida Territory, was not entirely conquered by American slaveholders. Its population was too international and too networked. Even slavery here was "global, interconnected, and transient." Traditions endured below the cupolas of the Parish Prison, steps from where Native Americans had held their harvest festivals, where executioners performed rituals of terror. In the jail's shadow in Congo Square, men and women danced and drummed African beats on their instruments. Abraham was in the de facto capital of the Deep South, but it was also a mecca of Creoles, Haitians, French, Spanish, free people of color, and Afro-Indigenous *griffes*.

The Love brothers had their "identified" prisoners. Abraham now made his own mental list of who was in prison. Many of the sheriff's captives, the chief discovered, weren't related at all. Of thirty-three detainees, only twelve were descendants of Dolly and Pompey.

Depositions in the case were likely taken at the Cabildo, the austere former seat of the Spanish colonial government, on what is now Jackson Square. George Allen, commander of the U.S. Barracks, argued that the captives were his rightful prisoners of war. He explained to the judge that he had "in his possession some of the arms" they had surrendered, that "some . . . in the garrison . . . [were] free" and were not enslaved even in name. A Black Seminole witness, a thirty-five-year-old woman named Eliza, whose freedom "no one contests," also took the stand. She testified that her people had been allied with the Seminoles for many years, that this was the second war she had lived through with them, and that after "the first war all the negroes claimed by the whites went home." Cross-examined, she clarified that she didn't know anyone who had belonged to any Creek enslavers, and that she didn't know a soul covered by the Loves' claim. She even said that she didn't know anyone named Dolly. She held her ground.

The judge ruled in the Black Seminoles' favor, on June 18.

By law, the captives had to remain in jail for ten days, to allow time for an appeal. The lawyer returning from the Indian Territory made it back to New Orleans before that period expired. Collins settled in at the Hotel D'Orleans on Chartres Street, in a room facing a spacious inner courtyard, steps from the riverfront. Unlike the Love brothers, he was not inclined to use the courts. He didn't have to. He had orders from Commissioner Harris and a stamp of approval from the War Department. Collins claimed thirty-one of the thirty-three seized.

Abraham didn't need a legal argument to free them. He needed a friendly face. The obvious choice was Isaac Clark, the assistant quartermaster in New Orleans. Clark was already irked with Commissioner Harris for delaying the ships, did not report to him, and outranked Reynolds. If Abraham could convince Clark, Clark might stand up to Harris.

All the Sense Bearer had to do—as a man of color in Louisiana in 1838—was challenge the legitimacy of orders that came from the highest levels of the U.S. government. The Interpreter's account of the prisoners did not portray Collins as a liar. Not outright. Abraham and Holatoochee disputed the lawyer through subtler means, muddling the claim. Jesup's Creek mercenaries had, the chiefs freely admitted, captured some of the prisoners, including descendants of Dolly. But Abraham downplayed the true number captured and sold, excluding at least seven people, most of them children: Nancy, twelve, and her mother, Teena; Katy and her baby; Toney, eleven; Argus, seven; and Nellie, twenty. The result made the claim look more random, and the lawyer himself like another prospector, like the Love brothers.

On June 26, Clark rebuffed Collins based on Abraham's statement, along with the general stink of fraud hovering around "the claims of white persons upon the same" individuals. The assistant quartermaster decided that "very few of the negroes claimed by Collins were taken by the Creeks" and concluded that "they should not be given up." Not a single person. The officer summoned Collins and "even had the hardihood to state that, by an examination of the lists, none of those negroes in New Orleans were embraced in" his client's claim.

Thirty-three people had been imprisoned since May 22. Peggy, mother to Hagar, gave birth in jail; thirty-four were freed on the evening of June 27, released to the army the day after Collins left New Orleans in failure. When the lawyer received news of their release, the next day, he was irritated to learn that they had already departed, having "immediately embarked and dispatched west" that night, with twenty-five days' rations. He accused Clark of secretly hiring a boat for their escape—one not under court orders to remain in the city.

Collins was incensed, foiled, he complained, by "so much duplicity." He could not understand how Clark had simply "determined not to respect the order he had received." Commissioner Harris was just as agitated with Lieutenant Reynolds. "It would seem that there has been a great disregard, if not a violation," he protested to his subordinate, "of the orders of the War Department in this matter." The Love brothers were irate, as was the ex–Indian agent Humphreys, who sent his own agitated letter to the Secretary of War.

Abraham spent some two weeks in New Orleans. After freeing his friends and their children, he left on the U.S. Transport *Columbia* for Fort Brooke. The trip hadn't been entirely limited to business. He and Holatoochee took in a vaudeville show at the St. Charles Theater, a performance of "light and interesting musical and farcical pieces," including George Holland's "'The Whims of a Comedian' consisting of Ventriloquism." Holatoochee's wife, "Mrs. Co-na-hai-kee . . . convulsed with laughter" when Holland imitated "the crying of a child in one of his songs." Another attendee, "Sa-ha-slo-chee, young, unmarried," fell asleep.

The *Times-Picayune* announced the honored guests in advance. Abraham was listed under his Indian name, as "principal Interpreter to the Nation" and "Chief of the *Iste-lustes*." In Muscogee, *este* means "person" or "people." *Lvstes* means "black" or "dark."

The Sense Bearer returned to Florida on July 5, 1838, days after the Green Corn festival, hours after the fireworks lit up the night sky over Tampa.

He was unsure how much "service" he had left to fulfill.

With Holatoochee, he walked toward Pease Creek, to search for "some of their people." He and others, unarmed, followed "the trail of 3 Indians" to a swamp before returning, together, "from apprehensions of being fired on." He could only hope not to die from a stray bullet, or from the whims of some drunk soldier, or of some disease.

The Florida War continued. An abandoned fort blazed to ashes. A bridge on the Withlacoochee smoldered. A skirmish went down near the Okefenokee Swamp, all the way up in Georgia. Dragoons carefully swept the area and found no one. In December, troops near the Econfina River were surprised by warriors, and ran away.

Statesmen held a convention in Tallahassee and drafted a constitution that mimicked Alabama's. The draft allowed them to forbid the abolition of slavery and to bar free Black people from entering the territory entirely. Settlers debated their banking scandals. Tired locals hoped to finally win the war, hoped for statehood, and to live to see it.

23

The Devil's Garden

Fever and "swimming in the head" plagued Zachary Taylor as he, like Jesup before him, grasped how Florida would destroy his army. The commander shed thirty pounds in his first weeks on the job, riding in the tropical sun, with "the worst water for drinking imaginable." Abiaka and his allies were "determined to use their legs instead of their arms" and have the climate "battle for them," he noted, "which has proved much more fatal [and] . . . is more to be dreaded than their rifles & scalping knives." By August of 1838, Taylor was dreaming of being replaced and leaving the peninsula. Better that than suffer and die for no reason, on lands that could not be "settled in all probability by the whites for several centuries." By November, he had "abandoned all ideas of pursuing" Abiaka's resistance through the "swamps, hammocks, and Everglades . . . as totally useless" and likely only to "break the men down."

"All we can do is get in sight of the Indians," he informed the War Department, "and when they choose to elude us, we have never been able . . . to overtake them."

The Everglades were an ideal refuge. Twisting rivulets and streams stretched across the width of the lower peninsula, allowing the Seminole and Miccosukee holdouts easy routes of retreat and thwarting any thoughts of a blockade. Hammocks and wildlife abounded and storms provided badly needed supplies. Ship after ship ran aground and offered up their cargoes. Three sloops and two brigs "laden with goods of every description" were plundered near Cape Florida, the crews killed. (A French brig and its passengers were spared, "as not being American.") Tobacco, sugar, clothes, and provisions were lost by Key Biscayne. Gale-force winds provided Abiaka's army with windfalls of the most precious provisions. Fourteen ships were wrecked during the hurricane season of 1838, including the brig *Alma*, the schooners *Carolina, Caldonia, Thracian,* and the sloops *Alabama, Caution, Export,* and *Dread*.

Troops at New Smyrna, living in an outbuilding of a wrecked labor camp beyond the ruins of a "princely mansion," set skulls of shipwreck victims on the sill. A fifer's boy, five or six, with a hat of sugar paper, beat a little drum morning, noon, and night.

Abiaka sent word to the army that he was sick with dysentery. The story was that he'd eaten salted meat from a wrecked ship, the meat spoiled from ocean water. The chief was oh-so-feeble, the messenger said, but he would surrender himself soon. Taylor hoped it was true and pressed on—"an odd kind of warfare, fighting and negotiating at the same time."

On Christmas, the soldiers at Fort Brooke feasted and the officers shot rifles. At Abraham's camp, as many as 140 Black Seminoles dressed up in "the gayest attire." Bedecked with bright streaming ribbons, they relaxed to the tunes of a fiddler who marched back and forth playing "Sugar in the Gourd" and other hoedowns. On New Year's Day, the Interpreter and the families celebrated to songs "play'd on a crack'd fiddle & tinpan." Women dressed "with considerable taste" in white frocks, and the couples danced, and the children feasted on the "roasted pigs, sofke, sweet potatoes and hominy."

In early 1839, Abraham was released from his burdens. Before leaving along the same route as the others, through New Orleans, he freed his son Renty, whom he owned, documenting the act in one of the oldest surviving record books of Hillsborough County:

> Know all men . . . that I Abram a free Black man of the Seminole nation . . . being Seized and possessed in my own right *of full* and unrestricted property in and to a certain negro & Slave named Renty son of Hagar . . . in consideration of the natural affection which I bear for said Renty as my own son by said woman Hagar do hereby emancipate said Renty from Slavery . . . I hereby warrant and defen[d] him against the claims of all persons whomsoever.
>
> In witness hereof I . . . set my hand and Seal this Twenty third day of February.

Judge Steele of Tampa Bay witnessed the manumission. Several days later, armed with that brittle legal guard, the Sense Bearer and his children left Florida behind.

Abraham, his family, and the Black Seminoles left Fort Brooke on a sailboat and on the U.S. Transport *Columbia,* on February 26 and March 1. Holatoochee and Cudjo went with them, as did Toney and Polly Barnett and their children. A writer for the *Daily Georgian* seemed to think that Abraham had won the day, and dismissed him as "well known as an interpreter and a wily and treacherous rascal." Most of the departing were ready for new lives, and looking to the future. The Black Seminole families were not weeping; they smiled and laughed. A witness at Little Rock was disturbed over why Abraham and his group seemed to be so "fat and good humored," as "if they had been living a life of indolent ease, instead of being hunted like wild beasts from fastness to fastness." The passengers waited for the river waters to rise, and reached Fort Gibson, in modern-day Oklahoma, on April 13, 1839. A single passenger, of over two hundred in total, died during the journey. No legal claims were made on Abraham's people.

After March of 1839, according to the Sense Bearer, there were only "twenty or thirty negroes left in the Nation." Nearly all Black Seminoles left with their allies. Some of the bondservants from the labor camps returned to owners in the forted cities. Of the estimated five hundred laborers who were freed or taken from the enslavement farms, at least one hundred fifty were turned over, either by Jesup's Creek warriors or by Seminoles, as part of the clemency deal.

Others left for the British Bahamas, where slavery was being abolished. As early as July of 1836, "a large schooner had been observed . . . at Indian Key," full of Afro-descendant families "escaping from Florida." Jesup had predicted that "all the negroes in the nation who can find the means of escape [would] follow" them "to those islands." For years, troubled enslavers wrote letters filled with names of those who'd never returned, and never would.

Abraham lost dear friends, as they all did. Both July and Murray were ordered to remain in the territory as interpreters and guides. Neither man would live to the end of their duties. July "was killed by hostile Indians, and was buried by the troops." Murray, while on the march with U.S. soldiers near Fort King, was killed by one of the Americans.

Jumper died in New Orleans, after Commissioner Harris delayed the ship. His "funeral was attended by the Military, and conducted with the honors of war."

For all of the worst possible outcomes, Abraham had guided most of his wards through the nightmare. Black Seminole families remained free, with lives left to cherish. Neither he nor his men ever faced consequences for destroying Dade's command.

In May of 1839, Alexander Macomb, Commanding General of the U.S. Army, waited at Fort King to meet resistance leaders, to discuss a truce. He would have been clad in the attire of his rank, in silk undergarments, a hat of ribbons, tassels, and swan feathers, golden epaulets sparkling on his coat, his figure booted and gloved and girdled by a sky-blue sash. For over a week, the highest-ranking officer in the nation lingered. When the warriors finally showed up, Abiaka wasn't with them. Neither was the Seminole chief Holata Micco. Abiaka was ill, the envoy's promised, and no longer led the Nation, and was really not so important.

Macomb offered every concession. The Indians could have a ceasefire, a trading house, and remain in Florida. Abiaka agreed, and Macomb released the captives being held at Garey's Ferry. Abiaka even appeared in the flesh on June 22 at Fort Lauderdale, "a tall, spare, old man, with locks as white as . . . crane feathers," to approve the deal. After the merchant's store opened, his warriors attacked the nearby troops, killed eleven, and made off with thousands of dollars in silver, liquor, Colt rifles, gunpowder, and other essential provisions.

Abiaka "feigned complete ignorance" of the attack.

Taylor played defense. He divided the inland into twenty-mile-square districts, each guarded by a garrison, in the hopes of bringing settlers and would-be sugar barons back into Alachua County. He also occupied lowland forts during the sickly season. "Bilious fever" killed or crippled his soldiers and officers, leveled Taylor himself, and sickened 90 percent of his men. "I should have a greater chance for my life," an officer at Fort Lauderdale reasoned, "were a mill-stone tied round my neck, and I thrown into the sea."

Healthy soldiers buried the dead and attended the dying. "And this is warfare," a soldier grieved, "glorious, noble, chivalrous warfare!" In February of 1840, Taylor asked to be relieved of command. He was obliged. More colonists died that year than in any other of the conflict. The military was reduced to bribery, offering Abiaka $10,000 to leave Florida.

In late 1841 and early 1842, the U.S. Navy led riverine excursions into the unmapped Everglades, a "place not fit for the white man" and a search area larger than Connecticut. The so-called Mosquito Fleet was originally equipped with three schooners, five barges, and canoes ten to forty feet long. The vessels struggled against currents and rapids, passed beautiful lagoons, navigated serpentine channels, and pushed through dense sedges. Sawgrass "inflicted deep wounds on the arms and legs of the men as they paddled through vast tracts of the vegetation" on "slow and tortuous" expeditions to nowhere. Seamen got lost amid meandering streams, unable to navigate by dead reckoning. On one seven-day excursion, sailors camped on solid ground for a single night. The Everglades was melancholic, disorienting, and tedious.

Skirmishes were initiated by the "hunted," by Seminoles and Miccosukees who "attacked the sailors and marines as they paddled and poled through the trackless wastes." Expeditions found homes on isle hammocks, but their occupants were always a step ahead. One island, "a most beautiful spot," revealed twenty acres of "extremely rich" soil, "well protected by immense live oak and wild fig trees, and an almost impenetrable thicket of mangroves." Here were two towns, two dancing grounds, a council lodge, and a plot of "fine Cuba tobacco." The "whole clearing [was] overrun with pumpkin, squash and melon vines, with occasionally Lima beans in great luxuriance and of a most excellent quality." Sugarcane and corn grew nearby. Here was the final answer to the U.S. military: networked sanctuaries hidden within the tree islands, connected by canoes and civilized by chickee homes and "acres of corn, beans, rice, tobacco, pumpkins and squashes." The region where Abiaka and the families survived, north of what is today the Big Cypress Reservation, became known, in the chief's honor, as the Devil's Garden.

In 1842, the Boston Liberty Party Association called for an immediate end to the Seminole war, an effort the group denounced as "barbarous in the extreme." There was hardly any to need for the outcry. The national mood had soured against the fight and fermented. Van Buren was out of office, and the Whig Party had begun a push to cauterize the "bleeding artery" draining the treasury. The Florida tribes would soon become a fading memory.

Abiaka won the land, as Abraham saved his people. Neither

achieved the national recognition of Osceola, the stereotype, who suffered and died.

Territorial Governor Richard Call still dreamed of victory before the year was out, even as he lamented the costs and the condition of Florida's banks, which were "still in a state of suspension . . . because their debtors are unprepared to pay them." In the end, the army simply gave up. In a special message to Congress on May 10, 1842, President John Tyler announced that only 240 Indigenous people remained in the territory, less than half the likely number.

Giving up was a noble restraint, to spare a few stragglers.

To commemorate the occasion, what was left of the army in Florida dug up the bodies of sixty officers and surgeons, and all of Major Dade's command, and reinterred "wagonloads of bones" under a three-pyramid coquina monument in St. Augustine.

24

Ink & Lead

One thousand four hundred and sixty-six army regulars died in the Second Seminole War, 328 of them in combat, at a cost of an estimated $35 million. Sixty-nine navy men and hundreds of settlers also perished. Unrecorded deaths among the thirty thousand militiamen who served could number another two to three thousand. For all of the emphasis on Native trauma, American fatalities may have been ten times worse. Allied Seminole forces lost several hundred in total, including forty Black Seminoles.

In 1842, Florida residents petitioned Congress for statehood, arguing that the region had been "deeply injured, nay well nigh ruined, by the deplorable war." Profitable and "most fertile fields . . . [were] now lying waste, with every house and cabin, on a frontier of upwards of four hundred miles, burned to the ground, and hundreds of the best plantations deserted by their former possessors and grown up in bushes." Locals claimed they had been "put back ten years" by the troubles of the last six.

Compared to the Northwest, the peninsula's growth was paltry.

Between 1830 and 1840, Michigan gained some 180,000 residents and Ohio lured a whopping 580,000, while the Florida Territory added fewer than 20,000 residents for a total of 54,477—still short of the statehood benchmark of 60,000 set by the Northwest Ordinance. In a bid to lure more immigrants to the newly peaceful territory, Congress passed an act offering free land to gun-toting settlers willing to brave the outback.

Miseries vexed the land. Yellow fever tore through Tallahassee, killing a reported four hundred of sixteen hundred residents. Victims included dozens of public figures and civil leaders. The "yellow jack" spread to the northern labor camps, claiming eight or nine a day and killing in as little as six hours. The port town of St. Joseph's was nearly decimated. Desperate locals took "calomel by the ounces." Bingeing on the mercury-based medicine, residents looked "more like walking skeletons than like live persons."

In May of 1843, a fire consumed Tallahassee. Starting in the Washington Hall Hotel, across from the territorial Capitol, flames ate their way north. Governor Call's businesses burned to ash, as did the Planter's Hotel. After three hours, eighty-nine properties had been turned to smoking sooty piles of cragged ruins, with "not a solitary store, shop or theatre of business" standing. Few of the gutted buildings were insured.

In September, in the Panhandle, a hurricane razed Port Leon, sending a tidal surge of nearly ten feet into the streets and flattening the settlement. "Our city is in ruins," the *Commercial Gazette* reported. "Every building but the lighthouse is gone—and dreadful to relate 14 lives lost! And among them some of our most valued citizens." Residents evacuated their dream city, abandoning it as a wrecked ghost town.

Florida seemed cursed by Abiaka, by debt and scandal, drought and disease, and pestering vermin. Caterpillars chomped on cotton as prices for the staple fell from 13.4¢ a pound in 1839 to 5.6¢ six years later. Banks fell into ruin. Speculators who had mortgaged their property were left in dire financial straits. Legislators, hoping to ease the crisis, indefinitely suspended taxes on land and enslaved people. By 1845, when Florida gained admission to the Union, there wasn't a single solvent bank in the territory.

Florida limped into statehood, hampered by lingering wounds of war, joining the United States on March 3, 1845, as the twenty-seventh state. It was the least populated state in the south—with less than a tenth of the population, in 1850, of both Virginia and neighboring Georgia. Florida statesmen dutifully pledged to protect "the interests and institutions peculiar to ourselves, and the South generally," especially from the "renewed vehemence" of the abolitionists. Vast swaths of the interior remained unsettled.

On June 23, the state General Assembly met for its first session, and on June 24, news arrived that Andrew Jackson, the "first American Governor of Florida"—whose "sword first drew aside the curtain and exposed this lovely 'Land of Flowers'" —was dead.

Legislators halted the General Assembly and penned floral tributes. The state Senate saluted America's seventh chief executive as "the ninth President of the United States." The House forgave past transgressions, praised Jackson as a steadfast friend, and applauded him for acquiring the peninsula from Spain. "Floridians," House members declared, "should be among the first and foremost to cherish his fame as identified with their own State." Newspapers celebrating statehood paused to mourn their founding hero.

Jackson died painfully. When Jesup visited him, on May 29, he was confined to his bedroom and unable to sleep much without opiates. Thirty visitors lined up with the quartermaster at the Hermitage to pay respects. Jesup found his "old friend" deep in the throes of edema, fluid swelling his body's tissues, a ghoulish symptom of nephrotic kidneys. Jackson's feet and legs ballooned first, followed by his hands and abdomen and face. His breathing grew so short and feeble that the ex-president feared he would suffocate.

"I am a blubber of water," he said. "How far my God may think proper to bear me up under my weight of afflictions, He only knows." He was "a bloated shell," in his own words: "a perfect Jelly from the toes to the upper part of my abdome, in any part of which a finger can be pressed half an Inch and the print will remain for minutes." His face grew "sunken and rayless" as he was carried from bed to chair and back again. "I am greatly afflicted, suffer much," he wrote, "swollen from the toes to the crown of my head, and in bandages to my hips." An enslaved servant, a man named George, fanned the flies off of him.

Jackson died on June 8, surrounded by family and enslaved people. One of the president's most respected biographers later removed all Afro-descendant persons from his side and placed them on the porch beyond the bedroom. Two lithographs also erased all uncomfortable facts from the scene. In reality, Jackson asked to have his pillows fluffed, George pulled out two from behind him, and he "gave one breath, hunched up his shoulders and all was over." His heart failed, his lungs froze, his brain shut down. Carbon dioxide built up in his blood, increasing its acidity. Clinical death was recorded that afternoon, at 6 p.m.

The Interpreter's Western home was cold in winter, but thousands of grouse roamed, and good fishing could be had where beavers swam. Wild horses, deer, and buffalo grazed prairies. Bears, panthers, and wolves ranged dense woods. Rich river-bottom soils welcomed corn kernels, bean germs, pepitas, melon seeds, and rice grains.

Indian and Black Seminole families camped below Fort Gibson, in the Indian Territory, not far from the riverine cliff rocks where the keelboats anchored, at the crossroads of the Arkansas, Verdigris, and Neosho Rivers. In time, they built settlements to the west at Deep Fork and at Wewoka, where they farmed and raised children.

Micanopy became Chief of the Seminole Nation in the west, with Abraham as his confidant. The Sense Bearer "commanded a good deal of respect among the Indians" and tribal leaders. His people lived freely, "uncontrolled by anyone," which outsiders found "singular and anomalous." As before, most families were "only slaves in name," as one Indian agent reported. "In nine cases out of ten they live with their masters, or not, as they please; work, if they work at all, when and where they please, and make their own bargains; come and go according to their own inclination; sit at the table with their masters and speak to them as . . . equals."

The situation, he wrote, "would scarcely be believed without being witnessed."

Jesup was blamed for the "*nuisance* of a free colony of [Black people] in a slave country." The acting U.S. attorney general insisted that a "settlement of free negroes" lay beyond the law. "There is no such thing in the states," he determined, in 1848, "where slavery exists as the qualified freedom which General Jessup seems to have promised." In his legal opinion, Jesup had never possessed the power to have negotiated terms with Seminole "property."

Fraudulent claims on the families continued, as Micanopy rebuffed them. Acquisitive Creeks in Indian Territory "claimed almost all of the Black Seminoles, alleging that either they or their ancestors had fled from the Creeks before the Florida conflict . . . [or] from Georgia and South Carolina plantations." Tribes jostled over limited resources, and Creek and white "aristocratic mixed bloods" targeted the Black Seminoles for profit. Some African Seminoles were betrayed by Seminoles who faced economic hardship. At least eighteen were forced into slavery.

In 1845, with tensions high, Micanopy and Abraham entered into talks with their Creek neighbors and negotiated a treaty. As a concession, the Creeks pledged not to interfere with the African Seminoles, and agreed that all disputed ownership claims would be adjudicated by the U.S. president. But Creek attempts to seize Abraham's wards as property went on.

Raiders descended on a settlement at Deep Fork in 1846; seventy-two armed Black Seminoles convinced them to turn around. A Creek enslaver named Hardridge tried to take August's brother; the would-be victim drew a pistol and knife and engaged him. A Cherokee Indian tried to take a Black Seminole named Walking Joe;

armed warriors got in his way and warned the Cherokee to tell his chiefs that if they tried it again, "*some person might get hurt.*" Facing enslavement, Abraham's men preferred "to die where they were."

Many Seminoles held true and "backed them in their defiance" when it mattered. In one instance, a Creek enslaver rode into Wewoka with four white men and three Cherokee Indians, "to take forcible possession of a number of" victims. But their Seminole allies, hearing word of the raid, "asserted their firm determination to assist . . . [them] in defending themselves." Seminole fighters "painted themselves for war" and made it clearly known that they had not abandoned their friends and were "determined to stand or fall with them."

In 1850, to escape the troubles, a party of over two hundred Indians and Black Seminoles fled to Mexico, where slavery was outlawed. Abraham and the others remained in Indian Territory. Frustrated by their defiance, the Creek Council had passed an act prohibiting enslaved people from owning guns. But the Sense Bearer and his neighbors simply ignored the decree, and retained their arms, and lived, as they had for many years, "under no restraint whatever from their owners," on lands where the laws were still written with powder and lead.

25

Autumn in New York

He was Old Abraham now. In his sixties, sporting a "woolly moustache," he remained as "venerable," dignified, and poised as in his youth.

Before the diplomatic trip began, in early 1852, a Southern newspaper described the Interpreter as "one of the oldest and most noted warriors" of the Seminole Nation. But after he appeared, after Southerners saw him, that description became intolerable. It was as if his existence became more impossible as the delegation neared the great cities. When the Sense Bearer reached North Carolina, he was relegated to being "a negro man, who appears to be interpreter." Six Seminoles, not seven, were heading north.

The Washington summit was as an act of calculated coercion, a final attempt to force the tribes and bands in Florida off the land without another costly fight. Envoys arrived from both the South and the West. The late Jumper's son John Jumper, who had witnessed Dade's defeat as a boy, was soon to be head chief in Indian Territory. Holata Micco, known to Americans as Billy Bowlegs, born to the royal Alachua line of Abraham's youth, led the Nation in Florida in tandem with Abiaka, who had declined to attend and sent a subchief.

For Abraham, the mission was little more than a junket, a paid vacation to enjoy with old friends. Why not see Washington City, and tour New York?

The "shrill *steam whistle*" on the steamship to Georgia startled him. In Savannah, the party was shown a printing press and saw "the skill with which the compositors placed the letters," and watched "sheet after sheet thrown off" lightning fast, as if the hosts wanted to demonstrate how quickly and widely their storytelling gadgets could lie about them.

Coach, steam, and rail led them on a whirlwind tour of metropolises, crowds, handshakes, and the "smiles of the ladies and the welcome of all good citizens." They passed through Charleston and Wilmington on the way to Washington, to the marbled halls. In the White House, President Millard Fillmore spoke about obligation and honor. At the Washington Arsenal, they perused the armaments factory. Smiles. Gifts. Lavish hotels. Fine entertainments. Cannons. Shells. Destruction. Big carrots. Big sticks.

All to get Bowlegs and the Miccosukees to abandon Florida.

Visiting the Smithsonian, the delegation gazed at paintings of Native leaders that hung on the walls like scalps on polls. Museum-goers eyed Abraham, Bowlegs, and Jumper as they walked the galleries and inspected "the old Florida Chiefs." Abraham and Bowlegs bantered as friends, "apparently on familiar terms," and the chiefs exchanged glances, and eyed the outsiders. To Bowlegs, American women "all looked very pretty, but they all looked alike." No African Seminole chiefs appeared in the paintings.

Well-read observers and insiders understood who Abraham was. At the highest levels, his reputation preceded him. The latest Commissioner of Indian Affairs could not believe, when they met, how young he looked, and asked if Abiaka was older.

"I can't tell exactly," Abraham replied. "I am the straightest man." The truest.

"They say [Abiaka] walks with a crutch or a staff," the commissioner prodded.

"They say so."

"I should have been glad if you had brought [him] along with you."

"He wouldn't come."

Bowlegs interjected to tell the commissioner that he could not expect the chief to visit unless they killed him and brought a piece of his flesh to the War Department.

The Seminoles laughed. The commissioner didn't find it funny.

In Washington, they attended a concert. In Philadelphia, theater.

Abraham reached New York on September 23, 1852. For him and the other Western delegates, the journey had been a long one. For nearly a year, since December 1851, they had lived on the road. Steamboat after steamboat, chartered vessels, hired cooks and hired horses. The Western Verandah Hotel in New Orleans, the Pulaski House in Savannah, the Carolina Hotel in Wilmington, the Indian Queen Hotel in Washington on Pennsylvania Avenue, the Girard House in Philadelphia. Last stop was the Empire City.

Horses hauled coaches through the business district and stopped at 229 Broadway, beside City Hall Park, at the American Hotel. Two rooms had been reserved on the top floor, where the windows overlooked the seat of local government, trees and triangles of lawn, and a hundred-foot fountain that could spout a jet fifty feet, as high as the flagpoles, using water pumped from the aqueduct. Official duties behind them, the chiefs arrived on a Thursday, with a long weekend ahead to indulge in the amusements of Gotham.

On Friday, after breakfast and drinks "from the bar," the delegates and several relatives (including Bowlegs' sister) piled into coaches for the most timeworn of New York activities: shopping. On a taxpayer-funded budget of $600, they perused the flagship store of Grant & Barton, pouring "over the richest ribbons" and "high-colored calicos." Stewart's Store, off City Hall Park, was even more extravagant, showcasing imported luxury items. The audacious

"Marble Palace" boasted Corinthian columns, towering plate-glass windows, mahogany and maple counters, and a rotunda under a dome of Italian frescos.

On Pearl Street, the delegates patronized a hardware store stocked with handsome firearms, and purchased various rifles, scissors, and "small cutlery."

Silk, guns, and knives weren't the only hauls. Beyond being paid for the trip—Abraham was due $365—necessities and pleasures were also gratis. Oysters, mackerel, venison, pork, Madeira wine, fine whiskey. French brandy, raspberry syrup, Goshen butter, cheese, crackers, and cigars. Abraham favored porter ale, when he could get it, and plug tobacco. Other pickups included $8 calfskin boots, pocketknives, a shiny set of dinner cutlery, cups and saucers, a coffee boiler, earrings, a tablecloth, and a gingham umbrella.

Brick wall advertisements clamored for eyeballs. At least in Washington there was space to walk. Here the crowds clustered as thick as grass, with children everywhere, "nothing but children." Urchins swarmed outside the offices of a New York newspaper, where the visitors were presented with still more whirling gadgets of the printed word. Abraham was quick to "appreciate the merits of what was being shown," and took it all in with a sense of humor, with a knowing glint. Children whooped at them like "Injuns."

At the Meade Brothers' Daguerreotype Gallery, the delegates posed for a photographic portrait. Skylights brightened snapshots of Count d'Orsay, the frontiersman Kit Carson, Shakespeare's home at Stratford-upon-Avon, and Niagara Falls. Four chiefs crammed tightly onto a white couch, with Abraham behind them flashing a hint of a smile. Newspapers printed a sketch of the photo in which much of the awkward comedy had been eliminated. In the drawing, the cramped couch was made spacious, and the Sense Bearer looked glum.

In Barnum's Museum, the chiefs puzzled at the Happy Family exhibit, where predators and prey were caged together in apparent harmony. Cats, rats, doves, owls, dogs, a hawk, a rooster, a raccoon, anteaters, monkeys, woodchucks, an opossum, an armadillo, foxes, rabbits, owls, and guinea pigs. Barnum had pacified natural enemies by devising strict feeding schedules and a precise sequence of adding new animals to the cage to make them feel "clanship" and "dependence." Troublemakers were removed at night.

From "the Museum they returned to the American Hotel," where most of the exhausted party collapsed into "their chairs and gazed moodily into the street" below. Inquisitive callers visited, "but they were unwilling to converse, and even old Abram acted as if he would rather be allowed to enjoy quiet than anything else."

Bowlegs visited City Hall, where civil leaders had hung paintings of men that the Seminoles beat in battle. He scoffed at Scott's and Taylor's portraits.

"I licked him," Bowlegs said, of Taylor.

A gentleman asked how many warriors he had left in Florida.

"Maybe ten," he answered, laconically. Americans always asked him that. "Myself, five more, and old Abraham," he told them, on another occasion.

At Mechanics' Hall, on Broadway between Broome and Grand, Abraham and Bowlegs shared the front row for a nighttime performance of Christy's Minstrels. White men smeared their faces with burnt cork and painted on ivory clown mouths and danced and sung ditties, including a sentimental tune about a labor camp on the Suwannee River. The chiefs weren't laughing at the start of the show, but they laughed after.

Then they were gone, leaving Americans with vague memories of six or seven Indians and dull diatribes on calico frocks, bright shawls, ornamental beads, and the glinting silver gorgets on their chests. Questions about Abraham lingered. What explained his proud manner? Wasn't it odd he wore "the full costume of the Seminoles. *Turban, á la Turk* . . . hunting shirt, leggings"? Who was the "old negro interpreter" really?

His headwrap lent him the look of "a Persian or Copt," a puzzling stranger, beyond their known sphere. His aura, regal posture, and attire hinted at Othello reborn. He carried "more of an air of confidence than is usually apparent in Africans South of the Potomac." He could not truly have come from the Deep South, but only from a place of majordomos and lords chancellor, a country of exalted keepers "of the King's conscience."

Chiefs called him their "interpreter" but there was "little necessity for such an assistant." Bowlegs himself spoke English "with great ease and correctness." Did "they regard him more as an *odieur* [*sic*]"? A pleasant perfume? Remarkably, to one outside observer, Abraham seemed to be "the Mentor of the delegation . . . obviously confided in by all the young and vigorous chiefs who surround[ed] him, as if he were their father."

Journalists in the know described him discreetly as "no unimportant personage." Others could not shake the dissonance of the "most peculiar member of the group" and wondered why the army, after the damage done in Florida, had not hung "him instantly." Oddly, too, Abraham did "not seem inclined to do justice to the memory of Osceola," and when asked about him, dismissed him "as a *Creek*—not a native Seminole."

Little was heard of Abraham after the 1852 trip, after he returned to the West. In Florida, between 1855 and 1858, the Americans tried again to expel the remaining Miccosukee and Seminole resistance—and failed again. For a final time, Abiaka outwitted the army. Like Abraham, his life and deeds faded into folklore.

The last recorded sighting of Sawanok' Tustenuggee came in 1870, when a traveler in Indian Territory reported that he was "still alive on Little River at the advanced age" of 120. Historians never did discover when or where he died.

The grave marker sits outside of the fence, beyond the formal boundary of the maintained cemetery, in a little town that was once named after his daughter's band, in Seminole County, Oklahoma. Finding the site requires crawling through vines and dense brush, onto private land currently occupied by cattle and oil rigs. A wide swath of empty space cuts through the middle of the cracked, split tombstone. From the remnants of the native rock, a faded hand-carved date catches shadows: " . . . PR. 10 1874"—April 10, 1874. The grave's occupant is listed only partially, as "ABRA . . . ," with no discernible last name. Only the neighboring stone, which marks the grave of his wife, confirms his identity.

Abraham died as an old man, as a great-grandfather, surrounded by loved ones. He lived to watch his son Peter serve in the Union Army in Kansas, and to see the fall of the Confederacy. He survived to see his daughter Rachel fight for the dues that the Americans owed her, and to behold her daughter, his granddaughter Nancy, become a mother herself. He survived eleven years after the Emancipation Proclamation, long enough to see his people celebrate their own hard-won freedoms, their very own Fourth of July.

August 4, Emancipation Day, commemorated the date when their Creek rivals granted Afro-descendant citizens full and equal rights, in 1865. Both Indian and white people were welcome to attend the annual celebrations. Horses were well-groomed, and decorated with embellishments and fringes and fine German silver. A queen was crowned with a silk headdress. She wore a divided riding skirt on an ornate steed.

Barbecue sizzled while the idle spun jokes and tall tales. Festivities began with a cannon and the flag. Bands came down in turns. You could hear them galloping from miles off, the laughing and yelling. Near Wewoka, the cannon fired and the Bruner Band rode down and circled the Stars and Stripes. The cannon fired again, and the next band circled around the American flag that promised a future of freedom and equality. Few of them could have imagined the battle ahead for what had been promised. But for some years, on August 4, the people were happy, and no one got drunk or fought.

Coda

In the 1950s, descendants of the Florida survivors recorded the folktales that had been passed down by Abiaka's storytellers, including the legend of the "long war." In the beginning, the elders said, the "Indians lived near Kissimmee where they had many hogs and cows and grew rice." When the white men's "army arrived . . . there was nothing for the Seminoles to do but run." Abiaka fought the colonists, and after a battle near the Loxahatchee, U.S. troops "put up a white flag." The chief warned that it was a trick, but many traveled to the American camp, where they were provided food. While the families were eating, soldiers "encircled them . . . took them prisoners aboard a ship, and sent them to Oklahoma."

Betty Mae Jumper, of the Snake Clan, later collected another tale that spoke to Jesup's deeds through fable. One day, the story went, a "lying rabbit" came upon a gathering of old men. Eager to impress them, the rabbit claimed he could trap the eight-foot-long rattlesnake by the river. "You can't," the old men warned. But the rabbit hopped over to the big snake anyway. "See all those people over there?" he asked the serpent. "They said you were a very short snake and not even as long as this string in my hand." He convinced the rattler to stretch out to prove that he was longer than the twine, jumped on the reptile's neck, and stuffed him into a sack. The old men were shocked when the rabbit returned, and the serpent rolled out of the bag.

"I told you I could," the rabbit said.

"Yes, with his lies," the snake said.

The lying rabbit appears often in Seminole folktales. Storytellers used the trickster as an example, to teach children to tell the truth.

Acknowledgments

This book would have been impossible without help from the many dedicated archivists who keep our history. I'm indebted to: Charles Tingley of the St. Augustine Historical Society; William Locascio of the Ah-Tah-Thi-Ki Museum Tribal Historic Preservation Office; Gary Marshall of the Eustis Historical Museum; Jana Gowan of the Gilcrease Library and Archives; Joanna Bouldin of the Knox County Library East Tennessee History Center; Marianna Stell and Patrick Kerwin at the Library of Congress; Cindy Murphy and Mia Sigler at the Maine Historical Society; Grace Doeden at the Massachusetts Historical Society; Rose Buchanan at NARA; Gregory Osborn at the New Orleans City Archives & Special Collections; Arlene Shane of the New York Academy of Medicine; Tal Nadan at the New York Public Library; Matthew Storey of the State Archives of Florida; Bridget Mary Bihm-Manuel and Caleb Del Rio of the University of Florida; Matthew Fraas of the U.S. Army Transportation Museum; Terry Eagan at the University of South Florida; Corey Flatt at the United States Military

Academy; and Mary Ellen Budney and Adrienne Sharpe-Weseman at Yale.

My gratitude goes out to Jimmie Abraham, Abraham's great-great-grandson, who was of vital help in the early phases of research and has been a source of encouragement along the way. His own father remembered Abraham's son Peter gifting him his first horse, Polly, a Florida Cracker horse, when he was a boy. Mr. Abraham is still raising livestock in the Little River Community, near the Abraham Family Cemetery. He also races Paint horses. I am also in debt to Carol Scott, who, in researching her husband Melvin Bruner's Seminole genealogy, knew of and located Abraham's grave.

Thanks go to my family: Nancy Maull, Stephen Holmes, Alexa Holmes, and Lapo Holmes, for their love and support, and in particular to my brother Francesco Holmes, for our early conversations about the evidence regarding Chief Abiaka. Khasad Yahu ZarBabal provided highly insightful notes on an early draft. Jack Martin, of William and Mary, was indispensable for his translations, advice, and help. Terrance Weik, at the University of South Carolina, was a valuable sounding board early in my research, and a wise guiding hand.

My editor Nicholas Ciani has proven to be a steady mentor and a trustworthy partner. Without Nick's faith in me and in the project, unwavering from the opening bell, the book wouldn't exist. One Signal's publisher Alessandra Bastagli has been just as supportive. I'd also like to thank Abby Mohr for her help and Davina Mock-Maniscalco for her beautiful design work. My agent Eric Lupfer has been, and continues to be, a friend and a skillful advisor.

Notes

ABBREVIATIONS

AAH	Alabama Department of Archives & History, Montgomery, AL
AHS	St. Augustine Historical Society, St. Augustine, FL
AMC	Ah-Tah-Thi-Ki Museum Collections, Clewiston, FL
ASP:IA	*American State Papers: Indian Affairs*
ASP:MA	*American State Papers: Military Affairs*
DLG	Digital Library of Georgia
DUA	Duke University Archives, Durham, NC
E	entry
EHM	Eustis Historical Museum, Eustis, FL
F	folder
FHQ	*Florida Historical Quarterly*
FSU	Florida State University Special Collections & Archives, Tallahassee, FL
GLA	Gilcrease Archive/Library Collection, Tulsa, OK
GLC	The Gilder Lehrman Collection, New York, NY
HM	*The Historical Magazine*
KCL	Knox County Library East Tennessee History Center, Knoxville, TN
LOC	Library of Congress, Washington, DC
MHS	Maine Historical Society, Portland, ME
MSA	Massachusetts Historical Society, Boston, MA
NAMP	National Archives Microfilm Publication
NARA	National Archives and Records Administration, Washington, DC, and College Park, MD
n.d.	no date
NHHS	New Hampshire Historical Society, Concord, NH
NOCA	New Orleans City Archives & Special Collections, New Orleans, LA
NYAM	New York Academy of Medicine Archives and Manuscripts, New York, NY
NYPL	New York Public Library Archives & Manuscripts, New York, NY
PQH	ProQuest History Vault, Papers of Quartermaster General Thomas S. Jesup
RG	Record Group
SLAF	State Library and Archives of Florida, Tallahassee, FL
SULF	State University Libraries of Florida, PALMM Digital Collections
THQ	*Tennessee Historical Quarterly*
TP	*The Territorial Papers of the United States*
UFA	University of Florida George A. Smathers Libraries, Collections, Gainesville, FL
UMA	University of Miami Libraries, Special Collections, Coral Gables, FL

UOA	University of Oklahoma Archives, Norman, OK
USAT	United States Army Transportation Museum Archives, Fort Eustis, VA
USF	University of South Florida Libraries, Special Collections, Tampa Bay, FL
USMA	United States Military Academy Library Archives and Special Collections, West Point, NY
UWF	University of West Florida, PALMM Florida Heritage Collection
YLA	Yale University Library, Manuscripts and Archives, New Haven, CT

EPIGRAPHS

v *"You're writing for"*: *Meeting The Man: James Baldwin in Paris*, film directed by Terence Dixon (France, United Kingdom: Buzzy Enterprises Ltd., 1970); Potter, *War in Florida*, 56. The Holata Micco quoted is not Billy Bowlegs, who later went by the same title. I have in cases, throughout the text, corrected spelling or changed the casing of words or altered punctuation in minor ways, for clarity.

INCITING EVENTS

xi Kimball, *Seminole & Creek War Battles*, 40–42, 47–49; Remini, *Jackson and the Course of American Empire*, 352–53, 388, 399. Jackson may have entered Florida on March 11, depending on how many miles his command made on March 10. Mahon, *History of the Second Seminole War*, 29, 46–47, 62: Brown, "Florida Crisis of 1826–27," 431–32; Laumer, *Dade's Last Command*, 116; Patrick, *Aristocrat in Uniform*, 70n1; Monaco, *Second Seminole War*, 214n5.

PRELUDE

xiii *folklorist, in the 1930s*: "Uncle Monday," USF; Congdon, *Uncle Monday and Other Florida Tales*, 54–58; Pamala Bordelon, ed., *Go Gater and Muddy the Water: Writings by Zora Neale Hurston from the Federal Writers' Project* (New York: W. W. Norton, 1999), 114–18.

ONE: THE FUNCTIONARY

3 *picturesque hillock*: Laumer, *Amidst a Storm of Bullets*, 9; Frank J. White, "Macomb's Mission to the Seminoles: John T. Sprague's Journal," *FHQ* 35, no. 2 (1956): 161; Laumer, *Dade's Last Command*, 115; City of Ocala Recreation and Parks Department, *Fort King: National Historic Landmark Master Plan* (Ocala, FL: Fort King National Historic Landmark Park Development Project, 2020), 37–39.

3 *tangled and primordial thicket*: Harris to Gibson, December 30, 1835, *ASP:MA* 6:561.

3 *the Seminole Agency house*: Kokomoor, *Indian Agent Gad Humphreys*, 46; City of Ocala, *Fort King*, 30, 37–39; Laumer, *Dade's Last Command*, 115–16.

3 *two hundred armed troops*: Fanning, "Post Return of Fort King Florida for the Month of April, 1835," NARA RG 94, Returns from U.S. Military Posts, 1800–1916, NAMP M617, roll 581.

4 *bathed in a fresh spring*: Simmons, "Recollections of the Late Campaign," 548; White, "Macomb's Mission," 161–62.

4 *Removal without war*: Donald L. Fixico, *Indian Treaties in the United States* (Santa Barbara, CA: ABC-CLIO, 2018), xix–xx, 107–25.

4 *could be printed in newspapers*: "From the *Columbus Enquirer* of Feb 5," *Cheraw Gazette*, February 16, 1836, 2; "Treaty with the Seminole Indians," *New-Orleans Commercial Bulletin*, February 27, 1836, 2.

4 *spent late March*: *ASP:MA* 6:71–72.

4 *estimated three to five thousand:* "Extract of a Letter from Lieutenant Joseph W. Harris," September 29, 1835, *ASP:MA* 6:80; Lewis Cass, "To the Public," March 6, 1837, 4, in Adjutant General, *Florida War*; Lewis Cass to William Carroll, July 14, 1832, 25, *ASP:MA* 5:25.

4 *six months, his lithe:* Thompson first arrives at Fort King in late 1833. Laumer, *Dade's Last Command*, 116. He spends some time in early 1834 in Tallahassee and then appears to be permanently stationed at Fort King starting in the fall of 1834, with a visit home to Georgia in early 1835. See Thompson to DuVal, January 20, 1834, *ASP:MA* 6:451–53; Thompson to DuVal, January 1, 1834, *ASP:MA* 6:453–55; Thompson to Herring, November 24, 1834, *ASP:MA* 6:476.

4 *physically resembled the president:* Fort King Heritage Foundation, "Wiley Thompson: Seminole Indian Agent," *Fort King Post*, April 7, 2022, accessed February 28, 2025, https://ftking.org/wiley-thompson-seminole-indian-agent/.

4 *was a drunk:* Gibson to Thompson, August 26, 1835, *ASP:MA* 6:542; Thompson to Gibson, September 21, 1835, *ASP:MA* 6:545–46. To be fair, as Thompson later reports, Yancey seems to have gotten himself together after making a poor early impression on the Indian agent.

4 *"workmanlike manner":* Gibson to Thompson, April 1, 1835, *ASP:MA* 6:529.

5 *only traded in his seat:* Wiley Thompson, "Circular," March 7, 1833, in Thompson to John Weeks, April 29, 1833, John Wingate Weeks Papers, 1804–99, NHHS. This document also appears as Thompson, "Circular," *Richmond Enquirer*, April 26, 1833; "Gen. Wiley Thompson's Last Will and Testament," Letters from Forgotten Ancestors Pre-1920 Letters, TNGenWeb Project, 2005, accessed February 28, 2025, https://www.tngenweb.org/tnletters/ga/18360516.html.

5 *as dicey as it sounded:* George Gibson to Thompson, April 3, 1835, *ASP:MA* 6:530.

5 *all of two weeks:* Two weeks minimum. One supply run in April of 1835 took twenty days, although that included a five-day stop at Palatka. Morris S. Miller to Sarah Miller, April 29, 1835, USMA.

5 *enclave cordoned off:* Mahon, *History of the Second Seminole War*, 50. The boundary lines of the reservation were amended several times.

5 *closer to the mangrove-choked:* Joseph Buttinger, *A Dragon Defiant: A Short History of Vietnam* (New York: Praeger, 1972), 7; Chris Mayda, *A Regional Geography of the United States and Canada: Toward a Sustainable Future* (Lanham, MD: Rowman and Littlefield, 2013), 234.

5 *under his wife's bed:* Laumer, *Dade's Last Command*, 230.

5 *campfires meant more people:* Thompson, Joseph Harris, and D. L. Clinch to Lewis Cass, April 24, 1835, *ASP:MA* 6:73; M. S. Miller to S. Miller, April 29, 1835, USMA. Miller's letter also references the stars, the neon parrakeets, blackened oranges, the troops visiting the campfires and eating corn and coontie root, the women's quarters, shillings and picayunes, and the welcoming ceremony.

5 *leaders of the:* Abraham himself used these designations, which overlap in cases and are not exhaustive, when he was interrogated in 1837. John C. Casey to Thomas Jesup, July 24, 1837, NARA RG 94 E159-Q, Box 6, Casey.

6 *lit up uncanny forests:* Laumer, *Amidst a Storm of Bullets*, 14.

6 *officers who attended were:* Simmons, "Recollections of the Late Campaign," 545.

6 *After sunrise, the leader:* Ibid., 546–48; Morris S. Miller to Maria Miller, May n.d., 1835, USMA.

6 *fragmented coalition:* Casey to Jesup, July 24, 1837, NARA; Covington, *Seminoles of Florida*, 55–56; Sprague, *Origin, Progress, and Conclusion*, 97.
6 *derived from the Spanish:* Covington, *Seminoles of Florida*, 13.
6 *Hefty, gentle, and:* Sprague, *Origin, Progress, and Conclusion*, 97.
7 *opened the meeting with:* Simmons, "Recollections of the Late Campaign," 547.
7 *an old treaty:* Thompson, Harris, and Clinch to Cass, April 24, 1835; Sprague, *Origin, Progress, and Conclusion*, 72–80.
7 *government had a playbook:* Monaco, *Second Seminole War*, 20, 24; Tocqueville, *Republic of the United States*, 367–72; Thompson, "Creek Indians in Georgia"; Report of Proceedings, October 25, 1834, *ASP:MA* 6:68.
7 *Thompson announced, reading:* D. L. Clinch to General R. Jones, April 1, 1835, *ASP:MA* 6:71–72; Andrew Jackson, "To the chiefs and warriors of the Seminole Indians in Florida," February 16, 1835, *ASP:MA* 6:524. This speech was read by Thompson in late March 1835, not at the April meeting, but it provides a good summary of the tenor and tactics of the talks in general.
7 *were not settling all:* General Jesup repeatedly makes this point in his letters. See, for example, Thomas Jesup to Alexander Macomb, May 10, 1837, NARA RG 94, E159-Q, Box 36, 11. (Some boxes in Jesup's papers are bound volumes with numbered pages. In those cases, I provide the page numbers.)
7 *They weren't hungry:* Jumper points this out in April: "They tell him . . . he is starving here; the country he lives in is good enough, he does not starve." M. S. Miller to M. Miller, May n.d., 1835, USMA.
7 *brashly informed the chiefs:* Simmons, "Recollections of the Late Campaign," 548; Miller to Miller, May n.d., 1835; Thompson, Harris, and Clinch to Cass, April 24, 1835.
8 *and did not show:* Simmons, "Recollections of the Late Campaign," 548; Miller to Miller, May n.d., 1835. The collapsing floor incident is also drawn from these sources.
8 *Eight chiefs voted:* Thompson, Harris, and Clinch to Cass, April 24, 1835. The total of thirteen refers to principal chiefs and does not include subchiefs.
8 *From the Agency house:* Thomas Lera, email to author, January 12, 2024; Thomas Lera, *The Seminole Agency Post Office, 1828–1837* (Dade City, FL: Seminole War Foundation and Florida Postal History Society, 2024); James W. Milgram, *The Express Mail of 1836–1839* (Chicago: Collectors Club of Chicago, 1977); Deane R. Briggs, ed., *Florida Stampless Postal History, 1763–1861* (North Miami, FL: David G. Phillips Publishing, 1999); Richard J. Stanaback, "Postal Operations in Territorial Florida, 1821–1845," *FHQ* 52, no. 2 (1973): 157–74.
8 *902-mile trek:* Postmaster General, *Table of the Post Offices in the United States Arranged by States and Counties* (Washington: Duff Green, 1831), 170.
9 *"His Excellency":* Gibson to Andrew Jackson, October 9, 1835, *ASP:MA* 6:92.
9 *as he did for portraits:* Sean Wilentz, *Andrew Jackson* (New York: Henry Holt, 1999), 1; Metropolitan Museum of Art, *A Walk Through the American Wing* (New Haven, CT: Yale University Press, 2010), 160.
9 *ruined the president's health:* Ludwig M. Deppisch et al., "Andrew Jackson's Exposure to Mercury and Lead: Poisoned President?," *JAMA* 282, no. 6 (1999): 569–71.
9 *from the War Department:* C. A. Harris to Thompson, May 22, 1835, Seminole Papers Collection, 3826.1442, GLA.
9 *turned them down:* Thompson to Gibson, April 27, 1835, *ASP:MA* 6:533–34.
9 *With Jackson's blessing:* R. K. Call to Andrew Jackson, March 22, 1835, Seminole Papers Collection, 3826.1440, GLA; Thompson to Cass, April 27, 1835,

ASP:MA 6:533–34; Elbert Herring to R. K. Call, March 26, 1835, Seminole Papers Collection, 3826.1441, GLA.

10 *Tribal law prohibited:* Thompson to C. A. Harris, June 17, 1835, *ASP:MA* 6:470–71.

10 *"slaves but in name":* Gad Humphreys to William McCarty, September 6, 1827, *TP* 23:911.

10 *in-kind tax:* Weik, *Archaeology of Antislavery Resistance,* 140; Mulroy, *Seminole Freedmen,* 38–39.

10 *Indians exercised:* William DuVal to Thomas McKenney, January 12, 1826, *TP* 23:413–14. Duval writes, "One Chief who was 70 slaves has not raised corn to feed his own family." Also see William DuVal to Thomas McKenney, March 2, 1826, in *TP* 23:453–54: "An Indian who has 20 Slaves has no corn annually from their labor, to feed his wife and Children."

10 *a Southern slaveholder:* "Gen. Wiley Thompson's Last Will and Testament."

10 *As of 1830:* "Census of the Colored Population of the U.S.," *Abolitionist* 1, no. 1 (January 1833): 10; Clair Clarke, ed., *Abstract of the Returns of the Fifth Census* (Washington: Duff Green, 1832), 32–33, 44.

10 *the president denied:* Callie Hopkins, "The Enslaved Household of President Jackson," White House Historical Association, August 1, 2019, accessed March 1, 2025, https://www.whitehousehistory.org/slavery-in-the-andrew-jackson-white-house.

000 *One Louisiana slaver:* Edwin Adams Davis, *Plantation Life in the Florida Parishes of Louisiana, 1835–1846* (New York: Columbia University Press, 1943), 406–10.

11 *governor whined that:* DuVal to McKenney, January 12, 1826; DuVal to McKenney, March 2, 1826.

11 *most powerful Americans:* Duncan Clinch, Edmund Gaines, James Gadsden, John Eaton, Richard Call, Robert Butler, and Wiley Thompson all served under Jackson or had close ties to him. Gaines, notably, opposed Indian Removal. See also Herbert J. Doherty Jr., "Andrew Jackson's Cronies in Florida Territorial Politics," *FHQ* 35, no 1. (1955): 3–29.

11 *board controlling land claims:* Doherty, "Andrew Jackson's Cronies," 6.

11 *on behalf of his dear:* Call to Jackson, March 22, 1835, Seminole Papers Collection, 3826.1440, GLA; Herring to Call, March 26, 1835, Seminole Papers Collection, 3826.1441, GLA.

12 *conveyed the president's position:* C. A. Harris to Thompson, May 22, 1835, Seminole Papers Collection, 3826.1442–3826.14421, GLA.

12 *the targets held rights:* Simmons, *Notices of East Florida,* 76; Thompson to Cass, April 27, 1835.

TWO: ABRAHAM'S TOWN

13 *Native shout echoed:* Deposition of Anthony Rutant, July 7, 1835, *ASP:MA* 6:498; "Deposition by Harman H. Holliman," November 24, 1832, *TP* 24:781–83.

13 *would likely have been:* MacCauley, *Seminole Indians of Florida,* 483. Abraham may have had a bandolier bag.

13 *His title was:* Previously, I believe, there were only two mentions of Abraham's Indian name known to scholars. His name appears as "Sohanac" in Samuel Forry, "Letters of Samuel Forry, Surgeon U. S. Army, 1837–1838. Part II," *FHQ* 6, no. 4 (1927): 214. The second mention appears in "Abraham, interpreter to Micanopy. Transcript of 'talk' to Cae Hajo, Tampa Bay. Sept. 11, 1837," UFA Digital Archives, accessed March 1, 2025, https://original-ufdc

.uflib.ufl.edu/AA00021285/00001/2j. The UFA transcript at the link is incomplete, but it lists Abraham's name as "Souanaffe Tustenukke." Porter, "Negro Abraham," 39–40, has a reproduction of this letter, and this is the accepted version of Abraham's name that appears in the literature.

After spending months reading hard-to-decipher cursive, and in light of the fact that the meaning of *Souanaffe* remains unknown, I suspected that this might be a transcription error and requested a photostat of the original from the University of Florida archives. My thanks go to Caleb Del Rio, of the George A. Smathers Libraries, for providing me with a scan of a photostat of the original letter: "Abraham Sends His Talk to Cae Hadjo," September 11, 1837, UFA, Miscellaneous Manuscripts, 00, 106. At first the *ff* appeared to me to be *ss*, which was commonly written in the cursive of the time as *fs*, but on closer inspection, the name actually reads "Souanagk Tustenukke." To determine this I had to figure out who actually wrote the letter that was dictated by Abraham. A note on the photostat reads, "Enclosure in letter from Acting Adjutant General, Headquarters, Army of the South to Captain P. H. Galt, Fort King, dated September 17, 1837." At the time that was Thomas B. Linnard, which is confirmed by T. B. Linnard to P. H. Galt, September 17, 1837, NARA RG 94, Letters Received, J186, in which Linnard informs Galt that he is forwarding Abraham's letter to him. I found numerous samples of Linnard's handwriting, and he does not write *f* in the style in which it appears in the photostat. He does write *g* in that manner, and in Abraham's letter he writes the word *tongue* twice; the second time the *g* is written in the same manner as it appears in *Souanaffe*. The second letter is trickier but it is clearly a *k*, which Linnard also writes distinctly, often finishing the letter with a curl between the shape of a *u* and a *c*.

In addition, I discovered a third mention of Abraham's name: It appears as "So-anhk-tuste-nuggee" in "Seminole Indians," *Times-Picayune*, June 23, 1838, 3. I ran all three versions by Professor Jack Martin, of William & Mary, an expert in Muscogee, and he replied (email to author, November 23, 2024) with the following information: "The word for 'Shawnee' in Muscogee is Sawvnoke /sa:wanoki/ . . . the first word in two-word names in Muscogee is commonly shortened, so Sawvnok-Tvstvnvke would be fine for Shawnee Tustennuggee." Martin also provided me a spelling in English, which I have used in the book: Sawanok' Tustenuggee, or Shawnee Warrior. Interestingly, in Porter, "Negro Abraham," 10, Porter notes that Abraham's name had been interpreted in the past as meaning Shawnee Warrior.

13 *was a chief:* Potter, *War in Florida*, 9; "Seminole Indians," *Times-Picayune*, June 23, 1838, 3; "Naval Museum," *Evening Post*, August 2, 1852, 4; Coe, *Red Patriots*, 46; "Indians," *Emancipator* 1, no. 45 (March 9, 1837), GLC.

13 *hailed as a prophet:* Motte, *Journey into Wilderness*, 211; Missall and Missall, *Miserable Pride of a Soldier*, 118.

13 *Seminoles as Yahola:* Cohen, *Notices of Florida*, 239, states Abraham was referred to by Indians as Yobly. Porter, "Negro Abraham," 14, expounds, "The meaning of Yobly is unknown. It cannot be translated by authorities either in African or Muskhogean linguistics." The word is being written down phonetically by a non-native speaker. Yahola appears in many variations in the archives, including as Yoholy. For example, see "Yoholy Hadjo" in "Muster Roll of a Party of Emigrating Indians," NARA RG 94, E159-Q, Box 21, Indian Affairs and Correspondence. My supposition is that Cohen, who, as Porter notes, appears to have never met Abraham and who wrote his book quickly, was scribbling down notes

secondhand, could not read his own hurried cursive writing, and later mistranscribed the *ho* as a *b*. Hence *Yobly*.

13 *over six feet:* Porter, "Negro Abraham," 4.

13 *"full blooded":* Cohen, *Notices of Florida*, 239.

13 *in the parlance of:* "Movements of Billy Bowlegs," *New York Times*, 8.

13 *brilliant and "artful":* Porter, "Negro Abraham," 15; McCall, *Letters from the Frontiers*, 302.

13 *in his left eye:* Porter, "Negro Abraham," 4, 34.

14 *Hogs shot dead:* "Affidavits of Abraham Daniels and Enoch Daniels," July 10, 1835, and "Affidavit of Grandison Barker," September 1, 1835, NARA RG 75, Records of the Bureau of Indian Affairs, NAMP M234 roll 800, 477–81.

14 *Indians promised:* For background regarding these negotiations, and the centrality and sensitivity of the issue of enslavement, see *TP* 23 and *TP* 24.

14 *An Alabama woman:* Littlefield, *Africans and Creeks*, 121.

14 *a man called Waters:* James Dill to James D. Westcott, August 27, 1830, NAMP M234 roll 287, 515–16.

14 *a proposal sent to:* James D. Westcott to the Secretary of War, October 11, 1830, NAMP M234 roll 287, 513–14.

14 *one of the lawmen:* Cohen, *Notices of Florida*, 239. In another instance, Abraham returned horses stolen by an Indian to the same settler's home. Weik, *Archaeology of Antislavery Resistance*, 141; Reuben Charles Papers, 1816–32, 2:15, UFA Digital Collections.

14 *Micanopy's top advisors:* Cohen, *Notices of Florida*, 239.

14 *locals believed that:* See the subsequent citation, in this chapter, for *Four hundred self-liberated people*.

15 *five known African Seminole:* Mulroy, *Seminole Freedmen*, 35–36; George Klos, "Blacks and Seminoles," *South Florida History Magazine* 2 (Spring 1991): 13.

15 *some of "considerable size":* Joel W. Jones, "Memoir: Transcribed by Leigh V. Stephens," 63, George A. Smathers Libraries, UFA Digital Collections. Hereafter referred to as Jones, "Memoir Transcript."

15 *twenty to three hundred acres:* Horatio S. Dexter, "Observations on the Seminole Indians, 1823," NAMP M271 roll 4, 505–19.

15 *the rainy seasons:* William P. DuVal to Thomas L. McKenney, February 22, 1826, *ASP:IA* 2:688–89.

15 *the land became:* Jones, "Memoir Transcript," 63; Cohen, *Notices of Florida*, 238; McCall, *Letters from the Frontiers*, 160.

15 *from clay pipes:* Cohen, *Notices of Florida*, 176.

15 *an emerald bottle:* Weik, *Archaeology of Antislavery Resistance*, 145.

15 *In the Muscogee language:* DuVal to McKenney, February 22, 1826. Some sources, including the official historical town marker, report that the name is Mikasuki-Hitchiti in origin. Bernard Fisher, ed., "Pilaklikaha / Abraham's Town," Historical Marker Database, revised July 22, 2018, https://www.hmdb.org/m.asp?m=114467. According to Jack Martin (email to author, January 22, 2024), "Pilaklakaha looks Muscogee rather than Mikasuki. The element pil- appears in several words relating to swamps or bottom lands: (o)pelwv ((o) pílwa) swamp; vpelofv (apil-ó:fa) hummock; pelofv (pil-ó:fa) swamp; akpelofv (ak-pil-ó:fa) swamp. The final -ofv in these words means 'inside,' but has other uses: eto (itó) tree; eto-ofv (ito-ó:fa) woods. The prefix ak- usually relates to water or a low place. So Pilaklakaha looks like pil- 'swamp' + ak- 'in water' + an element likaha . . . Pel-aklvkahe would be 'spotted swamp,'" i.e., a lowlands area

spotted with hammocks. See also Weisman, *Unconquered People*, 13. Abraham would have used Muscogee in his duties as interpreter.

15 *Abraham's Town:* Porter, *Black Seminoles*, 55.

15 *biblical, classical, or African names:* Bateman, "Naming Patterns in Black Seminole," 231; Littlefield, *Africans and Seminoles*, 205–55.

15 *Some used aliases:* For example, see the letters relating to "Lucy Joe—alias Lydia, Jenny & Diana" in "Slave Owner Claims of Runaway Slaves Living among Seminole Indians, Affidavits," Requests from Owners of Slaves Living with Seminoles, 1837, PQH.

15 *offered another to outsiders:* Lorenzo and Mock, *My Black Seminole Ancestors*, 12; "List of Negroes left in Tampa on 3d May without Authority," in "Lists of Indian and Black Prisoners Taken in Indian Wars," Reports and Lists of Indians and Negroes (hereafter referred to R&L), F1, PQH. Carolina, Tena, Rose, Bob, and Juan are listed as nos. 14–18; War Department, "Negroes, &c., captured from Indians in Florida, &c," February 27, 1839, Ho. of Reps., Doc. No. 225, 25th Cong., 3rd Sess., hereafter referred to Doc. No. 225; "Abram's Will," in John Casey, "Memoranda Concerning the Seminoles," 32, 127, USMA, hereafter referred to as Casey, "Memoranda Concerning the Seminoles." Casey's is a remarkable document, from a reliable witness who was taking notes from Native and Black Seminole sources, that has not received its due attention in the literature. To my knowledge, all of the following that appear in Casey's journal are new to the literature: Abraham's will; with other information, a full accounting of Abraham's nuclear families; the lists of Black Seminole soldiers, companies, and their commanders; a Native account of the coup of June 2, 1837; a Black Seminole account of the battle of December 31, 1835; Abraham's account of the Miccosukee and Seminole Council divide at the siege of Camp Izard; Abraham's account of the conflict between the Seminole and the Yamasee people; an account of Cowkeeper and King Payne's family and familiar relations, including the true relationship between Micanopy and Holata Micco or Billy Bowlegs, likely provided by Abraham. There appears to be only one existing citation of Casey's 1837 journal, which appears in West, "Abiaka, or Sam Jones," 369, as a citation for the names and backgrounds of Abiaka's wives. Casey spells *Tainy* phonetically as *Tenny*. I've used the spelling listed on the 1860s census: *1860 United States Federal Census*, Arkansas, Indian Lands, Free Inhabitants of Seminole County West, June 1, 1860, NAMP M653 roll 52, 1221–22.

15 *For nearly 150 years:* Porter, *Black Seminoles*, 4; Morgan, "Precarious Lives," 19; Dixon, *Florida's Negro War*, 9–12; Twyman, *Black Seminole Legacy*, 1.

16 *Africans fought for:* Clavin, *Battle of Negro Fort*, 12; Porter, *Black Seminoles*, 8–9; Morgan, "Precarious Lives," 20; Belko, *America's Hundred Years' War*, 47; Landers, "Spanish Sanctuary," 301.

16 *warriors perished when:* Clavin, *Battle of Negro Fort*, 123.

16 *a sizable African army:* "Affair at Bowleg's Town," 16 April, 1818, NARA RG 94, Returns of Killed and Wounded in Battles or Engagements with Indians, British Troops, and Mexican Troops, 1790–1848, NAMP 1832 roll 6, 256.

16 *Tena walked:* Lorenzo and Mock, *My Black Seminole Ancestors*, 10–14.

16 *added three guns:* "Negro Warriors in the Sem Nation: Abram's Company," Casey, "Memoranda Concerning the Seminoles," 11.

17 *Black Seminole royalty:* These include Toney Barnett's family. See Doc. No. 225, 69; *Record Book of Hillsborough County, Territory of Florida, 1838–1846* 1:142,

PALMM Digital Collections, SULF. Abraham was emancipated by Micanopy on June 18, 1830.

17 *four hundred self-liberated people:* James Horn et al. to Andrew Jackson, January 1834, *ASP:MA* 6:465–66. At one point, by another estimate, the Black Seminole population reached fourteen hundred people, with only two hundred of that number being enslaved people: Littlefield, *Africans and Seminoles,* 12. A third estimate of how exactly these two populations were split demographically appears in "Extract from the Private Journal of a Late Field Officer," *Army and Navy Chronicle,* March 7, 1838, 8, 10, which states, "It would appear that the force of the Indians in Florida amounts to about 1,450 warriors and 250 negroes: one hundred of the latter are Indian slaves, and the one hundred and fifty are runaways." Monaco, *Second Seminole War,* 63, writes that if Micanopy didn't let his bondservants fight, it would "have certainly hindered the war effort." Abraham puts Micanopy's enslaved warriors at only fifteen fighters: Casey to Jesup, July 24, 1837, NARA RG 94, E159-Q, Box 6, Casey. The typically American reductionist tendency to force these groups into separate categories is in large part beside the point. See Smith, *Sketch of the Seminole War,* 21n1: "Micanopy possesses upwards of a hundred negro slaves; they do no work except to make him a little corn, and he is not apparently the richer for them than any other Indian." As Jane Landers has said, "I don't think some modern U.S. audiences can get that neither the Spaniards nor the Seminoles nor the blacks themselves considered them slaves—only the Americans did": West Palm Beach, "Early Florida," n.d., accessed March 5, 2025, https://wpbequalitytaskforce.org/early-florida/.

17 *to guard their freedoms:* Orin Marsh to James Riz, January 22, 1834, Glunt, "Plantation and Frontier Records," 1:260.

17 *likely a mixture of:* Mulroy, *Freedom on the Border,* 11.

17 *enslaved other Native Americans:* Ibid., 8.

17 *known Seminole children since:* Jarvis, "Floridian War: Transcript," 50, NYAM.

17 *nearly his own entire life:* William Armstrong to J. H. Crawford, October 17, 1840, Office of Indian Affairs, Letters Received 1824–1881, Western Superintendency, 1840–1846, NAMP M234 roll 923. Micanopy had at least one other residence in addition to Pilaklikaha.

17 *Abraham's people appeared:* "More Seminoles," *Weekly Arkansas Gazette,* June 6, 1838, 2; Testimony of A. B. Benjamin, May 10, 1838, *Heirs of Love vs. E. P. Gaines,* 15.975 (1st Dist. 1838), F2, NOCA.

17 *a free Black Seminole woman:* Testimony of Eliza, May 10, 1838, *Heirs of Love vs. E. P. Gaines,* 15.975 (1st Dist. 1838), F2, NOCA.

17 *others were listed as chiefs:* Joseph Hernández to Thomas Jesup, October 22, 1837, in War Department, "Seminole Indians—Prisoners of War," April 11, 1838, Ho. of Reps., Doc. No. 327, 25th Cong., 2nd Sess., 5; Zachary Taylor to Thomas Jesup, December 7, 1837, Zachary Taylor Papers, Series 2, LOC; "Seminoles of Philip's Band," R&L F3, PQH; "Registry of negro prisoners," Doc. No. 225, 69; Thomas Jesup to Joel Poinsett, September 25, 1838, NARA RG 94 E 159Q, Box 38, 140; Thomas Jesup to W. L. Marcy, July 1, 1838, NAMP M547 roll 13, Special File 96; Jesup, "Diary," E for April 23, 1837. "The Florida Indians," *Daily National Intelligencer,* May 18, 1837, 3.

18 *laid fresh paths:* Weik, *Archaeology of Antislavery Resistance,* chap. 6; Dixon, *Florida's Negro War,* 10–13; Dixon, "Black Seminole Ethnogenesis."

18 *some of the noblest:* Mahon, *History of the Second Seminole War,* 128; Bateman,

"Naming Patterns in Black Seminole," 230; Mock, *Dreaming with the Ancestors*, 209.

18 *forged in the 1790s:* Weisman, "Labor and Survival," 70.

18 *By the 1830s, two generations:* Wasserman, *People's History*, 286; Kly, *Invisible War*, 156–59.

18 *had likely never known:* The wide acceptance of Abraham as a self-liberated former bondservant who escaped from Dr. Eugenio Sierra in Pensacola appears to have originated in Porter, "Negro Abraham," 2. Porter writes that Abraham "had been a slave in Pensacola to Dr. Sierra," as if the matter were settled. In footnote 3, however, he details that while Hitchcock, Cohen, and McCall claim that Abraham was a "runaway" from Pensacola, John Casey reported that Abraham had "been all his life among the Indians." Porter does not specify that McCall is the only source to name Sierra. Porter then concludes that McCall was correct on the grounds that "McCall knew Abraham earlier, and probably more intimately, than Casey." McCall did meet Abraham before Casey, but did not know him better. In fact, when McCall first met Abraham in 1826, McCall reports that the population of Pilaklikaha was made up of "chiefly runaway slaves from Georgia": McCall, *Letters from the Frontiers*, 160. Years later, when he meets Abraham during the war, McCall does not appear to be aware that he is meeting the same person and incorrectly describes Micanopy as Abraham's "master," clearly unaware that Micanopy formally emancipated the interpreter in 1830. Cohen seems to have never met Abraham.

From what I can tell, the white officers circulating the claim that Abraham was a "runaway" more or less intended the term as a pejorative: They mean to say that he is disloyal, illegitimate, and not to be trusted. McCall, in particular, is clearly a biased source. Sierra was alive for years after the war, as well, and there is no mention of an Abraham in Sierra's entries in the relevant deed books. Given the sensitivity of the "runaway" issue in the 1820s and '30s, it would have been unwise to place a self-liberated former bondservant in charge of the Black Seminoles and put him in the most exposed position possible, as chief interpreter. Casey, on the other hand, had a baseline of respect for Abraham and the African Seminoles and eventually got to know the interpreter well. Here are a few descriptions of Casey: "John G. Casey, an officer who has served all the war in Florida, and knows more of the Indians and negroes than any other man"; "When the Indians and negroes now at Tampa shall be ordered to move, I desire that such as, Colonel Taylor may designate, or that Mr. Casey (from his intimate knowledge of their characters and capacity for usefulness) may consider. . . ." See Doc. No. 225, 27, 118. An officer once said of why the Seminole's trusted Casey, "He never deceived them; never told a lie, and never made a promise he did not fulfill if within his power. . . . By this means he gained the confidence of the whole nation": Missall and Missall, *Seminole Struggle*, 279.

Anyone stationed at Fort Brooke in Tampa Bay during the period Abraham was living there, from June of 1837 to mid-November 1837, would be better informed than the three officers floating the Pensacola story. Nathan Jarvis and Amos Eaton were. See Eaton, "Journal," E for November 10, 1837, UMA: "These marks were described to Old Abram, a celebrated negro of great shrewdness formerly a slave of Micanopy, now in pay as guide and interpreter to this Army, who was born and raised among the Seminoles." Also see Nathanial Jarvis, "Floridian War: Transcript," 50, NYAM, which reads, "I have lately observ'd among them a deformity resembling club foot and which I suppos'd was a natural malformation. . . . I was told these were owing to their being bitten by snakes and their feet had rotten'd off in consequence. This Abraham says was the cause & he has known them from childhood." Additional evidence comes from Luther Blake, who spent over a year working with Abraham as military escort during the 1852 Washington trip. "Correspondence of the *Journal of Commerce*," *Weekly Journal of Commerce*, 2, reports, regarding Abraham, "He speaks English fluently, and also Indian, as his mother tongue. He came up among the Seminole in Florida, but cannot tell where or when he was born"; "Local Matters," *Republic*, 2.

Porter further speculated that Abraham must have been present at the attack on the African Fort. Examining the lists of those at the African Fort, we do find an "Abraham" present, but not one owned by Sierra: "Correspondence from the Commander of Panzacola, 1815," May, Archivo General de Indias, Seville, Papeles de Cuba, Legajo 1796 Part IX, Box 3070, Letter 513, 768–74. We could speculate that Sierra sold Abraham to Innerarity, who claims him, but there is no evidence for that. Francis Belton links Abraham to a man named Harry, and there is a Harry at the African Fort, but that person cannot be the one Abraham is close to in 1835 because that individual returned to Innerarity, and the Abraham listed appears to have as well. My thanks go Claudio Saunt for this information (email to author, March 1, 2024), drawn from his research: John Innerarity to James Innerarity, 3 June 1815, Forbes-Innerarity Papers, 73/17, reel 147 Q, P. K. Yonge Library, original in Mobile Public Library, Mobile, AL, which reads, [water damaged] "the carpenter James Crook, like most [?] of this country, is rather too spry of spirits to [???]. I expect he will return. If not, I do not care as I am happy to inform you that I this morning got sipinter [?] Harry back. He came round with 2 other negroes in a very small canoe . . . [?] . . . and reports that Marie, Abraham, Sophy, Stephen and some of the others will come as soon as . . . [?] . . . get an opportunity (not being able to depart at present as the canoe was too small)."

18 *Asked directly*: "Correspondence of the *Journal of Commerce*," *Weekly Journal of Commerce*, 2; "Local Matters," *Republic*, 2.

18 *His freedom papers*: "Extract of a Letter," *Vermont Phoenix*, 2.

18 *Later records list*: *1860 U.S. Federal Census*, Arkansas, Indian Lands, Seminole County West, roll 52, 1221–22; "Enrollment for Seminole Census Card 703," NARA RG 75, Enrollment Cards, Card 703, is the card for Peter Lincoln, Abraham's son with Pacy. Abraham's great-great-grandson Jimmie Abraham was of great help in the early stages of my research in pinning down Abraham's lineage: Jimmie Abraham, interview with author, July 19, 2023. Abraham never used the last name Lincoln in his lifetime to my knowledge, but he used others. See Lantz, *Seminole Indians of Florida, 1850–1874*, and Lantz, *Seminole Indians of Florida 1875–1879*, for the various annuity rolls that list Abraham's family.

18 *"the happiness of his people"*: Porter, "Cowkeeper Dynasty," 341.

18 *to avoid any senseless fighting*: Cusick, "King Payne and His Policies," 42–43. Also see James Seagrove to King Payne, April 14, 1793, *ASP:IA* 1:380.

19 *honey water*: Bartram, *Travels*, 164.

19 *outside every home*: Covington, *Seminoles of Florida*, 13.

19 *fifteen hundred cattle*: Blakney-Bailey, "Archaeology of the Payne Town Seminoles," 353.

19 *early as 1802*: Saunt, *New Order of Things*, 207, 207–8n12. The Harry mentioned here may be the one Abraham was purportedly close to.

19 *the early 1820s*: Glunt, "Plantation and Frontier Records," 1:150, 153–58; Littlefield, *Africans and Seminoles*, 8.

19 *visit Washington City in 1826:* Brown, "Florida Crisis of 1826–27," 431–32; Missall and Missall, *Seminole Struggle*, 102.

19 *around forty-five years:* Porter, "Negro Abraham," 2.

19 *he had two wives:* Casey, "Memoranda Concerning the Seminoles," 9, 32. Washington's and Rachel's ages are taken from Doc. No. 225, 67–68, in which their ages are listed in 1837 as eleven and twenty-five. Rachel's child Nancy is listed as one year old. Porter, "Negro Abraham," 11, correctly lists Hagar but suggests she was "the widow of the former chief of the nation." That assumption is due to a transcription error where the description of Toney Barnett is lumped in with that of Abraham. Doc. No. 225, 69, correctly distinguishes the two. The woman in question is Polly Barnett, Toney Barnett's wife.

20 *President Jackson insisted: ASP:MA* 6:65, 68. Jack Martin provided the Muscogee translations with assistance in one case from Linda Wood.

20 *officer complained that Abraham:* "Domestic Intelligence: Seminole War," June 15, 1837, 4.

20 *as a political animal:* Missall and Missall, *Miserable Pride of a Soldier*, 118.

20 *Many Indians knew English:* Wickman, *Osceola's Legacy*, 6.

20 *spoke in a low tone:* Coe, *Red Patriots*, 45.

20 *lenient views of servitude:* Landers, *Black Society in Spanish Florida*, 7–8. Also see Zephaniah Kingsley, "Address to the Legislative Council of Florida on the Subject of Its Colored Population," 1823, 3, SLAF, in which Kingsley argues, in vain, that the Americans should continue the Spanish system of having "three classes or casts of people," including free people of color, instead of two classes.

20 *slow to appreciate:* Porter, "Negro Abraham," 14–15. This confusion most often expresses itself in the biased and contradictory idea of the Black Seminoles as enslaved people who ruled their masters.

20 *formal position akin to:* "Domestic Intelligence: Seminole War," June 15, 1837, 4; Susan A. Miller, "Seminoles and Africans Under Seminole Law: Sources and Discourses of Tribal Sovereignty and 'Black Indian' Entitlement," *Wicazo Sa Review* 20, no. 1 (Spring 2005): 37.

20 *two other interpreters:* James Gadsden to Lewis Cass, November 1, 1834, *ASP:MA* 6:507–8.

21 *Europeans were:* Many writers of the time use "white men," but others, including General Jesup, repeatedly use "whitemen." My use of it is intended more as a comic note than as a historical representation of the standard term of the era. See, for example, Thomas Jesup to William Harney, April 26, 1837, NARA RG 94, E159-Q, Box 36; Samuel Forry to John W. Phelps, July 3, 1837, Box 1, F4, NYPL.

21 *he and the president: ASP:MA* 6:67.

21 *alive and plotting:* Ibid., 6:68.

21 *preceded him were crooks:* Drake, *Biography and History of the Indians*, 4:122; Thompson to Lewis Cass, December 12, 1834, ASP:MA 6:520–21; Thompson to Lewis Cass, July 19, 1835, *ASP:MA* 6:460; Potter, *War in Florida*, 25; Humphreys to McCarty, September 6, 1827, *TP* 23:911.

21 *In 1822, Gad Humphreys:* Kokomoor, "Indian Agent Gad Humphreys," 38.

21 *An undated sketch:* Frederick Humphreys, M.D., *The Humphreys Family in America* (New York: Humphreys Print, 1885), 528.

21 *the U.S. government forbade him:* Thomas L. McKenney to William P. DuVal, May 8, 1826, *TP* 23:536; Humphreys to McCarty, September 6, 1827. Jesup later writes, of Humphreys claims on the Black Seminoles, "The principle claimant of this class was a former Agent of the Seminoles, but had the trade been

recognized he, as Agent, was forbidden by law—all the purchases of slaves made by him from the Indians while he was there agent were therefore illegal and void. After he ceased to be Agent he could not legally trade with the Indians unless licensed as a trader," which there does not appear to be evidence of: Thomas Jesup to William Marcy, April 3, 1848, Thomas Sidney Jesup Papers, Box 15, 5, LOC.

21 *targeted one woman:* Orin Marsh to James Riz, January 22, 1834, Glunt, "Plantation and Frontier Records," 1:260. "Speculat[ing] in Negro claims" also derives from this source.

21 *ally, Toney Barnett:* "Chiefs of the Creek Nation to the Honorable Secretary of War," July 25, 1843, NARA RG 75, M234 roll 227, 125–26; John Page to J. H. Crawford, September 6, 1842, NARA RG 75, M234 roll 289, 450–51. The year 1816 is a rough estimate; the letter puts the date between 1813 and 1818.

21 *Toney also had children:* Casey, "Memoranda Concerning the Seminoles," 9.

22 *likely squatting on: Articles of Agreement and Association of Florida Peninsula Land Company* (New York: Edward S. Mesier, 1836), 14.

22 *Twenty-nine Black Seminoles remained:* See the chapter 11 note for *Twenty-nine African Seminoles.*

22 *charged with corruption and fired:* Kokomoor, "Indian Agent Gad Humphreys," 101–2, 119.

22 *even more bent:* Childs, "Correspondence with His Family," *HM* 3, no. 4 (1874): 281.

22 *$1.25 a day:* Abraham worked from September 25, 1832, to May 7, 1833, for 225 days and was owed $281.25. *Document 512: Correspondence on the Subject of the Emigration of Indians Between the 30th of November, 1831 and 27th December, 1833* (Washington: Duff Green, 1835), 328–29.

22 *an additional $200:* "Treaty of Payne's Landing, 1832," May 9, 1832, 1, SLAF Reference Collection.

22 *the army painted Abraham:* Mahon, *History of the Second Seminole War,* 78; Guinn, *Our Land Before We Die,* 58.

22 *Phagan never paid:* Thomas Jesup to Luke Lea, October 5, 1852, NARA RG 75, M234 roll 801, 929–35; Drake, *Biography and History of the Indians,* 4:122.

22 *Phagan was charged:* Klos, "Blacks and the Seminole Removal," 155–56n82, 84.

22 *not particularly intelligent:* Monaco, *Second Seminole War,* 43.

22 *He promised that:* Thompson to Cass, April 27, 1835, *ASP:MA* 6:534.

22 *profoundly unnerved them:* Andrew Jackson, "Indorsement of the President," July 6, 1835, *ASP:MA* 6:478.

23 *spurred on by citizens:* Call to Jackson, March 22, 1835, GLA; James Horn et al. to Andrew Jackson, January 1834, *ASP:MA* 6:465–66; DuVal to McKenney, January 12, 1826, *TP* 23:414; DuVal to McKenney, March 2, 1826, *TP* 23: 452–54.

23 *Abraham told Thompson:* McCall, *Letters from the Frontiers,* 302; *ASP:MA* 6:66–67.

THREE: THINGS LOST

24 *into Thompson's office:* Thompson to Gibson, June 3, 1835, *ASP:MA* 6:76.

24 *he told Thompson that:* Simmons, "Recollections of the Late Campaign," 548.

24 *hurled it against them:* Monaco, *Second Seminole War,* 35.

24 *leave their corpses:* Missall and Missall, *Seminole Struggle,* 121; "Billy Bowlegs in New Orleans," *Harper's Weekly* 2, no. 76 (June 12, 1858): 376.

24 *singled him out as:* Thompson to Lewis Cass, December 28, 1834, *ASP:MA* 6:70.

25 *stalked about outside:* Viator, "Florida," 2, 13.

25 *enforcer for the Miccosukee:* Wickman, *Osceola's Legacy*, 13, 143. Before the war, Osceola is sometimes associated instead with Holata Micco. For instance: "Osceola's chief, Holata Micco of the Tallahassee Creeks": Brown, *Ossian Bingley Hart*, 32. Early on, however, before the war even begins, he associated himself with the Miccosukees. The warriors that Osceola attacked Thompson with were widely reported to be Miccosukees, and Casey, "Memoranda Concerning the Seminoles," 25, provides a description of the December 31, 1835, engagement: "Powell commanded having collected less than 100 Miccosukees Apiakka being absent." This information comes from Cudjo's son Ned. Simmons, "Recollections of the Late Campaign," correctly associates Osceola with the Miccosukees, as does Viator, "Florida."

25 *face of the conflict:* Loftman, "Broward History." Mike Osceola describes the relationship of Jones to Osceola correctly here.

25 *the athleticism in his:* Simmons, "Recollections of the Late Campaign," 543.

25 *important to index:* Wickman, *Osceola's Legacy*, 291–95.

25 *ideal Indian warrior:* Thompson to Elbert Herring, October 28, 1835, *ASP:MA*6 63–64.

25 *"leader of the Seminoles":* Joint Committee on Printing, of the House and Senate, *A Compilation of the Messages and Papers of the Presidents*, vol. 4 (New York: Bureau of National Literature, 1897), 1682. The most accurate description would be that Osceola was "a" subordinate leader among many.

25 *concealed his own power:* Loftman, "Broward History"; West, "Abiaka, or Sam Jones," 377; Casey, "Memoranda Concerning the Seminoles," 23–25; Monaco, *Second Seminole War*, 70. The pattern repeats itself in the Third Seminole War: The most visible chief is William or Billy Bowlegs; he becomes the "sacrificial lamb" while Jones remains in the background and repeatedly downplays his power. See Knetsch, Missall, and Missall, *History of the Third Seminole War*.

26 *dressed plainly:* Simmons, "Recollections of the Late Campaign," 543.

26 *Abolitionists would claim:* Porter, "Episode of Osceola's Wife," 93.

26 *was drunk or that:* Viator, "Florida"; Boyd, "Asi-Yaholo or Osceola," 275; Potter, *War in Florida*, 76.

26 *two hundred yards:* Boyd, "Asi-Yaholo or Osceola," 275.

26 *glad to keep the dissident:* Thompson to S. V. Walker, June 23, 1835, *ASP:MA* 6:78–79.

26 *had to be punished:* "Reported confidentially," October 23, 1834, *ASP:MA* 6:66.

26 *For centuries, residents:* Searcy, "Introduction of African Slavery," 21; Saunt, "English Has Now a Mind," 157–58.

27 *Creeks raided rival:* Snyder, "Enemies, Adopted Kin," 255–57.

27 *new culture of acquisitiveness:* Ibid., 259, 285; Saunt, "English Has Now a Mind," 164–65.

27 *practiced the old:* Bartram, *Travels*, 164; Pressly, *Southern Underground Railroad*, 158. Black Seminole history appears to be rooted primarily in the Creek and Seminole story and the problems that arose with Creek acculturation. General Jesup to Marcy, April 3, 1848, Thomas Jesup Papers, Box 15, LOC, puts their population into four categories. One, "descendants of negroes taken from citizens of Georgia in former wars by the Creek or Muscogee Confederacy, of which the Seminole formed a part." Two, bondservants purchased by the Indians from the Spanish. Three, individuals freed from the plantations of Florida prior to 1832. Fourth, "Negroes claimed under pretended purchases from the Indians." After the First Seminole War, the Black Seminole population was estimated at four hundred. If accurate, that is not much population growth from 1818 to 1835.

Littlefield, *Africans and Seminoles*, 8. Another thing to consider is that recently self-liberated former bondservants would have been safer to leave the country entirely, as many Afro-descendant people did after Spain ceded the territory. There is a reason the Black Seminoles remained in Florida, with their allies. The bonds went back many years.

27 *Lucy, aka Lydia:* See, in "Slave Owner Claims of Runaway Slaves," PHQ, the "Deposition of Richard Leake," March 6, 1833; the "Deposition of Sally Wallen," August 21, 1834; the "Deposition of Kent," September 15, 1834; and the "Deposition of Jim Edinboro," November 3, 1836.

28 *Many of them spoke:* Covington, *Seminoles of Florida*, 13, 30; Simmons, *Notices of East Florida*, 76; Dixon, *Florida's Negro War*, 13.

28 *supplanted conventional communities:* Saunt, *New Order of Things*, 47, 55, 97, 99, 149.

28 *around ten:* Wickman, *Osceola's Legacy*, 5.

28 *around 1814, after:* Boyd, "Asi-Yaholo or Osceola," 252.

28 *some eight hundred:* Susan M. Abram, "Cherokees in the Creek War: A Band of Brothers," in *Tohopeka: Rethinking the Creek War & the War of 1812*, ed. Kathryn E. Holland Braund (Auburn: University of Alabama Press, 2012), 125.

28 *Only fifteen or twenty:* Remini, *Jackson and the Course of American Empire*, 216.

28 *pompous functionary, livid:* Thompson to Lewis Cass, December 28, 1834, *ASP:MA* 6:70.

28 *he had argued in Council:* "Reported Confidentially," October 23, 1834, *ASP:MA* 6:66.

28 *the Creek Confederacy fractured:* Saunt, "English Has Now a Mind," 159–60.

29 *muscular Apalachee cattleman:* Monaco, *Second Seminole War*, 53; Viator, "Florida," 13.

29 *protested, pointing to: ASP:MA* 6:66; Monaco, *Second Seminole War*, 22–23.

29 *life and his people: ASP:MA* 6:63, 69, 72, 569–70.

29 *Osceola cooled off:* Thompson to Gibson, June 3, 1835, *ASP:MA* 6:76.

29 *After six days:* Call, "Journal: Transcription," 313, SLAF.

29 *that moment, he seemed to:* Ibid., 89–90; "To the Editors," *Georgia Constitutionalist*, March 3, 1838, 2.

29 *organized a cordial competition:* Wickman, *Osceola's Legacy*, 15.

30 *brimming with certitudes:* Thompson to Gibson, June 3, 1835.

30 *Salt water mingled with:* "Report of Buckingham Smith, Esq., on His Reconnaissance of the Everglades, 1848," June 1, 1848, in *Everglades of Florida, Acts, Reports, and Other Papers, State and National, Relating to the Everglades of the State of Florida and Their Reclamation*, U.S. Sen. Doc. No. 89, 62nd Cong., 1st Sess. (Washington: Government Printing Office, 1911), 47; Michael Grunwald, *The Swamp: The Everglades, Florida, and the Politics of Paradise* (New York: Simon & Schuster, 2006), 9; "Mem. of Suggestions by Captain John C. Casey," in *Memoir of Reconnaissances with Maps During the Florida Campaign, April 1854–February 1858*, NAMP M1090, roll 1, 1:68; Mahon, *History of the Second Seminole War*, 216.

30 *old rafts and snagging:* George W. Long to William H. Chase, January 18, 1835, *TP* 25:96.

30 *As of early 1835:* K. B. Gibbs, "Presentment of the Grand Jury of the St. Johns and Mosquito Counties," December 20, 1834, *TP* 25:82, FN 82; Miller to Miller, April 29, 1835, 4, USMA.

30 *tree stumps sawed off:* Sivilich, Norman, and Dean, *Fort King Road*, 27.

30 *terrain so interspersed:* F. L. Dancy to Thomas Jesup, September 30, 1835, *TP* 25:66n75.

30 *a water route:* Thomas McKenney, *A History of the Organization and Movements of the Army of the United States* (Philadelphia: William S. Young, 1840), 20.
31 *It took a full year:* Sivilich, Norman, and Dean, *Fort King Road*, 15.
31 *This sort of work:* Missall and Missall, *Miserable Pride of a Soldier*, 103.
31 *surveyor avoided beachy hills:* Sivilich, Norman, and Dean, *Fort King Road*, 4, 27.
31 *mule, on August 11:* Duncan Clinch to R. Jones, September 12, 1835, *ASP:MA* 6:80.
31 *barely drinkable:* Mahon, "Journal of A. B. Meek," 309; Covington, "Life at Fort Brooke," 326.
31 *sugar-sand elevation:* Morris and Hough, *Fort King Road*, 10, 12–13, 16–18.
31 *Miccosukees allied with:* D. L. Clinch to Lewis Cass, November 13, 1835, *ASP: MA* 6:555–56.
31 *That task fell to:* Lewis Cass to D. L. Clinch, December 4, 1835, *ASP:MA* 6:559.
31 *over 250 pounds:* Bemrose, *Reminiscences*, 59.
32 *Christian who had been:* Patrick, *Aristocrat in Uniform*, 31–32, 80.
32 *necessary tit for tat:* Clinch to Jones, September 12, 1835.
32 *the idea that ten companies:* Lewis Cass to Duncan Clinch, October 22, 1835, *TP* 25:188; Duncan L. Clinch to the Adjutant General, October 8, 1835, *TP* 25:183.

FOUR: LABYRINTHS OF DOUBT

33 *Abraham recruited soldiers:* "Copy of a Letter, Dated Fort Brooke, Tampa Bay, April 13," *Maryland Gazette*, May 12, 1836, 2.
33 *dipped in red paint:* Scott McCabe, "Web Chronicles Little-Known Fla. Slave Revolt," *Palm Beach Post*, July 21, 2005, accessed March 2, 2025, http://www.johnhorse.com/black-seminoles/news/072105.htm.
33 *and his companion:* "Copy of a Letter," *Maryland Gazette*, May 12, 2, reports the chief's name as Ko-ho-ha-jo, or Mad Wolf. Porter, "Florida Slaves and Free Negroes," 394, instead, has his name as Yaha Hadjo. Difficult to say which is true, if either.
33 *Romeo, a fifty-one-year-old:* "List of Negroes taken from Messrs de Peyster & Cruger Plantation December 27, 1835," William de Peyster to Thomas Jesup, April 13, 1837, in "Slave Owner Claims of Runaway Slaves," PQH. One of the two men in question writes his own name twice here as de Peyster and once as De Peyster, on the outside of the letter. Wayne, *Sweet Cane*, 119, has it has DePeyster. I've opted for the format he used to sign his name in his letter to Jesup.
33 *sister to the prophet's*: Thomas Jesup to William Preston, January 4, 1841, in "William Depeyster and Henry N. Cruger [To accompany Senate bill No. 68]," February 3, 1843, Ho. of Reps., Rep. No. 146, 2, 27th Cong., 3rd Sess; "Talk of Tustennuk Kochokkonnee," April 13, 1838, in Casey, "Memoranda Concerning the Seminoles," 69.
34 *six-hundred-acre plot:* Wayne, *Sweet Cane*, 42, 119–20.
34 *authorities in St. Augustine intervened:* John W. Phelps, "Journal (Loose Leaves)," E for January 25, 1839, NYPL.
34 *a squat stone factory:* Visit by author, June 12, 2024; George Harvey, *Ruins of Sugar House*, ca. 1836–37, watercolor on paper, 7¼ × 10½ in., Harn Museum of Art, University of Florida, accessed December 3, 2024, https://harn.emuseum.com/objects/23581/ruins-of-sugar-house; Wayne, *Sweet Cane*, 98, 122–27.
34 *sugar farms were forced:* "It is generally planted in December and cut in October and November," according to Brown, "Diary," 60, YLA.

34 *240 degrees:* Wayne, *Sweet Cane,* 29.
34 *for this reason, a minder:* Brent Staples, "A Fate Worse than Slavery, Unearthed in Sugar Land," *New York Times,* October 27, 2018.
35 *his hands severed:* Donald B. Armstrong, *The Journey: From Shackles and Chains to the White House* (Pittsburg, PA: Dorrance, 2021), 19; Rasmussen, *American Uprising,* 142.
35 *stretching forty miles:* Rasmussen, *American Uprising,* 148.
35 *mutilated, cut into pieces:* John W. Cromwell, "The Aftermath of Nat Turner's Insurrection," *Journal of Negro History* 5, no. 2 (April 1930): 212, 218.
35 *mailed southward 175,000 copies:* Bertram Wyatt-Brown, "The Abolitionists' Postal Campaign of 1835," *Journal of Negro History* 50, no. 4 (October 1965): 228.
35 *Threatening ideas carbonized:* Wyly-Jones, "1835 Anti-Abolition Meetings," 289.
36 *European observed, after visiting:* Alexis de Tocqueville, *Democracy in America* (New York: J & H. G. Langley, 1841), 412.
36 *dared to print that slavery:* "Slavery a Sin [From the Declaration of Sentiments of the Ohio Anti-Slavery Convention]," *Anti-Slavery Record* 1, no. 7 (July 1835): 75.
36 *Georgia, Alabama, Virginia:* Wyly-Jones, "1835 Anti-Abolition Meetings," 294.
36 *abolitionist petitions in Congress:* Abraham Eustis to Frederic Eustis, February 12, 1837, USAT; Abraham Eustis to Frederic Eustis, February 12, 1837, in "Copies of Letters from Abraham Eustis to his Son Frederic Eustis 1831–1841," EHM; Ivy, *Distinguished Light,* 159. "It is the beginning of the end," Eustis notes of the prevailing feeling among Southern members of Congress.
36 *over 150:* Wyly-Jones, "1835 Anti-Abolition Meetings," 291–92.
36 *visitor was warned that:* Bemrose, *Reminiscences,* 109.
36 *residents urged laws:* Brown, *Ossian Bingley Hart,* 32.
36 *assured readers of how:* "Abolition Meeting at Utica," *Jacksonville Courier,* November 19, 1835, 2.
36 *townspeople watching a slaveholder:* Fogg, letter to his parents, MSA.
36 *In 1833, the Legislative Council:* Kathryn T. Abbey, "The Union Bank of Tallahassee: An Experiment in Territorial Finance," *FHQ* 15, no. 4 (1936): 208–9.
37 *some 250 people:* T. Frederick Davis, *History of Jacksonville and Vicinity, 1513 to 1924* (St. Augustine: Florida Historical Society, 1925), 74–75, 415.
37 *several dozen scattered:* Fogg, letter to his parents; Davis, *History of Jacksonville,* 63, 68. I have assumed that a seventh store did not open between Christmas and New Year's of 1834.
37 *woman described it:* Denham and Huneycutt, *Echoes from a Distant Frontier,* 10.
37 *cotton production was centered:* Smith, *Slavery and Plantation Growth,* 10–11; Wayne, *Sweet Cane,* 40.
37 *waterways, delivering sugar boilers:* "History of Sugar Cane in Osceola Was Short but Sweet," *Orlando Sentinel,* February 12, 1995; Schene, *Hopes, Dreams, and Promises,* chap. 6.
37 *In October 1835:* Joseph M. Hernández to John Eaton, October 26, 1835, *TP* 25:189–90.
37 *owned three plantations:* Nicholas J. Linville, "Cultural Assimilation in Frontier Florida: The Life of Joseph M. Hernández, 1788–1857" (MA/nonthesis paper, University of Florida, 2004), 5–10; House of Representatives, *Hispanic Americans in Congress: 1822–2012* (Washington: U.S. Government Printing Office, 2013), 70–78.
38 *forwarded the letter:* Hernández to the Secretary of War, October 26, 1835, *TP* 25:189.

38 *warned Washington:* Duncan L. Clinch to the Adjutant General, October 8, 1835, *TP* 25:182–84.

38 *commander complained:* Duncan L. Clinch to the Adjutant General, November 3, 1835, *TP* 25:192–93. The attack may have happened November 1. Clinch says he heard the news on November 2 and was informed then that the event took place "a few days since." It depends on what Clinch means by "since."

38 *received orders to muster:* Brown, *Ossian Bingley Hart,* 32.

38 *did next to nothing:* In Cass to Clinch, October 22, 1835, *TP* 25:188, Clinch cites Jackson's limited executive capacity to act in self-defense of the country, blaming his refusal to authorize mounted men on congressional war powers. To me, this reads more as an excuse than a legitimate justification. Jackson was very aware—as he demonstrated, by invading Spanish Florida in 1818—of how flexible the notion of self-defense could be. See Schlesinger, *Imperial Presidency,* 35–37. Perhaps Jackson hoped to provoke a conflict to claim self-defense, but Jackson's later near-complete underestimation of the Florida War and dismissal of its seriousness suggests that he believed the warnings from Florida to be alarmist.

38 *over the abolitionists:* A. Eustis to F. Eustis, February 12, 1837.

38 *denied Clinch's:* Cass to Clinch, October 22, 1835. Later on, Cass authorizes the governor to supply Clinch with any militia that can be mustered. Lewis Cass to John Eaton, December 9, 1835, *ASP:MA* 6:1026. That order would not have reached Florida until after hostilities began.

39 *Cass also rebuffed:* Lewis Cass to Joseph M. Hernández, November 10, 1835, *TP* 25:194.

39 *speculators who were possessed:* Alexander C. W. Fanning to the Adjutant General, April 29, 1835, *TP* 25:132.

39 *directly to Jackson:* Thompson to Andrew Jackson, June 14, 1835, *ASP:MA* 6:478.

39 *the president reversed course:* Jackson, "Indorsement of the President," July 6, 1835, *ASP:MA* 6:478. While Thompson mentions that one officer will brief Jackson, in the event two were present.

40 *owned his son:* "Slaves of Harriet Bowlegs," in Casey, "Memoranda Concerning the Seminoles," 9.

40 *After Renty was born:* Ibid.

40 *transactions were duly transcribed:* Ibid.; Monaco, *Second Seminole War,* 212n81; "Deed of Sale, Micanopy, Chief of the Seminole Tribe of Indians (Ft. King)," May 6, 1834, Ancient Records Deed Book B, 66, Alachua County Clerk of the County Court, Gainesville, FL.

40 *had their three children's freedom:* "Letters Sent and Received Relating to Indian Affairs," Apr. 30, 1840–Aug. 27, 1851," Headquarters Records Fort Gibson, Indian Territory 1830–57, RG 393, NAMP M1466, roll 1, target 5, 28.

40 *their trained dogs:* John Walker and Jim Walker to Thompson, July 28, 1835, *ASP:MA* 6:463.

40 *as Thompson called them:* Thompson to Elbert Herring, November 24, 1834, *ASP:MA* 6:476;

40 *ever eager to cheat:* Thompson to Lewis Cass, December 2, 1833, *TP* 24:917.

40 *date for emigration:* Joseph W. Harris to Lewis Cass, October 12, 1835, *ASP:MA* 6:548; Thompson to Elbert Herring, October 28, 1835, *ASP:MA* 6:64.

41 *if an auction was held:* Thompson to Gibson, August 1, 1835, *ASP:MA* 6:541; Thompson to Gibson, August 29, 1835, *ASP:MA* 6:543; Thompson to George, September 21, 1835, *ASP:MA* 6:545; Gibson to Thompson, October 15, 1835, *ASP:MA* 6:549.

41 *would likely kill them:* Fanning to the Adjutant General, April 29, 1835.

41 *set a date for December:* Wiley Thompson, "Indian Affairs: Sale of Indian Cattle," *Jacksonville Courier*, November 19, 1835, 3; Thompson, "Indian Affairs: Sale of Indian Cattle," *Floridian*, December 5, 1835, 1; Thompson, "Indian Affairs: Sale of Indian Cattle," *Florida Herald*, October 22, 1835, 3.

41 *refused to reverse:* Potter, *War in Florida*, 96–97; William Hartley and Ellen Hartley, *Osceola: The Unconquered Indian* (New York: Hawthorn, 1973), 132.

41 *another recorded version of events:* Wickman, *Osceola's Legacy*, 16; Sprague, *Origin, Progress, and Conclusion*, 88; Porter, *Black Seminoles*, 35. I take issue with Wickman's assumption, echoed by Monaco, that Osceola was acting on behalf of the full Council. The "pro-removal" chiefs were part of the Council. By this logic, Emathla voted to have himself murdered. Additionally, why would an identical law punishing any who "agreed" to emigrate need to be passed after Micanopy's deposal if the law already existed? See chapter 16. If such a law existed and was agreed on, why would Abraham object to the killing? There is little reason to believe that Bemrose was doing anything but guessing. In Bemrose, *Reminiscences*, 31, he gets the date wrong by two months and qualifies his statement as a guess.

41 *more mundane report:* Reid to Forsyth, December 3, 1835, UFA.

41 *the Miccosukees had applied:* Jesup, "Diary," E for March 31, 1837.

41 *The victim either:* Boyd, "Asi-Yaholo or Osceola," 277–78; Call, "Journal and Transcriptions," 314, SLAF; Gloria Jahoda, *River of the Golden Ibis* (New York: Holt, Rinehart and Winston, 1973), 124.

42 *white journalists spread word:* "Indian Affairs," *Charlestown Courier*, December 9, 1835; "Indian Affairs," *Florida Herald*, December 3, 1835; "Indian Affairs," *Southern Patriot*, December 9, 1835.

42 *Fanning immediately messaged commander Clinch:* Mahon, *History of the Second Seminole War*, 109; Fanning to Clinch, November 27, 1835, *TP* 25:200; Fanning to Clinch, November 28, 1835, *TP* 25:203–4.

42 *Thompson appeared to react:* Thompson to Gibson, November 30, 1835, *ASP: MA* 6:80.

43 *published a new announcement:* Thompson, "To the Public," *Charlestown Courier*, December 9, 1835. This announcement would have appeared in the St. Augustine *Herald* on Thursday, December 3, 1835. Thompson, "To the Public," *Southern Patriot*, December 9, 1835, gets the date right.

FIVE: THE END

44 *St. Augustine's harbor:* The opening description of St. Augustine comes from An Invalid, *A Winter in the Indies and Florida* (New York: Wiley and Putnam, 1839), 142, 144–45, 157; Edward A. Mueller, "East Coast Florida Steamboating, 1831–1861," *FHQ* 40, no. 3 (1961): 242, 259; William W. Dewhurst, *The History of St. Augustine, Florida* (New York: G. P. Putnam's Sons, 1881), 147; Forbes, *Sketches, Historical and Topographical*, 87–89; Harper, "Ante-Bellum Census Enumerations," 46; U.S. Department of Commerce, *Fifteenth Census of the United States: 1930, Population* (Washington: U.S. Government Printing Office, 1931), 1:196.

45 *Travelers described the port:* Invalid, *Winter in the Indies*, 152; Moore, "South Carolina Lawyer," 366.

45 *loved drinking and dancing:* Nathan S. Jarvis to William Jarvis, August 9, 1837, in Jarvis, "Typescript of Letters," NYAM; Van Arsdol, *Frontier Soldier*, 33.

45 *John Audubon dismissed:* James Audubon to Lucy Audubon, December 5, 1831, in *Letters of John James Audubon, 1826–1840* (Boston: Kraus Reprint Co., 1930), 163.
45 *Northerners passing the:* Bemrose, *Reminiscences*, 109.
45 *a distinctly multiethnic flavor:* Ibid., 9–11; Patrick, *Aristocrat in Uniform*, 84; Motte, *Journey into Wilderness*, 113; Patricia C. Griffin, *Mullet on the Beach: The Minorcans of Florida, 1768–1788* (Gainesville: University of Florida Press, 2017), 24–25.
45 *Over one hundred:* Harper, "Ante-Bellum Census Enumerations," 45–46; Porter, "Negroes and the Seminole War," 433.
45 *Abraham visited in November:* Testimony of Captain G. S. Drane, in Gates, W—1844, File No. G62, NAMP M567 roll 285, 741.
45 *prophet had likely frequented:* "Deposition by Harman H. Holliman," November 24, 1832, *TP* 24:782.
46 *55 percent of items:* Weik, *Archaeology of Antislavery Resistance*, 144.
46 *included blankets, felt:* Glunt, "Plantation and Frontier Records," 2:246.
46 *organize the covert delivery:* Thomas Jesup to Lucien Webster, January 21, 1837, Webster, L B—1837, File No. W49, NAMP M567 roll 154, 151.
46 *fifty-three armed men:* R. Jones to Lewis Cass, February 9, 1836, *ASP:MA* 6:57.
46 *confiscated all the guns:* Joseph S. Sanchez to Frederick Weedon, [illegible] December 1835, Frederick Weedon Family Papers, SPR251 F1, file Q35738–40, AAH.
46 *veterans of past wars:* Joseph M. Hernández to [illegible, likely Frederick Weedon], December 18, 1835, Frederick Weedon Family Papers, SPR251 F1, file Q35856–57, AAH.
46 *Terrifying hearsay spread wildly:* James B. Mason to Sarah Mason, December 3, 1835, James B. Mason Letters, 1833–48, F1, UFA; Reid to Forsyth, December 3, 1835, UFA.
47 *the largest white settlement:* Chris Monaco, "Fort Mitchell and the Settlement of Alachua County," *FHQ* 79, no. 1 (2000): 21–22; Susan Yelton, "Newnansville: A Lost Florida Settlement," *FHQ* 53, no. 3 (1974): 322.
47 *Crossing the river:* Reid to Forsyth, December 3, 1835; Duncan Clinch to Acting Governor G. K. Walker, December 5, 1835, *TP* 25:208; D. L. Clinch to John Warren, December 3, 1835, Letters from General Clinch, 1820–47, F7, UFA. Reid is the local judge referenced.
47 *Destruction came:* Monaco, *Second Seminole War*, 54.
48 *three of Hernández's investments:* Committee of Claims, "Joseph M. Hernández," January 26, 1843, Ho. of Reps., Rep. No. 104, 27th Cong., 3rd Sess., 20–21, 53–56.
48 *that year, he'd borrowed:* Siebert, "Early Sugar Industry in Florida," 314.
48 *guard the city, he declined:* Hernández to Weedon, December 18, 1835. I have assumed, as the archivist has, that this letter is to Weedon. Note that on December 18, 1835, Hernández has already given the order to militiamen to guard the intracoastal labor camps. His men are committed elsewhere.
48 *Clinch pledged to counterattack:* Duncan Clinch to the Adjutant General, December 9, 1835, *TP* 25:209.
48 *The president advised the commander:* Jackson, Andrew. Referred to the Secretary of War that General Duncan L. Clinch move into the Indian towns, December 16, 1835, Pioneer Days in Florida, UF Digital Collections, UFA. Jackson and Clinch seem to be reacting to rumors.

48 *Clinch did not invade:* Duncan Clinch to the Adjutant General, December 26, 1835, in Clinch, "Clinch Letterbook." The pages of this bound volume are not numbered and the letters are not strictly chronological. By the time Clinch is writing this letter, the so-called Battle of Black Point has already taken place outside the boundaries of the Indian reservation, only eight days prior, on December 18, 1835.

48 *abandoned his pledge:* "I shall proceed immediately to Fort King," Clinch writes, on November 29, 1835. Duncan Clinch to the Adjutant General, November 29, 1835, *TP* 25:199. From the datelines that appear in *TP* 25 and the "Clinch Letterbook," we can see that Clinch was at Newnansville on December 5, Fort Defiance on December 9, and at Fort Drane by December 15, 1835. He is still based there on December 29 and returns there after the battle of December 31, 1835.

48 *Auld Lang Syne labor camp:* "Mortgage, Lang Syne Plantation," May 3, 1834, Legal and Land Documents for General Clinch, 1834–53, F6, Duncan Clinch Papers, Digital Collections UFA.

48 *some 180 sugar casks:* Potter, *War in Florida*, 5–6.

48 *Primus, a man with:* "Mortgage, Lang Syne Plantation," May 3, 1834; John W. Phelps to his sisters, January 16, 1837, Miscellaneous Manuscripts Collection, J. W. Phelps, LOC; Cushman, "Journal: 1836–1837," E for Wednesday, March 9, MHS.

48 *a half million dollars:* Patrick, *Aristocrat in Uniform*, 173, details that Clinch was compensated for losses of 205,000 pounds of sugar at the low price of eight cents a pound. Using Potter's estimate of Clinch's annual sugar production, that would correspond to a cask size of one thousand pounds of sugar, which is what is found in Committee of Claims, "Joseph M. Hernández," 9. Using an estimate of ten cents per pound, 180 hogsheads would bring $18,000. That was converted using www.officialdata.org/us/inflation.

48 *twenty-six miles northwest:* Robert Charles Stafford, "The Bemrose Manuscript on the Seminole War," *FHQ* 18, no. 4 (1939): 287.

48 *built pickets 12 feet high:* Patrick, *Aristocrat in Uniform*, 70.

49 *The site remained:* Monaco, "Alachua Settlers," 25.

49 *ordered all but one company:* Joseph W. Harris to Gibson, December 30, 1835, *ASP:MA* 6:561.

49 *Fort King's defensive walls:* Ibid.; Simmons, "Recollections of the Late Campaign," 543.

49 *an irregular pentagonal:* Gary D. Ellis, *Final Report: An Archaeological Study to Locate the Stockade Walls of Historic Fort King* (Crystal River, FL: Gulf Archaeology Research Institute, 1999), 18.

49 *entered from below:* Davis, *History of Jacksonville*, 77.

49 *Indian forces intercepted:* Clinch to the Adjutant General, December 16, 1835, *TP* 25:214.

49 *agent was warned:* "The Murder of Gen. Wiley Thompson," *Alexandria Gazette*, January 22, 1836.

49 *filled newspapers:* Wiley Thompson, "Communication. To the Editors," *Daily National Intelligencer*, July 18, 1826; "Congress Proceedings of Yesterday: Protest," *Alexandria Gazette*, May 10, 1826; "Congressional Summary: House of Representatives," *Augusta Chronicle*, December 31, 1825.

000 *one session with the president:* Thompson, "Creek Indians in Georgia"; "Letter from Wiley Thompson, a Representative in Congress from Georgia, to the editors of the *Georgia Journal*," *American Advocate*, June 20, 1829.

50 *Bedridden, a lame duck:* Reid, "Diary," E for May 12, 1835.

50 *watched the Stars and Stripes:* Herbert J. Doherty Jr., "The Governorship of Andrew Jackson," *FHQ* 33, no. 1 (1954): 10, 22–23.

50 *melting pot in the South:* Marquis James, *Andrew Jackson: The Border Captain* (Indianapolis, IN: Bobbs-Merrill, 1933), 340.

50 *men and women of color:* Landers, *Atlantic Creoles*, 3.

50 *gleaned the knowledge:* James, *Andrew Jackson*, 340.

51 *with other biters:* "Seminole War—First Campaign," May 30, 1837, 2.

51 *Jackson conveyed his instructions:* Lewis Cass to Duncan Clinch, December 9, 1835, NAMP M6 roll 14, vol. 14, January 2, 1834–January 18, 1836, 368–69.

51 *Clinch withdrew troops:* J. B. Crane, "Post Return of Fort King Florida for the Month of December, 1835," NAMP M617 roll 581.

51 *around three thirty in the afternoon:* Harris to Gibson, December 30, 1835.

SIX: PROPHECY

52 *Epigraph:* "Domestic Intelligence," *Army and Navy Chronicle*, November 3, 1836, 3.

52 *a pan-Indigenous alliance:* Gregory E. Dowd, "Thinking and Believing: Nativism and Unity in the Ages of Pontiac and Tecumseh," *American Indian Quarterly* 16, no. 3 (Summer 1992): 309; Kevin Kokomoor, *Of One Mind and of One Government: The Rise and Fall of the Creek Nation in the Early Republic* (Lincoln: University of Nebraska Press, 2019), 331; Michelene E. Pesantubbee, "When the Earth Shakes: The Cherokee Prophecies of 1811–12," *American Indian Quarterly* 17, no. 3 (Summer 1993), 302.

52 *Holy women protested:* Saunt, *New Order of Things*, 267.

52 *saw the vision:* Ibid., 234. As Saunt notes, Tecumseh's brother is known both as Tenskwatawa and as the Shawnee Prophet. Abraham's Indian title could be a reference to his role as a prophet.

52 *The Redstick prophet:* Frank L. Owsley, "Prophet of War: Josiah Francis and the Creek War," in *American Indian Prophets: Religious Leaders and Revitalization Movements*, ed. Clifford E. Trafzer (New Castle, CA: Sierra Oaks Publishing, 1986), 35. Prophecy itself, to be sure, was not new to La Florida.

52 *many subordinate sages:* Theron A. Nunez Jr., "Creek Nativism and the Creek War of 1813–1814," *Ethnohistory* 5, no. 1 (Winter 1858): 11.

53 *leading to what textbooks called:* Owsley, "Prophet of War," 40–41, 50; "Struggle for Survival, 1817–1858," Ah-Tah-Thi-Ki Museum, 2022, accessed March 3, 2025, https://www.ahtahthiki.com/struggle-for-survival-18171858/struggle-for-survival-one-war/.

53 *Master of Breath:* John T. Ellisor, *The Second Creek War* (Lincoln: University of Nebraska Press, 2010), 10; Bryan C. Rindfleisch, *Brothers of Coweta: Kinship, Empire, and Revolution in the Eighteenth-Century Muscogee World* (Columbia: University of South Carolina Press, 2021), 19.

53 *looked more like:* Donald L. Chamberlin, "Fort Brooke: Frontier Outpost," *Tampa Bay History* 7, no. 1 (1985): 6–29; Laumer, *Dade's Last Command*, 16; Mahon, "Journal of A. B. Meek," 308. The original reads "ornamented" not "ornamental." Meek, *Journal of the Florida Expedition*, E for March 6.

53 *sat off a grand shoreline:* McCall, *Letters from the Frontiers*, 133; Francis Belton to Harriet Kirby Belton, December 11, 1835, NYPL.

53 *hundred-some local civilians:* Belton to the Adjutant General, December 12, 1835, *TP* 25:211.

54 *only one hundred men:* Ibid.; F. S. Belton, "Autobiography," 48, NYPL.
54 *companies of soldiers:* Clinch to the Adjutant General, December 16, 1835, *TP* 25:214; Laumer, *Dade's Last Command*, 28.
54 *planned to attack:* Belton, "Autobiography," 49, puts the date as the thirty-first. Belton, "Major Belton's Official Report," 2, puts the date as the thirtieth. Clinch's plan is also mentioned in Harris to Gibson, December 30, 1835, *ASP:MA* 6:562. Belton's report and autobiography also contain the details about Abraham intercepting the letter.
54 *sense as a staging:* Clinch to the Adjutant General, December 16, 1835; Clinch to the Adjutant General, December 9, 1835, *TP* 25:210.
54 *ranking officer disembarked:* Belton, "Major Belton's Official Report." Dade arrives from Key West, not Louisiana. I have assumed "39 strong" includes Dade.
55 *London barrister:* Belton, "Autobiography," 2.
55 *communications blackout:* Belton to Kirby, December 11, 1835.
55 *preferred to resign:* Steele, "Last Command: The Dade Massacre," 6.
55 *Most officers agreed:* Laumer, *Dade's Last Command*, xvii, 24, 28.
55 *an unexpected event:* Belton, "Autobiography," 49.
56 *Dade reassured the:* Laumer, *Dade's Last Command*, 25, 34–47. The one-hundred -some soldiers is assuming the full strength of two companies.
57 *would terrify the Indians:* Belton, "Autobiography," 50.
57 *Nine years prior:* Brown, "Florida Crisis of 1826–1827," 432–35.
57 *twelve miles north:* Weisman, *Like Beads on a String*, 68.
57 *under Jackson during the invasion:* Laumer, *Dade's Last Command*, 83.
58 *he assured the captain:* Belton, "Autobiography," 50.
58 *three best civilian horses:* Belton, "Major Belton's Official Report."\
58 *linguist Louis Pacheco:* Porter, "Three Fighters for Freedom," 66.
58 *The enslaved interpreter:* Porter, "Early Life of Luis Pacheco," 52.
58 *a mix of Northern rabble:* Laumer, *Dade's Last Command*, 63.
58 *Dade messaged Belton again:* Belton, "Autobiography," 49–50.
58 *Halley's Comet tore across:* "The Comet," *Florida Herald*, October 29, 1835, 3.
59 *Spies sent word that:* Sprague, *Origin, Progress, and Conclusion*, 90. Sprague is the source of the strategy session with Osceola.
60 *fifty Miccosukee warriors:* Harris to Gibson, December 30, 1835, *ASP:MA* 6:562.
60 *held fast in the woods:* Sprague, *Origin, Progress, and Conclusion*, 89.
60 *saw Halley's Comet:* Michael J. Carlowicz and Ramon E. Lopez, *Storms from the Sun: The Emerging Science of Space Weather* (Washington, DC: Joseph Henry Press, 2002), 38.
60 *lured Thompson's spirit:* Weisman, *Like Beads on a String*, 106.
60 *three hundred yards:* Harris to Gibson, December 30, 1835.
60 *shrill battle cry:* Boyd, "Seminole War," 72–73; Potter, *War in Florida*, 111.
60 *was shot twice:* Harris to Gibson, December 30, 1835.
60 *the murdered sutler's cook:* Potter, *War in Florida*, 111.
60 *shoring up defenses:* Sprague, *Origin, Progress, and Conclusion*, 89; Harris to Gibson, December 30, 1835.
61 *the fourth quarter of 1835:* J. W. Harris, "Florida Removal: Statement of Agents for 4th Quarter 1835," n.d., 1835 Seminoles (Emigration), Statement of Agents, PQH.

SEVEN: TRESPASS

62 *Epigraph: The Book of the Prophet Jeremiah*, translated by S. R. Driver (London: Hodder and Stoughton, 1906), 125; *The Holy Bible: Containing the Old Testament and the New* (Concord, NH: Morrill, Silsby, and Co., 1843), 700.

62 *Seminoles routinely burned:* Gamble, "Extracts from Journal," 31–32, FSU.

62 *first to wander into:* Ibid.; Smith, *Slavery and Plantation Growth*, 22, 49–50; Marquis James, *Andrew Jackson: The Border Captain* (Indianapolis, IN: Bobbs-Merrill, 1933), 341; Kimelman, "Examination of Poor Whites," 1; Baptist, *Creating an Old South*, 16–17.

63 *alcoholics, gunfighters:* Denham, "'Rogue's Paradise.'"

63 *nephew Achille Murat:* A. J. Hanna, *A Prince in Their Midst: The Adventurous Life of Achille Murat on the American Frontier* (Norman: University of Oklahoma Press, 1946), 87.

63 *A society woman called them:* Denham and Huneycutt, *Echoes from a Distant Frontier*, xxiv.

63 *who followed by coach:* Hanna, *Prince in Their Midst*, 87.

63 *enslaved people cleared woods:* Smith, *Slavery and Plantation Growth*, 4, 15.

63 *cattleman of this sort:* Ibid., 4; Charles E. Whitehead, *The Camp-Fires of the Everglades or Wild Sports in the* South (Edinburgh: David Douglas, 1891), 37.

63 *general, the migrants:* Denham and Huneycutt, *Echoes from a Distant Frontier*, 20.

63 *only 0.6 inhabitants:* Harper, "Ante-Bellum Census Enumerations," 43.

63 *U.S. Census Bureau would not:* Hoffman, *Florida's Frontiers*, 283–84. This is a later standard, hence the wording "would not."

63 *standard of the Northwest Ordinance:* Peter S. Onuf, *Statehood and Union: A History of the Northwest Ordinance* (Indianapolis: Indiana University Press, 1987), xiv, xx, 59–60, 64.

64 *over ten thousand settlers shy:* Harper, "Ante-Bellum Census Enumerations," 44.

64 *advertisers championed the soil:* Hoffman, *Florida's Frontiers*, 294–95; "Life in Florida: Female Prowess," *New Hampshire Gazette*, April 18, 1837, 3.

64 *pledged rosy futures:* Whipple Aldrich, "For Sale," *Jacksonville Courier*, December 17, 1835, 3; I. D. Hart and James Dell, "Land at St. Pablo for Sale," *Jacksonville Courier*, December 17, 1835, 4; James Eslick, "Land for Sale," *Floridian*, December 12, 1835, 3; Willis Alston, "Plantations for Sale on a Long Credit," *Floridian*, December 5, 1835, 3.

64 *in roast turkey:* Kevin M. McCarthy, *Christmas in Florida* (Sarasota, FL: Pineapple Press, 2000), 24.

64 *sand pines too spindly:* Ruth Stanbridge, "Local History: Early Florida Settlers Used Native Trees for Christmas," *TCPalm*, December 1, 2021.

64 *shot pistols after dark:* McCarthy, *Christmas in Florida*, 26.

64 *men to meet Dade's:* Sprague, *Origin, Progress, and Conclusion*, 90, provides Alligator's estimate of 180. General Jesup puts the Indian force facing Dade at 170: Thomas Jesup, "Dade's battle," n.d., Papers of Thomas S. Jesup, Box 25, Seminole War Period, LOC.

64 *commanded eighty warriors:* The figure could be higher. This is the number given to Hitchcock by Black Dirt, in reference to the fight with Gaines. Drake, *Biography and History of the Indians*, 4:93; "Extract of a Letter from Captain Hitchcock, dated Tampa, March 20," *Daily Pittsburgh Gazette*, April 21, 1836, 2.

64 *ranks numbered around fifty:* Barr, *Indian War in Florida*, 10; Cohen, *Notices of Florida*, 72. Both of these sources draw from Ransom Clark's later and rather fanciful accounts. Both state, in my view unreliably, that the Black Seminoles somehow arrived after the battle was over, on horseback. Clark's August 1836

account makes no such claim (and reports merely that "the Indians are supposed to have been 800 strong with 100 negroes, who were more savage than the Seminoles"): "The Last of Major Dade's Command," *Niles' Register*, August 20, 1836. Belton's report, written days after the event based on what Clark and another survivor told him immediately afterward, also does not make that assertion. Belton, "Major Belton's Official Report," 3, instead reports that "about 100 Indians were well-mounted, naked, and painted." Nor does Belton's report attempt to define an artificial end to the battle or attempt to claim that the Black Seminole warriors somehow arrived after the fight was over. Belton merely reports that "many negroes were in the field." Alligator's report in Sprague, similarly, does not exclude them from the battle.

The famous sketch by Lieutenant Duncan that went with Belton's report clearly marks the "Position of Mounted Indians Who Did Not Participate." See Laumer, *Dade's Last Command*, 219–21. Somehow, these one hundred mounted Indians who did not participate became forty or fifty Black Seminoles who did not participate. Laumer, who claims that Abraham's men were not recognized as warriors, either engaged in an attempt at censorship or was poorly informed about the war writ large. McCall, *Letters from the Frontiers*, 311, similarly reports Bassinger's killer as Indian, as if August would admit culpability and contrary to the earliest, most reliable reports. McCall acknowledges that August was at the battle. He fought under Juan. Dembo Factor, whose first-person account puts him at the battle, fought under Abraham. Using Casey's 1837 lists, those two companies total forty-five fighters. Old Primus' men, allied with the Miccosukees, may not have been present and may have been with Osceola. See "Population of Flo. Indians: Seminole Forces," 2, and "Negro Warriors in the Sem Nation," 11–14, in Casey, "Memoranda Concerning the Seminoles"; "Story of a Former Slave: The Massacre of Major Dade's Command by Seminole Indians," *Atlanta Constitution*, March 12, 1888.

64 *trusted counselor and skilled soldier:* Doc. No. 225, 77, 68. See entries 72 and 73. As others have noted, "Ino" is a transcription error. The original reads "Juan." See entries 70 and 71 in "Register of Indian and Negro Prisoners Captured in '36 '37," R&L F1. For the ages and familial relationships listed see Doc. No. 225, 67–68, 75–77, 79, 84–86; Lorenzo and Mock, *My Black Seminole Ancestors*, 12.

65 *for over a year:* Sprague, *Origin, Progress, and Conclusion*, 90.

65 *had purchased gunpowder:* Thompson to Elbert Herring, October 28, 1835, *ASP:MA* 6:64; Thomas Douglas, *Autobiography of Thomas Douglas: Late Judge of the Supreme Court of Florida* (New York: Calkins and Stiles, 1856), 121, SULF.

65 *women and children had evacuated:* Thompson to Gibson, December 7, 1835, *ASP:MA* 6:560; Potter, *War in Florida*, 109; "Copy of a Letter received at the office of the *Times and Gazette*, dated Fort Brooke, Tampa Bay, April 13, 1836," *Cheraw Gazette*, May 3, 1836, 2.

65 *eight miles west of Pilaklikaha:* Potter, *War in Florida*, 109.

65 *good head-collars for horses:* Gamble, "Extracts from Journal," 45.

65 *sixty-three-thousand-acre wetland:* Monaco, *Second Seminole War*, 52–53; Brent Weisman, "The Cove of the Withlacoochee: A First Look at the Archaeology of an Interior Florida Wetland," *Florida Anthropologist* 39, nos. 1–2 (March–June 1986): 4.

65 *natural fortifications:* J. W. Phelps to John Phelps, July 10, 1837, NYPL.

66 *On December 28, 1835:* Sprague, *Origin, Progress, and Conclusion*, 90.

66 *Known as "the Lawyer"*: George E. Harral to E. A. Hitchcock, October 9, 1836, *ASP:MA* 7:435; Foreman, "Jumper Family," 273; "List of Seminole Indians & Negro Prisoners at Fort Pike La this 28th day of Feby 1838," R&L F3, PQH.
66 *against Andrew Jackson's forces:* William Warren Chapman, "A West Point Graduate in the Second Seminole War," *FHQ* 68, no. 4 (1989): 469–70.
66 *he was of the Yamasees:* Foreman, "Jumper Family," 279; Swanton, *Early History,* 107, 412.
66 *insisted that he came:* Cohen, *Notices of Florida,* 239; *ASP:MA* 6:66.
66 *deeply loyal:* Clay MacCauley, *Seminole Indians of Florida,* 508.
66 *On the contrary:* Sprague, *Origin, Progress, and Conclusion,* 90.
67 *a semicircle:* Boyd, "Seminole War," 92; Clark, "Dade Massacre."
67 *the "Big Hillsborough" River:* W. T. B., "Dade Massacre," 2. Louis Pacheco's account is drawn from this source and Lynn Dale, "Interesting Account by Eye Witnesses, and the Two Sole Survivors of the Dade Massacre by the Seminole Indians in 1836," *Florida Metropolis,* November 29, 1913.
67 *town of Thlonoto-sassa:* Laumer, *Dade's Last Command,* 61–62; Kenneth Wiggins Porter, "Thlonoto-Sassa: A Note on an Obscure Seminole Village of the Early 1820s," *Florida Anthropologist* 13, no. 4 (December 1960): 115–19.
68 *to the Indians as Capikch:* "O. Bowlegs story about the abduction on 2d June," July 24, 1837, in Casey, "Memoranda Concerning the Seminoles," 3. The index in the back of Casey's journal provides full titles, by topic, for his entries.
68 *slept behind the trunks:* Boyd, "Seminole War," 90.
69 *hounds behaved strangely:* W. T. B., "Dade Massacre," 2.
69 *Dade was calm and confident:* Clark, "Dade Massacre."
69 *around 9:00 a.m.:* Sprague, *Origin, Progress, and Conclusion,* 90. Belton's report, cited above, puts the time at ten o'clock, as Pacheco does. Clark says 9:00 a.m. Steele, "Last Command," 12, 15.
69 *silvery mare:* In Steele, "Last Command," 15, the horse is gray; in W. T. B., "Dade Massacre," the horse is white.
69 *Micanopy yelled Dade's name:* "Story of a Former Slave," *Atlanta Constitution.*
69 *Jumper gave the war cry:* Sprague, *Origin, Progress, and Conclusion,* 91.
69 *Micanopy, to the end:* Laumer, *Dade's Last Command,* 180–81; A. C. M. Azoy, "Dade and His Command," *Esquire,* April 1944, 61.

EIGHT: KINSHIP

70 *Epigraph:* Jesup to John Bell, June 8, 1841, NAMP 574 roll 13, Special File 96.
70 *women ennobled men:* "Extract of a Letter," *Vermont Phoenix,* 2.
70 *husbands were all chiefs:* Monaco, *Second Seminole War,* 50; Kieffer, *Maligned General,* 155; Porter, *Black Seminoles,* 35, 69; Wickman, *Osceola's Legacy,* 24.
70 *Philip was most formidable:* Sprague, *Origin, Progress, and Conclusion,* 324; George Catlin, *Letters and Notes on the Conditions and Customs of the North American Indians* (London: Tosswill and Myers, 1841), 2:220.
70 *Philip reportedly commanded:* Drake, *Biography and History of the Indians,* 4:93, puts Micanopy, Jumper, and Abraham's total troops at 190; Casey to Jesup, July 24, 1837, NARA RG 94, E159-Q, Box 6, Casey, puts Miccosukee forces at 295 in total and Philip's forces at 350. These numbers come from 1837 and are of course imprecise. "Population of Flo. Indians: Seminole Forces," in Casey, "Memoranda Concerning the Seminoles," 87–88, puts Miccosukee forces in 1836 at 265.
70 *succession rules were flexible:* Harry A. Kersey Jr., *The Seminole and Miccosukee Tribes: A Critical Bibliography* (Indianapolis: Indiana University Press, 1987), 20.

70 *a compromise candidate:* "King Payne's Family," in Casey, "Memoranda Concerning the Seminoles," 72–73, states that Micanopy was related to William or Billy Bowlegs but that he had "≠ relation to King Payne" and was "elected during William's minority."
71 *brother was made a chief:* Hughes, "Diary: Transcript," 53, USF; Jarvis, "Floridian War: Transcript," 46, NYAM.
71 *Among the elite, marriages:* Dixon, *Florida's Negro War*, 24.
71 *who were candid:* Jesup to Poinsett, June 16, 1837, NARA RG 94, E159-Q, Box 36, 201.
71 *interrupted by nine Indians:* Ibid., 62; Jane Murray Sheldon, "Seminole Attacks near New Smyrna, 1835–1856," *FHQ* 8, no. 4 (1929): 189.
71 *in a long line:* Laumer, *Dade's Last Command*, 182; W. T. B., "Dade Massacre," 2; Sprague, *Origin, Progress, and Conclusion*, 90–91; Boyd, "Seminole War," 92.
71 *A dazed lieutenant:* Clark, "Dade Massacre."
72 *one-ounce lead balls:* Laumer, *Dade's Last Command*, 186–87, 192–93.
72 *Men met in a clinch:* Belton, "Major Belton's Official Report," 3.
72 *cannon smoke cleared:* Sprague, *Origin, Progress, and Conclusion*, 91.
72 *velvet case:* Simmons, "Recollections of the Late Campaign," 557.
72 *was shot in the thigh:* "The Last of Major Dade's Command," *Niles' Register*, August 20, 1836.
72 *entered near his temple:* Clark, "Dade Massacre."
73 *tomahawked him:* Ibid.; Belton, "Major Belton's Official Report," 2; "Slaughter of a Detachment of U.S. Troops by the Seminoles, on the 28th of December," *Hartford Courant*, February 1, 1836, 2; Edward P. Lawton, "William Elon Basinger: A Georgian Who Died for Florida," *Georgia Historical Quarterly* 45, no. 2 (June 1961): 107.
73 *included a castration:* Laumer, *Dade's Last Command*, 206.
73 *Jumper said:* W. T. B., "Dade Massacre," 2.
73 *around a pole of scalps:* Sprague, *Origin, Progress, and Conclusion*, 91.
73 *the form of a dog:* Boyd, "Seminole War," 90.
74 *stalked by beasts:* Steele, "Last Command," 14; Clark, "Dade Massacre."
74 *He was treated:* Laumer, *Dade's Last Command*, 212; Frank Laumer, "The Incredible Adventures of Ransom Clark," *Tampa Bay History* 3, no. 2 (1981): 11; "Last of Major Dade's Command," *Niles' Register*; Bemrose, *Reminiscences*, 65.
74 *long enough to pen:* Francis Belton to Harriet Kirby Belton, January 1, 1835, NYPL.
74 *Belton set fire to:* Ibid.; Cushman, "Journal: 1836–1837," E for Wednesday, February 10, MHS; Belton, "Major Belton's Official Report," 3.
74 *dance were invited:* Sheldon, "Seminole Attacks Near New Smyrna," 189–92; Carrier, "Trade and Plunder Networks," 74; "From the *St. Augustine Herald* of January 13, 1835," *ASP:MA* 6:21.
75 *an estimated seventy-five others:* "War with the Seminoles," *Niles' Register*, January 30, 1836.
75 *never used to produce:* Wayne, *Sweet Cane*, 120.
75 *160 souls were liberated:* "From the *St. Augustine Herald*," *ASP:MA* 6:21–22.
75 *Barges floated away:* Carrier, "Trade and Plunder Networks," 75, 78–81, 138. Details of the destruction and its costs come from Monaco, *Second Seminole War*, 58; Wayne, *Sweet Cane*, 42–43, 99, 132; Siebert, "Early Sugar Industry in Florida," 316; "From the *St. Augustine Herald*," *ASP:MA* 6:22; Douglas, *Autobiography of Thomas Douglas*, 120–22, SLUF; Jones, "Memoir Transcript," 59–60; Cohen, *Notices of Florida*, 79, 89–90; Boyd, "Seminole War," 66.

77 *to trek up the coast:* Jones, "Memoir Transcript," 60.
77 *scarlet glow was visible:* Boyd, *Florida Aflame*, 116.

NINE: FIDELITY

78 *Epigraph:* "Seminole War—First Campaign," May 9, 1836, 3.
78 *Abraham met the enemy:* Francis Belton to the Adjutant General, January 14, 1836, NARA RG 94, Letters Received, B92, 2, reads, "He says *Abram* was on the ground at Withlacoochee but made off on the first fire." This information comes from a POW interrogation at a moment when the Americans are afraid and trying to ascertain Abraham's intentions. It reads to me like a perfect way to protect an ally in case he was spotted by others at the battle. You don't command eighty men and run off at the first shot and retain command, no matter what side you're fighting on. Warriors fired from concealed positions during this battle. Monaco, *Second Seminole War*, 61; Porter, "Negro Abraham," 19–20.
78 *200 men with 120 warriors:* Frank Laumer "Encounter by the River," 323; Thomas Jesup, "Clinch's battle," n.d., Papers of Thomas S. Jesup, Box 25, Seminole War Period, LOC, lists one hundred Miccosukees and twenty Black warriors present for "Clinch's battle." Likewise, according to Cudjo's son Ned, Osceola was in command of "less than 100 Miccosukees" that day. "Mem. of Clinch's Battle of 31 Dec.," in Casey, "Memoranda Concerning the Seminoles," 25; Andrew Jackson, "Message from the President of the United States," February 9, 1836, Doc. 152, 424th Cong., 1st Sess., in Adjutant General, *Florida War*, reports two hundred regulars. *Sprague, Origin, Progress, and Conclusion*, 92, has higher Indigenous forces. I have gone with Jesup's figure—the Americans tended to exaggerate the strength of Seminoles forces, which in my mind makes the lower number more credible.
78 *double-breasted military jacket:* Laumer, "Encounter by the River," 331.
78 *the most visible man:* Boyd, "Seminole War," 76–78.
78 *spanned for nearly a mile:* Bemrose, *Reminiscences*, 56.
78 *Indians lost three:* Jesup, "Clinch's battle"; "Mem. of Clinch's Battle," in Casey, 25.
79 *storytelling and self-promotion:* Laumer, "Encounter by the River," 323; Stanley, "Tennessee Volunteers," *THQ* 2, no. 3 (1943): 252.
79 *with five hundred militiamen:* Monaco, *Second Seminole War*, 60.
79 *army of the era:* Covington, *Seminoles of Florida*, 77; Coffman, *Old Army*, 6, 66–67; Monaco, *Second Seminole War*, 69.
79 *Clinch publicly outed:* "D. L. Clinch's Reply to Governor Cass," *Niles' Weekly Register*, July 15, 1837; "Gov. Call to Gen. Clinch," *Floridian*, July 22, 1837, 1; "D. L. Clinch to the People of Florida," *Army and Navy Chronicle*, December 21, 1837, 1.
80 *officers and enlisted men testified:* Laumer, "Encounter by the River," 336n37.
80 *few volunteers who did cross:* Journal of a Private, "Battle of the Ouithlacoochee," *New Hampshire Gazette*, May 16, 1837, 3.
80 *Floridians demanded to know:* Civis, "Communications," *Jacksonville Courier*, December 31, 1835, 3.
80 *unable to protect the people:* Childs, "Correspondence with His Family," *HM* 2, no. 5 (1873): 301; McGaughy, "Lynch's Journal," 77. The McGaughy citation refers to 1837, but the same sentiment pervaded in early and mid-1836. "United States," *St. George Chronicle and Grenada Gazette*, April 9, 1836, 119; Winfield Scott, "General Order," *Niles' Register*, June 4, 1836.
81 *gloating in private letters:* William Llyod Garrison to George Thompson, May 24, 1836, in *A House Divided Against Itself: The Letters of William Lloyd Garrison*, ed. Louis Ruchames (Cambridge, MA: Belknap Press, 1971), 2:105–6.

81 *Jackson's January 2, 1836, bill:* Meacham, *American Lion*, 321–22; Remini, *Life of Andrew Jackson*, 281–82; Bassett, *Correspondence of Andrew Jackson*, 5:382–3.
81 *in 1834, a blaze sparked:* Remini, *Jackson and the Course of American Democracy*, 184–85, 187.
81 *faux Grecian colonnade:* Ibid., 332; Remini, *Life of Andrew Jackson*, 281.
82 *issuing placid directives:* Cass to Clinch and Cass to Thompson, January 11, 1836, *ASP:MA* 6:564.
82 *spread slowly, south to north:* "Indian Hostilities," *Alexandria Gazette*, January 13, 1836, 2; "Indian War!," *Richmond Enquirer*, January 7, 1836, 2; "The Indians in Florida," *Charlotte Journal*, January 15, 1836, 3.
82 *come to be known:* Joel Poinsett to Thomas Jesup, August 3, 1837, *TP* 25:411.
82 *a Jackson ally insisted:* "Debates in Congress: Extracts from the Speech of Mr. Cambreleng," *Vermont Phoenix*, March 18, 1836.
82 *editor blamed troops:* "Florida," *Fall River Monitor*, May 12, 1836, 2.
82 *published a column expressing: Burlington Weekly Free Press*, February 5, 1836, 3.
83 *reached the War Department:* Lewis Cass to D. L. Clinch, January 16, 1836, *ASP:MA* 6:564.
83 *from an old ally:* James Gadsden to Andrew Jackson, January 14, 1836 *TP* 25:224–26; James Gadsden to Andrew Jackson, January 14, 1836, Andrew Jackson Papers, LOC. I have added the quotes around "something must be done" for clarity.
84 *short by roughly one thousand:* Casey to Jesup, July 24, 1837, NARA RG 94 E159-Q, Box 6, Casey.
84 *longest American wars:* Stephen Hahn, *A Nation Without Borders: The United States and Its World in an Age of Civil Wars, 1830–1910* (New York: Penguin, 2016), 4.
84 *at 11:00 a.m., members of:* "Proceedings of the Legislative Council," *Floridian*, February 6, 1836, 2.
84 *two-story brick building:* "The Capitol," Florida Department of State, accessed December 25, 2024, https://dos.fl.gov/florida-facts/florida-history/the-capitol/; Writers Program, "Capitol Building of Tallahassee," April 28, 1838, UFA.
84 *two dozen officials who:* Charles Bowen, *The American Almanac and Repository of Useful Knowledge for the Year 1836* (Boston: Charles Bowen, 1835), 257.
84 *fighting together, had decimated:* John Eaton to Lewis Cass, January 17, 1836, in Abraham Eustis to the Adjutant General, NARA RG94, Letters Received, E16 1836, 1, NAMP M567 roll 122, 629.
84 *spread to the North:* For instance, see "Slaughter of a Detachment of U.S. Troops by the Seminoles, on the 28th of December," *Connecticut Courant*, February 1, 1836, 2, which notes Belton's report as having already appeared in the "Washington papers" and excerpts it. See also "Indian Massacre!," *Mobile Commercial Register and Patriot*, January 11, 1836, in Ethan Hitchcock to the Adjutant General, January 12, 1836, NARA RG 94, Letters Received, H19 1836, NAMP M567 roll 124, 751.
85 *no mention of a rebellion:* "Indian Devastations," *New Orleans Commercial Bulletin*, February 27, 1836, 2.
85 *who knew better drafted:* See chap. 930 [No. XIX] in *Acts of the Governor and Legislative Council of the Territory of Florida Passed at the Fourteenth Session* (Tallahassee, FL: William Wilson, 1836), 13–15, 19.
85 *Black Seminole messengers visited:* "Seminole War: First Campaign," *New Hampshire Gazette*, May 9, 1837, 3; Wickman, *Osceola's Legacy*, 84; Bemrose, *Reminiscences*, 52.

86 *Cooley, a squatter:* Joe Knetsch, "William Cooley and the Land Office: A Note on Frontier Settlement," *Broward Legacy* 16, nos. 1–2 (1993): 21; Cooper Kirk, "William Cooley: Broward's Legend," *Broward Legacy* 1, no. 1 (1976): 12, 17; Committee on Claims, "William Cooley," July 10, 1840, Ho. of Reps., Rep. No. 695, 26th Cong., 1st Sess., American Indian and Alaskan Native Documents in the Congressional Serial Set: 1817–99, UOA.

86 *Cooley was barely literate:* William Cooley to Thomas Jesup, February 29, 1837, NARA RG 94, E 159-Q, Box 19, Letters Received Relating to Creek and Seminole Affairs, May 1836.

86 *Cooley took the assassins:* Kirk, "William Cooley," 17.

86 *Philip's men raided:* West, "Abiaka, or Sam Jones," 382, attributes the raid to Abiaka, but King Philip appears to have been responsible. John H. Winder to H. Garner, May 1, 1837, "Florida Military Post Supplies and Operations during Indian Wars, Lieutenant John Winder Correspondence," F1, PQH. It reads, "I have been told by several people that a man by the name of Cooley has declared that he meant to kill the Indian chief Philip when ever he saw him be the consequences what they may."

86 *Philip's son Wild Cat:* Monaco, *Second Seminole War*, 58.

TEN: GRACE

87 *Epigraph:* Secretary of War, "Court of Inquiry—Operations in Florida, &c.," January 8, 1838, Ho. of Reps., Doc. No. 78, 25th Cong., 2nd Sess, 173. Hereafter referred to as Doc. No. 78.

87 *Regulars and volunteers:* Monaco, *Second Seminole War*, 64–65.

87 *an astonished private observed:* McGaughy, "Lynch's Journal," 13.

87 *a single company of fifty-five:* "Enlisted Soldiers," *Army and Navy Chronicle*, June 13, 1839.

87 *Greenhorns yearned for:* Monaco, *Second Seminole War*, 65; Clinch to Call, February 7, 1836, Clinch, "Clinch Letterbook," LOC.

87 *made up the rest:* "For the Floridian," *Floridian*, January 16, 1836, 3. The basic error of attributing to Osceola primary leadership of the war, widely and incorrectly reported at the time, still appears in American history books.

87 *Newspapers promised soldiers:* "From the *St. Augustine Herald* of January 13, 1835," *ASP:MA* 6:21.

88 *Patriots seemed eager:* Cushman, "Journal: 1836–1837," E for February 10, MHS.

88 *New Orleans, word spread:* Canter Brown Jr., "Persifor F. Smith, the Louisiana Volunteers, and Florida's Second Seminole War," *Louisiana History: The Journal of the Louisiana Historical Association* 34, no. 4 (Autumn 1993): 395–97.

88 *a recruit testified:* Cushman, "Journal: 1836–1837," E for February 7.

88 *thirteen hundred troops:* Ibid., E for February 10.

88 *disturbed to find:* Barr, *Indian War in Florida*, 4–5; Mahon, "Journal of A. B. Meek," 307–8.

88 *included not only:* McCall, *Letters from the Frontiers*, 310; Francis Belton to Commander Dallas, February 1, 1835, NARA RG 45, Records Collection of the Office of Naval Records and Library, Correspondence, 1798–1918, Press Copies of Reports Sent Concerning Navy and Marine Corps Service in the Second Seminole War, 1835–42, E-61, I-18 1:38.

88 *explained to his wife:* Francis Belton to Harriet Kirby Belton, February 12, 1836, NYPL. The date of February 12 is assumed, since Belton informs his wife that he will march the next day, and the troops marched on the thirteenth.

89 *eleven hundred soldiers:* Cushman, "Journal: 1836–1837," E for February 15, 1836.

89 *ten days' provisions:* Barr, *Indian War in Florida*, 5.

89 *Military staples of the era:* A. C. S., "Provisions Remaining on Hand at Garey's Ferry Fla. October 29, 1837," NARA RG 94 E 159-Q, Box 17, Letters Received from Officers, Lieutenant John Winder, F2; John Casey, "Statement of Subsistence Stores on hand at the Depots of Fort Brooke Flo. on the 16th day of April, 1838," NARA RG 94, E 159-Q, Box 6.

89 *over eighteen thousand pounds:* Potter, *War in Florida*, 135; Cushman, "Journal: 1836–1837," E for December 2, 1836; McGaughy, "Lynch's Journal," 80.

89 *infested with weevils:* Irwin, "Memoir, 1836," 18, UFA.

89 *camp of twenty tents:* Motte, *Journey into Wilderness*, 49–50.

89 *twelve pounds of corn:* Truman Cross, "Memorandum for the Secretary of War," November 3, 1836, NARA RG 94 E 159-Q, Box 7, Letters Received from Officers, Lieutenant T. Cross, F1.

89 *seven miles the first day:* Laumer, *Amidst a Storm of Bullets*, 11. Prince also mentions the lieutenant's accident and the disenchanted volunteers.

90 *sun and rain had weathered:* Ibid., 12–13; Cushman, "Journal: 1836–1837," E for February 20, 1836; Belton, "Autobiography," 52, NYPL; Laumer, *Dade's Last Command*, 3–4.

90 *thirty or so bodies:* Hitchcock, *Fifty Years in Camp and Field*, 90.

90 *if they had been scalped:* Laumer, *Amidst a Storm of Bullets*, 13.

90 *Sallow skulls rested on:* McCall, *Letters from the Frontiers*, 306.

90 *Belton wrote:* Laumer, *Dade's Last Command*, 8.

90 *dental work, and jewelry:* Cushman, "Journal: 1836–1837," E for February 20, 1836. According to Cushman, the song was "Scots Wha Hae."

90 *buried as a group:* Ibid.; Belton, "Autobiography," 52.

90 *the funereal song drifted west:* "Mem. of Gaines' campaign," in Casey, "Memoranda Concerning the Seminoles," 22. "Abram" is credited as the source at the bottom of page 24.

91 *Oranges, plums, and grapes:* "Seminole War—First Campaign," April 25, 1837, 3.

91 *could harvest coontie root:* Phelps, "Journal (Loose Leaves)," E for March 19, 1838; Kirby, "Diary," E March 18, 1838, UFA.

91 *Abraham said, as:* "Domestic Intelligence," *Army and Navy Chronicle*, November 3, 1836. Abraham may well have said this later in the year, but the same sentiment would have held in February.

91 *few outsiders who heard:* Irwin, "Memoir, 1836," 33; Hollingsworth, "Tennessee Volunteers," *THQ* 2, no. 1 (March 1943): 61–62. The Irwin document is mislabeled; it is identical, with a few differences, to the series of Hollingsworth articles. In cases where the differences (what has been edited out) are important, I continue to cite them independently.

91 *Hewn-log homes:* R. K. Call to the Secretary of the Navy, November 27, 1836, 2, Richard Keith Call Papers, SLAF.

91 *Five hundred more:* Cushman, "Journal: 1836–1837," E for March 6, 1836.

91 *Payne's army had routed the Georgia:* Cusick, "King Payne and His Policies," 47.

91 *claimed few warriors:* "Affair at Bowleg's Town," 16 April, 1818, NAMP 1832 roll 6, 256; A. Arbuthnot to John Arbuthnot, April 2, 1818, *ASP:MA* 1:722, which reads, regarding Jackson's planned attack on Suwannee Old Town, "So soon as the Sahwahnee is destroyed, I expect the Americans will be satisfied and retire."

92 *by the orange tree:* Cohen, *Notices of Florida*, 174.
92 *rainy cold, around 4:00 p.m.:* Cushman, "Journal: 1836–1837," E for February 27, 1836.
92 *rapid, 120-foot-wide:* McCall, *Letters from the Frontiers*, 325.
92 *could still not cross:* Cushman, "Journal: 1836–1837," E for February 28, 1836.
92 *Warriors followed them:* McCall, *Letters from the Frontiers*, 326–27.
92 *the corner of his eye:* Belton, "Autobiography," 54. Izard died on March 5, according to Cushman's entry of that day, around 10:00 a.m.
92 *"to cross the river without":* Cushman, "Journal: 1836–1837," Es for February 28 and February 39, 1836; McCall, *Letters from the Frontiers*, 327.
93 *catching two dislodged teeth:* Hitchcock, *Fifty Years in Camp and Field*, 93.
93 *reportedly numbered over eleven hundred:* Belton, "Autobiography," 54.
93 *small-caliber bullets:* Laumer, *Dade's Last Command*, 192; Cushman, "Journal: 1836–1837," E for February 28, 1836. Also see Cushman's entries for March 1, 2, and 3.
93 *lighting large fires:* Barr, *Indian War in Florida*, 17.
93 *March 4, the troops:* Cushman, "Journal: 1836–1837," E for March 4, 1836.
93 *ammunition grew scarce:* Barr, *Indian War in Florida*, 17.
93 *Orleans were reduced to:* Monaco, *Second Seminole War*, 70.
93 *Soldiers foraged for roots:* Barr, *Indian War in Florida*, 17; Belton, "Autobiography," 64; Laumer, *Amidst a Storm of Bullets*, 26.
94 *Miccosukees held a Council:* "Mem. of Gaines' campaign," in Casey, 22.
94 *Given no other option:* Hitchcock, *Fifty Years in Camp and Field*, 94, 138.
94 *Abraham approached:* Potter, *War in Florida*, 154–55; Testimony of Captain Thistle, Doc. No. 78, 173.
95 *Word of the promised visit:* Testimony of Captain Thistle, Doc. No. 78, 173; Cushman, "Journal: 1836–1837," E for March 6, 1836; Laumer, *Amidst a Storm of Bullets*, 24–25. Potter says eight thirty; Prince says seven thirty. I've split the difference.
95 *the Creek rebel looking:* McCall, *Letters from the Frontiers*, 329.
95 *the talks, through Abraham:* Potter, *War in Florida*, 156–58; George E. Harral to E. A. Hitchcock, October 9, 1836, Doc. No. 78, 766–67.
95 *let the famished men fish:* Testimony of Captain Thistle, Doc. No. 78, 173.
95 *afternoon, the same envoys:* Hitchcock, *Fifty Years in Camp and Field*, 138; Childs, "Correspondence with His Family," *HM* 3, no. 4 (1874): 280; Laumer, *Amidst a Storm of Bullets*, 74; Monaco, *Second Seminole War*, 71–72; *ASP:MA* 7:454. The encounter in which the army refuses to continue talks after Clinch arrives derives from Childs and Hitchcock.
96 *emaciated soldiers were rescued:* Bemrose, *Reminiscences*, 77.

ELEVEN: CONTAGION

97 *Epigraph:* Cushman, "Journal: 1836–1837," E for December 13, 1836, MHS.
97 *gathered in the west:* "Seminole War—First Campaign," June 6, 1837, 2.
97 *summer deluges came:* Childs, "Correspondence with His Family," *HM* 2, no. 5 (1873): 301.
98 *the crowded steamships:* Ivy, *Distinguished Light*, 149.
98 *Dry seasons brought rare gusts:* Jarvis, "Diary: Army in Florida," E for October 1, 1838, 148, NYAM.
98 *the skies escorted:* N. S. Jarvis to W. Jarvis, August 9, 1837, "Typescript of Letters," NYAM.

98 *roaming Abraham's former home:* Jones, "Memoir Transcript," 63, UFA.
98 *Soldiers marched toward the Cove:* Monaco, *Second Seminole War,* 73–75; Mahon, *History of the Second Seminole War,* 151–52.
98 *who dreamed of war:* Allan Peskin, *Winfield Scott and the Profession of Arms* (London: Kent State University Press, 2003), 33.
98 *The military pamphlet:* "Artillery Tactics," Robert Anderson Papers, 1836–39, Box 2, Mar. 9–Sep. 21, LOC.
98 *settled in and marches became:* "Colonel Lindsay's testimony," December 8, 1836, Doc. No. 78, 152; Jones, "Memoir Transcript," 65.
98 *multiplied in limestone sinks:* "General Eustis in continuation," December 9, 1836, Doc. No. 78, 159–60.
98 *the Suwannee River, maladies:* Irwin, "Memoir, 1836," 9, UFA.
99 *recorded the terminal causes:* "Register of Soldiers Killed in Action During the Florida War, 1835–42," NARA RG 94, Records of Divisions, Appointment, Commission and Personal Branch, 1783–1917, Box 1 PI 17 E 331, 332.
99 *a mosquito-infested marsh:* Bemrose, *Reminiscences,* 33; Assistant Surgeon [illegible] to J. A. Chambers, April 23, 1837, NARA RG 94, E 159-Q, Box 2, Letters Received from Adjutant General's Office August 1837, Surgeon General's Office 1837.
99 *slept in the slave:* Mahon, *History of the Second Seminole War,* 107.
99 *temporary shed badly roofed:* Bemrose, *Reminiscences,* 34, 95.
99 *forced labor camp were healthy:* Assistant Surgeon to Chambers, April 23, 1837.
99 *Desperate cases filled:* Bemrose, *Reminiscences,* 95–96.
99 *Aggressive interventions included:* C. S. Monaco, "Shadows and Pestilence: Health and Medicine During the Second Seminole War," *Journal of Social History* 48, no. 3 (Spring 2015): 568.
100 *requested at Fort Drane:* W. P. Bowles, "Requisition for Medicines, Hospital Stores, Books, Instruments &c for use of the Hospital at Fort Drane E. Florida & Army in the field," November 11, 1836, and "Invoice of Medicines, Instruments, Hospital Stores, &c," November 13, 1835, NARA RG 94 E 159-Q, Box 20, Letters Received Relating to Creek and Seminole Affairs, September–December 1836.
100 *Eleven regulars died:* The earliest on April 25. The "sickly season" in Florida started in April. "Register of Soldiers Killed in Action," NARA RG 94, E 331, 332, Box 1.
100 *not comprehensively recorded:* Monaco, *Second Seminole War,* 139.
100 *claimed many names:* Bemrose, *Reminiscences,* 79, 98.
100 *After one grueling march:* Monaco, "Shadows and Pestilence," 572; Irwin, "Memoir, 1836," 29–30.
100 *a man shrieked, before:* Bemrose, *Reminiscences,* 99, 102–3.
100 *outpost was finally evacuated:* Monaco, *Second Seminole War,* 78.
100 *soldiers fled and their enemies:* "Further News from Florida," *Long-Island Star,* May 12, 1836, 5. Forts Drane and King were evacuated a bit later than this report; the quote holds true.
100 *took over Fort Drane:* Porter, *Black Seminoles,* 58–59; Hollingsworth, "Tennessee Volunteers," *THQ* 1, no. 4 (December 1942): 356–57.
101 *resigned from the military:* Patrick, *Aristocrat in Uniform,* 143, 145–46. Troops were aware of the hypocrisy involving both Fort Drane and Clinch's brother-in-law's plantation, Oaklands, and did not like it. See for example Knetsch, *Fear and Anxiety,* 88.

101 *an estimated five hundred bondservants:* William Harney to Thomas Jesup, May 18, 1837, "Florida Military Post Supplies and Operations during Indian Wars, Colonel William Harvey Correspondence," F2, 19, PQH.

101 *least twenty-two cash-crop estates:* Wayne, *Sweet Cane*, 3.

101 *a soldier reported:* Humphreys, "Seminole War Field Journal," 215.

101 *assault on Fort Defiance:* Monaco, *Second Seminole War*, 77.

101 *three hundred yards east:* Committee on Military Affairs, "Gad Humphreys," February 10, 1846, Ho. of Reps, Rep. No. 203, 29th Cong., 1st Sess., 4. Hereafter referred to as Doc. No. 203.

101 *Twenty-nine African Seminoles:* Humphreys, "Seminole War Field Journal," 218.

101 *Barnett spread word:* Porter, "Florida Slaves and Free Negroes," 395; R. B. Lee to Lt. Col. Bankhead, May 22, 1836, NARA RG 94, Letters Received, L147, filed in E84; Humphreys, "Seminole War Field Journal," 219.

101 *Jumper instigated the jailbreak:* R. B. Lee to Lt. Col. Bankhead, May 21, 1836, NARA RG 94, Letters Received, L150, filed in E84.

102 *soldier puzzled over:* Humphreys, "Seminole War Field Journal," 218–19.

102 *Humphreys endured:* Doc. No. 225, 106.

102 *in smoke went:* Doc. No. 203, 2–3.

102 *already elevated:* Sidney Walter Martin, "Richard Keith Call, Florida Territorial Leader," *FHQ* 21, no. 4 (1942): 341–42.

102 *Tennessee Volunteers attacked:* Hollingsworth, "Tennessee Volunteers," *THQ* 1, no. 4 (1942): 365–66, and *THQ* 2, no. 1 (1943): 61–62.

102 *One month later:* Ibid., *THQ* 2, no. 2 (1943): 168–69; Irwin, "Memoir, 1836," 33.

103 *Call led his men:* Monaco, *Second Seminole War*, 84–86. Monaco, citing Call, gives credence to the notion that Native losses numbered over one hundred. Given Call's record of exaggerating his deeds, that seems unlikely. Van Arsdol, *Frontier Soldier*, 28, references "Gov. Call's romanced account" of the Battle of Wahoo Swamp. Call himself, in one letter, only claims twenty-five enemy deaths on November 18: Call to the Secretary of the Navy, November 27, 1836, 7, Richard Keith Call Papers, SLAF.

103 *a soldier remarked:* Van Arsdol, *Frontier Soldier*, 25.

103 *with a reported fifteen hundred troops:* Ibid., 30; B. F. Butler to Richard Call, November 4, 1836, *ASP:MA* 6:992; John Casey to his mother, December 12, 1836, M.C.1964.43 no. 4026.3802, John Charles Casey Manuscript Collection, GLA; Sprague, *Origin, Progress, and Conclusion*, 164–65; Mahon, *History of the Second Seminole War*, 184–85; Call to the Secretary of the Navy, November 27, 1836, 11.

103 *Jackson seethed:* Andrew Jackson to Richard Call, November 1, 1836, Andrew Jackson Papers, 1775–1874, Series 12, Addenda, 1806–1874, Manuscript Division, LOC.

103 *attacked him for his:* For reaction to the war, see "Mr. Clay's Speech," *Niles' Weekly Register*, September 3, 1836; "The Florida War," *Rutland Weekly Herald*, November 1, 1836; "General Jackson," *Morning Post*, October 27, 1836, 3. This is an excerpt from the *Revue des Deux Mondes*.

104 *nature reclaimed Florida's interior:* Patrick, *Aristocrat in Uniform*, 157.

104 *two were ever even rebuilt:* Wayne, *Sweet Cane*, 3.

104 *erased pathways and concealed shards:* Jarvis, "Diary: Army in Florida," E for February 10, 1838, 52, NYAM; "Seminole War—First Campaign," April 25, 1837, 3; Phelps, "Journal (Loose Leaves)," E for April 17, 1839, NYPL.

TWELVE: THE QUARTERMASTER

107 *didn't look like much:* Kieffer, *Maligned General*, 2, 36–37, 128.

107 *the best bureaucrats:* T. D. Allman, *Finding Florida: The True History of the Sunshine State* (New York: Grove Press, 2013), 168.

107 *quartermaster had led a life:* Lewis Collins, *Collins' Historical Sketches of Kentucky: History of Kentucky* (Covington, KY: 1874), 2:586.

107 *a one-horse cart hauled:* Truman Cross, "Memorandum for the Secretary of War," November 3, 1836, NARA RG 94 E 159Q, Box 7, Cross, F1.

108 *was a numbers game:* Thomas Jesup, "Probably Expenses of Transporting One Thousand Indians to West of the Mississippi," Thomas Sidney Jesup Papers, 1836–38, Box 6, LOC.

108 *as a store clerk:* Collins, *History of Kentucky*, 2:586.

108 *scolded another general:* Thomas Jesup to Winfield Scott, June 18, 1836, Settlement, Commerce, Revolution and Reform: 1393–1859, Documents Relating to 1836, GLC02640, GLC.

108 *tapped him to take over:* B. F. Butler to Thomas S. Jesup, November 4, 1836, *ASP:MA* 6:993.

108 *he grumbled:* Remini, *Jackson and the Course of American Democracy*, 311. For Jackson raving, see Cushman, "Journal: 1836–1837," E for December 16, 1836, MHS.

109 *left Washington for Tennessee:* Remini, *Jackson and the Course of American Democracy*, 331–33; Meacham, *American Lion*, 325–26.

109 *war budget was ballooning:* Mahon, *History of the Second Seminole War*, 138; Monaco, *Second Seminole War*, 76.

109 *high-ups realized that the Indians:* Jones, "Memoir Transcript," 60–61, UFA.

109 *promotions came slowly:* Coffman, *Old Army*, 49–51, 74.

109 *troops grew more:* N. S. Jarvis to William Jarvis, November 2, 1837, "Typescript of Letters," NYAM.

110 *a surgeon wrote:* Ibid., October 4, 1837. I'm jumping forward a bit in time, but this sentiment held in late 1836.

110 *Everglades in the summer:* Coffman, *Old Army*, 51–52.

110 *north without a guide:* "Seminole War—First Campaign," May 9, 1837, 3.

110 *simmering resentment:* B. F. Butler, "Officers Resigned in 1836, and Companies Employed in Seminole War," March 2, 1837, Ho. of Reps., Doc. No. 183, 24th Cong., 2nd Sess., 3–5. Hereafter referred to as Doc. No. 183.

110 *eleven artillery companies:* Coffman, *Old Army*, 54.

110 *three field officers served:* Doc. No. 183, 8.

110 *a colonel noted:* Jeffrey J. Winters, "Justifiable or Self-Serving? An Analysis of the Resignations of Ninety-Eight West Point Graduates as a Result of the Seminole War," November 15, 1996, 8, USMA.

110 *During Scott's 1836 campaign:* R. Jones to B. F. Butler, November 26, 1836, *ASP:MA* 6:827.

110 *"consequently knew not":* Irwin, "Memoir, 1836," 22, UFA.

110 *couldn't find anyone to pay:* Andrew Jackson to the Adjutant General's Office, October 14, 1836, NARA RG 393-1 E 85, Orders Issued and Received Fort Brooke, Fla., Nov. 28, 1835–Dec. 30, 1836. Hereafter referred to as Fort Brooke Order Book.

110 *Basic reports went unfiled:* Jones to Butler, November 26, 1836, *ASP:MA* 6:828.

111 *equipment and rations:* Humphreys, "Seminole War Field Journal," 209.

111 *forlornly through tent flaps:* John W. Phelps to his father, July 10, 1837, Box 1, Part 2, NYPL.

111 *Jackson could barely stand:* Jackson to the Adjutant General, October 14, 1836, Fort Brooke Order Book.

111 *Jesup pitched a plan:* Thomas Sidney Jesup to Andrew Jackson, July 23, 1836, Andrew Jackson Papers, 1775–1874, Series 1, General Correspondence and Related Items, 1775–1885, MSS 27532, vol. 95, Manuscript Division, LOC. Jesup sent the letter in July; Jackson read it in August.

111 *force him to reveal:* Ibid., Jackson to Jesup, August 3, 1836, 200–202. In the August 2 letter, cited below, the relevant quote is "where the Indian women are." Same idea.

111 *not contain his zeal:* Jackson to Jesup, August 2, 1836, NARA RG 94 Letters Received, J156, NAMP M567 roll 126, 196–98. The August 2 letter also appears in Andrew Jackson's LOC files, but Jackson's byline is missing and the document is incorrectly labeled online as having been written by Jesup, to Jackson: Thomas Sidney Jesup to Andrew Jackson, August 2, 1836, Andrew Jackson Papers, 1775–1874, Series 1, General Correspondence and Related Items, 1775–1885, MSS 27532, vol. 95, LOC. The August 3 letter from Jackson to Jesup does not appear in the LOC files.

112 *also suffered sickness:* Jonathan R. Watson and Jacob Vickers, "From the *Mobile Chronicle*, June 11," *Daily Pittsburgh Gazette*, June 29, 1836, 2.

112 *Jumper lost many men:* Monaco, *Second Seminole War*, 90.

112 *items they would need:* Jarvis, "Floridian War: Transcript," 18–19, 22, NYAM; Phelps, J. W. Phelps correspondence and journal entries, J. W. Phelps to Helen M. Phelps, August 15, 1837.

112 *others joined:* John Tyler, "Seminole War—Slaves Captured: Message from the President of the United States," Ho. of Reps., Doc. No. 55, 27th Cong., 2nd Sess., 5; Doc. No. 225, 66–68.

112 *learned of the law:* Jesup to Hernández, March 29, 1837, NARA RG 94, E159-Q, Box 35.

112 *by decree, now risked:* This act was repealed on January 14, 1837, although clearly Jesup and Abraham were not aware of that when they were negotiating. *Acts of the Governor and Legislative Council of the Territory of Florida Passed at the Fifteenth Session* (Tallahassee, FL: William Wilson, 1837), 3.

113 *soldiers would get tired:* Van Arsdol, *Frontier Soldier*, 28.

113 *as alien to their enemy:* Sprague, *Origin, Progress, and Conclusion*, 200.

113 *where, as Jumper said:* Forry, "Letters: Part I," 135–36.

113 *red and black oaks:* Hollingsworth, "Tennessee Volunteers," *THQ* 2, no. 3 (September 1943): 244–45.

113 *and Jumper resettled:* W. W. Morris to Brig. Gen. Armistead, January 9, 1836, NARA RG 94 E 159-Q, Box 4, Armistead, April 1836–April 1837, F1.

113 *joining Micanopy's brother-in-law:* Monaco, *Second Seminole War*, 88.

113 *Jesup arrived in Tampa:* Jesup, "Diary," E for October 1, 1836, SLAF.

113 *Jesup promised them:* T. B. Linnard, "Orders No. 116," June 2, 1837, Doc. No. 225, 3.

114 *claimed that the Seminoles:* Gregory Evans Dowd, *Groundless: Rumors, Legends, and Hoaxes of the Early American Frontier* (Baltimore: Johns Hopkins University Press, 2015), 223–24.

THIRTEEN: PRISONERS

115 *mercenary was good-looking:* J. M. Stanley, *Portraits of North American Indians* (Washington: Smithsonian Institution, 1852), 10–11; Childs, "Correspondence with His Family," *HM* 3, no. 4 (1874): 281. Tustenuggee Emathla wasn't the only

Muscogee leader fighting with Jesup in Florida but was one of the most prominent, along with Paddy Carr.

115 *remove his own people*: Peter Cozzens, *A Brutal Reckoning: Andrew Jackson, the Creek Indians, and the Epic War for the American South* (New York: Alfred Knopf, 2023), 360.

115 *he had once marched*: Thomas L. McKenney, *History of the Indian Tribes of North America, with Biographical Sketches and Anecdotes of the Principal Chiefs* (Philadelphia: Frederick W. Greenough, 1838), 2:95–96.

115 *of assault and fraud*: Feller, *Papers of Andrew Jackson*, 7:107; J. R. Poinsett, "Letter from the Secretary of War: Contract—General Jesup, Creek Chiefs, &c.," Ho. of Reps., Doc. No. 274, 25th Cong., 2nd Sess., 24–25.

115 *and that he exhibited*: Kathryn H. Braund, *The African American Experience and the Creek War, 1813–14: An Annotated Bibliography* (Auburn, AL: National Park Service and Auburn University, 2017), 48, 57; John Casey to Isaac Clark, July 11, 1838, Doc. No. 225, 121.

115 *to join Jesup's army*: Monaco, *Second Seminole War*, 87.

115 *delirious U.S. officer*: John W. Phelps to his father, July 10, 1837, Box 1, Pt. 2, NYPL.

116 *eighth of the monthly*: R. Jones, "Army of the United States," *Niles' Register*, April 27, 1833. I am referring to privates among Mounted Dragoons.

116 *U.S. forces stayed in boats*: Clavin, *Negro Fort*, 2, 117–18.

116 *Suwannee Old Town in 1818*: "Affair at Bowleg's Town," April 16, 1818, NAMP 1832 roll 6, 256.

116 *dispersed in small groups*: Thomas Jesup to William de Peyster, n.d., "Slave Owner Claims of Runaway Slaves," PQH.

116 *The job was to*: Jesup to Poinsett, June 6, 1838, Thomas Sidney Jesup Papers, Box 7, LOC; Thomas Jesup to Major T. Cross, April 26, 1837, NARA RG 94 E195-Q, Box 35.

116 *general had to rely*: R. Jones, "Proceedings of Military Courts of Inquiry on the Operations of the Army Under Command of Major General Scott and Major General Gaines, and on the Course Pursued by Those Officers Respectively," March 3, 1837, *ASP:MA* 7:197.

116 *seized Jumper's nephew*: Jesup to Jackson, October 8, 1836, NARA RG 94 E 159-Q, Box 34, 76. Jesup located Jumper's nephew in a jail in Columbus, as he explained to the governor of Georgia. See Thomas Jesup to William Schley, September 21, 1836, NARA RG 94, Letters Received, J47 1837.

116 *a philanderer*: Jarvis, "Diary: Army in Florida," E for March 10, 1839, 195, NYAM.

116 *The quartermaster also formed*: R. K. Call to Thomas Jesup, September 8, 1836, NARA RG 94 E 159, Box 6, Call, F1; Jesup to Poinsett, June 15, 1837, NARA RG 94, Box 36, 183–84; Jesup to Jones, December 5, 1836, Doc. No. 78, 51; J. A. Chambers, "Orders No. 124," June 12, 1837, Doc. No. 225, 3–4.

117 *Fighting battles*: Jesup to Marcy, April 3, 1848, NAMP M547 roll 13, Special File 96.

117 *not for seizing families*: Jesup to Jones, March 10, 1838, NAMP M547 roll 13, Special File 96. Again, dated a bit later than Jesup's early days as commander, but this general realization and strategy were apparent from the start.

117 *taking prisoners in earnest*: Irwin, "Memoir, 1836," 41, UFA; Hollingsworth, "Tennessee Volunteers," *THQ* 2, no. 3 (September 1943): 240–41; Jesup to Jones, December 5, 1836, *ASP:MA* 7:820; Jesup, "Diary," Es for December 2 and 3, 1836, SLAF.

117 *spearheaded the interrogations:* Jesup, "Diary," E for December 6, 1836.
117 *Jesup wrote on December 18:* Jesup to Butler, December 18, 1836, NAMP M567 roll 126, 190.
117 *Wahoo Swamp with eighty warriors:* Cushman, "Journal: 1836–1837," E for December 16, 1836, MHS.
118 *Jim Boy and two hundred Creek:* Hollingsworth, "Tennessee Volunteers," *THQ* 2, no. 3 (September 1943): 240, 246; Jesup, "Diary," E for December 17, 1836; Jesup to Butler, December 23, 1836, *ASP:MA* 7:822.
118 *Creek forces captured:* Jesup to R. Jones, January 12, 1837, *ASP:MA* 7:825; Porter, "Negroes and the Seminole War," 436; "Register of Indian and Negro Prisoners Captured by the Troops Commanded by Major Thomas Jesup in 1836 and 1838 and owned by Indians," n.d., R&L F1, PQH. Note that the list of those taken at the Panasoffkee as it appears here is only fifty-one, not fifty-two.
118 *Many were close with:* Morris to Armistead, January 9, 1836, NARA RG 94 E 159-Q, Box 4, Armistead.
118 *Jim Boy and forty-seven:* Missall and Missall, *Miserable Pride of a Soldier*, 71–72; Jesup to R. Jones, January 21, 1837, *ASP:MA* 7:827.
118 *smuggling connection:* Jesup to Hernández, January 21, 1837, NAMP M567 roll 154, 151.
118 *opening the road:* Jesup, "Diary," E for January 22, 1837.
118 *petrified five-year-old:* John W. Phelps to his sisters, January 16, 1837, LOC.
118 *the ransackers found:* Ibid.; "Extract of a Letter," *Vermont Phoenix*, 2; Kirby, "Diary," E for March 23, 1838, UFA. I'm writing here generally about what soldiers found after raids, not strictly chronologically about January of 1837.
119 *reached Lake Apopka:* David Cawlfield to W. H. Armistead, January 25, 1837, NARA RG 94 E 159-Q, Box 6, Cawlfield.
119 *out of the water:* Childs, "Correspondence with His Family" *HM* 2, no. 6 (1873): 372.
119 *wrote up the accident:* Jesup, "Diary," E for January 24, 1837.
119 *died on January 2:* "Powell the Seminole Indian," *Cheraw Gazette*, February 16, 1836, 2; Wickman, *Osceola's Legacy*, 93–94; Watson and Vickers, "From the *Mobile Chronicle*, June 11," *Daily Pittsburgh Gazette*, June 29, 1836, 2; *Tarboro Press*, September 10, 1836, 2, and July 23, 1836, 2; "Osceola or Powell," *Daily Selma Reporter*, March 19, 1836, 2.
120 *If he didn't die:* Jesup, "Diary," E for January 10, 1837; Irwin, "Memoir, 1836," 16–17.
120 *departed the Panasoffkee Swamp:* Morris to Armistead, January 9, 1836.
120 *claimed that the enforcer:* Ibid.; Jesup to B. F. Butler, January 19, 1837, NAMP M567 roll 144, 51.
120 *high, rolling country:* Washington Hood and J. J. Albert, *Map of the Seat of War in Florida* (Washington City: U.S. Topographical Engineers, 1838), Map Division, LOC; "Extract of a Letter," *Vermont Phoenix*, 2; Laumer, *Amidst a Storm of Bullets*, 72; Childs, "Correspondence with His Family" *HM* 2, no. 6 (1873): 372.
120 *toward Philip's settlements:* Cohen, *Notices of Florida*, 79.
120 *maze of prairies:* "Extract from a Private Journal," March 7, 1839.
120 *loaded onto fifty ponies:* Archibald Henderson to Thomas Jesup, January 28, 1837, Doc. No. 78, 71.
120 *Abraham's belongings included:* Childs, "Correspondence with His Family," *HM* 3, no. 4 (1874): 282–83.

120 *Jesup himself were combing:* Childs, "Correspondence with His Family," *HM* 2, no. 6 (1873): 373; Jesup to R. Jones, February 7, 1836, *ASP:MA* 7:828; Henderson to Jesup, January 28, 1837, 69–71.

121 *engaged the attackers:* Ibid., 69; Coe, *Red Patriots,* 73. By another report, the pack train was seized prior to the Creek pursuit in the swamp. See Henderson to Jesup, January 28, 1837, 69.

121 *Alone in the swamp:* Childs, "Correspondence with His Family," *HM* 3, no. 4 (1874): 283. The opening of chapter 14 derives from this source.

FOURTEEN: THE WARDEN'S RATIONS

122 *dripping through the canvas:* Childs, "Correspondence with His Family," *HM* 2, no. 6 (1873): 373.

122 *His soldier Ben:* "Negro Warriors in the Sem Nation: Abram's Company," in Casey, "Memoranda Concerning the Seminoles," 11.

122 *by the Creek Volunteers:* T. B. Linnard, "Orders No. 116," Doc. No. 225, 3. "List of Negroes taken by the Creek Warriors," R&L F1, PQH, lists Ben as captured by the "2d Battalion," commanded by Morris or, as Jesup refers to them, "Morris' Creek Volunteers." See Thomas Jesup, "Orders No. 47," January 27, 1837, NARA RG 94 E195-Q, Box 43, General Orders, June 6, 1836–February 13, 1837.

122 *at least sixty:* "Register of Indian and Negro Prisoners Captured," R&L F1, PQH. This estimate comes from totaling those taken at the Panasoffkee Swamp and Cabbage Hammocks and adding nine as the Great Cypress estimate (fourteen of twenty-three taken in that engagement are listed as having been enslaved by local whites).

122 *Abraham, Ben claimed:* Childs, "Correspondence with His Family," *HM* 3, no. 4 (1874): 283.

123 *had recently fallen ill:* "Domestic Intelligence: Late from Florida," *Army and Navy Chronicle,* April 13, 1837.

123 *killed near St. Augustine:* Mahon, *History of the Second Seminole War,* 197.

123 *claimed over 130 captives:* "Register of Indian and Negro Prisoners Captured," R&L F1.

123 *suggest but do not confirm:* Abraham's family members appear on the previous list of people seized at the Great Cypress Swamp, but the thirty-seven captives under that heading exceeds the total number of prisoners taken during the raid. The Childs extracts make clear that Abraham believed that his wife might have been taken prisoner, and he was acting under that possibility, but where, when, and if they were actually taken is not conclusively apparent.

123 *their young children:* Doc. No. 225, 67; "Extract from a Private Journal," March 7, 1839.

123 *the hostages' ages:* Ibid.; "Register of Indian and Negro Prisoners Captured," R&L F1.

123 *stopping at the outskirts:* Childs, "Correspondence with His Family," *HM* 3, no. 4 (1874): 283.

123 *known as Camp Childs:* Jesup, "Orders No. 49," January 28, 1837, NARA RG 94 E195-Q, Box 43.

123 *a hundred miles long:* "Extract from a Private Journal," March 7, 1839.

123 *description of the site:* Childs, "Correspondence with His Family," *HM* 2, no. 6 (1873): 373.

124 *who knew all about:* Ibid., 374; Irwin, "Memoir, 1836," 19, UFA.

124 *first white he saw said:* Childs, "Correspondence with His Family," *HM* 3, no. 4

(1874): 283. This source also has Abraham's description of the meeting with Jesup. Jesup's description is in Jesup, "Diary," E for January 31, 1837, SLAF.

124 *Ben's wife was:* "Extract from a Private Journal," March 7, 1839.

124 *white men saw him:* "Domestic Intelligence: Seminole War," June 15, 1837; Childs, "Correspondence with His Family" *HM* 2, no. 6 (1873): 374. Childs has the date as January 30, Jesup has it as January 31. I've used Jesup's date since he kept a daily diary: Jesup, "Diary," E for January 31, 1837.

125 *a commander's paraphernalia:* This generalized, speculative list is drawn from items that were available at the time. "List of Quarter Master Stores &c. on hand at Garey's Ferry Fla.," July 1, 1837, RG 94 E 159-Q, Box 7, Clark, F2.

126 *near a deep morass:* Jesup, "Diary," E for February 3, 1837; Childs, "Correspondence with His Family," *HM* 3, no. 3 (1874): 169.

126 *to send out runners:* T. F. Hunt to R. Jones, February 15, 1837, NAMP M567 roll 143, 291.

126 *attacked Camp Monroe:* Kimball, *Seminole & Creek War Battles*, 72. The estimate of 650 total men in the fight comes from an estimate of 350 Indian and allied warriors and 300 U.S. soldiers.

126 *Bullets pierced sleeves, and tents:* McGaughy, "Lynch's Journal," 44–50. This source has the reported deaths and the write-up of whom Lynch saw as heroic.

126 *word of the truce:* "Domestic Intelligence: Seminole War," June 15, 1837.

126 *Three hours:* Mahon, *History of the Second Seminole War*, 199.

126 *arrived at Fort Dade:* Childs, "Correspondence with His Family," *HM* 3, no. 3 (1874):169–70; Jesup, "Diary," E for February 18, 1837.

127 *the following days:* "Off-Hand Notes of a Moving Gentleman," *New-Yorker* 3, no. 2 (April 1, 1837): 27–28. This source also has the sister and brother encounter in Tampa.

127 *after a misunderstanding:* Jesup, "Diary," E for March 19, 1837. Jesup notes his meetings with Abraham in this diary.

128 *offered the warriors clemency:* "Florida: Treaty with the Seminoles," *New-Yorker* 3, no. 2 (April 1, 1837): 28.

128 *caught a turkey:* Childs, "Correspondence with His Family," *HM* 3, no. 4 (1874): 280–81. This source also describes Micanopy's appearance, the food Jesup served, and Jim Boy feeling snubbed.

128 *a bit of gaslighting:* Laumer, *Amidst a Storm of Bullets*, 84.

128 *surprised American explained:* "Domestic Intelligence: Late from Florida," *Army and Navy Chronicle*, April 13, 1837.

129 *beyond upset: Florida Herald*, April 19, 1837, 2. The report of the planters' anger derives from this source also.

129 *sway and martial power:* Jesup to Hernández, March 29, 1837, and Jesup to Call, April 18, 1837, RG 94 E 159Q, Box 35.

130 *Miccosukees were too weak:* Jesup, "Diary," E for March 5, 1837.

FIFTEEN: WAITING FOR OSCEOLA

131 *Washington was close to eleven:* "Registry of negro prisoners," Doc. No. 225, 67; Deed of Sale, Micanopy to Abraham, April 17, 1841, NAMP 640 roll 3, 857.

131 *Armstrong, on April 2:* Childs to Chambers, April 2, 1837, NARA RG 94 E 159-Q, Box 6, Childs, F1.

131 *fast and slim, and:* Josiah Fogg to his parents, May 12, 1837, Howe-Fogg family papers, 1834–1955, Fogg family papers, 1837, Box 1, F2, MSA.

131 *raid, and wept:* Childs, "Correspondence with His Family," *HM* 3, no. 4 (1874): 282.

131 *was delayed in reaching:* Childs, "Correspondence with His Family," *HM* 3, no. 4 (1874): 282–83. I have changed Wann to Juan. I have also changed "I 'fraid" to "I'm afraid." Childs has cartooned the dialogue. A multitude of sources confirm that Abraham spoke fluent, elegant English.

132 *twenty-one bovines in the pen:* [Illegible] to Lt. Searle, April 24, 1837, NARA RG 94 E 159-Q, Box 4, Armistead, F1.

132 *a fraction of his:* Cross-Examination of George W. Allen, May 10, 1838, *Heirs of Love vs. E. P. Gaines*, 15.975 (1st Dist. 1838), F2, NOCA.

132 *Fort King Road toward:* Morris and Hough, *Fort King Road*, 99, 128, 135, 145.

133 *miles to Fort Foster:* William Bainbridge, "Distances from Fort Brooke to Fort Armstrong, and intermittent places," NARA RG 94 E 159-Q, Box 4, Bainbridge.

133 *chief was reportedly:* Jesup, "Diary," E for March 23, 1837, SLAF. The report does not specify when the incident occurred. Mahon, *History of the Second Seminole War*, 385, notably lists Juan or John Philip as King Philip's son in the index, a claim that does not appear in the main text. Rivers, *Slavery in Florida*, 198, also has Juan Philip as King Philip's son. Abraham may simply have used *father-in-law* and *father* as shorthand for his son-in-law's father.

133 *surgeon recorded:* John F. Brown, "Morning Report of Sick at Micanopy's Camp 10 Miles from Fort Brooke," R&L F1, PQH. Jesup describes the camp as eight miles away, but Brown is on-site; I've compromised with nine. Jesup to Poinsett, June 7, 1837, NARA RG 94 E195-Q, Box 36, 144.

133 *Philip was apparently:* Harney to Jesup, May 1837, *ASP:MA* 7:870. When King Philip finally appears at Fort Mellon, he was reported to be "looking emaciated." See "Domestic Intelligence: Interesting and Authentic from Florida," *Army and Navy Chronicle*, June 29, 1837.

133 *sent word they were:* Jesup, "Diary," Es for April 29, May 7–8, 1837.

133 *camped and drew rations:* John Casey, "Memoranda of Indians Enrolled on the 29th April," April 29, 1937, includes a list of rations drawn on April 28, 1837, R&L F3, PQH.

133 *inspected a steamboat:* Jesup, "Diary," E for April 24, 1837. John Horse appears in the E for May 1, as does the threat to Jumper's life.

133 *Abraham deposited money:* "From the *St. Augustine Herald*, June 9," *Army and Navy Chronicle*, January 22, 1837.

134 *next territorial governor:* Reid, "Diary 1833–35," E for August 13, 1833, UWF.

134 *deposed suspected enemy:* Moore, "South Carolina Lawyer," 369–70.

134 *did Mayor Gould:* "Florida Citizen Petitions," 5, PQH.

134 *he petitioned Jesup:* Gould to Hernández, February 8, 1837, PQH. Ned was interviewed, but he faced no punishment. See also Kly, *Invisible War*, 172.

134 *statesmen in Tallahassee:* See chap. 930 [No. XIX] in *Acts of the Governor and Legislative Council of the Territory of Florida Passed at the Fourteenth Session* (Tallahassee, FL: William Wilson, 1836), 13–15, 19.

134 *crooks would claim:* Jesup to Call, April 18, 1837, RG 94 E 159Q, Box 35.

134 *with lurking speculators:* Forry, "Letters: Part I," 134.

134 *Jesup heard it, Cooley:* Jesup, "Diary," E for May 5, 1837.

134 *a major reported:* Childs to Chambers, March 21, 1837, RG 94 E 159Q, Box 6, Childs, F1.

135 *compelled to issue:* J. A. Chambers, "No. 79," April 5, 1837, RG 94 E 159Q, Box 44, 20.

135 *chaired a public meeting:* E. B. Gould to Jesup, April 27, 1837, "Florida Citizen Petitions," 12, PQH.

135 *ceded the land:* "Government House: The 1935 U.S. Post Office and Customs House St. Augustine, Florida," *Historic Structure Report,* May 31, 2012, 17; Franklin B. Hough, *American Constitutions* (Albany, NY: Weed, Parsons and Company), 1:209.

135 *market where they sold:* Kennedy Dendy, "They Sold Human Beings; St. Augustine's Old Slave Market," *Action News Jax,* February 28, 2023.

135 *a resentful letter:* "Public Meeting," *Florida Herald,* April 26, 1837, 3; Doc. No. 225, 108–10.

136 *dependent on the military:* "Ration of Troops in the Service of the United States in the 2d Mily Dist of E Florida with the numbers of persons at each post for whom Rations are required," Returns of Troops, January 1837, F1, 41, PQH.

136 *Martha Hull drew aid:* "Correspondence, Reports, Rolls &c. on the subject of the formation of settlements and in reference to the suffering inhabitants of Florida," RG 393 Part I E 74, 122–26.

136 *funerals plagued the city:* Moore, "South Carolina Lawyer," 368–69, 374–76.

136 *no intention of sitting idly:* Humphreys to Downing, May 30, 1838, Doc. No. 225, 106–7.

136 *Jesup's peace deal:* Jesup to Brown, April 26, 1837, NARA RG 94 E 159Q, Box 35.

136 *Cooley made it to Tampa:* Jesup to Miller, March 27, 1837, Doc. No. 225, 9.

136 *carrying military dispatches:* Chambers to Crane, April 8, 1837, and Chambers to McClintock, March 31, 1837, NARA RG 94 E 159Q, Box 35.

137 *began to die in May:* "List of negro prisoners who have died from January to 31st May '37," R&L F3, PQH.

137 *Osceola looked:* McGaughy, "Lynch's Journal," 67; Hughes, "Diary: Transcript," 111, USF.

137 *arrived late at Fort Mellon:* Harney to Jesup, April 1837, "Florida Military Post Supplies and Operations during Indian Wars, Colonel William Harvey Correspondence," F2, 15–17, PQH.

137 *sold cows and calves:* McGaughy, "Lynch's Journal," 63; Jesup to Harney, April 8, 1837, NARA RG 94 E 159Q, Box 35.

137 *doubted they could plant twice:* Forry, "Letters: Part I," 135.

137 *Mellon was a sprawling:* N. S. Jarvis to William Jarvis, December 3 and 16, 1837, "Typescript of Letters," NYAM.

137 *eager to see him:* Hughes, "Diary: Transcript," 111; McGaughy, "Lynch's Journal," 66, 70. The daily evening ball games are referenced in this source.

138 *types of ball games:* Motte, *Journey into Wilderness,* 284n12, 308n4; Swanton, *Indians of the Southeastern United States,* 678.

138 *two goal-style:* Author visit to the Ah-Tah-Thi-Ki Museum, June 9, 2024; Weisman, *Like Beads on a String,* 29, 154–55.

138 *as a powerful athlete:* Weisman, *Like Beads on a String,* 155; Sprague, *Origin, Progress, and Conclusion,* 101.

138 *inflamed and swollen:* Harney to Jesup, May 25, 1837, Harney F2, 22, PQH; Wickman, *Osceola's Legacy,* 22. Harney is the officer writing up the detailed reports to Jesup. See also Harney to Jesup, May 4 and 26, 1837, Harney F2, 22, PQH.

138 *Newspapers marked:* "Something Curious" and "From Florida," *United States Gazette,* May 20, 1837, 1; "Jacksonville, May 11," *Charleston Mercury,* May 19, 1837, 2; "From Florida," *Wyoming Republican and Farmer's Herald,* May 24, 1837, 3; "From the Theater of War," *Lancaster Intelligencer,* May 30, 1837, 3; "Highly Important from Florida," *Vermont Mercury,* May 26, 1837, 3.

138 *A soldier described:* Fogg to his parents, May 12, 1837.
138 *Osceola dined and drank:* Harney to Jesup, May 1837, *ASP:MA* 7:870–71.
139 *Americans could finally enjoy:* Harney to Jesup, March 16, 1837, Harney F1, 5, PQH.
139 *would soon subjugate:* "The Great Oseola Surrendered," *Evening Post*, February 21, 1837, 2.
139 *a letter promised:* Harney to Jesup, April 1837, Harney F1, 15, PQH.
139 *Micanopy had been dethroned:* Harney to Jesup, May 24, 1837, Harney F2, 25, PQH.
139 *Micanopy was blindsided:* "New Council 1st June," June 1, 1837, NARA RG 94 E 159-Q, Box 21, Indian Affairs and Correspondence.
139 *close to nothing:* Harney to Jesup, May 1837, *ASP:MA* 7:871; NARA RG 94 E 159Q, Boxes 33–35.
139 *locals came to call:* Jumper, *Legends of the Seminoles*, xix.

SIXTEEN: THE OLD MAN

140 *a parody:* West, "Abiaka, or Sam Jones," 378; Hughes, "Diary: Transcript," 52, USF.
140 *dismissed him as a gossip:* McCall, *Letters from the Frontiers*, 411–12.
140 *so they borrowed one:* H. A. Wise, *Captain Brand of the "Centipede": A Pirate of Eminence in the West Indies* (New York: Harper and Brothers), 195.
140 *chatty, while in reality:* West, "Abiaka, or Sam Jones," 377; Cori Brosnahan, "A Place to Remember," November 5, 2021, *American Experience*, accessed January 21, 2025, https://www.pbs.org/wgbh/americanexperience/features/swamp-place-to-remember-abiaki/.
140 *a surgeon wrote:* Hughes, "Diary: Transcript," 52.
140 *messengers said he:* West, "Abiaka, or Sam Jones," 378–79, 399. The physical description of Abiaka comes from this source, 379–80, as does his relationship to Micanopy, 368, 399.
141 *anything of substance:* Potter, *War in Florida*, 9–11, 30, 84; Cohen, *Notices of Florida*, 54; Smith, *Sketch of the Seminole War*, 104–6. See also Williams, *Territory of Florida*, 275.
141 *troops taunted one Northerner:* J. W. Phelps to his sister, August 15, 1837, LOC.
141 *placed in the spotlight:* West, "Abiaka, or Sam Jones," 377. Also see Knetsch, Missall, and Missall, *History of the Third Seminole War*, chap. 10.
142 *"never consented":* Hughes, "Diary: Transcript," 87.
142 *the bands held:* Peyton to Harney, May 24, 1837, Harney F2, 34, PQH; Harney to Jesup, May 25, 1837, Harney F2, 41, PQH; Harney to Jesup, May 24, 1837, Harney F2, 25, PQH.
142 *Abiaka only commanded:* Casey to Jesup, July 24, 1837, NARA RG 94 E159-Q, Box 6, Casey; Drake, *Biography and History of the Indians*, 4:93.
142 *threatened Chief Coa Hadjo:* McGaughy, "Lynch's Journal," 68; Motte, *Journey into Wilderness*, 283n11.
142 *elevating them to:* West, "Abiaka, or Sam Jones," 377.
142 *demanded that Micanopy:* Peyton to Harney, May 24, 1837.
142 *one chief reported:* Forry, "Letters: Part II," 208.
142 *brought Micanopy to power:* "King Payne's Family," in Casey, "Memoranda Concerning the Seminoles," 11, 72. Details on Holata Micco Chee, later Holata Micco, aka William or Billy Bowlegs, derive from this source.
143 *fool the Americans:* Harney to Jesup, May 24, 1837, 25–28. Details on the new Council's law derive from this source.

143 *Abiaka dispatched warriors:* "Bowlegs story about the abduction on 2d June," in Casey, "Memoranda Concerning the Seminoles," 3–4, 11. According to Old Bowlegs, Wild Cat and Pahosee Emathla were assigned this task. This information fits with what Jesup learned immediately after the coup, as revealed by his chronologically arranged letters in NARA RG 94 E159Q, Box 36.

143 *likely only harbored:* Another report, by Coa Hadjo, puts the raiding party at two hundred, while the number of people in Micanopy's camp has been estimated to be as high as seven hundred: Mahon, *History of the Second Seminole War*, 204. The smaller figures seem more plausible to me. Regarding the size of Micanopy's camp, on April 28, 1837, rations are drawn for 261 people, and then about 30 people leave for their families, leaving an estimated 23 people on April 29, 1837: Casey, "Memoranda of Indians Enrolled on the 29th April," April 29, 1937, L&R F3, PQH. It does not appear that the numbers in camp grew substantially after this date, since the measles had already broken out by late April. See Thomas Jesup to J. R. Poinsett, June 7, 1837, NARA RG 94 E195-Q, Box 36, 144, which reads, "Soon after the Indians had begun to assemble in this neighborhood the measles . . . broke out among them, after which very few came in—the Indian negroes had been alarmed by the arrival in camp of individuals who had lost their slaves during the war—most of them fled." Jesup later states, "After the measles broke out in the Seminole camp, not a single woman or child came in": Thomas Jesup to J. R. Underwood, November 20, 1837, NARA RG 94 E195-Q, Box 39, 74. Old Bowlegs' lower estimate of the size of the raiding party also aligns closely with the figure Micanopy and Jesup discuss when they hear Abiaka's warriors are coming, cited below.

143 *Alligator's brother:* Jesup to Chambers, July 10, 1837, NARA RG 94 E195-Q, Box 36, 279.

143 *did not list Osceola:* He explicitly reports that John Horse was not there, by implication suggests that Sam Jones was not there, and makes no mention of Osceola: "Bowlegs story about the abduction," in Casey, 3–4, 11. Jesup makes no attributions to Osceola, John Horse, or Sam Jones as being present in the raid in the days following the coup, either in his diary or in his letters. Neither does anyone else. Only months later, when Jesup is trying to deflect blame for having seized Osceola under a white flag, does he target Osceola and John Horse: Jesup to Underwood, November 20, 1837. Jesup puts the blame on Osceola; the two Hicks brothers, whom he also just captured under a white flag; John Horse, also just captured under a white flag; and Wild Cat. Note that this is a letter to a representative of Congress written in a moment where Jesup is afraid that he might be investigated for his actions. Before Jesup captures the party under a white flag, he expresses no uncertainty about who did it. In Jesup to Thomas Cross, November 17, 1837, Doc. No. 327, 11, Jesup writes to his confidant that "Coacoochee carried off Micanopy by force, and, if he had been a white man, I would have executed him." No mention of Osceola or the Hicks brothers. In essence, Jesup retroactively plants guns in the hands of the people he is accused of wronging. This sort of behavior is very much in Jesup's character and tendencies. Note also that when Jesup gave the orders to Hernández to seize Osceola and the others, Jesup cited "a recent murder" as the reason, not Osceola's—or anyone else's—alleged involvement in the coup: Thomas Jesup to Gen. J. M Hernández, October 21, 1837, in "No. 3," *Maryland Gazette*, December 21, 1837, 2.

143 *Abraham was absent:* Jesup to Armistead, June 6, 1837, NARA RG 94 E195-Q, Box 36, 142.

144 *called them cowards:* Jesup to Poinsett, June 15, 1837, Enclosure A, *ASP:MA* 7:875.
144 *were escorted east:* "Bowlegs story about the abduction," in Casey, 4–5.
144 *letter to an allied:* Abraham, "Abraham Sends His Talk."
144 *women and children:* Jesup to Gadsden, June 14, 1837, Doc. No. 225, 18, provides an excerpt of the letter, which appears in full as Jesup to Gadsden, June 14, 1837, NARA RG 94 E 159-Q, Box 36, 170–71.
144 *Loved ones could not:* "Register of Negro Prisoners who have died from January to May 31st 1837," R&L F1, PQH; "Register of Indian Prisoners who have died from January to May 31st '37," R&L, F3, PQH; Jesup to Gadsden, June 14, 1837, NARA RG 94 E 159-Q, Box 36, 171.
145 *Abraham had heard:* "New Council 1st June," June 1, 1837, NARA RG 94 E 159-Q, Box 21, Indian Affairs and Correspondence. This source contains an account of Jesup's meeting with Micanopy.
145 *sent an envoy to Jesup:* "Bowlegs story about the abduction," in Casey, 4; Jesup to Armistead, June 6, 1837, 141–42.
145 *he seized the messenger:* Jesup to Gadsden, June 14, 1837, Doc. No. 225, 18; Jesup to Gadsden, June 14, 1837, NARA RG 94 E 159-Q, Box 36, 171.
145 *Order No. 116:* T. B. Linnard, "Orders, No 116," June 2, 1837, Doc. No. 225, 3; Jesup to Isaac Clark, June 2, 1837, NARA RG 94 E 159-Q, Box 36, 129.
145 *Toney Barnett:* J. A. Chambers, "Order No. 131," June 21, 1837, NARA 94 E 159Q, Box 44, 69; Casey, "List of negroes Left at Tampa on 3d May without authority," R&L F1, PQH.
145 *sunrise, breakfast, dinner:* Major Hoffman, "Orders No. 5," January 12, 1838, Fort Brooke Order Book. These orders are a few months ahead of our time frame, but are generally indicative of the routine Abraham would have witnessed.
145 *tended to the horses:* "Lists of Men on duty in the Quarter Masters Department at Fort Brooke E.F.," January 2, 1837, Returns of Troops Jan 1837 F1, 7 PQH.
146 *water at Fort Brooke:* Mahon, "Journal of A. B. Meek," 309.
146 *vinegary whiskey mix:* Hughes, "Diary: Transcript," 95.
146 *didn't only sign up:* Monaco, *Second Seminole War*, 56; Cushman. "Journal: 1836–1837," Es for November 11, 13, 14, 16, 1836, MHS.
146 *soldiers enjoyed:* Jones, "Memoir Transcript," 60, UFA.
146 *ordered to a fort:* N. S. Jarvis to William Jarvis, October 4, 1837, "Typescript of Letters," NYAM.
146 *kept getting arrested:* Forry, "Letters Part I," 144, and "Letters Part II," 216, 218–19.
146 *were so undisciplined:* Monaco, *Second Seminole War*, 157.
146 *doctor was:* Cushman, "Journal: 1836–1837," E for December 18, 1836.
146 *the worst reputations:* "Seminole War—First Campaign," May 9, 1837, 3.
146 *feared the militia, and:* Jarvis, "Floridian War: Transcript," 52–53, NYAM.
146 *who left Florida:* Samuel Miller to Jesup, July 16, 1837, NAMP M567 roll 145, 323.
146 *his children drowned:* McKenney, *History of the Indian Tribes*, 2:96.
147 *assigned twenty warriors:* Jesup to Zachary Taylor, October 28, 1837, NARA RG 94 E 159Q, Box 38, 270.

SEVENTEEN: LIVE

148 *Epigraph:* Abraham to Jesup, April 25, 1838, UFA.
148 *demoralizing reports:* Jesup to C. A. Harris, June 5, 1837; Jesup to R. Jones,

June 5, 1837; and Jesup to Poinsett, June 7, 1837, NARA RG 94 E 159Q, Box 36, 136–37, 143–44.

148 *locals, in particular:* Jesup began to blame nearly all of these targets before the coup and continued afterward with renewed energy. His complaints appear in Jesup to Call, May 21, 1837; Jesup to Trueman Cross, June 16 and 24, 1837, NARA RG 94 E 159Q, Box 36, 91–92, 198, 234; Jesup to B. Boykin, April 28, 1837, NARA RG 94 E 159Q, Box 35.

149 *$8 million:* War Department, "Florida War, &c: Letter from The Secretary of War," January 30, 1838, Ho. Doc. No. 133, 25th Cong., 2nd Sess., 2. Hereafter referred to as Doc. No 133.

149 *government had expended:* Levy Woodbury to James K. Polk, June 27, 1838, "Official Public Expenditure from 1824 to 1838: Letter from the Secretary of the Treasury," June 27, 1838, LOC, accessed January 24, 2025, https://www.loc.gov/item/ca14000307. The figure is exclusive of expenses related to public debt.

149 *never pursued the job:* Jesup to R. Jones, June 5, 1837, NARA RG 94 E 159Q, Box 36, 139–40.

149 *leave the peninsula:* Jesup to Armistead, June 18, 1837; and Jesup to Archibald Henderson, July 4, 1837, NARA RG 94 E 159Q, Box 36, 216, 257.

149 *Removal policy truly was:* Jesup to Cross, June 16, 1837, ibid., 200.

149 *he concluded:* Jesup to Edmund Gaines, June 10, 1837, ibid., 154.

149 *His journal ends:* The journal itself appears to have run out of pages. If Jesup continued on in another book, I am not aware of its existence.

149 *twenty-six ships:* Monaco, *Second Seminole War,* 93; Kieffer, *Maligned General,* 170.

149 *cracked his ankle:* Jesup to A. Steele, July 17, 1837, NARA RG 94 E 159Q, Box 37, 22. Jesup's being confined to his hotel room comes from this source.

149 *overrun with scurvy:* Jesup to Macomb, June 38, 1837, NARA RG 94 E 159Q, Box 36, 247.

149 *on Treasury Street:* George R. Fairbanks, *The History and Antiquities of the City of St. Augustine, Florida* (Gainesville: University of Florida Press, 2017), xxi.

150 *mood among residents:* "St. Augustine," *Florida Herald,* June 22, 1837, 2; *Florida Herald,* July 7, 1837, 2.

150 *pulled up stakes:* James B. Mason to his mother, January 21, 1836, UFA Digital Collections, Mason, James B. Letters 1833–1848, F1. Mason is the Jacksonville resident.

150 *an inhabitant declared: Florida Herald,* July 21, 1837; *Floridian,* July 8, 1837, 2.

150 *St. Augustine newspapers: Florida Herald,* June 22, 1837, 2.

150 *Jesup's top officers:* Abraham Eustis to Frederick Eustis, June 7, 1837, Abraham Eustis Papers, 1811–43, F31, USAT.

150 *Colonists concluded that: Florida Herald,* June 22, 1837, 2.

150 *he could not accept:* NARA RG 94 E 159Q, Box 36, 134–282; Jesup to Harney, June 18, 1837, NARA RG 94 E 159Q, Box 36, 214.

150 *The general grew:* Monaco, *Second Seminole War,* 93; "Another Campaign," *Floridian,* June 17, 1837, 2.

150 *spent his hours ordering:* See, for instance, orders Nos. 128, 131, 134, 144, 153 of June 18, 21, and 23, and July 9 and 20, 1837, in RG 94 E 159Q, Box 44, 65, 68, 71, 97, 113.

150 *had deserters tattooed with:* T. B. Linnard, "Orders No. 139," June 20, 1837, ibid., 90; T. B. Linnard, "Orders No. 148," July 14, 1837, ibid., 103–4.

151 *blunt and bloodthirsty:* Jesup to Harney, June 1, 8, and 11, 1837, NARA RG 94 E 159Q, Box 36, 126, 150, 160.

151 *who couldn't be grabbed:* Jesup to Armistead, June 6, 1837; and Jesup to John Crowell, June 17, 1837, ibid., 141–42, 212.
151 *could use bloodhounds:* Jesup to John McNeil, June 20, 1837, ibid., 221.
151 *a thousand Shawnee:* Thomas Jesup to William Clark, June 11, 1837, ibid., 165; Jesup to [illegible], August 9, 1937, NARA RG 94 E 159-Q, Box 20, Letters Received Relating to Creek and Seminole Affairs, 1837.
151 *insisted, to the ranking:* Jesup to Miller, July 8, 1837, NARA RG 94 E 159Q, Box 36, 270.
151 *interrogation of:* Casey to Jesup, July 24, 1837, NARA RG 94, E159-Q, Box 6, Casey; Casey, "Memoranda Concerning the Seminoles," 1.
151 *probably took place inside:* "Plot of Government Reservation, Fort Brooke Florida," NARA RG 94, Military Reservation Division, E 464 P-17, Reservation File, Box 18, Fort Brooke, FL.
152 *than twelve of them:* Drake, *Biography and History of the Indians,* 4:93; Casey to Jesup, July 24, 1837, NARA. Casey repeats the information in his journal here, namely that Wild Cat and Pahosee Emathla carried off Micanopy with eighty men, information derived from Alligator's brother.
152 *third prisoner:* "Toney Barnett's acct.," Casey, "Memoranda Concerning the Seminoles," 2, 11–14.
152 *current locations:* Ibid., 4–5; Casey to Jesup, July 24, 1837.
152 *Jumper's voices countered:* Jesup to Jones, August 13, 1837; and Jesup to Trueman Cross, August 16, 1837, NARA RG 94 E 159Q Box 38, 8–9, 25.
152 *he missed and "wished":* Casey to Jesup, July 14, 1837, NARA RG 94 E 159Q, Box 20, Letters Received Relating to Creek and Seminole Affairs, 1837.
153 *horses were stolen:* Casey and Graham to Jesup, August 19, 1837, NARA RG 94 E 159Q, Box 6, Casey.
153 *storms hit Florida:* "St. Augustine," *Florida Herald,* August 10, 1837, 2; N. S. Jarvis to William Jarvis, August 9 and September 13, 1837, NYAM; T. B. Linnard, "Orders No. 162," August 8, 1837, NARA RG 94 E 159Q, Box 44, 139; "Loss of the Schr. S.S. *Mills,*" *Charleston Courier,* August 18, 1837.
153 *visited the reconstructed:* Jesup to Jones, August 13, 1837, *ASP:MA* 7:846.
153 *"influence of Micanopy and Jumper":* Jesup to Cross, August 16, 1837, NARA RG 94 E 159Q Box 38, 25.
153 *emissaries explained:* Details of the meeting appear in Jesup to Poinsett, August 22, 1837, *ASP:MA* 7:879–80; Forry, "Letters Part II," 207.
154 *Coa Hadjo argued:* Forry, "Letters Part III," 94. The quote regarding Abiaka's power can be found here.
154 *family among Jesup's captives:* Ibid.; Jesup to Poinsett, August 22, 1837. This latter source contains the information regarding Miccosukee prisoners.
154 *planned to muster:* Jesup to P. H. Galt, August 13, 1837, NARA RG 94 E 159Q, Box 38, 10–12. The troop levels, the quote about the northern Indians, and the wider threat of enslavement derive from this letter.
155 *met with Abraham:* There is no record of the date of this meeting, but it is clear by the timeline that it took place in early September. Jesup is back at Fort Brooke by August 28, Abraham is promoted from $1 (A. Chambers, "Order No. 131," June 21, 1837, NARA 94 E 159Q, Box 44, 69, see the citation on Barnett) a day to $2.50 on September 1, and Jesup refers to his deal with Abraham, his promise to Abraham, and his purchase of Black Seminole prisoners from the Creeks as connected in Thomas Jesup to C. A. Harris, September 24, 1837, Doc. No. 225, 21–22. See "Letter from the Secretary of War: Persons Employed in the Indian Department—1838," January 19, 1839, Ho. of Reps., Doc. No. 103, 25th Cong.,

3rd Sess., 12, hereafter referred to as Doc. No. 103; T. B. Linnard, "Orders No. 169," August 28, 1837, and "Orders No. 175," September 6, 1837, NARA RG 94 E 159Q, Box 44, 147, 155–56; Jesup to F. Searle, September 9, 1837, Doc. No. 225, 20.

EIGHTEEN: WALK

156 *Epigraph:* Jarvis, "Floridian War: Transcript," 16, NYAM.
156 *avoided liquor:* "Jackson's Last Night as President," *Weekly Register*, August 27, 1879, 1; Remini, *Jackson and the Course of American Democracy*, 419.
156 *longest presidential goodbye:* Sarah Pruitt, "A History of the Presidential Farewell Address," January 10, 2017 (updated October 29, 2023), History Channel, accessed January 27, 2025, https://www.history.com/news/a-history-of-the-presidential-farewell-address.
156 *Jackson did not bother:* Andrew Jackson, "Farewell Address," March 4, 1837, American Presidency Project, accessed January 27, 2025, https://www.presidency.ucsb.edu/documents/farewell-address-0.
157 *forcibly relocated west:* Remini, *Andrew Jackson and His Indian Wars*, 277.
157 *longest, costliest, and deadliest:* Ibid.; Porter, *Black Seminoles*, 106–7.
157 *had been singled out:* Remini, *Andrew Jackson and His Indian Wars*, 276.
157 *not a nice thing:* Joseph White to J. Knowles, February 15, 1837, *TP* 25:37–39.
157 *a headline read:* "Gen. Jackson vs. Florida," *Florida Herald*, March 29, 1837, 2.
158 *six private letters:* Jackson to Poinsett, August 27, 1837, Andrew Jackson Papers 1775–1874, Series 6, Additional Correspondence, 1779–1855, MSS 27532, vol. 164, LOC; Jackson to Poinsett, September 14, 1837, Andrew Jackson Papers 1775–1874, Series 1, General Correspondence and Related Items, 1775–1885 MSS 27532, vol. 99, LOC; Poinsett to Jackson, September 6 and 23, 1837, ibid. The letter of August 27 references a fifth letter from Poinsett to Jackson on August 19; the sixth is an October 1 letter from Jackson to Poinsett found in Jesup's LOC papers, see "Excerpt of a private letter from General Jackson to the Secretary of War dated Hermitage Oct 1st 1837," Thomas Jesup Papers, Box 6. The excerpted Jackson letter can be found in Bassett, *Correspondence of Andrew Jackson*, 5:512–13. The letters also cover unrelated subjects.
158 *he promised Poinsett:* Jackson to Poinsett, August 27, 1837, 4. Jackson's assumption about Osceola and Emathla appears in this source.
158 *Abiaka, the war leader:* Rodenbough, *Everglade to Canyon*, 27.
158 *Jesup seized Osceola:* Monaco, *Second Seminole War*, 96.
158 *scene should have:* "Latest from Florida—Surrender of Osceola," *Herald* (New York), February 21, 1837, 2.
159 *another paper reported:* "Latest from Florida—the Indian War Ended. Osceola Surrendered," *Herald of the Times* (Newport, RI), February 23, 1837, 3.
159 *had never commanded:* Osceola was subordinate to Abiaka throughout the war and was, at the start of the war at least, not even a chief. "Mem. of Clinch's Battle of 31 Dec.," Casey, "Memoranda Concerning the Seminoles," 25; Wickman, *Osceola's Legacy*, 11.
159 *real thing went down:* Hernández to Jesup, October 22, 1837, in War Department, "Letter from the Secretary of War: Seminole Indians—Prisoners of War," April 11, 1838, Ho. of Reps., Doc. No. 327, 25th Sess., 3rd Cong., 5–6. Hereafter referred to as Doc. No. 327.
159 *waiting for the colonists:* Jarvis, "Army Surgeon's Notes," *Journal of the Military Service Institution* 39, no. 143 (1906): 278.

159 *fabric was scarce:* Phelps, "Journal (Loose Leaves)," Es for February 14 and 28, 1839, NYPL.
159 *In this case:* Jesup, "Account of the capture of Osceola," YLA.
159 *Osceola seemed content:* Jarvis, "Diary: Army in Florida," 7–8, NYAM. The dialogue with Hernández comes from this source as does some of the description of the scene, along with Rodenbough, *Everglade to Canyon*, 26; Forry, "Letters Part III," 90; Motte, *Journey into Wilderness*, 138–39.
159 *Jesup apprised Jackson:* Jesup to Andrew Jackson, October 24, 1837, Andrew Jackson Papers, 1775–1874, Series 1, General Correspondence and Related Items, 1775–1885, MSS 27532, vol. 99, LOC.
160 *strange markings:* Eaton, "Journal," E for November 7–8, UMA.
160 *recorded the image:* Casey, "Diary for 1850," John Charles Casey diaries and papers, 7, 154, USMA.
160 *an icon appears:* Abraham, "Abraham Sends His Talk."
160 *only waiting for:* Jesup to Zachary Taylor, October 27, 1837, NARA RG 94 E 159Q, Box 38, 271.
160 *Sense Bearer dictated:* "Abram's will," in Casey, "Memoranda Concerning the Seminoles," 32.
160 *Acting Paymaster:* [illegible] to Jesup, June 21, 1837, NARA RG 94 E 159Q, Box 6, Casey.
161 *as Abraham's relative:* This interpretation would fit with his "ownership" of his son Renty and his attempts to purchase Romeo, as the reported husband to a "close relation." Tenebo (or Charles) and his wife, Taymour, their three children, and her mother, Sarah, her brother, her sister, and her father, Old Jack, were among the group who tried to come into Tampa Bay the day after the coup. Casey, "List of negroes Left at Tampa on 3d May without authority," R&L F1, PQH. Also see Walker Armistead to Jesup, January 22, 1838, NARA RG 94 E 159Q, Box 4, Armistead, F4, which reads, "The rest of the negroes that came in with Jumper—consisting of Charles and his family and the connections of Abraham, I have permitted to remain here 'till the return of Abraham."
161 *Abraham and Toney:* Missall and Missall, *Miserable Pride of a Soldier*, 118–19.
161 *a rainstorm hit:* Eaton, "Journal," Es for November 14 and 15, 1837. The description of the motley characters derives from this source.
162 *colonel in command:* Missall and Missall, *Miserable Pride of a Soldier*, 118; W. Foster to B. Foster, November 13, 1837, KCL.
162 *he secured concessions:* "List of persons in the service of the Indian department at any time during the year 1838," Doc. No. 103, 12; Forry, "Letters Part II," 214.
162 *Every prisoner captured:* Jesup to Harris, September 24, 1837, Doc. No. 225, 21.
162 *would have their freedom:* Gad Humphreys to C. Downing, ibid., 95–96, 106; J. B. Bird, "Tally of plantation slaves in the Black Seminole slave rebellion, with sources," October 29, 2012, accessed January 31, 2025, http://www.johnhorse.com/toolkit/numbers.htm; Harney to Jesup, May 4, 1837, Harney F2, 9, PQH; Jesup to Marcy, April 3, 1848, Thomas Jesup Papers, Box 15, 5, LOC; Humphreys, "Seminole War Field Journal," 218.
162 *Jesup had threatened:* Jesup to Harris, September 24, 1837, Doc. No. 225, 22.
162 *work with the army:* Doc. No. 103, 12; John Casey, "Memorandum of Indians & negroes to be detained at Tampa Bay as Guides and Interpreters," April 17, 1837, R&L F1, PQH.
162 *course of their efforts:* See chapter 23 citations regarding July and Murray.
162 *no time to be:* Foreman, *Five Civilized Tribes*, 234.
163 *the soldiers hiked:* Missall and Missall, *Miserable Pride of a Soldier*, 119–20.

163 *Pease Creek:* Jesup to Call, October 30, 1837, NARA RG 94 E 159Q, Box 38, 284.
163 *met with Micanopy:* Monaco, *Second Seminole War,* 99; Missall and Missall, *Miserable Pride of a Soldier,* 122–23; Jesup to Cross, December 3, 1837, NARA RG 94 E 159Q, Box 39, 130.
163 *Jumper was too sick:* Jarvis, "Floridian War: Transcript," 16.

NINETEEN: RUN

164 *Epigraph:* Sprague, *Origin, Progress, and Conclusion,* 326.
164 *paraded the prisoners:* Jarvis, "Floridian War: Transcript," 8, NYAM.
164 *Castillo:* Author's visit, June 13, 2024; Albert C. Manucy, *The Building of Castello de San Marcos* (Washington: U.S. Government Printing Office, 1955), 1–3, 11. Americans called it Fort Marion.
165 *bragged about capturing:* Jesup to Call, October 22, 1837, NARA RG 94 E 159Q, Box 38, 245.
165 *his men only seized:* L. B. Webster to Hernández, October 22, 1837, Doc. No. 327, 8.
165 *a surgeon wrote:* Forry, "Letters Part III," 95.
165 *the detainees:* "List of Indian Prisoners. St. Augustine," n.d., R&L F3, PQH.
165 *Americans had found:* Moore, "South Carolina Lawyer," 367.
165 *human waste:* Harvey Brown, "Orders No. 27," September 13, 1837, NARA RG 94 E 159Q, Box 4, Brown F3.
165 *dank stone rooms:* Porter, "Seminole Flight from Fort Marion," 115.
165 *Osceola had poisoned himself:* Forry, "Letters Part III," 95.
165 *contracted head lice:* Wickman, *Osceola's Legacy,* 19, 27, 228.
165 *Jesup seized more:* Ibid., 26–27.
165 *hostages became increasingly:* A. G. W. Fanning to Lt. Chambers, December 13, 1837; and George Turner to P. Morrison, December 12, 1837, Fanning F2, PQH; Sprague, *Origin, Progress, and Conclusion,* 325–26.
166 *John Hicks died:* Wickman, *Osceola's Legacy,* 137; "List of Indian Prisoners. St. Augustine: Miccosukees of A-pai-ah-keis Band," R&L F3, PQH. Wickman has confused Billy and John Hicks.
166 *southwest of the Castillo:* Porter, "Seminole Flight from Fort Marion," 115, 124.
166 *Wild Cat:* Ibid., 116, 118, 127; Jarvis, "Floridian War: Transcript," 15; Sprague, *Origin, Progress, and Conclusion,* 325–27. Reports of the jailbreak appear in Harvey Brown to J. A. Chambers, November 30, 1837, NARA RG 94 E 159Q, Box 4, Brown F3; E. B. Gould, J. H. Drum, and E. A. Capron, "Board of Inquiry Report," November 30, 1837, Letters from Officers, G, 19–20, PQH. The "Board of Inquiry Report" can also be found as MC16.4 Fldr. 4a Report, AHS.
167 *twenty men and women:* "List of prisoners who made their escape from Fort St. Marks on the night of the 29th of November 1837," NARA RG 94 E 159Q, Box 21, Indians Affairs and Correspondence; "List of Indian Prisoners. St. Augustine: Miccosukees."
167 *chased the jailbreakers:* Major Creighton to Harvey Brown, December 2, 1837, NARA RG 94 E 159Q, Box 4, Brown, F3.
167 *Tennessee Volunteers:* J. A. Chambers to William Lauderdale, December 2, 1837; and Chambers to Harvey Brown, December 2, 1837, NARA RG 94 E 159Q, Box 39, 124–25.
167 *ditched a mule:* Sprague, *Origin, Progress, and Conclusion,* 327.
167 *Jesup lost:* Chambers to Lauderdale, December 2, 1837, 124. I don't mean to imply that Osceola was not "a leader," only that he was never "the leader."

167 *part of the story:* Monaco, *Second Seminole War,* 96–97.
167 *his resignation:* Kieffer, *Maligned General,* 188–89; "Gen. Jesup," *Newbernian,* January 12, 1838, 3.
167 *framing Osceola for:* See the chapter 16 citation for "*did not list Osceola.*"
167 *sullied for capturing:* Jesup, "Account of the capture of Osceola," YLA.
167 *condemnation was: Vermont Chronicle,* November 15, 1837, 3; *Madisonian,* December 12, 1837, 4; "Gen. Jesup," *Newbernian,* 3; *South-Western Farmer,* November 24, 1837, 1l.
167 *snatched Osceola sooner: Natchez Daily Courier,* December 13, 1837.
168 *paper ribbed him: Pennsylvania Republican,* January 3, 1838, 1.
168 *busy scheming to capture: Recorder,* February 27, 1838, 3.
168 *South Carolina representative:* "Debate in the House of Representatives in the Seminole War," *Daily National Intelligencer and Washington Express,* January 25, 1838, 2.
169 *a Southern war:* "The Seminole War," *Liberator,* November 24, 1837, 4.
169 *Abolitionists forced:* Ibid.; John W. Phelps, who fought in Florida, was a prominent abolitionist. Upton Fraser was another. See Laumer, *Dade's Last Command,* 177.
169 *extended beyond Jesup: Recorder,* January 23, 1838, 1.
169 *did not defend Jesup:* Ibid. I could find no letters from Jackson to Jesup after Osceola's seizure in Jackson's LOC archives, Jesup's LOC archives, or in Jesup's records at NARA.
169 *Abraham was unfamiliar:* Taylor to Jesup, December 4, 1837, Zachary Taylor Papers: Series 2, LOC.
169 *no choice but:* Taylor to Jesup, December 17, 1837, ibid.; Missall and Missall, *Miserable Pride of a Soldier,* 122–23.
169 *cost the Interpreter:* Taylor to Jesup, November 26, 1837, Zachary Taylor Papers: Series 2, LOC; Jesup to Taylor, October 27, 1837, NARA RG 94 E 159Q, Box 38, 272.
169 *true to his word:* Monaco, *Second Seminole War,* 99.
170 *thirty-seven of:* "Enrollment of Jumpers party Jany 19th 1838," NARA RG 94 E 159Q, Box 4, Armistead F4.
170 *had five hundred fighters:* Rodenbough, *Everglade to Canyon,* 31.
170 *army had eighty-nine hundred:* "Abstract of the table marked Z, of the printed document No. 3, showing the strength of the Florida army," Doc. No. 133, 6.
170 *Taylor alone had over:* Monaco, *Second Seminole War,* 103.
170 *projecting weakness:* Jesup to Taylor, November 27, 1837; Jesup to Cross, December 3, 1837; Jesup to Harvey Brown, December 4, 1837, NARA RG 94 E 159Q, Box 39, 104, 131, 134.
170 *the messengers insisted:* Jesup to Taylor, November 27, 1837, 104.
170 *battlefield was expertly chosen:* White, "Journal of Robert C. Buchanan," 145–46; Zachary Taylor to R. Jones, January 4, 1838, in War Department, "Report from the Secretary of War," February 21, 1838, Ho. of Reps., Doc. No. 227, 25th Cong., 2nd Sess. Hereafter referred to as Doc. No. 227.
170 *from the tops:* Monaco, *Second Seminole War,* 104.
170 *so exhausted:* White, "Journal of Robert C. Buchanan," 148.
171 *Taylor described the scene:* Taylor to Jones, January 4, 1838, Doc. No. 227, 6.
171 *the 6th Infantry:* Zachary Taylor, "The Battle on the Kissimmee," *Madisonian,* February 3, 1838, 1.
171 *Lake Okeechobee marked:* West, "Abiaka, or Sam Jones," 389. Abiaka's losses and escape derive from this source.

171 *Taylor claimed "victory"*: Monaco, *Second Seminole War*, 105.
171 *whipped the army*: "Lieut. Powell's Battle," *Martinsburg Gazette*, February 14, 1838, 2; Buker, *Swamp Sailors*, 61–63; Jarvis, "Floridian War: Transcript," 31–32.
171 *she escaped, was caught*: Jarvis, "Floridian War: Transcript," 58. Jesup's march south is described in, ibid., 32–35.
171 *Troops met Abiaka near*: Monaco, *Second Seminole War*, 105; Robert McLane to Louis McLane, January 29, 1838, Papers of Louis McLane, Box 2, General Correspondence, Nov. 16, 1831–Sept. 1839, LOC; Rodenbough, *Everglade to Canyon*, 30; Kieffer, *Maligned General*, 200.
172 *knocking off his glasses*: Jarvis, "Army Surgeon's Notes," *Journal of the Military Service Institution* 39, no. 144 (1906): 451.
172 *described Jesup's injury*: "Message from the President of the United States: Indian War in Florida," March 12, 1838, Ho. of Reps., Doc. No. 219, 25th Cong., 2nd Sess., 2. Casualties appear in this source.

TWENTY: TRUST

173 *Epigraph*: Abraham to Jesup, April 25, 1838, UFA.
173 *with the other captives*: A. G. W. Fanning to J. A. Chambers, January 2, 1838, Fanning F2, 18, PQH.
173 *detainees were dying*: George Turner to P. Morrison, December 12, 1837, ibid., 4–5.
173 *prisoners arrived on*: Wickman, *Osceola's Legacy*, 141.
173 *the Ellis Island*: Linda Conley, "Sullivan's Island Marking History of Slave Landings," *Herald-Journal*, June 27, 1999.
173 *long and sandy*: I take Poe's description of the island, although it appears in a work of fiction, as more or less accurate. See "The Gold Bug" in Edgar Allan Poe, *The Essential Tales and Poems of Edgar Allan Poe* (New York: Race Point Publishing, 2015), 30; George Catlin, "Osceola," *Native American*, February 10, 1838, 1; Moore, "South Carolina Lawyer," 363–64.
173 *a celebrity*: Wickman, *Osceola's Legacy*, 141–44.
174 *the demand was so great*: Van Arsdol, *Frontier Soldier*, 37–38.
174 *attended a play*: Coe, *Red Patriots*, 104.
174 *who seemed at peace*: Catlin, "Osceola," 1; "Death of Osceola," *Martinsburg Gazette*, February 14, 1838, 2.
174 *Poets, painters, and writers*: Viola, "Osceola," *Southern Argus*, April 10, 1838, 1; Catlin, "Osceola," 1; Wickman, *Osceola's Legacy*, 115; Frederick Weedon's diary pages, January 28–31, 1838, Weeden/Howell Collection Transcriptions, 4594, AAH.
174 *was confused and*: George Catlin to C. Harris, January 31, 1838, NAMP M234 roll 290.
174 *January 26*: May McNeer Ward, "The Disappearance of the of Osceola" *FHQ* 33, no. 3 (1954): 195–96, 198; Wickman, *Osceola's Legacy*, 146–47.
175 *a plaque*: Conley, "Sullivan's Island Marking History."
175 *lived year-round*: Jarvis, "Army Surgeon's Notes," 451.
175 *sliced the soldiers*: Jarvis, "Army Surgeon's Notes," *Journal of the Military Service Institution* 39, no. 144 (1906): 452; Rodenbough, *Everglade to Canyon*, 30; Jesup to H. Whiting, January 29, 1838; and Jesup to L. M. Powell, January 28, 1838, NARA RG 94 E 159Q, Box 40, 58, 59.
176 *between 1,300 and 1,400 horses*: N. S. Jarvis to his father, February 18, 1838, Nathanial Jarvis Papers, "Typescript of Letters," NYAM.

176 *five miles away:* J. B. S. Todd to Edwin Morgan, February 21, 1838, accessed February 4, 2025, https://www.christies.com/en/lot/lot-3918439.
176 *Abiaka had occupied:* Jarvis to his father, February 18, 1838; Phelps, "Journal (Loose Leaves)," E for February 7, 1838.
176 *The warriors were:* Phelps, "Journal (Loose Leaves)," E for February 3, 1838.
176 *commander caved:* Jesup to Taylor, February 2, 1838, NARA RG 94 E 159Q, Box 40, 69.
176 *requested peace talks:* Jarvis to his father, February 18, 1838; Jesup to R. Jones, February 9, 1838, NARA RG 94 E 159Q, Box 40, 86.
176 *the Secretary of War:* Jesup to Poinsett, February 11, 1838, ibid., 94–97; Kirby, "Diary," E for February 13, 1838, UFA; Robert Anderson, "Pocket Diary and Almanac for 1838," E for February 14, 1838, LOC.
176 *knew what it was:* Phelps, "Journal (Loose Leaves)," Es for February 8, 10, 13, and 25, 1838; Todd to Morgan, February 21, 1838.
177 *two days after Abraham:* Phelps, "Journal (Loose Leaves)," Es for February 22 and 24, 1838.
177 *a surgeon noted:* Jarvis, "Floridian War: Transcript," 43–44, NYAM.
177 *Motte fumed:* Motte, *Journey into Wilderness*, 210. Motte describes the female speaker on 209.
177 *brother to the late Cooper:* Monaco, *Second Seminole War*, 108.
177 *how she had earned:* Ibid.; also see Laurel Clark Shire, *Threshold of Manifest Destiny: Gender and National Expansion in Florida* (Philadelphia: University of Pennsylvania Press, 2016), 129–30.
177 *an astonished chief asked:* Phelps, "Journal (Loose Leaves)," E for February 26, 1838. Phelps also writes about the chiefs' avoidance of Jesup's ploy here, as does Anderson, "Pocket Diary and Almanac," E for February 27, 1838.
177 *a strange agreement:* Jesup to Poinsett, February 24, 1838, NARA RG 94 E 159Q, Box 40, 129.
178 *Washington's response:* Monaco, *Second Seminole War*, 112.
178 *capturing 513:* Ibid.; Jesup to J. A. Lagnel, March 21, 1838, NARA RG 94 E 159Q, Box 40, 216.
178 *to purchase Romeo:* J. P. Taylor to Zachary Taylor, January 31, 1838, Zachary Taylor Papers: Series 2, LOC; Jesup to Zachary Taylor, February 8, 1838, Doc. No. 225, 23.
178 *de Peyster didn't appreciate:* Thomas Jesup to [illegible], n.d., "Slave Owner Claims of Runaway Slaves," PQH.
178 *Jesup knew not to risk:* Ibid.; T. B. Linnard to W. de Peyster, March 25, 1838, Doc. No. 225, 25–26.
178 *Pacheco, and Primus:* Alcione M. Amos, "The Life of Luis Fatio Pacheco: Last Survivor of Dade's Battle," *Seminole Wars Foundation Pamphlet* 1, no. 1 (2006): n40.
178 *independent villages:* Jesup to Marcy, April 3, 1848, NAMP M547 roll 13, Special File 96. According to Jesup, the deal with the Black Seminoles was "that they should be sent to the West as a part of the Seminole Nation, and be settled in a separate village under the protection of the United States."
178 *Historians have described:* Wasserman, *People's History of Florida*, 288; Kristen T. Oertel, "The 'First' Emancipation Proclamation: Black Rebellion, Removal, and Freedom during the Seminole Wars," *Civil War History* 69, no. 4 (December 2023): 11–35.
178 *lively episodes:* Phelps, "Journal (Loose Leaves)," Es for February 26, March 6, and March 19, 1838.

179 *ship full of rice:* Ibid., E for February 2, 1838; Zachary Taylor to Jesup, February 5, 1838, Zachary Taylor Papers: Series 2, LOC.

179 *Soldiers marched past:* Forry, "Letters Part I," 138, 140; Forry, "Letters Part III," 98; Phelps, "Journal (Loose Leaves)," E for March 13, 1838.

179 *camp was dubbed:* Phelps, "Journal (Loose Leaves)," E for March 19, 1838.

179 *visited Fort Jupiter:* Ibid., E for February 22, 1838; Abraham to Jesup, April 25, 1838; Jesup to Taylor, March 24, 1838, NARA RG 94 E 159Q, Box 40, 232.

179 *came in with his people:* Taylor to Jesup, April 4, 1838, Zachary Taylor Papers: Series 2, LOC.

179 *designated as the:* J. Steele and J. M'Campbell, eds., *Laws of the Arkansas Territory* (Little Rock, AK: J. Steele, 1835), 300.

180 *going by water:* John Eaton to Lewis Cass, March 8, 1835, *ASP:MA* 6:493.

180 *he was ambushed:* See "Chief John Blount: Apalachicola Band of Creek Indians," *Calhoun Country Public Library*, n.d., accessed February 14, 2025, https://ccpl-fl.net/history/chief-john-blount/, which draws on written sources as well as on information from "current tribal Chief Mary Sixwomen Blount of the Apalachicola Band of Creek Indians (Texas Branch) and Ann McClellan, Chief of the Apalachicola Band of Creek Indians (Blountstown Branch)." The article seems to have been written around 2022. A slightly different version of events with the same essential facts appears in Edwin C. McReynolds, *The Seminoles* (Norman: University of Oklahoma Press, 1957), 129, 132–35. Note that this occurred under a separate treaty. Thompson reports Blount's death in Thompson to Herring, January 19, 1835, *ASP:MA* 7:485.

180 *fenceless little camp:* "Fort Denaud," NARA RG 94 E 464, PI-17, Box 37.

180 *dictated a letter:* Abraham to Jesup, April 25, 1838.

181 *he received new orders:* Ibid., which stipulates that Abraham's letter was received on April 30. Jesup learns that he is to turn over command to Taylor on April 29. Jesup to Taylor, April 29, 1838; Jesup to R. Jones, April 29, 1938, NARA RG 94 E 159Q, Box 40, 334–35.

TWENTY-ONE: STAND

182 *Epigraph:* "Journal of J. G. Reynolds," NAMP M234 roll 290. Hereafter cited as Reynolds, "Journal."

182 *arrived in Tampa Bay:* Dennis Kirk, "Finding the 'Real' Florida Along the Peace River," *Florida Weekly: Charlotte County Edition*, February 16, 2023; "Negroes who came in at Peas Creek," n.d.; "Negroes who surrendered to General Taylor," n.d.; and "Negroes bought in by August and Latty at Fort Jupiter," n.d., Thomas S. Jesup Papers, Box 25, Seminole War Period, LOC; J. P. Taylor to Zachary Taylor, January 31, 1838, Zachary Taylor Papers: Series 2, LOC; J. A. Chambers, "Orders No. 63," February 27, 1838, Doc. No. 225, 6.

182 *twenty-five packhorses:* Taylor to Jesup, March 21, 1838, Zachary Taylor Papers: Series 2, LOC.

182 *through lands that were:* Taylor to Jesup, March 14, 1838, ibid.

182 *arrived in New Orleans:* Littlefield, *Africans and Seminoles*, 30.

182 *vessels had shallow wooden hulls:* National Park Service and Middle Tennessee State University, *Rivers, Rails & Roads: Transportation During the Cherokee Removal, 1837–1839* (Murfreesboro, TN: CESU Task Agreement P18AC01316, 2020), 2. Also see Works Projects Administration, *Ship Registers and Enrollments of New Orleans, Louisiana*, vol. 3 (Baton Rouge: Louisiana State University, 1942), which has details on some of the ships.

183 *used little galley stoves:* Contract between J. G. Reynolds and George Whitman,

n.d., in Reynolds, "Journal," following Reynolds' advertisement of March 22, 1838. I have assumed that the requirements set out by Reynolds in the contract were the basic necessities generally arranged by the army.

183 *was eager to follow:* Abraham to Jesup, April 25, 1838, UFA.

183 *5 percent of passengers:* Mahon, *History of the Second Seminole War*, 252. Mortality rates varied depending on the voyage, to be sure.

183 *trauma was another:* Lozano and Mock, *My Black Seminole Ancestors*, 16.

183 *Jesup left a note:* Thomas Jesup, May 15, 1838, NARA RG 94 E 159Q, Box 41, 17.

183 *the New Orleans sheriff:* See Frederick Buisson's addition to John Reynolds to C. A. Harris, September 20, 1838, in Doc. No. 225, 116.

183 *suffered nine months:* The order was given on June 2, 1837, for the hostages to be immediately transferred to New Orleans. They would have arrived in mid-June 1837. See Linnard, "Orders, No. 116," June 2, 1837; and J. A. Chambers, "Orders, No. 124," June 12, 1837, Doc. No. 225, 3.

183 *persevered as captives:* See Thomas Jesup to R. Jones, July 20, 1837, Doc. No. 225, 65. On September 9, nine days after Jesup hires Abraham as an interpreter, Jesup checks in on his prisoners and asks Lieutenant F. Searle to make an accurate count of them (and record their names, ages, height, and sex, and to get them new clothes): Thomas Jesup to F. Searle, September 9, 1837, Doc. No. 225, 20. The list Jesup ordered appears in R&L F2, PQH, hereafter referred to as "Fort Pike List 1." Another version of this list appears as "List of Indian and Negro Prisoners turned over by Lieutenant George H. Terrett U.S. Marine Corps to Major Zantzinger U.S. Army Comdg Fort Pike La this 22 day of September 1837," NARA RG E 159Q, Box 17, Letters Received from Officers, Major R. A. Zantzinger, F2, hereafter referred to as Terrett, "Fort Pike List 2." The names and count between the two lists are identical; only the first list has gender, ages, and heights.

183 *foundation of cypress logs:* U.S. Department of the Interior, National Park Service, "National Register of Historic Places: Fort Pike," August 13, 1972, NARA RG 79, National Register of Historic Places and National Historic Landmarks Program Records: Louisiana, 2, accessed March 4, 2025, https://catalog.archives.gov/id/73974262.

184 *ten years old or younger:* "Fort Pike List 1."

184 *Jesup raised Abraham's salary:* J. A. Chambers, "Order No. 131," June 21, 1837, NARA 94 E 159Q, Box 44, 69; Doc. No. 103, 12; Thomas Jesup to C. A. Harris, September 24, 1837, Doc. No. 225, 21–22; Jesup to Searle, September 9, 1837, 20.

184 *a compound located:* U.S. Department of the Interior, "National Register of History Places: Jackson Barracks," n.d., NARA Record Group 79, National Register of Historic Places and National Historic Landmarks Program Records: Louisiana, 2–3, accessed March 4, 2025, https://catalog.archives.gov/id/73974264. See the Old Jackson Barracks Map in Rhett Breerwood, "Jackson Barracks Historic Garrison Overview," *New Orleans Historical*, September 19, 2023, accessed February 15, 2025, https://neworleanshistorical.org/items/show/760.

184 *in Louisiana:* Reynolds, "Journal," E for March 26, 1838; Littlefield, *Africans and Seminoles*, 41.

184 *eyeing the emigrants:* J. G. Reynolds to C. A. Harris, March 22, 1838, Doc. No. 225, 8.

184 *wrote, on March 22:* J. G. Reynolds to C. A. Harris, March 26, 1838, Doc. No. 225, 82.

184 *Fort Pike prisoners reached:* J. G. Reynolds to C. A. Harris, March 28, 1838; and C. A. Harris to J. G. Reynolds, March 22, 1838, in Reynolds, "Journal."

185 *inner circle:* Cody Lynn Berry, "Carey Allen Harris," *Encyclopedia of Arkansas*, June 16, 2023, accessed February 15, 2025, https://encyclopediaofarkansas.net/entries/carey-allen-harris-9370/.

185 *summer diseases:* J. Clark to C. A. Harris, May 1, 1838, in Foreman, *Transcripts* 6:170–71.

185 *As a result:* Henry W. Wharton to R. Jones, June 4, 1838, NARA RG 94, Letters Received, W261.

185 *named Buisson:* Doc. No. 225, 31, 116. The writ itself was dated May 2, 1838.

185 *Judge Buchanan:* Reynolds, "Journal," E for May 21, 1838; *Heirs of Love vs. E. P. Gaines*, 15.975 (1st Dist. 1838), F2, NOCA.

185 *walked up the wharf:* Reynolds, "Journal," E for May 21, 1838; Breerwood, "Jackson Barracks Historic Garrison."

185 *names and heights:* "Fort Pike List 1"; "Muster Roll of Thirty three Seminole Indian slaves claimed at New Orleans by civil authority from 21st May to 28th June 1838 about to emigrate west under the charge of Asst Conductor J. B. Benjamin 28th June 1838," NAMP M234 roll 290. Two Scipios are listed. The second is three feet, five inches tall.

186 *when that didn't work:* "Claims on the Indians," *Charleston Mercury*, May 30, 1838, 2.

186 *with a misfitting:* J. Campbell to Hugh Love, April 21, 1834, NAMP M234 roll 235, 480–81; J. Campbell to Elbert Herring, May 9, 1834, NAMP M234 roll 236, 435.

186 *Love's story went:* John H. Love to James Logan, July 4, 1840, NAMP M234 roll 923.

186 *given a valuation:* "*Heirs of Love vs. E. P. Gaines:* Judgement on Rule," Doc. No. 225, 31.

187 *he had hired someone:* Love to Logan, July 4, 1840, 101.

187 *listed sixty-seven Black Seminole captives:* "Fort Pike List 1"; Terrett, "Fort Pike List 2"; "Muster Roll of Thirty three Seminole," NAMP M234 roll 290.

187 *her granddaughter Abby:* "Muster Roll of Thirty three Seminole," NAMP M234 roll 290; Littlefield, *Africans and Seminoles*, 42.

187 *was hauled downtown:* "Extract of a letter from Lieutenant Reynolds," June 28, 1838, Doc. No. 225, 104; J. Reynolds to J. B. Benjamin, May 21, 1838, in Reynolds, "Journal."

187 *apparently left Fort Brooke:* George H. Griffin, "Orders No. 13," Doc. No. 225, 7; John Casey to Isaac Clark, July 11, 1838, Doc. No. 225, 119; Jarvis, "Diary: Army in Florida," 115.

187 *smaller and faster than:* Works Projects Administration, *Ship Registers*, 3:44.

187 *made the Alabama coast:* "Domestic Intelligence: New Orleans, June 14," June 28, 1838.

187 *reaching New Orleans:* "More Seminole Indians," *Courier*, June 14, 1838, 3. The *Columbia* was traveling with the *Tomachichi*, and I have assumed they arrived together (the phrasing is vague). The article says that the *Tomachichi* arrived on the thirteenth and that the *Columbia* was "in the river." It's possible the *Columbia* arrived on June 14, the day after the *Tomachichi*.

188 *had already departed:* Reynolds, "Journal," E for May 22, 1838.

188 *chased them upriver:* N. F. Collins to C. A. Harris, July 29, 1838, Doc. No. 225, 111.

TWENTY-TWO: TELL

189 *Epigraph:* Casey to Clark, July 11, 1838, Doc. No. 225, 119.
189 *at three knots:* Reynolds, "Journal," Es for May 22–25, 1838.
189 *gas streetlights:* John Magill, "Turning on the Streetlights in the French Quarter," *French Quarterly Magazine,* August 2, 2013, accessed March 4, 2025, https://frenchquarterly.com/history/turning-streetlights-french-quarter.
190 *displayed on the shores:* Rasmussen, *American Uprising,* 148.
190 *for fresh beef:* Reynolds, "Journal," Es for May 25 and 26, 1838.
190 *dispatched a boat:* Ibid., E for May 26, 1838; Reynolds to Harris, May 26, 1838, Doc. No. 225, 97–98; N. F. Collins to Harris, July 29, 1838, Doc. No. 225, 11; Harris to S. Cooper, May 9, 1838, Doc. No. 225, 45.
190 *had visited Washington:* Harris to S. Cooper, May 9, 1838, 28.
190 *then sold the claim:* "Report No. 724: Legal Representatives of James C. Watson," June 23, 1848, Ho. of Reps., Report No. 724, 30th Cong., 1st Sess., 1. Hereafter referred to as Report No. 724.
190 *loaned Harris:* Mary E. Young, "The Creek Frauds: A Study in Conscience and Corruption," *Mississippi Valley Historical Review* 42, no. 3 (December 1955): 430n75.
190 *resign amid scandal:* Ibid.; Berry, "Carey Allen Harris," *Encyclopedia of Arkansas,* June 16, 2023, accessed February 15, 2025, https://encyclopediaofarkansas.net/entries/carey-allen-harris-9370/.
190 *brother-in-law:* Mahon, *History of the Second Seminole War,* 251.
190 *mandate had been approved:* C. A. Harris to P. Morrison, May 9, 1838, Doc No. 225, 45; Harris to S. Cooper, May 9, 1838, 45.
190 *he told Reynolds:* Reynolds to [Harris], June 2, 1838, in Reynolds, "Journal."
191 *for fifty years:* Armstrong to Crawford, October 17, 1840, NARA Series M234 roll 923, 96.
191 *Reynolds forwarded a letter:* Reynolds to Sam Roane, June 3, 1838, Doc. No. 225, 102.
191 *reported to Washington:* "Extract of a letter from Lieutenant Reynolds," Doc. No. 225, 100.
191 *wanted no part of:* Sam Roane to Reynolds, June 4, 1838, Doc. No. 225, 102.
191 *also declined:* M. Arbuckle to Reynolds, June 13, 1838; and N. F. Collins to C. A. Harris, July 29, 1838, Doc. No. 225, 102–4, 111.
191 *edge of a swamp:* Henry Castellanos, *New Orleans as It Was* (Gretna, LA: Pelican Publishing Company, 1990),104; John K. Bardes, *The Carceral City: Slavery and the Making of Mass Incarceration in New Orleans, 1803-1930* (Chapel Hill: University of North Carolina Press, 2024), 63–64; Roulhac Toledano and et al., *New Orleans Architecture* (Gretna, LA: Pelican Publishing Company, 2003), 6:63.
192 *cauldrons of bats spun:* New Orleans Press, *Historical Sketch Book and Guide to New Orleans* (New York: Will H. Coleman, 1885), 298.
192 *forced into hard labor:* Andrea Armstrong, *The Impact of 300 Years of Jail Conditions* (New Orleans: Data Center, 2018), 3.
192 *executed the disobedient:* Rashauna Johnson, *Slavery's Metropolis: Unfree Labor in New Orleans During the Age of Revolutions* (New York: Cambridge University Press, 2016), 160.
192 *Micanopy's nephew:* Monaco, *Second Seminole War,* 90.
192 *visited the captives in person:* Clark to Reynolds, September 13, 1838; and John Casey to Isaac Clark, July 11, 1838, Doc. No. 225, 118–19.
192 *for his taste:* Laumer, *Amidst a Storm of Bullets,* 111.

192 *total residents would surpass:* Ned Sublette and Constance Sublette, *American Slave Coast: A History of the Slave-Breeding Industry* (Chicago: Lawrence Hill, 2016), 507.

192 *went hand in hand:* Bardes, *Carceral City*, 64.

192 *was the town hero:* Castellanos, *New Orleans as It Was*, 141.

192 *slavery here was:* Johnson, *Slavery's Metropolis*, i.

192 *held their harvest festivals:* Richard Brent Turner, *Jazz Religion, the Second Line, and Black New Orleans after Hurricane Katrina* (Bloomington: Indiana University Press, 2017), 19.

193 *danced and drummed:* Willie Lee Rose, ed., *A Documentary History of Slavery in North American* (Athens: University of Georgia Press, 1999), 515.

193 *the chief discovered:* Casey to Clark, July 11, 1838, 121.

193 *taken at the Cabildo:* My thanks go to Gregory Osborn, Library Associate III, at the New Orleans City Archives & Special Collections, for the information (email to author, September 24, 2024).

193 *argued that the captives:* Testimony of George W. Allen, *Heirs of Love vs. E. P. Gaines*, 15.975 (1st Dist. 1838), NOCA, F2.

193 *Eliza whose freedom:* Testimony of Henry W. Wharton and Testimony of Eliza, ibid.

193 *jail for ten days:* Tod Robinson to J. G. Reynolds, October 2, 1838, Doc. No. 225, 125.

193 *at the Hotel D'Orleans:* Collins to Clark, June 26, 1838, Doc. No. 225, 114; New Orleans Press, *Historical Sketch Book*, 71.

194 *thirty-one of the thirty-three:* Collins to Harris, July 29, 1838, 111.

194 *downplayed the true number:* Casey to Clark, July 11, 1838, 119–21; "Fort Pike List 1"; Terrett, "Fort Pike List 2"; "Muster Roll of Thirty three Seminole," NAMP M234 roll 290; "Register of Indian and Negro Prisoners . . . owned by Indians," R&L F1, PQH; a similar list, untitled and undated, appears in R&L F3, PQH.

194 *basis of Abraham's statement:* Clark to Reynolds, September 13, 1838, 118; Casey to Clark, July 11, 1838, 119–21.

194 *general stink of fraud:* Clark to Reynolds, September 13, 1838, 118; Collins to Harris, July 29, 1838, 111.

194 *gave birth in jail:* "Muster Roll of Thirty three Seminole," NAMP M234 roll 290.

194 *left New Orleans:* The entire incident is covered in detail in Doc. No. 225. See Tod Robinson to J. G. Reynolds, October 2, 1838, 124–25; "Extract of a letter from Lieutenant Reynolds," June 28, 1838, 104; George Whitman to Reynolds, September 12, 1838, 116–17; N .F. Collins to C. A. Harris, August 8, 1838, 112; C. A. Harris to J. G. Reynolds, August 27, 1838, 50.

195 *After freeing his:* Jarvis, "Diary: Army in Florida," E for July 5, 1838, 115. Jarvis has Abraham's return date and the mention of the Green Corn festival, which also appears in N. S. Jarvis to his father, July 4, 1838, "Typescript of Letters," NYAM.

195 *a vaudeville show:* "Vaudevilles," *Times-Picayune*, June 17, 1838, 2; "How D-Ye Do?," *Times-Picayune*, July 10, 1838, 3; *Times-Picayune*, June 24, 1838, 2; "The Seminole Indians," *Times-Picayune*, June 23, 1838, 3.

195 *announced the honored guests:* "The Seminole Indians," *Times-Picayune*, June 23, 1838, 3.

195 *walked toward Pease Creek:* Jarvis, "Diary: Army in Florida," 122, 124–25.

195 *Florida War continued:* Kimball, *Seminole & Creek War Battles*, 82–83.
195 *Statesmen held a convention:* Hoffman, *Florida's Frontiers*, 308–9.

TWENTY-THREE: THE DEVIL'S GARDEN

197 *plagued Zachary Taylor as:* Zachary Taylor to Hancock Taylor, August 14, 1838, Series 6, Additions, 1820–63, mss42440, Box 1, LOC.
197 *likely only to:* Jarvis, "Diary: Army in Florida," E for November 6, 1838, 157, NYAM.
197 *informed the War Department:* Monaco, *Second Seminole War*, 116.
198 *sloops and two brigs:* Jarvis, "Diary: Army in Florida," E for September 22, 1838, 145.
198 *hurricane season of 1838:* Ibid., Es for October 13 and 16, 1838, 150–52; Buker, *Swamp Sailors*, 73–78; Cooper Kirk, "Edward Zane, Carroll Judson, Alias Ned Buntline," *Broward Legacy* 3, no. 3–4 (1979): 17.
198 *skulls of shipwreck victims:* John Phelps to Helen Phelps, December 17, 1838, J. W. Phelps Papers, Box 214, LOC.
198 *hat of sugar paper:* John Phelps to Helen Phelps, March 6, 1839, ibid.
198 *sent word to the army:* Jarvis, "Diary: Army in Florida," E for October 25, 1838, 154.
198 *true and pressed on:* John Phelps to Helen Phelps, October 18, 1838, J. W. Phelps Papers, Box 214.
198 *feasted and the officers:* Jarvis, "Diary: Army in Florida," E for December 25, 1838, 170–71.
198 *140 Black Seminoles:* Motte, *Journey into Wilderness*, 210.
198 *celebrated to songs:* Jarvis, "Diary: Army in Florida," E for January 1, 1839, 175.
199 *he freed his son: Record Book of Hillsborough County*, 1:142.
199 *Several days later:* Jarvis, "Diary: Army in Florida," Es for February 26 and March 1, 1839, 191, 193; "Muster Roll of a Party of Seminole Indians about to emigrate west of the Mississippi River, under the direction of P. Morrison," NAMP M234 roll 291, 253–55.
199 *Abraham had won:* "Domestic Intelligence: Florida War," *Army and Navy Chronicle*, March 28, 1839.
199 *smiled and laughed:* Jarvis, "Diary: Army in Florida," E for March 1, 1839, 193; "Emigrating Seminoles," *Army and Navy Chronicle*, April 25, 1839.
199 *reached Fort Gibson:* Amanda L. Paige, Fuller L. Bumpers, and Daniel F. Littlefield Jr., *The North Little Rock Site on the Trail of Tears National Historic Trail: Historical Contexts Report* (Little Rock, AK: American Native Press Archives, 2003), 38–39; "Muster Roll of a Party of Seminole Indians," 255.
200 *according to the Sense Bearer:* Motte, *Journey into Wilderness*, 210.
200 *at least one hundred fifty were:* Thomas Jesup to James Gadsden, June 14, 1837, Doc. No. 225, 18, lists eighty-four; "Testimony written by C. C. Heriot (typescript)," n.d., 1845, Civil War Collection, Stuart A. Rose Manuscript, Archives, and Rare Book Library, DLG, lists seventy people returned to the Woodruff estate after two years, which if accurate puts that date as December 1837. A number were turned over after Osceola was captured, but many of those individuals were claimed by the Woodruff estate. See "List of Indians who arrived at Fort Mellon," November 30, 1837, Indian Documents, MC16.93, AHS. It is difficult to calculate this figure with certainty without cross-referencing more detailed, dated lists than appear to exist.
200 *for the British Bahamas:* Kenneth W. Porter, "Notes on Seminole Negroes in

the Bahamas," *FHQ* 25, no. 1 (1945): 59; Jesup to Joseph McBride, June 8, 1837, Doc. No. 225, 17.

200 *enslavers wrote letters:* Jesup to Joseph McBride, June 8, 1837, Doc. No. 225, 17; "Florida Citizen Petitions and Claims," PQH; "Claims against the Seminole Indians for property loses, treaty of 1832. 1835–1839," NAMP M547 roll 27, Special File 125; "Seminole claims to certain Negroes, 1841–49," NAMP M547 roll 13, Special File 96.

200 *would live to the end:* "Statement of the Claim of the Heirs of Sally Factor," NAMP M234 roll 802, 398–99; Littlefield, *Africans and Seminoles,* 33n19, 34n40.

200 *Jumper died in New Orleans:* "Another Chief Gone," *Martinsburg Gazette,* May 2, 1838, 3.

200 *waited at Fort King to meet:* Mahon, *History of the Second Seminole War,* 255–57.

200 *the attire of his rank:* Monaco, *Second Seminole War,* 122.

201 *warriors finally showed:* Ibid., 124–26; Mahon, *History of the Second Seminole War,* 256–57, 261–62.

201 *feigned complete ignorance:* Monaco, *Second Seminole War,* 127.

201 *divided the inland:* Rodenbough, *Everglade to Canyon,* 35.

201 *killed or crippled:* Monaco, *Second Seminole War,* 128.

201 *officer at Fort Lauderdale:* "Copy of a Letter from a Young Officer of the Army," *Army and Navy Chronicle,* August 8, 1839.

201 *a soldier grieved:* Mahon, *History of the Second Seminole War,* 269.

201 *be relieved of command:* Ibid., 274; Monaco, *Second Seminole War,* 128.

201 *More colonists died:* Kimball, *Alachua Ambush,* iii.

201 *offering Abiaka $10,000:* West, "Abiaka, or Sam Jones," 404.

201 *Navy led riverine excursions:* Ibid.; Monaco, *Second Seminole War,* 110, 132; George E. Buker, "The Mosquito Fleet's Guides and the Second Seminole War," *FHQ* 57, no. 3 (1978): 310; Coe, *Red Patriots,* 121.

202 *pushed through dense sedges:* Buker, "Mosquito Fleet's Guides," 310, 313.

202 *One island:* "Second Expedition of Colonel Harney in the Everglades," *Niles National Register,* April 3, 1841.

202 *by chickee homes and:* West, "Abiaka, or Sam Jones," 404.

202 *Abiaka and the families survived:* Ibid.; Deanna Butler, "The Devil, Abiaka: The Legacy of Sam Jones," September 21, 2023, Ah-Tah-Thi-Ki Museum, accessed February 22, 2025, https://floridaseminoletourism.com/the-devil-abiaka-the-legacy-of-sam-jones/.

202 *called for an immediate:* "Texas and the United States," *Liberator,* April 15, 1842.

202 *a push to cauterize:* Monaco, *Second Seminole War,* 115.

203 *still dreamed of victory:* "Florida," *Charleston Daily Courier,* January 15, 1842, 2.

203 *special message to Congress:* James D. Richardson, ed., *A Compilation of the Messages and Papers of the Presidents,* vol. 4, no. 2 (Washington: Bureau of National Literature and Art, 1908), 154–55. The address is dated May 10 and was delivered to Congress on May 11, 1842. "Senate, May 11," *Georgia Constitutionalist,* May 19, 1842, 4.

203 *To commemorate the occasion:* Monaco, *Second Seminole War,* 133–34; Kimball, *Seminole & Creek War Battles,* 100.

TWENTY-FOUR: INK & LEAD

204 *army regulars died:* Monaco, *Second Seminole War,* 139. Militiamen often served shorter terms, so it would be inappropriate to apply the same fatality rate as that suffered by the army regulars.

204 *cost of an estimated:* Mahon, *History of the Second Seminole War,* 326.

204 *lost several hundred:* Hoffman, *Florida's Frontiers*, 305. This is deaths in combat, to be clear.

204 *petitioned Congress for:* "Memorial to Congress by Inhabitants of Leon County," July 1, 1842, *TP* 26:491–94.

204 *peninsula's growth was paltry:* James W. Covington, "The Armed Occupation Act of 1842," *FHQ* 40, no. 1 (1961): 41.

205 *fever tore through Tallahassee:* Baptist, *Creating an Old South*, 187–89. The epidemic hit in 1841.

205 *a fire consumed Tallahassee:* Ibid., 189; Gerald Ensley, "1843 Tallahassee Fire Started at Hotel Dixie," *Tallahassee Democrat*, October 10, 2014; Ana Goñi-Lessan, "'Perfect and Entire Ruin': How Tallahassee Survived After 1843 Inferno," *Tallahassee Democrat*, April 23, 2024; F. Eppes, "The Tallahassee Fire of 1843," *FHQ* 7, no. 2 (1928): 165.

205 *hurricane razed Port Leon:* "After a Hurricane, Port Leon Vanished," *Orlando Sentinel*, October 25, 1992; Jeff Burlew and Gerald Ensley, "A History of Hurricane Hits and Near Misses for Tallahassee and the Big Bend," *Tallahassee Democrat*, September 25, 2024.

205 *Florida seemed cursed:* Baptist, *Creating an Old South*, 189.

205 *chomped on cotton:* Ibid., 187; Hoffman, *Florida's Frontiers*, 307.

206 *indefinitely suspended taxes:* Hoffman, *Florida's Frontiers*, 307.

206 *single solvent bank:* James C. Clark, *A Concise History of Florida* (Charleston, SC: History Press, 2014), chap. 9.

206 *the least populated state:* Ibid.

206 *statesmen dutifully pledged: Journal of the Proceedings of the Senate of the Territory of Florida at Its Seventh Session* (Tallahassee: Joseph Clisby, 1845), 62.

206 *the state General Assembly met: Journal of the Proceedings of the Senate of the General Assembly of the State of Florida at Its First Session* (Tallahassee: Joseph Clisby, 1845), 3.

206 *news arrived that Andrew Jackson:* Ibid., 4, 6.

206 *saluted America's seventh:* Ibid., 6; "Death of Gen. Jackson," *Star of Florida*, June 27, 1845, 2.

206 *celebrating statehood paused to mourn:* "Death of Gen. Jackson," *Star of Florida*, June 27, 1845, 2.

206 *Jesup visited him, on May 29:* "Biographical Sketch of Gen. Jackson," *Indiana State Sentinel*, July 3, 1845, 1; Remini, *Jackson and the Course of American Democracy*, 517–21, 524. Jackson's death is drawn from Remini.

207 *George, fanned the flies:* Remini, *Jackson and the Course of American Democracy*, 519. Remini describes the individual as "a servant boy." This would have been George, Jackson's personal "manservant," who "slept in the president's bedroom, on a pallet next to his bed, so that he was accessible any time Jackson needed him": Callie Hopkins, "The Enslaved Household of President Jackson," White House Historical Association, August 1, 2019.

207 *removed all Afro-descent:* Remini, *Jackson and the Course of American Democracy*, 524.

207 *lithographs also erased:* Hopkins, "Enslaved Household"; Nathaniel Currier, "Death of Genl. Andrew Jackson. President of the United States from 1829–1837," 1845, D'Amour Museum of Fine Arts; J. Baillie, "The Death of President Andrew Jackson in Washington," 1845, accessed February 23, 2025, https://wellcomecollection.org/works/jphjt9d2.

207 *George pulled out two:* "'Old Hannah's' Narrative of Jackson's Last Days," June 1845, in Bassett, *Correspondence of Andrew Jackson* 6:415.

207 *Clinical death was recorded:* Remini, *Jackson and the Course of American Democracy,* 525; Jonathan Jarry, "In Death, Our Body Feasts on Itself," McGill Office for Science and Society, May 20, 2021, accessed February 23, 2025, https://www.mcgill.ca/oss/article/general-science/death-our-body-feasts-itself.

207 *thousands of grouse roamed:* Grant Foreman and Carolyn Thomas Foreman, *Fort Gibson: A Brief History* (Norman: University of Oklahoma Press, 1936), 3–8; "Report of a Survey of the Military Reservation at Fort Gibson," November 1842, NAMP M1302 roll 8.

207 *camped below Fort Gibson:* Porter, *Black Seminoles,* 111–12, 126.

207 *Abraham as his confidant:* Littlefield, *Africans and Seminoles,* 100.

207 *people lived freely:* "Affidavit of J. L. Hill in Relation to the Seminole Indians," February 10, 1841, NARA RG 393 Part 1, E 73A Box 1.

207 *which outsiders found:* B. Marshall, G. W. Stidham, and George Scott to William Medill, April 26, 1848, NAMP M547 roll 13, Special File 96. See the summary on the exterior of the folded letter.

208 *one Indian agent reported:* Porter, *Black Seminoles,* 121; Charles W. Dean to George Mannypenny, June 24, 1856, NAMP M234 roll 802, 105.

208 *Jesup was blamed:* Marcellus Duval to John Mason, May 20, 1848, NAMP M547 roll 13, Special File 96.

208 *attorney general insisted:* "Opinion of J. Y. Mason," June 28, 1848, ibid.

208 *claims on the families continued:* Armstrong to Crawford, October 17, 1840, NAMP M234 roll 923; Littlefield, *Africans and Seminoles,* 81, 102–4.

208 *Creeks in Indian Territory:* Porter, *Black Seminoles,* 119.

208 *Creek and white:* Littlefield, *Africans and Creeks,* 143.

208 *eighteen were forced:* Porter, *Black Seminoles,* 117–18.

208 *entered into talks:* Littlefield, *Africans and Seminoles,* 89–90, 102.

208 *descended on a settlement:* Ibid., 121.

208 *take August's brother:* Littlefield, *Africans and Seminoles,* 108, 145.

209 *named Walking Joe:* Porter, *Black Seminoles,* 127.

209 *Abraham's men preferred:* Ibid., 126.

209 *Seminoles held true and:* Littlefield, *Africans and Creeks,* 210.

209 *word of the raid:* Porter, *Black Seminoles,* 132–33; F. Dent to F. Flint, July 15, 1850, NARA RG 94, Letters Received, D210, also available as NAMP M567 roll 427, 416–18.

209 *made it clearly known:* John Drennen to Newman McIntosh, June 30, 1850, NAMP M567 roll 427, 424.

209 *to escape the troubles:* Littlefield, *Africans and Seminoles,* 200.

209 *prohibiting enslaved people from owning:* Littlefield, *Africans and Creeks,* 145.

209 *ignored the decree:* Porter, *Black Seminoles,* 127.

TWENTY-FIVE: AUTUMN IN NEW YORK

210 *his sixties, sporting:* Abraham's year of birth is often put at 1787, which was arrived at by backdating the 1837 list, which has him as fifty years old. See "Registry of negro prisoners," Doc. No. 225, 66–67; "Arrival of Indians at Washington," *Sun,* September 16, 1852, 2.

210 *a Southern newspaper described:* "Florida Indians," *Weekly Southern Standard,* February 7, 1852, 2.

210 *he was relegated to being:* "Billy Bowlegs," *Wilmington Journal,* September 7, 1852, 2.

210 *soon to be head chief:* Susan A. Miller, *Coacoochee's Bones: A Seminole Saga* (Lawrence: University Press of Kansas, 2003), 176; Porter, "Negro Abraham," 36.

210 *witnessed Dade's defeat:* D. M. Marrs., ed., "Biographical Sketch of John Jumper," *Indian Chieftain* 15, no. 7 (1896). Reproduced in Seminole Nation, Box 1 F7, John Jumper Collection 1874–1928, Islandora Repository, UOA, accessed February 25, 2025, https://repository.ou.edu/islandora/object/oku%3A34932.

211 *the Nation in Florida:* Knetsch, Missall, and Missall, *History of the Third Seminole War*, chap. 1.

211 *steamship to Georgia:* George L. B. to Manne, January 25, 1850, transcript #366, AMC. The transcribed year date should be 1853.

211 *shown a printing press:* "Distinguished Arrivals," *Boston Herald*, September 20, 1852, 2nd ed., 1.

211 *a whirlwind tour of metropolises:* "Indian Delegations in Washington—Billy Bowlegs," *Baltimore Patriot and Commercial Gazette*, September 16, 1852, 2.

211 *Fillmore spoke about obligation:* "What Bowlegs Thinks of New York," *Richmond Enquirer*, November 12, 1852, 2; "Seminole Interview with the President," *New York Daily Times*, September 21, 1852, 3.

211 *perused the armaments factory:* "The Seminole Indians," *Republic*, September 20, 1852, 3.

211 *Visiting the Smithsonian:* "Indian Chiefs in a Picture Gallery," *Boston Semi-Weekly Advertiser*, Saturday Morning, September 25, 1852; "What Bowlegs Thinks of New York," November 12, 1852, 2.

211 *appeared in the paintings: Portraits of North American Indians, with Sketches of Scenery, Etc., Painted by J. M. Stanley. Deposited with the Smithsonian Institution* (Washington: Smithsonian Institution, 1852), 5–8. Cudjo appeared in one of the paintings as a "negro Interpreter."

211 *how young he looked:* "The Seminole Indian Delegation," *Republic*, September 17, 1852.

212 *they attended a concert:* "Halls of the Metropolis," *New-London Democrat*, Saturday Morning, September 25, 1842, 1.

212 *Philadelphia, theater:* Report of the Secretary of the Interior, "Abstract of expenses incurred by Luther Black, special agent, &c., in taking delegation, consisting of Billy Bowlegs and other Indians (seven in number), from Florida to Washington and New York, and returning," June 16, 1854, Executive Document No. 71, 33rd Cong., 1st Sess., 29. Hereafter referred to as Ex. Doc. No. 71.

212 *reached New York on:* "The Seminoles En Route for Florida," *Charleston Courier*, September 30, 1852.

212 *the journey had been:* Ex. Doc. No. 71, 29, 34, 62; "Billy Bowlegs," *Wilmington Journal*, September 17, 1852, 2.

212 *stopped at 229 Broadway:* Details of the New York itinerary appear in "Arrival of Billy Bowlegs and Suite," *New York Times*, September 24, 1852, 8; "Movements of Billy Bowlegs and His Companions," *New York Times*, September 25, 1852, 8; "Billy Bowlegs in Gotham," *New York Times*, September 27, 1852, 8; "Arrival of Billy Bowlegs and His Companion Seminole Indians," *Evening Mirror*, September 25, 1852, 3; "Departure of Billy Bowlegs and Suite," *Baltimore Patriot and Commercial Gazette*, September 28, 1852, 2; also see Matthew Dripps, "Map of the City of New York Extending Northward to Fiftieth St. Surveyed and Drawn by John F. Harrison," 1852, David Rumsey Map Collection, accessed February 26, 2025, https://www.davidrumsey.com/maps2977.html.

212 *fountain that could spout:* "City Hall Park," n.d., accessed February 26, 2025, https://www.nycgovparks.org/parks/city-hall-park/history.

212 *taxpayer-funded budget:* L. Lea to Luther Blake, September 22, 1852, Ex. Doc. No. 71, 14. For the Marble Palace see Sam Roberts, *A History of New York in*

27 Buildings: The 400-Year Untold Story of an American Metropolis (New York: Bloomsbury, 2019), 64–74.

213 *necessities and pleasures:* Ex. Doc. No. 71.

213 *a photographic portrait:* "'Billy Bowlegs' and Suite," *Illustrated London News,* May 21, 1853, 395–96; "Daguerreotype Galleries of the Meade Brothers," *History of Photography* 1, no. 4 (1977): 348.

213 *a sketch of the photo:* Reproductions of the sketch and the photo appear in Orlando Museum of Art, "Enduring Beauty: Seminole Art & Culture. From the collection of: I. S. K. Reeves V & Sara W. Reeves," n.d., 14, accessed February 26, 2025, https://omart.org/wp-content/uploads/2024/09/Enduring_Beauty_Edited_Catalogue_Complete_Final.pdf.

213 *predators and prey were caged:* Adrienne Saint-Pierre, "PTB Letters (#57) The Secret Has Cost Me Much Trouble," Barnum's Museum, June 4, 2021, accessed February 26, 2025, https://barnum-museum.org/the-secret-has-cost-me-much-trouble/; "Billy Bowlegs in Gotham," September 27, 1852, 8.

214 *how many warriors:* "Departure of Billy Bowlegs and Suite," September 28, 1852, 2.

214 *he told them, on:* "What Bowlegs Thinks of New York," November 12, 1852, 2.

214 *laughing at the start:* "Movements of Billy Bowlegs," September 25, 1852, 8.

214 *diatribes on calico frocks:* "Arrival of Billy Bowlegs and Suite," September 25, 1852; "'Billy Bowlegs' and Suite," *Illustrated London News,* May 21, 1853, 395; "The Seminole Delegation," *Daily National Intelligencer,* September 15, 1852.

214 *odd he wore:* Porter, "Negro Abraham," 34.

214 *headwrap lent him:* "Indian Chiefs in a Picture Gallery," September 25, 1852.

215 *attire hinted at Othello:* "Calumnies Against General Scott—Billy Bowlegs and the Florida Indians," *New York Daily Times,* September 21, 1852, 6.

215 *the Deep South, but only:* "The Seminole Delegation," *Daily National Intelligencer,* September 15, 1852; "Indian Chiefs in a Picture Gallery," September 25, 1852; "Correspondence of the *Journal of Commerce,*" *Weekly Journal of Commerce,* September 30, 1852, 3.

215 *him their "interpreter" but:* "Halls of the Metropolis," September 25, 1852, 1.

215 *Bowlegs himself spoke English:* "Arrival of Billy Bowlegs and Suite," September 25, 1852.

215 *pleasant perfume:* "Halls of the Metropolis," September 25, 1852, 1.

215 *one outside observer:* "Indians at Washington," *Preston Chronicle and Lancashire Advertiser,* October 16, 1852, 2.

215 *described him discreetly:* "Billy Bowlegs and Suite," *New-York Evangelist,* September 30, 1852, 159.

215 *the dissonance of the:* "Billy Bowlegs, &c," *Sunday Dispatch,* September 26, 1852.

215 *when asked about him:* "Correspondence of the *Journal of Commerce,*" September 30, 1852, 3.

215 *last recorded sighting:* Porter, "Negro Abraham," 36; "A Veteran," *Daily Missouri Republican,* December 21, 1870, 5.

215 *sits outside of the fence:* Lantz, *Seminole Indians of Florida: 1850–1874,* 70, 156–57, 207, 259; Lantz, *Seminole Indians of Florida: 1875–1879,* 51, 91. My thanks for this information go to Carol Scott, a local resident in Oklahoma who knew of the graves and took pictures of them (email to author, July 21, 2023). I am being intentionally vague about the precise location, to protect the site.

215 *watch his son Peter:* "Bruner, Peter; Lincoln Peter," Veterans Administration Master Index Card 2500824, accessed February 27, 2025, https://www.familysearch

.org/ark:/61903/1:1:QPZ9-QWNX; author interview with Jimmie Abraham, July 19, 2023; "Peter Lincoln, Aged Freedman, Taken by Death," *Seminole Producer*, December 8, 1936, 2; Lantz, *Seminole Indians of Florida: 1850–1874*, 259; Chairman to Peter Lincoln, April 25, 1905, NARA RG 75, Applications for Enrollment in the Five Civilized Tribes, Dawes Enrollment Jacket for Seminole, Seminole Card #744.

216 *Rachel fight for the dues:* Rachel Abraham to Baldwin, July 15, 1870, NAMP M234 roll 804, 506.

216 *become a mother herself:* Lantz, *Seminole Indians of Florida: 1850–1874*, 258; Seminole Nation Freedman Roll, Charles Bruner, NARA RG 75, Enrollment Cards, Enrollment for Seminole Census Card 777, accessed February 27, 2025, https://catalog.archives.gov/id/268351?objectPage=2.

216 *granted Afro-descendant citizens:* Gary Zellar, *African Creeks: Estelvste and the Creek Nation* (Norman: University of Oklahoma Press, 2007), 160; C. W. Dawson, "Remembering Tradition: Marking August 4 as Emancipation Day," *Columbia Missourian*, August 3, 2021.

216 *people were welcome to attend:* "An Interview of Aaron Grayson" by Billie Byrd, September 10, 1937, University of Oklahoma Western History Collections, Indian-Pioneer Papers, UOA, accessed February 27, 2025, https://repository.ou.edu/islandora/object/oku%3A13570.

CODA

217 *recorded the folktales:* Evans, "Seminole Folktales," 482–85.

217 *spoke to Jesup's deeds:* Jumper, *Legends of the Seminoles*, 79.

Selected Sources

ARCHIVAL MATERIAL

Abraham. "Letter to Thomas S. Jesup. Fort Deynand," April 25, 1838. Pioneer Days in Florida, P. K. Yonge Library Special Collections, University of Florida Smathers Libraries, Gainesville, FL.

———. Photostat of original letter, "Abraham Sends His Talk to Coe Hadjo," September 11, 1837. Pioneer Days in Florida, Miscellaneous Manuscripts, 00, 106. P. K. Yonge Library Special Collections, University of Florida Smathers Libraries, Gainesville, FL.

Adjutant General, ed. *Florida War*, n.d. Record Group 94: Records of the Adjutant General's Office, 1780s to 1917, Oversize Documents Withdrawn from Various AGO Files, Roller Drawer No. 5, Box 12. National Archives and Records Administration, Washington, DC.

Anderson, Robert. "Pocket Diary and Almanac for 1838." Robert Anderson Papers, 1819–1948, MSS10967, Box 1. Manuscript Division, Library of Congress, Washington, DC.

———. Robert Anderson Papers, 1819–1948, MSS10967, Box 2: March 9, 1836–September 31, 1839. Manuscript Division, Library of Congress, Washington, DC.

Belton, Francis Smith. "Autobiography." Dade Belton-Kirby-Dawson-Todd Families Papers, 1763–1892, MssCol 258, Papers of Francis Smith Belton, 1818–53, V7. Manuscripts and Archives Division, New York Public Library, New York, NY.

———. "Letters to His Wife Harriet Kirby Belton, 1834–1836." Dade Belton-Kirby-Dawson-Todd Families Papers, 1763–1892, MssCol 258, Papers of Francis Smith Belton, 1818–1853, V10. Manuscripts and Archives Division, New York Public Library, New York, NY.

Call, Richard Keith. "Richard Keith Call Journal and Transcriptions of Journal," n.d. Richard Keith Call Papers, N2013–5. Historical Records, State Library and Archives of Florida, Tallahassee, FL.

Carter, Clarence Edwin, ed. *The Territorial Papers of the United States.* 28 vols. Washington: U.S. Government Printing Office, 1934–75.

Casey, John Charles. "Memoranda Concerning the Seminoles," 1837. John Charles Casey Diaries and Papers, CU 551, Box 1. Special Collections, U.S. Military Academy, West Point, NY.

Clinch, Duncan Lamont. "Clinch Letterbook—1834–35 Ft. King, Fla." Duncan Lamont Clinch, 1787–1849. Manuscript Division, Library of Congress, Washington, DC.

Cushman, Hosea Lewis. "Journal, 1836–1837." Hosea Lewis Cushman, 1806–39, Coll. 1406. Special Collections, Maine Historical Society, Portland, ME.

SELECTED SOURCES

Dickens, Asbury, and John W. Forney, eds. *American State Papers: Military Affairs*. 7 vols. Washington: Gales and Seaton, 1832–60.

Eaton, Amos Beebe. "Journal of Amos B. Eaton," July 31, 1837–August 24, 1838. Amos Beebe Eaton Papers, ASM0239, Box 1. Archives and Special Collections, Otto G. Richter Library, University of Miami, Coral Gables, FL.

Eliza. Testimony and Cross-Examination of Eliza, May 10, 1838. *Heirs of Love vs. E. P. Gaines*, 15.975 (1st Dist. 1838). New Orleans City Archives & Special Collections, New Orleans, LA.

Fogg, James P. Letter to his parents, December 25, 1834. Howe-Fogg Family Papers, 1834–35, N-2342, Fogg Family Papers, Box 1, F1. Massachusetts Historical Society, Boston, MA.

Foster, William. Letter to Betty Foster, November 13, 1837. William Stanhope Foster Papers, MSC 0686, F55. McClung Historical Collection, Knox County Library East Tennessee History Center, Knoxville, TN.

Gamble, Robert. "Extracts from Journal of Robert Gamble," 1900, 1970. Gamble Family Papers, 1818–53, 1898, 1962, MSS105 B147, F02. Florida Manuscript Collections, Special Collections & Archives, Florida State University Libraries, Tallahassee, FL.

Hitchcock, Ethan Allen. *Fifty Years in Camp and Field: Diary of Major-General Ethan Allen Hitchcock*. New York: G. P. Putnam's Sons, 1909.

Hughes, Ellis. "Ellis Hughes Diary: Transcript," 1838. Select Florida Studies Manuscripts, H38-00002. Tampa Special Collections, Digital Commons: University of South Florida Libraries.

Irwin, John R. "Memoir, 1836," July–December 1836. Florida Miscellaneous Manuscript Collection 01, 007. George A. Smathers Library, Special and Area Studies Collections, University of Florida, Gainesville, FL.

Jackson, Andrew. "Excerpt of a private letter from General Jackson to the Secretary of War dated Hermitage Oct 1st 1837." Thomas Sidney Jesup Papers, 1780–1907, MSS27789, Box 6, February 25, 1836–April 6, 1838. Manuscript Division, Library of Congress, Washington, DC.

———. Letter to Thomas Jesup, August 2, 1836. Record Group 94: Records of the Adjutant General's Office, 1780s to 1917, Letters Received, J156, NAMP M567 roll 126, frames 196–98. National Archives and Records Administration, Washington, DC.

———. Letter to Thomas Jesup, August 3, 1836. Record Group 94: Records of the Adjutant General's Office, 1780s to 1917, Letters Received, J156, NAMP M567 roll 126, frames 200–202. National Archives and Records Administration, Washington, DC.

Jarvis, Nathan Sturgis. "M.S. N.S. Jarvis Diary . . . Army in Florida," June 1, 1837–August 30, 1839. Special Collections, New York Academy of Medicine Rare Book Room, New York, NY.

———. "Typescript of Letters in NYAM Library," February 5, 1837–August 1, 1839. Special Collections, New York Academy of Medicine Rare Book Room, New York, NY.

Jesup, Thomas Sidney. "Diary Seminole Campaign," 1836–37. State Archives of Florida, M86-12. Historical Records, Florida Memory, State Library and Archives of Florida, Tallahassee, FL.

———. General's Papers, 159Q, Boxes 1–44. Record Group 94: Records of the Adjutant General's Office, 1780s to 1917. National Archives and Records Administration, Washington, DC. These extensive holdings are also available in part within U.S. Army in the Era of Indian Removal. Papers of Quartermaster General Thomas S. Jesup, 1818–52. ProQuest History Vault.

———. "Major General Thomas Jesup, autograph manuscript account of the capture of Osceola," 1858. Ethan Allen Hitchcock Collection on Indian Removal, WA MSS S-2678, Box 5, F51. Beinecke Rare Book and Manuscript Library, Yale University, New Haven, CT.

Jones, Joel W. "A brief Narration of some of the Principle Events in the Life of Joel W. Jones with a few Observations," 1849. P. K. Yonge Library Special Collections, University of Florida Smathers Libraries, Gainesville, FL.

Kirby, Reynold Martin. "Diary," August 16, 1837–May 18, 1838. P. K. Yonge Library Special Collections, University of Florida Smathers Libraries, Gainesville, FL.

Lowrie, Walter, and Matthew St. Clair Clarke. *American State Papers: Indian Affairs*. 2 vols. Washington: Gales and Seaton, 1832–34.

Mason, James B. Letter to his mother, January 21, 1836. James B. Mason Letters, 1833–48, F1. P. K. Yonge Library Special Collections, University of Florida Smathers Libraries, Gainesville, FL.

Meek, Alexander Beaufort. "Journal of the Florida Expedition, 1836: Feb. 21–April 23." Meek, A. B., 1814–65, M-2380. Manuscript Department, William R. Perkins Library, DUA.

Miller, Morris Smith. Morris Smith Miller Papers, 1814–70, CU 763. Special Collections, U.S. Military Academy, West Point, NY.

Phelps, John Wolcott. "Journal (Loose Leaves)," January 15, 1838–May 15, 1839. John Wolcott Phelps Papers, 1833–84, MssCol 2399, Series III, S. 1. Manuscripts and Archives Division, New York Public Library, New York, NY.

———. J. W. Phelps correspondence and journal entries, 1836–62, MSS85739. Miscellaneous Manuscript Collection, Manuscript Division, Library of Congress, Washington, DC.

Reid, Robert Raymond. "Diary of Robert Raymond Reid," 1833, 1835, transcript, Historical Records Survey, 1939. Florida Heritage Collection, University of West Florida, PALMM Project.

Taylor, Zachary. Zachary Taylor Papers, Series 2, General Correspondence, 1814–50, mss42440, reel 1. Manuscript/Mixed Material, Manuscript Division, Library of Congress, Washington, DC.

Weedon, Frederick. "Pages from a diary kept by Dr. Frederick Weedon of St. Augustine, Florida, who served as the physician for Chief Osceola during his captivity," January 1838. Frederick Weedon Family Papers, SPR251 F1. Alabama Textual Materials Collection, Alabama Department of Archives and History, Montgomery, Alabama.

BOOKS AND DISSERTATIONS

Baptist, Edward E. *Creating an Old South: Middle Florida's Plantation Frontier Before the Civil War*. Chapel Hill: University of North Carolina Press, 2002.

Barr, James. *A Correct and Authentic Narrative of the Indian War in Florida*. New York: J. Narine, 1836.

Bartram, William. *The Travels of William Bartram*. New York: Macy-Masius, 1928.

Bassett, John Spencer, ed. *Correspondence of Andrew Jackson*. 7 vols. New York: Kraus Reprint, 1969.

Belko, William S., ed. *America's Hundred Years' War: U.S. Expansion to the Gulf Coast and the Fate of the Seminole, 1763–1858*. Gainesville: University of Florida Press, 2011.

Bemrose, John. *Reminiscences of the Second Seminole* War. Tampa, FL: University of Tampa Press, 2001.

Boyd, Mark F. *Florida Aflame: The Background and Onset of the Seminole War, 1835*. Tallahassee: Florida Board of Parks and Historic Memorials, 1951.

Pressly, Paul M. *A Southern Underground Railroad: Black Georgians and the Promise of Spanish Florida in Indian Country*. Athens: University of Georgia Press, 2024.

SELECTED SOURCES

Brown, Canter, Jr. *Ossian Bingley Hart, Florida's Loyalist Reconstruction Governor*. Baton Rouge: Louisiana State University Press, 1997.

Buker, George E. *Swamp Sailors in the Second Seminole War*. Gainesville: University of Florida Press, 2017.

Carrier, Toni. "Trade and Plunder Networks in the Second Seminole War in Florida, 1835–1842." Master's thesis, University of South Florida, 2005.

Clavin, Matthew J. *The Battle of Negro Fort: The Rise and Fall of a Fugitive Slave Community*. New York: New York University Press, 2019.

Coe, Charles H. *Red Patriots: The Story of the Seminoles*. Cincinnati, OH: Editor Publishing Company, 1898.

Coffman, Edward M. *The Old Army: A Portrait of the American Army in Peacetime, 1784–1898*. New York: Oxford University Press, 1986.

Cohen, Myer M. *Notices of Florida and the Campaigns*. Charleston, SC: Burges and Honour, 1836.

Congdon, Kristin G. *Uncle Monday and Other Florida Tales*. Jackson: University Press of Mississippi, 2001.

Covington, James W. *The Seminoles of Florida*. Gainesville: University of Florida Press, 1993.

Denham, James Michael. "'A Rogue's Paradise': Violent Crime in Antebellum Florida." PhD diss., Florida State University, 1988.

Denham, James Michael, and Keith L. Huneycutt, eds. *Echoes from a Distant Frontier: The Brown Sisters' Correspondence from Antebellum Florida*. Columbia: University of South Carolina Press, 2004.

Dixon, Anthony E. *Florida's Negro War: Black Seminoles and the Second Seminole War, 1835–1842*. Tallahassee, FL: AHRA Publishing, 2014.

Douglas, Marjory Stoneman. *The Everglades: River of Grass*. Sarasota, FL: Pineapple Press, 1997.

Drake, Samuel G. *The Book of the Indians; or, Biography and History of the Indians of North America, from Its First Discovery to the Year 1841*. 8th ed. Boston: Antiquarian Bookstore, 1841.

Feller, Andrew, ed. *The Papers of Andrew Jackson*. Vol. 7. Knoxville: University of Tennessee Press, 2007.

Forbes, James Grant. *Sketches, Historical and Topographical of the Floridas; More Particularly of East Florida*. New York: C. S. Van Winkle, 1821.

Foreman, Grant. *The Five Civilized Tribes: Cherokee, Chickasaw, Choctaw, Creek, Seminole*. Norman: University of Oklahoma Press, 1934.

———. *Indian Removal: The Emigration of the Five Civilized Tribes of Indians*. Norman: University of Oklahoma Press, 1972.

———, ed. *Transcripts: Commissioner of Indian Affairs* 6. Oklahoma City, OK: Oklahoma Historical Society, 1930.

Glunt, James David. "Plantation and Frontier Records of East and Middle Florida, 1789–1868." 2 vols. PhD diss., University of Michigan, 1930.

Guinn, Jeff. *Our Land Before We Die: The Proud Story of the Seminole Negro*. New York: Jeremy P. Tarcher / Putnam, 2002.

Hoffman, Paul E. *Florida's Frontiers*. Indianapolis: Indiana University Press, 2002.

Ivy, Richard F. *The Distinguished Light of Abraham Eustis: A Biography of an 1800 Artillery General*. Yorktown, VA: Citizen Publications, 1993.

Kieffer, Chester L. *Maligned General: The Biography of Thomas Sidney Jesup*. San Rafael, CA: Presidio Press, 1979.

Kimball, Chris. *Alachua Ambush: Bloody Battles of the 2nd Seminole War*.

———. *Seminole & Creek War Battles & Events*. 3rd ed. Christopher D. Kimball, 2018.

Kimelman, Jessica Slavin. "An Examination of Poor Whites and Crackers in Florida, 1845–1880." PhD diss., Tallahassee: Florida State University, 2000.

Kly, Y. N., ed. *The Invisible War: The African American Anti-Slavery Resistance from the Stono Rebellion Through the Seminole Wars*. Atlanta: Clarity Press, 2006.

Knetsch, Joe. *Fear and Anxiety on the Florida Frontier: Articles on the Second Seminole War*. Dade City, FL: Seminole Wars Foundation, 2008.

Knetsch, Joe, John Missall, and Mary Lou Missall. *History of the Third Seminole War, 1849–1858*. Philadelphia: Casemate, 2018.

Kokomoor, Kevin D. "Indian Agent Gad Humphreys and the Politics of Slave Claims on the Florida Frontier, 1822–1830." Master's thesis, University of South Florida, 2008.

Landers, Jane G. *Atlantic Creoles in the Age of Revolutions*. Cambridge, MA: Harvard University Press, 2010.

———. *Black Society in Spanish Florida*. Urbana: University of Illinois Press, 1999.

Lantz, Raymond C. *Seminole Indians of Florida, 1850–1874*. Westminster, MD: Heritage Books, 2008.

———. *Seminole Indians of Florida, 1875–1879*. Westminster, MD: Heritage Books, 2012.

Laumer, Frank ed. *Amidst a Storm of Bullets: The Diary of Lt. Henry Prince in Florida, 1836–1842*. Tampa Bay, FL: University of Tampa Press, 1998.

———. *Dade's Last Command*. Gainesville: University of Florida Press, 1995.

Littlefield, Daniel F, Jr. *Africans and Creeks: From the Colonial Period to the Civil War*. Westport, CT: Greenwood Press, 1979.

———. *Africans and Seminoles: From Removal to Emancipation*. Westport, CT: Greenwood Press, 1977.

MacCauley, Clay. *The Seminole Indians of Florida*. Gainesville: University of Florida Press, 2000.

Mahon, John K. *History of the Second Seminole War, 1835–1842*. Gainesville: University of Florida Press, 1995.

McCall, George A. *Letters from the Frontiers*. Philadelphia: J. B. Lippincott, 1868.

McGaughy, Felix P., Jr. "The Squaw Kissing War; Bartholomew M. Lynch's Journal of the Second Seminole War, 1836–1839." Master's thesis, Tallahassee: Florida State University, 1965.

Meacham, Jon. *American Lion: Andrew Jackson in the White House*. New York, Random House, 2009.

Missall, John, and Mary Lou Missall, eds. *This Miserable Pride of a Soldier: The Letters and Journals of Col. William S. Foster in the Second Seminole War*. Tampa: University of Tampa Press, 2005.

———. *The Seminole Struggle: A History of America's Longest Indian War*. Palm Beach, FL: Pineapple Press, 2020.

Mock, Shirley Boteler. *Dreaming with My Ancestors: Black Seminole Women in Texas and Mexico*. Norman, OK: University of Oklahoma Press, 2010.

Monaco, C. S. *The Second Seminole War the Limits of American Aggression*. Baltimore, MD: Johns Hopkins University Press, 2008.

Morris, Jerry C., and Jeffrey A. Hough. *The Fort King Road: Then and Now*. Dade City, FL: Seminole Wars Foundation, 2009.

Motte, Jacob Rhett. *Journey into Wilderness: An Army Surgeon's Account of Life in Camp and Field During the Creek and Seminole Wars, 1836–1838*. Gainesville: University of Florida Press, 1953.

Mulroy, Kevin. *The Seminole Freedmen: A History*. Norman: University of Oklahoma Press, 2007.

———. *Freedom on the Border: The Seminole Maroons, Florida, the Indian Territory, Coahuila, and Texas*. Lubbock, Texas: Texas Tech University Press, 1993.

Patrick, Rembert W. *Aristocrat in Uniform: General Duncan L. Clinch.* Gainesville: University of Florida Press, 1963.

Porter, Kenneth W. *The Black Seminoles: History of a Freedom-Seeking People.* Gainesville: University of Florida Press, 1996.

Potter, Woodburne. *The War in Florida: Being an Exposition of Its Causes, and an Accurate History of the Campaigns of Generals Clinch, Gaines, and Scott.* Baltimore: Lewis and Coleman, 1836.

Rasmussen, Daniel. *American Uprising: The Untold Story of America's Largest Slave Revolt.* New York: HarperCollins, 2011.

Record Book of Hillsborough County, Territory of Florida, 1838–1846. 4 vols. Jacksonville, FL: Works Progress Administration, 1938.

Remini, Robert V. *Andrew Jackson and His Indian Wars.* New York: Viking, 2001.

———. *Andrew Jackson and the Course of American Empire, 1767–1821.* New York: Harper and Row, 1977.

———. *Andrew Jackson and the Course of American Democracy, 1822–32.* New York: Harper and Row, 1984.

———. *Andrew Jackson and the Course of American Freedom, 1767–1821.* New York: Harper and Row, 1981.

———. *The Life of Andrew Jackson.* New York: Harper and Row, 1988.

Rivers, Larry E. *Rebels and Runaways: Slave Resistance in Nineteenth-Century Florida.* Champaign: University of Illinois Press, 2013.

———. *Slavery in Florida: Territorial Days to Emancipation.* Gainesville: University of Florida Press, 2009.

Rodenbough, Theophilus F. *From Everglade to Cañon with the Second United States Cavalry: An Authentic Account of Service in Florida, Mexico, Virginia, and the Indian Country, 1836–1875.* Norman: University of Oklahoma Press, 2000.

Saunt, Claudio. *A New Order of Things: Property, Power, and the Transformation of the Creek Indians, 1733–1816.* Cambridge, UK: Cambridge University Press, 1999.

Schene, Michael G. *Hopes, Dreams, and Promises: A History of Volusia County, Florida.* Daytona Beach, FL: News-Journal Corporation, 1976.

Schlesinger, Arthur M., Jr. *The Age of Jackson.* Boston: Little, Brown, 1945.

———. *The Imperial Presidency.* Boston: Houghton Mifflin, 1973.

Simmons, William H. *Notices of East Florida, with an Account of the Seminole Nation of Indians.* Charleston, SC: A. E. Miller, 1822.

Sivilich, Michelle, Sean Norman, and Jonathan Dean. *Fort King Road: Battlefields and Baggage Trains.* Crystal River, FL: Gulf Archaeology Research Institute, 2017.

Smith, Julia Floyd. *Slavery and Plantation Growth in Antebellum Florida, 1821–1860.* Gainesville: University of Florida Press, 2017.

Smith, William Wragg. *Sketch of the Seminole War, and Sketches During a Campaign.* Charleston, SC: Dan J. Dowling, 1836.

Sprague, J. T. *The Origin, Progress, and Conclusion of the Florida War.* New York: D. Appleton & Company, 1848.

Swanton, John R. *Early History of the Creek Indians and Their Neighbors.* Washington: U.S. Government Printing Press, 1922.

———. *The Indians of the Southeastern United States.* Washington: U.S. Government Printing Office, 1946.

Tocqueville, Alexis de. *The Republic of the United States of America, and Its Political Institutions, Reviewed and Examined.* Translated by Henry Reeves. New York: A. S. Barnes, 1877.

Twyman, Bruce Edward. *The Black Seminole Legacy and North American Politics, 1693–1845.* Washington, DC: Howard University Press, 1999.

Van Arsdol, Ted, ed. *Frontier Soldier: The Letters of Maj. John S. Hatheway, 1833–1853*. Vancouver, WA: Vancouver National Historic Reserve Trust, 1999.

Wasserman, Adam. *A People's History of Florida, 1513–1876: How Africans, Seminoles, Women, and Lower Class Whites Shaped the Sunshine State*. Sarasota, FL: CreateSpace Independent Publishing, 2009.

Wayne, Lucy B. *Sweet Cane: The Architecture of the Sugar Works of East Florida*. Tuscaloosa: University of Alabama Press, 2010.

Weik, Terrance M. *The Archaeology of Antislavery Resistance*. Gainesville: University of Florida Press, 2012.

Weisman, Brent Richards. *Like Beads on a String: A Culture History of the Seminole Indians in Northern Peninsular Florida*. Tuscaloosa: University of Alabama Press, 1989.

———. *Unconquered People: Florida's Seminole and Miccosukee Indians*. Gainesville: University of Florida Press, 1999.

Wickman, Patricia Riles. *Osceola's Legacy*. Tuscaloosa: University of Alabama Press, 2006.

Williams, John Lee. *The Territory of Florida: or, Sketches of the Topography, Civil and Natural History, of the Country, the Climate, and the Indian Tribes, from the First Discovery to the Present Time, with a Map, Views, &c.* New York: A. T. Goodrich, 1837.

Wright, J. Leitch, Jr. *Creeks and Seminoles: The Destruction and Regeneration of the Muscogulge People*. Lincoln: University of Nebraska Press, 1986.

MAGAZINES, NEWSPAPERS, AND PERIODICALS

"Another Chief Gone." *Martinsburg Gazette*, May 2, 1838, 3.

"Claims on the Indians." *Charleston Mercury*, May 30, 1838, 2.

"Copy of a Letter, Dated Fort Brooke, Tampa Bay, April 13." *Maryland Gazette*, May 12, 1836, 2.

"Copy of a Letter from a Young Officer of the Army." *Army and Navy Chronicle*, August 8, 1839.

"Correspondence of the *Journal of Commerce*." *Weekly Journal of Commerce*, September 30, 1852, 2.

"Domestic Intelligence." *Army and Navy Chronicle*, November 3, 1836, 3.

"Domestic Intelligence: Late from Florida." *Army and Navy Chronicle*, April 13, 1837.

"Domestic Intelligence: New Orleans, June 14." *Army and Navy Chronicle*, June 28, 1838.

"Domestic Intelligence: Seminole War." *Army and Navy Chronicle*, June 15, 1837, 4.

"Extract from a Private Journal of a Late Field Officer." *Army and Navy Chronicle*, March 7, 1839, 154.

"Extract of a Letter from an Officer in the U. States Army, in Florida, to His Correspondent in This Village." *Vermont Phoenix*, May 5, 1837, 2.

"Florida Indians." *Weekly Southern Standard*, February 7, 1852, 2.

"The Great Oseola Surrendered." *Evening Post*, February 21, 1837, 2.

"Indian Devastations." *New Orleans Commercial Bulletin*, February 27, 1836, 2.

"Indians at Washington." *Preston Chronicle and Lancashire Advertiser*, October 16, 1852, 2.

"Latest from Florida—Surrender of Oseola." *Herald* (New York), February 21, 1837, 2.

"Local Matters." *Republic*, September 18, 1852, 2.

"Movements of Billy Bowlegs and His Companions." *New York Times*, September 25, 1852, 8.

"The Murder of Gen. Wiley Thompson," *Alexandria Gazette*, January 22, 1836.

"The Naval Museum." *Evening Post*, August 2, 1852, 4.

"Off-Hand Notes of a Moving Gentleman." *New-Yorker* 3, no. 2 (April 1837): 27.

"The Seminole Indian Delegation." *Republic*, September 17, 1852.

"The Seminole Indians." *Times-Picayune*, June 23, 1838, 3,

"Seminole War—First Campaign: Extracts from the Journal of a Private." *New Hampshire Gazette*, April 25, 1837, 3

———. *New Hampshire Gazette*, May 9, 1836, 3.

———. *New Hampshire Gazette*, May 30, 1837, 2.

———. *New Hampshire Gazette*, June 6, 1837, 2.

Bateman, Rebecca B. "Naming Patterns in Black Seminole Ethnogenesis." *Ethnohistory* 49, no. 2 (2002): 227–57.

Belton, Francis. "Major Belton's Official Report." *Richmond Enquirer*, January 28, 1836, 3.

Blakney-Bailey, Jane Ann. "The Archaeology of the Payne Town Seminoles." In *Methods, Mounds, and Missions: New Contributions to Florida Archaeology*, edited by Ann S. Cordell and Jeffrey M. Mitchem. Gainesville: University of Florida Press, 2021.

Boyd, Mark F. "Asi-Yaholo or Osceola." *FHQ* 33, nos. 3 and 4 (1954): 249–305.

———. "The Seminole War: Its Background and Onset." *FHQ* 30, no. 1 (1951): 3–115.

Brown, Cantor, Jr. "The Florida Crisis of 1826–1827 and the Second Seminole War." *FHQ* 73, no. 4 (1994): 419–42.

Call, Richard. "Gov. Call to Gen. Clinch," *Floridian*, July 22, 1837, 1.

Childs, Thomas. "General Childs, U.S.A.: Extracts from Correspondence with His Family." *Historical Magazine* 2, no. 5 (1873): 299–304.

———. "General Childs, U.S.A.: Extracts from Correspondence with His Family." *Historical Magazine* 2, no. 6 (1873): 371–74.

———. "General Childs, U.S.A.: Extracts from Correspondence with His Family." *Historical Magazine* 3, no. 3 (1874): 169–71.

———. "Major Childs U.S.A.: Extracts from His Correspondence with His Family." *Historical Magazine* 3, no. 4 (1874): 280–84.

Clark, Ransom. "The Dade Massacre." *Niles' Weekly Register*, June 17, 1837.

Covington, James W. "Life at Fort Brooke, 1834–1826." *FHQ* 36, no. 4 (1957): 319–30.

Cusick, James G. "Historiography of Nineteenth-Century Florida." *FHQ* 94, no. 3 (2015): 295–319.

———. "King Payne and His Policies: A Framework for Understanding the Diplomacy of the Seminoles of La Chua, 1784–1812." In *America's Hundred Years' War: U.S. Expansion to the Gulf Coast and the Fate of the Seminole, 1763–1858*, edited by William S. Belko. Gainesville: University of Florida Press, 2011.

Dixon, Anthony E. "Black Seminole Ethnogenesis: Origins, Cultural Characteristics, and Alliances." *Phylon* 57, no. 1 (2020): 8–24.

Foreman, Carolyn Thomas. "The Jumper Family of the Seminole Nation." *Chronicles of Oklahoma* 34, no. 3 (1956): 272–85.

Forry, Samuel. "Letters of Samuel Forry, Surgeon U.S. Army, 1837–1838," *FHQ* 6, no. 2 (1927): 67–84.

———. "Letters of Samuel Forry, Surgeon U.S. Army, 1837–1838, Part I." *FHQ* 6, no. 3 (1927): 133–48.

———. "Letters of Samuel Forry, Surgeon U.S. Army, 1837–1838, Part II." *FHQ* 6, no. 4 (1927): 206–19.

———. "Letters of Samuel Forry, Surgeon U.S. Army, 1837–1838, Part III." *FHQ* 7, no. 1 (1928): 88–105.

Harper, Roland M. "Ante-Bellum Census Enumerations in Florida." *Florida Historical Quarter* 6, no. 1 (1927).

Horn, Stanley F., ed. "Tennessee Volunteers in the Seminole Campaign of 1836: The Diary of Henry Hollingsworth." *Tennessee Historical Quarterly* 1, no. 3 (1942): 269–74.

———. "Tennessee Volunteers in the Seminole Campaign of 1836: The Diary of Henry Hollingsworth." *Tennessee Historical Quarterly* 1, no. 4 (1942): 344–66.

———. "Tennessee Volunteers in the Seminole Campaign of 1836: The Diary of Henry Hollingsworth." *Tennessee Historical Quarterly* 2, no. 1 (1943): 61–73.

———. "Tennessee Volunteers in the Seminole Campaign of 1836: The Diary of Henry Hollingsworth." *Tennessee Historical Quarterly* 2, no. 2 (1943): 163–78.

———. "Tennessee Volunteers in the Seminole Campaign of 1836: The Diary of Henry Hollingsworth." *Tennessee Historical Quarterly* 2, no. 3 (1943): 236–56.

Jarvis, N. S. "An Army Surgeon's Notes of Frontier Service, 1833–48." *Journal of the Military Service Institution of the United States* 39, no. 142 (1906): 131–35.

———. "An Army Surgeon's Notes of Frontier Service, 1833–48." *Journal of the Military Service Institution of the United States* 39, no. 143 (1906): 275–86.

———. "An Army Surgeon's Notes of Frontier Service, 1833–48." *Journal of the Military Service Institution of the United States* 39, no. 144 (1906): 451–60.

———. "An Army Surgeon's Notes of Frontier Service, 1833–48." *Journal of the Military Service Institution of the United States* 40, no. 146 (1907): 469–77.

Klos, George. "Blacks and the Seminole Removal Debate, 1821–1835." In *The African American Heritage of Florida*, edited by David R. Colburn and Jane L. Landers. Gainesville: University of Florida Press, 1995

Landers, Jane. "Spanish Sanctuary: Fugitives in Florida, 1687–1790." *FHQ* 62, no. 3 (1983): 296–313.

Laumer, Frank. "Encounter by the River." *FHQ* 46, no. 4 (1967): 322–39.

Loftman, Simone. "Broward History: The Florida Seminoles." *Westside Gazette*, April 9, 2015. Accessed March 2, 2025. https://thewestsidegazette.com/broward-history-the-florida-seminoles/.

Mahon, John K. "The Journal of A. B. Meek and the Second Seminole War, 1836." *FHQ* 38, no. 4 (1959): 302–18.

Monaco, C. S. "Alachua Settlers and the Second Seminole War." *FHQ* 91, no. 1 (2012): 1–32.

Moore, John Hammond, ed. "A South Carolina Lawyer Visits St. Augustine—1837." *FHQ* 43, no. 4 (1965): 361–78.

Morgan, A. A. "Precarious Lives: Black Seminoles and Other Freedom Seekers in Florida Before the Civil War." Creative Commons License CC BY-NC-ND 4.0, 2020.

Pearcy, Matthew T., ed. "Documents: Andrew Atkinson Humphreys' Seminole War Field Journal." *FHQ* 85, no. 2 (2006): 197–230.

Porter, Kenneth W. "The Cowkeeper Dynasty of the Seminole Nation." *FHQ* 30, no. 4 (1951): 341–49.

———. "The Early Life of Luis Pacheco Né Fatio." *Negro History Bulletin* 7, no. 3 (1943): 52, 54, 62, 64.

———. "The Episode of Osceola's Wife: Fact or Fiction." *FHQ* 26 no. 1 (1947): 92–98.

———. "Florida Slaves and Free Negroes in the Seminole War, 1835–1843." *Journal of Negro History* 28, no. 4 (1943): 390–421.

———. "The Negro Abraham." *FHQ* 25, no. 1 (1946): 1–43.

———. "Negroes and the Seminole War, 1835–1842." *Journal of Southern History* 30, no. 4 (1964): 436

———. "Seminole Flight from Fort Marion." *FHQ* 22, no. 3 (1944): 113-33.

———. "Three Fighters for Freedom." *Journal of Negro History* 28, no. 1 (1943): 51–72.

Saunt, Claudio. "The English Has Now a Mind to Make Slaves of Them All: Creeks, Seminoles, and the Problem of Slavery." *American Indian Quarterly* 22, no. 1 (Winter 1998): 157–80.

Searcy, Martha Condray. "The Introduction of African Slavery into the Creek Indian Nation." *Georgia Historical Quarterly* 66, no. 1 (Spring 1982): 21–32.

Siebert, Wilbur H. "The Early Sugar Industry in Florida." *FHQ* 35, no. 4 (1957): 312–19.

Simmons, James W. "Recollections of the Late Campaign in East Florida." *Atkinson's Casket: Gems of Literature, Wit and Sentiment* 11 (November 1836): 542–57.

Steele, W. S. "Last Command: The Dade Massacre." *Tequesta* 1, no. 46 (1986): 6.

Snyder, Christina. "Enemies, Adopted Kin, and Owned People: The Creek Indians and Their Captives." *Journal of Southern History* 73, no. 2 (May 2007): 255–88.

Thompson, Wiley. "Circular." *Richmond Enquirer*, April 26, 1833.

———. "Creek Indians in Georgia." *Niles' Register*, May 30, 1829.

———. "To the Public." *Southern Patriot*, December 9, 1835.

Viator. "Florida." *Army and Navy Chronicle*, March 31, 1836, 2, 13.

Weisman, Brent R. "Labor and Survival Among the Black Seminoles of Florida." In *Florida's Working Class Past: Current Perspectives on Labor, Race, and Gender from Spanish Florida to the New Immigration*, edited by Robert Cassanello and Melanie Shell-Weiss. Gainesville: University of Florida Press, 2009.

West, Patsy. "Abiaka, or Sam Jones, in Context: The Mikasuki Ethnogenesis Through the Third Seminole War." *FHQ* 94, no. 3 (2016): 366–410.

White, Frank F., Jr., ed. "A Journal of Robert C. Buchanan During the Seminole War: The Battle of Lake Okeechobee." *FHQ* 29, no. 2 (1950): 132–51.

Wyly-Jones, Susan. "The 1835 Anti-Abolition Meetings in the South: A New Look at the Controversy over the Abolition Postal Campaign." *Civil War History* 47, no. 4 (2001): 289–309.

W. T. B. "The Dade Massacre: Louis Fatio's Thrilling Story." *Florida Times-Union*, October 30, 1892.

INTERVIEWS, ORAL HISTORIES, AND FOLKTALES

Abraham, Jimmie. Interview by author, July 19, 2023.

Evans, Hedvig Tetens. "Seminole Folktales." *FHQ* 56, no. 4 (1978): 473–94.

Grayson, Aaron. "An Interview of Aaron Grayson." Interviewed by Billie Byrd, September 10, 1937. Indian-Pioneer Papers, University of Oklahoma Western History Collections.

Greenlee, Robert F. "Folktales of the Florida Seminoles." *Journal of American Folklore* 58, no. 228 (1945): 138–44.

Jumper, Betty Mae. *Legends of the Seminoles*. Sarasota, FL: Pineapple Press, 1994.

Lozano, Alice Fay, and Shirley Boteler Mock. *My Black Seminole Ancestors: Running to Freedom*. San Antonio: Institute of Texan Cultures, 2004.

"Uncle Monday." Collected by Zora Neale Hurston. USF, Federal Writers' Project Collection (MS 1991-05), Box 1, Folder 11.

Index